You Can Travel Free

YOU CAN
Travel
FREE

Robert Wm Kirk

PELICAN PUBLISHING COMPANY
Gretna 1998

This is a completely rewritten book based on a previous work by
the author.

*The word "Pelican" and the depiction of a pelican are
trademarks of Pelican Publishing Company, Inc., and are
registered in the U.S. Patent and Trademark Office.*

Library of Congress Cataloging-in-Publication Data

Kirk, Robert William.
    You can travel free / Robert Wm Kirk.
      p. cm.
    Includes index.
    ISBN 1-56554-317-3 (alk. paper)
    1. Travel. 2. Free material. I. Title.
G151.K57 1998
910'.2'02—dc21   98-3425
                                                         CIP

*Information in this guidebook is based on authoritative data available
at the time of printing. Prices and hours of operation of businesses listed
are subject to change without notice. Readers are asked to take
this into account when consulting this guide.*

Manufactured in the United States of America

Published by Pelican Publishing Company, Inc.
1000 Burmaster Street, Gretna, Louisiana 70053

To Kathy—
With love, Dad

It is a good and safe rule to sojourn in every place as if you meant to spend your life there, never omitting any opportunity of doing a kindness or speaking a true word, or making a Friend.

—John Ruskin

Contents

CHAPTER 1

Traveling Without Money

McCheap's First Law of Travel:
The less money you spend at any destination,
the more enjoyable the experience.

THE PRICELESS VACATION ADVANTAGE

Despite their great desire to travel far and frequently, most Americans never get to go abroad. Many never get to visit the state next door. In 1997, according to the Travel Industry Association of America, the average traveler, on his or her longest trip of the year, spent a little over a thousand dollars. Sadly that amount bought Mr. and Ms. Average American Vacationer only short trips of five nights or less. Those trips took them no more than 700 miles—round trip.

Needless to say, the short-duration traveler visited a location within the U.S.A. or just across the border. Although surveys indicate that 80 percent of the trips Americans took were for pleasure, many of these rushed and stringently budgeted getaways were to visit relatives—relatives who don't charge for a night's lodging. Moreover, according to surveys, the Great American Vacation has been atrophying. Many budget travelers are reduced to three- to five-night hit-and-run, not-so-fun breaks. The reasons for shortened vacations aren't too complex: People claim to have less time due to busy work and school schedules, and they state that lack of money prevents them from taking longer overseas trips. It's too bad that lack of cash prevents would-be wanderers from seeing the world.

It's too bad, because being unable to afford travel is no longer a valid reason to postpone travel. When you've read this book you'll know how thousands of seasoned globe wanderers, bothered by a lack of cash but not by poverty of spirit, go where they wish, when they wish—without green stuff, traveler's checks, or credit cards. They've found that one can journey safely, legally, and comfortably without digging into a wallet or purse. These innovative adventurers have not only proven that there is indeed such as thing as a free lunch, but that one can eat it in Tahiti, Bermuda, Rome, Singapore, Rio, or wherever one chooses.

This book explains a multitude of free travel methods used by those who roam far and freqently—without paying. Only the names have been changed to protect the indigent.

HOW THIS BOOK CAME TO BE WRITTEN

I was born with a passion for travel. Chances are you were too. As a beginning teacher with a family, I desperately wanted to travel and learn on overseas summer vacations. I knew I'd be a better teacher as a result of getting to know other countries firsthand rather than only through books. When my wife, Barbara, and I paid a chunk of our savings to go to Europe for the first time, I realized that if I wanted to go again, I'd have to figure out ways to do it without passing around piles of money. My teacher's salary was too small to pile.

I look back at that first magic summer in Europe as one of the best investments I ever made. That's because people I met there opened my eyes to the truly amazing possibilities of traveling free.

My free-travel education began one August day when we paused in Nice, the flower-strewn capital of the French Riviera. After a rich bowl of bouillabaisse, a slice of melon, and a carafe of vin rosé, we settled back at the beach on soft mattresses and let the sun and wine make us drowsy. A gentle breeze stirred the warm afternoon air. Vacationers laughed and splashed in the lapping surf; waiters buzzed about refilling glasses. We stared at the azure sea, at the pure blue sky, at the relaxed bronzed sea bathers.

The young man reclining on the lounge next to us was Alex, a high-school teacher from Illinois. He and two of his students were discussing a projected excursion to the Picasso Museum in nearby Antibes. We had been to that treasure trove of modern art the day before, so we introduced ourselves and exchanged information and experiences with Alex and his companions, as travelers often do when they hear their own language spoken in another land.

Alex told us he was chaperoning a group of his pupils from their school near Chicago. They had traveled by bus and train in England, France, and Switzerland and were now resting after a seven-day Mediterranean cruise aboard a luxury liner. One of the students, a sandy-haired 16-year-old named Barry, told us enthusiastically that the ship had two swimming pools, four sun decks, a discotheque, a dance band, nightly floor shows, a casino, a movie theater, and two restaurants with lengthy menus.

As the two happy students headed for the water, Alex told us: "It's been a great trip, and the best part is that it hasn't cost me a cent. In fact, I'll go home a couple of hundred dollars richer." That statement really got our attention. Alex disclosed he had earned a complimentary trip for taking a group of students on the tour and cruise and had received a stipend as well. Until that moment we'd never doubted that everyone paid for their own vacation travel. We were astonished to learn that lots of people, like Alex, travel free. What Alex had told us was only our first stategy. It was the first step in what has been my quest since 1970 to learn about every free strategy that's both legal and ethical and that will prove of use to the general public.

Once alerted to the possibilities, we waited hardly any time at all to learn a second valuable strategy. We met John and Tina in Paris a week later. They were staying for a month in a sumptuous flat close to the Bois de Boulogne; the flat came with the services of a maid and a cook. They had exchanged homes with a French executive and his family; the French family was spending a month at John and Tina's second home at Lake Geneva, Wisconsin. Not only were John and Tina living quite well, but Tina told us they were saving thousands in hotel bills.

Jennifer taught us our third strategy. We met Jennifer two days later in London while we were queued up for theater tickets at the half-price booth at Liecester Square. She also was traveling without using any of her own money. Before that summer, although she was 21, Jennifer told us she had never been more than a hundred miles from McAllen, Texas. "London is so thrilling that I resisted going to sleep the first few days," she told us. The proud recipient of a Rotary Foundation Scholarship, Jennifer was studying television broadcasting for the entire academic school year in the British capital.

On the same day we met Jill, a charming 19-year-old art student from New York City. She taught us strategy number four. Jill had been traveling with an American family in Greece while caring for their two small children and getting paid for it. She told us that her golden tan came from watching these children on the beach on the Greek island of Mykonos.

Since that long ago summer, I've met dozens and dozens of people who have quit paying for vacation travel. These price-less travelers have taught me so many free travel strategies that it's taken a book this size to contain them. What I've learned from resourceful globetrotters, from research into just about everything written on the subject, as well as what I discovered by taking my family on free vacations is in this book.

A PASSION FOR TRAVEL

I'm convinced that you can get your next trip—and every trip after that—without paying. But in order to do so, you have to have a genuine passion for travel. If you're passionate but penniless, read on. Although handing around money to hotel desk clerks, waiters, taxicab drivers, transportation ticket sellers, and others is quick, easy, and final, it's not always possible. People *have* been known to experience shortages of the stuff. Nor does using money ensure that you'll get the most from your trip; it ensures only that you'll be a fairly typical tourist. Traveling free requires more than writing a check or signing a credit card slip.

Anyone who's going to use the tested free-travel strategies in this book must be passionate enough about exploring his planet to spend something more valuable than money. Free travelers need to give something of themselves—time, patience, expertise, interest. Such gifts will not only help them appreciate their experience more, but will help make the free traveler part of the exotic scene rather than a detached spectator with a sizable credit card debit.

Whether you pay something tangible for your experience, such as the use of your house or apartment while you're away, or something intangible, such as the pleasure of your company—which, incidentally, is all that's asked of some free travelers—you're bound to come home with an increased understanding of yourself, of others, and of the places you've visited rather than merely a pocket full of receipts.

GETTING STARTED

You Can Travel Free is a comprehensive tool, your master key to the world. It contains tried-and-true methods and tips, confirmed addresses, phone and fax numbers, and e-mail addresses that will prove invaluable to you. It contains titles of books that can help you find out even more about realizing your travel dreams. Furthermore, this book tells you how and where to obtain—without cost—essential brochures and maps from popular destinations nearly everywhere in the world.

After reading *You Can Travel Free*, you'll be able to select experiences and opportunities from a smorgasbord of free and super-low-cost experiences for a one-, two-, three-, or four-week vacation, or for a travel experience lasting three or four months or even a year or more. And you can do it year after year, whenever you have sufficient time.

Although this book contains a world of suggestions for trips without any cost, some opportunities aren't totally free. Occasionally it becomes necessary, in order to participate in an otherwise free travel program, to pay for your own airfare, to pay to attend an orientation session, to put up money as a registration fee, etc. This book will alert you to these possibilities and often make suggestions for lessening the bite. If you want to avoid paying anything at all, select a totally free strategy. You'll find them in every chapter.

All of the methods presented in *You Can Travel Free* have worked for someone, but not *all* are suitable for each and every reader. A vacationing octogenarian, for example, may find home exchanging less physically challenging than taking a group of 20-year-olds backpacking in the Alps. A teenager who lives under his parents' roof may find it more prudent to hop on a bike to see Holland than to swap Mom and Dad's home for a houseboat on an Amsterdam canal.

WHAT CAN *YOU* DO?

What can you do to get your next vacation gratis? Here are just a few options, a sneak preview of what's in the chapters that lie ahead: Recruit a group of friends for a tour of Scotland; volunteer to help destitute farmers in Africa; do a home exchange in the Caribbean; get a free flight to Japan; stay as a guest with a family in Istanbul; deliver a car to Florida; inoculate children in Honduras; teach English to Chinese speakers in Taiwan; pay a fraction of what everyone else pays for a suite at a tropical resort; try to see every free museum in London; study in Brazil on a Rotary scholarship; deal blackjack on a cruise ship; enjoy a brewery tour in Milwaukee; accompany a vacationer as his or her travel companion; teach children in Switzerland how to ski; join the crew on a yacht for a sail between Antigua and San Juan; travel around Brazil on a scholarship; or fly around the world as an air courier. Those ideas form only the tip of the proverbial iceberg. This book has a sufficient number of ideas. Your first challenge will be to select the one that's best for you.

CHOOSING THE RIGHT STRATEGY

After reading this book, make a list of strategies from *You Can Travel Free* that suit your abilities and interests. If you don't feel that teaching improved sanitation methods to villagers in Burundi is for you, leave it out. If you're shy and don't want to host a group on a tour of Western Europe, omit that strategy from your list. A short list is great; it'll be easier to zero in on one or more strategies that are sure to work for you. Then, decide where you want to go and for how long; that's the fun part. After that, get all the information you need, not only about getting your trip free, but about your destinations.

An example of how to complete these three steps comes readily to mind. Aurora, an administrative assistant in a natural gas supply company, wanted to cruise the Caribbean, but her paycheck was always running out before her supervisor handed her another. Aurora read *You Can Travel Free,* paid particular attention to the part about luxuriating on cruise ships, and decided she could actually tell passengers' fortunes in return for her cabin and five or six meals a day. Aurora is genuinely prescient and she has real theatrical ability. "I don't have a shy bone in my bod," Aurora once e-mailed me.

Aurora went to her nearest free public library and checked out the latest edition of a cruise ship guide that listed the address of every cruise line operating in the Caribbean. Then, Aurora threw a party. She invited 25 friends and entertained them by telling the fortunes of three friends. Aurora displayed her consummate sense of drama as she revealed that Penny would get a promotion, Franz would fall in love, and Clarita would become seriously wealthy. Aurora's boyfriend, Jack, made a video of her telling fortunes; Jack was careful to film the rapt attention and appreciative applause of Aurora's friends—her audience.

Aurora had 20 copies of the video made and called around to 20 cruise lines to find out the names of people hiring visiting lecturers and entertainers. She sent each cruise line—or the agency that supplied the ships with entertainers—a video of her performance. She also sent an eight-by-ten glossy picture of herself shuffling tarot cards, a brief biography, and a cover letter.

Here's what Aurora wrote on a postcard she sent me recently from Martinique:

> Hi, Bob. Thanks to your book I'm on my third cruise in the Caribbean. In three years I've been to 15 islands, some of them twice. The cruise line lets me take the companion of my choice. That's Jack. I'm having a ball telling passengers' fortunes. I get a bigger crowd than the cruise director gets at bingo. Want to know my fortune? More cruises! Fondly, Aurora.

Aurora's nothing if not resourceful. You can be too. Read on.

GETTING THE INFORMATION YOU NEED

When you've pinpointed one or more of the free travel strategies that are best for you, find out all you can about the places you want to visit. Chapters contain plenty of recommendations for further reading. Chapter 17, "A Wealth of Free Information," consists of sources of more pamphlets, maps, and books. Suggested books can be found in public, university, college, and school libraries. If the books aren't available, ask the librarian to order them for you on interlibrary loan. In addition, many libraries have travelogues on videotape, so you can travel vicariously before experiencing the real thing.

Some pamphlets and books recommended in the following pages are available only through mail order. If worse comes to worse and you can't get the information you need without cost, and you actually need to open your wallet to buy a book, addresses of publishers are included.

When you order a book, you need first to find out the price. You won't find prices in *You Can Travel Free*. It's not just that the author is allergic to spending money (which he is); it's because few inconveniences can be more time consuming and aggravating than to read that a book costs $9.95 plus $1.50 postage, so you send off your check and wait. Your wait ends a few weeks later when your check is returned from the publisher with the notation that the price has gone up to $11.95 and that you should reorder. That holds you up. You could have been in Bermuda by now. As a result, prices are omitted here. In this age of instant communication, it's easy enough to obtain the latest price: Write, call, fax, e-mail, or check websites to find current prices before ordering. Necessary addresses and numbers are included.

When writing for information, particularly from charities that utilize volunteers overseas, it's customary to send an SASE—an envelope with your address and a stamp so they can return the information you requested without incurring an expense. When the organization is located overseas, don't send them U.S. or Canadian stamps for their reply. Rather, send international reply coupons, available at your post office; this courtesy will help overseas charities conserve their choked budgets.

> $$$—Cousin Thrifty McCheap says: "When requesting information, use '800' numbers when they're available or use e-mail."

WHY A NEW EDITION?

The first edition of *You Can Travel Free* hit bookstore shelves in 1985. It was well received by a public eager for such useful information. Sometime later, Pelican's editors saw the need for a new edition of *You Can Travel Free* and asked me to update it. They realized that the book is unique and that nobody else has brought out a truly comprehensive guide to roaming the globe without money. The editors reminded me that readers who had written to express gratitude for free vacations they'd taken as a result of following the book's strategies sometimes noted that organizations mentioned had gone out of business or that addresses or phone numbers had changed.

Moreover, today, it's quite clear that the electronic super-information highway is a prime source of mountains of diverse information, including free travel strategies. As a result, it seemed even more obvious that the 1985 edition, which was without essential e-mail and website or home page addresses, was outdated.

When Pelican's editors first asked me to update the book, I wanted to do it. I wanted to expand the book substantially—in fact, to rewrite it almost completely. But I was too busy for such a time-consuming project. I was busy teaching and traveling free. When I wasn't producing chalk dust in front of a college class to earn a living, I was visiting villagers in the Marquesas Islands, riding a camel up to the Great Pyramid at Giza, climbing the symbolic steps at Boroburdur in Java, snapping photos of children in Thailand's Golden Triangle, visiting descendants of *Bounty* mutineers on Pitcairn Island, barging on China's Grand Canal, getting pretty darned seasick coming out of the Strait of Magellan, and so on.

Since 1985—when I thought I was telling all there was tell— I've learned a lot more about traveling free. The first edition's cover biographical sketch informed readers that I'd completed 166,000 miles of free travel. I had. But now I'm up to 470,000 miles with lots more planned.

I have stopped traveling long enough to write a second edition. It's virtually a new book. The first edition's 10 chapters have grown to 17 in the second. Not only have addresses and phone numbers been updated, the most recent editions of books and new books noted, and electronic addresses added, but copious amounts of additional information and several exciting new strategies also make their grand debuts.

DISCLAIMER

At the time writing was completed, addresses, phone numbers, Internet addresses, faxes, etc., were current. By the time you read this book, inevitably some organizations will have new addresses and phone and fax numbers, or have ceased to exist. The Internet will have sprouted a bumper crop of new travel sites, some of which will undoubtedly be useful to free travelers. Changes occur, which is why subsequent editions are published.

As was true for the first edition, neither the publisher nor I can accept responsibility for the actions or omissions of any organization, company, agency, government, or individual listed in this book. All are, to my knowledge, reputable, but their performance can't be guaranteed. Nor can Pelican Publishing Company or I accept responsibility for any of the curious things that can happen when you're out there exploring 180 or more countries during the next several decades. If you're swallowed by a crocodile in Queensland or become an indispensable ingredient in cannibal stew on some dangerous atoll, I claim no responsibility. Try not to look so tempting.

Crocs and cannibals not withstanding, may all your travels be fun, fascinating, and free.

CHAPTER 2

Free Accommodations

McCheap's Second Law of Travel:
If you paid anything at all for your last vacation,
you may have paid too much.

STAYING WITHOUT PAYING

If the collection agency, the IRS, and the mechanic who repaired your slightly used Studebaker have taken a heavy toll on the petty cash that once was your life's savings, and if your only vacation options are to stay home reading travel brochures or visit Aunt Wilda in Weedpatch, Wyoming—again—here's good news: Tens of thousands of people, rich and poor, with and without homes, vacation without paying for accommodations.

How do they save $50 to $1,000 or more a night that others pay to sleep in motel and hotel beds? The majority of the free-lodging crowd do home exchanges; others swap timeshares, boats, RVs, and vacation homes. In addition, a number of people are catching on to the idea of renting out their homes for a week or more and vacationing on the proceeds.

No home? You can get in on the action anyway. If you happen to be temporarily without shelter, or if Mom and Dad won't let you swap the ancestral estate for a room on the beach at Santa Monica so you can catch waves and meet babes, this chapter holds hope for you: You can become a qualified house-sitter. Houses virtually everywhere lie empty and waiting to be sat.

The tens of thousands who avoid paying for staying devote the money they'd normally hand over to a reception clerk to better uses, such as vacationing a few extra days; dining well instead of fast; riding everything at amusement parks that makes their hearts go "pumpy pump"; taking side trips and excursions; and attending concerts, plays, and ball games. Some folks actually save enough money to take a second trip. Home exchanging is the best option for most free travelers, so let's start there and after that move on to other strategies for getting free housing.

EXCHANGING YOUR HOME

Dollar-wise vacationers get free accommodations by residence-swapping for periods ranging from a weekend to a year—or more. Potential exchangers live in every state and in dozens of fascinating countries. The world of rent-free travel has become virtually unlimited. Just about anyone can benefit.

You can participate whether you own or rent; you qualify whether you have a house, an apartment, a mobile home, an RV, a timeshare, condominium, vacation cabin, or even a boat. The proud possessor of a condo on the beach at Maui will have a somewhat easier time of locating swapping partners than the folks with a studio apartment in Akron, but if your place has anything at all to offer visitors, you can holiday elsewhere rent free.

Warning: Home Exchanging Can Be Habit Forming

A neighbor of ours recently exchanged his home for one in Ireland. As a retired airline employee, neighbor Greg had no trouble getting a nearly free flight to Dublin, but he wanted to avoid paying two weeks' hotel-room rent. So he joined a home-exchange club and wrote to an Irish couple who had listed their names and address in the club's catalog. The Irish couple offered use of their flat, three miles from central Dublin. The flat was just steps from a coach stop and minutes from Trinity College and and from the train station that leads into the excruciatingly green Irish countryside.

We got to know Margaret and Sean, the couple from Dublin, when they were our temporary neighbors in Greg's house. We asked them if they had swapped residences before. Indeed they had and their free-holiday destinations make up a mini-gazetteer of posh places. In 1989 they spent two weeks in Tenerife in the Canary Islands off the coast of northwest Africa; in 1990, they had a fortnight in a cottage in Cornwall, England, and a week in a condo overlooking the Mediterranean in Malaga, Spain; in 1991, they spent three sunny weeks in an Italian villa just outside a Tuscan village; in 1993, they enjoyed a week of skiing in Grenoble, and later that year they stayed in Versailles, in a gigantic flat near Louis XIV's palace and just a short drive from Paris. In 1994, they bicycled in Bermuda in May and had a few days in Brighton, England, in July; in 1995 Margaret and Sean spent time sunning in Corfu in the Adriatic and later at St. Remo on the Italian Riviera. In 1996 they spent a week in Berlin; and in 1997, they swam in the azure waters at Costa Smeralda on the coast of Sardinia. April in Paris was their 1998 spring fling—in a flat on the Ile St.-Louis. "In all of those years," Sean told us, "we paid for a night's lodging no more than five or six times."

Major Advantages of Swapping Your Residence

There are a number of advantages to trading accommodations. Some are more obvious than others.

Above all, thanks to home exchanging, we, like Margaret and Sean, pay nothing for housing when we vacation, except perhaps for a night's lodging en route. Nevertheless, we enjoy the use of clean, well-furnished—and sometimes luxurious— homes, condominiums, and apartments in upper-middle-class neighborhoods or in verdant rural locations. In all honesty, we couldn't afford long vacations in similar areas if we had to settle with a cashier at checkout time. No money passes between us and the people with whom we exchange, unless it's for a long-distance call on a telephone bill. We do pay a small fee to a home-exchange club in order to receive the club's annual directory and periodic supplements and to be listed in that directory, but that's all we pay.

Second, we find swapping preferable to descending on friends and relatives for extended stays in cramped and often uncomfortable guest quarters. (I'm thinking particularly of Second-Cousin Tillie's hideaway bed). The desirability of a place of one's own should be apparent to anyone who's had a long-term guest—or been one.

Another obvious advantage is that we feel safer when someone is occupying our house while we're away, which minimizes the risk of burglary, vandalism, or undetected fire. Many of the people with whom we exchange—professionals, executives, or retired folks—could well afford the best hotel room in our community, but they prefer to swap so that a reliable party will be guarding their homes in their absence.

Having someone in your home to water the plants, feed the fish, walk Igor, take in the mail and the freebie advertising papers that accumulate on the porch to advertise that you're out of town and your home is ripe for the plucking, is a tremendous convenience. A great deal of trust is implicit when you exchange, and it could extend to allowing your exchanger to use your car or care for your valued pets and plants—if that person is willing.

In addition, house swapping makes traveling with children easier, especially if you occupy a home with a bedroom for each child. Having ample room is obviously preferable to climbing over extra cots in the Sleep 'n Save Motel to tuck the little grabbers in. Your pint-sized heirs may also enjoy a yard to play in, and if you exchange with families who have children, your own kids could reap the advantage of toys, strollers, playpens, or cribs. And by living in a residential community rather than a motel or hotel, the kids will probably enjoy the company of neighborhood playmates.

Moreover, the houses and apartments we use invariably have kitchen and laundry facilities, so we're able to maintain almost the same life-style that we do at home. Using stoves, dishwashers, and vacuum cleaners can be repulsive to the family member who handles cooking and housekeeping duties all year and wants to be liberated while on vacation; however, we find that the convenience of being able to do essential tasks for ourselves—*if* and when we wish—outweighs our desire to avoid chores. After all, eating three meals a day in restaurants over a period of many days and flagging down Patience the waitress every time we want a coffee refill or waiting for Pierre to bring the dinner check becomes a form of drudgery in itself. Having food preparation and laundry facilities at our disposal gives us options.

Above all, we find straightening up for ourselves preferable to having Gretchen the hotel housekeeper bang on our door every 15 minutes—while simultaneously flinging it opening and muttering "sorry"—so she can make the bed. When we're on vacation, we like to decide for ourselves what time to leave each morning rather than have to evacuate the room we've paid for dearly so a hotel employee can check the minibar.

House swapping can add real fun to a trip. Exchangers frequently make available their sail- or powerboats, jet skis, campers, off-road vehicles, RVs, bicycles, motorcycles, snowmobiles, horses, or other grown-up toys during our stay. In particular, use of the exchangee's car is a real advantage; we can fly to our destination and have a vehicle at our disposal at no extra cost. We also offer the use of our car and country club facilities and often get golf, swimming, tennis, fitness, yacht harbor, or country club privileges in return. Many homes come equipped with amenities we normally don't have the chance to enjoy: saunas, hot tubs, tennis courts, premium movie channels, private pools, and home gyms.

Best of all, when we live in someone else's home, we feel more a part of their community than we do when we stay at a hotel or resort. If your experience is anything like ours, your temporary neighbors—hospitable folks who've been informed of your impending arrival—will go out of their way to tell you the best places to shop or to eat, how to use local transportation, where to have your hair cut or permed, and what local sights to see. Your children may also find that the neighborhood kids have formed a welcoming committee, because they are eager to meet new playmates. We've been wined and dined by our temporary neighbors and on at least one occasion threw a party in our borrowed home to thank the several neighborhood families who had been so kind to us during our stay.

Another bonus is that living in someone else's residence allows you to sample a place to see if you'd really like to live there. Our former neighbors, Howard and Ellie, for example, exchanged their home near San Jose, California, for one in Tucson, Arizona. They were looking for the best place to retire. They sampled the Southwestern city and its environs for a month while meeting people, attending public events, shopping in local stores, and looking at homes for sale. When they finally decided to stay put in California, it was because their exchange had given them the opportunity to base their decision on their experience of being part of a community rather than to have visited Tucson as hurried tourists.

Potential Drawbacks

Nothing's perfect. There are several drawbacks to exchanging. Howard and Ellie found that Thomas Wolfe was right: You *can't* go home again. When Ellie wanted to return to California after two weeks in Tucson in the high heat of summer, she couldn't. She had agreed to let the family from Tucson use her house for another two weeks. If pressing business, illness, or another emergency calls you home, or even if you've become bored silly sitting on the porch at the hunting lodge you've contracted for in Bear's Lair, Saskatchewan, you can't go home—yet. "Home exchanging isn't for everybody," said Vacation Exchange Club founder David Ostroff. "You need a spirit of adventure and have to be flexible. It is not a substitute for conventional travel."

A second drawback, for some, is worry; but their concerns are usually unnecessary. These worriers are reluctant to have others stay in their homes because they value their possessions too much to entrust them to the care of non-family members. "I would never allow strangers to live in my house," my colleague Dick said. "What if they take my fishing gear or wreck the place?" Dick's point is well taken, and I didn't change his mind when I told him that by the time an exchange actually takes place, the people with whom he would correspond and call long-distance to arrange the swap would hardly be strangers any longer. I also pointed out that, although exchange clubs have been responsible for hundreds of thousands of house switches for close to half a century, each club admits to having received only a handful of valid complaints. These complaints are usually about dirty dishes left in the sink or about unwatered plants. In fact, when the Vacation Exchange Club sent questionnaires to their catalog subscribers, and four thousand responded, only three reported "unsatisfactory" experiences. Our own loss during a four-week exchange was a broken one-dollar wine glass. Following another swap, we had to wipe away a ring left around the sink. I call it our *$3,100 ring* because we had saved that amount in motel and hotel charges.

The most common home-exchange complaint has nothing to do with damage, theft, or messiness. It occasionally happens that at the last minute, when all arrangements have been made and the suitcases are all but locked, what was assumed to be a firm exchange falls through. It's usually due to something unavoidable such as illness or business, but sometimes your exchangees back out simply because they've found a sweeter deal elsewhere. Finding out you're not actually going to spend January at someone's condo in St. Barts is about as much fun as having a New Orleans hotel lose your reservation during Mardi Gras. This potential problem underscores the point that exchangers, like all free travelers, must remain flexible. You must be willing to switch plans when necessary, even if it means staying home or driving to Wyoming to descend on Aunt Wilda—again.

All in all, however, we feel the advantages of home swapping outweigh any potential disadvantages.

Two Weeks in a Dull Town

We once lived in a small city that a national news magazine characterized as "an unattractive town of gas stations, seedy bars and hamburger joints," located on "a sun-baked mosquito-plagued tableland." When we lived there, the town's population remained static; the mayor told us it was because every time a baby was born, a man left town. To make matters worse, the town is an hour from anything of even marginal interest to tourists. Yet people in that sorry place can almost always swap their homes for residences in more desirable locations. For example, our former neighbors there, the Daltons, exchanged with a family from Chapel Hill, North Carolina, who wanted to visit their relatives, Uncle Todd and Aunt Louise. Their uncle and aunt had only a small apartment and couldn't house the North Carolinians comfortably for 14 days, so the visitors became our temporary neighbors when they agreed to swap homes with the Daltons. Another neighbor was able to exchange his house for a ranch house in Idaho because its owner wanted to come to our town for the duck-hunting season.

Wherever you live, you may be certain that someone somewhere wants to stay in your community for one reason or another. Almost every place has an attraction for someone. After all, *you* live there, don't you?

THREE WAYS TO MAKE AN EXCHANGE

The first and most obvious way to arrange a home exchange is to do so with friends or relatives. The major advantages of coming to an agreement with someone you know are two: You don't have to pay club membership fees to find your exchange partners; and because you know them (presumably) well, you won't worry about the safety of your home and its contents while they're in residence.

Trading with friends is how we got started. When we were first married we lived in an apartment in California's Silicon Valley. Our memories of the 24-unit building and its tenants have always been of fun and camaraderie around a most inviting central pool and patio. We kept in touch with a couple from that complex and several years later offered to swap use of our home, which sat just above a large lake in a resort community, for their apartment. Marty and Marie readily agreed. The swap worked well, so well in fact that we soon lost these exchange partners. Within a few months they gave notice to their landlord and bought a house around the corner from us. Not only did we gain old friends as neighbors, but once we had experienced home exchanging, there was no going back. We've been hooked ever since.

We found that anyone can exchange homes with friends or relatives, relying on mutual trust built over the years. People we ask will occasionally refuse such a proposition for various reasons. But, we've never felt so much as a twinge of embarrassment for having offered and been refused; it's their lost opportunity for a nearly free vacation. You'll find most folks want to holiday affordably and will seriously consider your proposal.

> $$$—Cousin Thrifty McCheap says: "Swapping with someone you know costs absolutely nothing. You avoid advertising costs or exchange club fees when you've found your own exchange partner."

The second way to find exchange partners is to advertise your home. Try this: Place a classified ad in a newspaper published in the area you plan to visit. Even if you intend to stay only a couple of nights, a cheap ad costs a lot less than putting hotel-room rent on your credit card. Your ad could read something like this: "Home Exchange, 1st week Aug. Our 5-rm apt, Atlanta, slps 4, nr trans. Pool. Reliable party. [your phone number]." If it doesn't matter to you what part of the country you visit, place an ad describing your home and its location in a national periodical and choose from among the offers you're bound to receive.

Place an ad in a foreign paper if you're planning on an overseas trip; for example, if you want to go to London, send your offer to the classified columns of the *Evening Standard*. In any ad, you must mention the approximate dates your residence will be available, the number of people that can be accommodated comfortably, and your address, phone number, e-mail address, or fax number. It's also helpful to list amenities such as premium movie channels or Jacuzzis, nearby attractions, the proximity of public transportation, and any remarkable features that make your home a pleasure to live in. You should also announce how of many of you will be occupying the exchange house—for example: two adults and three children under age 10.

The third stategy is to join a home exchange club. By far, most exchanges are made through clubs. Clubs don't normally arrange trades for you; they're in the business of publishing directories that list offers of members who want to swap homes. It's up to the members to contact one another. Let's say a Salt Lake City family wants an apartment in Paris for three weeks in October. They scan the Paris listings in their club's directory and contact members in the French capital who have indicated that their homes will be available at that time and who either specify in their listing that they want to visit the American West or that they're open to offers from anywhere in the U.S. or, indeed, on this planet. Once the two parties have agreed in principle to swap, they agree by phone or letter on all the details a home swap entails.

Exchanges may be for one time only, or they can be repeated several times a year or annually—if the two parties agree. They can be for as short as a single day and night, for a weekend, or for a year or more. Duration and frequency are up to the participants. If you set up an ongoing periodic exchange for the next 20 years, you've still paid only one initial fee for your listing and for your copy of the club membership directory.

Annual dues, incidentally, are usually less than the tariff for one night in a moderately priced motel or hotel.

Because these for-profit clubs are matchmakers that facilitate introductions, the clubs' owners will assume no responsibility for their members' actions. If the Joneses' dog Chomp takes a bite out of your waterbed while his master is using your home, that's strictly a matter between you and the Joneses. Clubs don't screen or investigate members in advance. It's up to you to size up the other party and decide whether you're sufficiently comfortable having them use your home.

Because directories are published infrequently during the year, exchangers have to keep deadlines in mind. Nine or 10 months in advance isn't too long to start planning your vacation. Some participants make arrangements a year or more in advance. Others make reciprocal agreements with procrastinating swappers at the last minute. Thus, procrastinators have every potential of enjoying their exchange as much as do the long-term planners.

Try to be as flexible as possible about your destination. Travelers who announce they're open to a trade "anywhere" often get the best offers. Retirees and others who are open to swaps "anytime" get far more offers than those who must cram their vacation into a specific period such as the first two weeks of October.

INSIDE THE CLUB DIRECTORIES

Let's take a moment to flip through a few club directories. One offers a "spacious modern house" with a private pool in Acapulco: "Sailing, fishing, golf, tennis, beach—winter in tropical paradise." On the Spanish island of Minorca is a plush penthouse boasting four large balconies with an unobstructed view of the harbor. Nearby are "many good beaches." Another directory offers a Taos, New Mexico, ski cabin within walking distance of lifts. Then there's a chance to barter your home for a "beautiful" Palm Springs house with private pool. Or would you prefer a "comfortable" house overlooking Windsor Castle, only 20 minutes from central London? It too is in the same directory.

Another club's list tempted us with a "luxury three-plus bedroom loft cabin, one mile to Lake Tahoe, 3 miles to Heavenly Valley skiing, 4 miles to major gambling casinos." This Shangri-la has three decks from which to look at the lake. The owner expressed a willingness to swap "anywhere, anytime." In the same book was an offer of a furnished townhouse in the Florida Keys, with pool and terraces overlooking the ocean—"Moped and Rolls Royce available."

CLUBS, CLUBS, CLUBS

The popularity of house swapping is attested to by the large number of clubs that facilitate swaps. Many belong to The International Home Exchange Association. The IHEA includes 18 home exchange clubs worldwide. There's no reason to join more than one member of IHEA, because the catalog of each includes swap offers from all the clubs. IHEA members include Invented City, Landfair Home Exchange, Trading Homes International, and Vacation Homes. International members include Latitude Home Exchange (Australia), International Travel (Australia), Home Across the Sea (Australia), Global Home Exchange (New Zealand), Home Base Holidays (Britain), Greene Theme Home Exchange (Britain), Haney's Bolig Bytte (Denmark), Landfair Home Exchange (Canada), Holiday Exchange Club (Britain), Homenet (France), Interlink (France), Family Link (Italy), T.H.E.A. (Italy), and Fair Tours (Switzerland).

But not all clubs are in the IHEA. Here's a list of clubs in the U.S., some of which belong to IHEA and some of which are independent:

Faculty Exchange Center

College and university faculty members can swap not only houses, but professional lives—at least for a semester or year. The Faculty Exchange Center publishes both a directory of house exchange opportunities and a directory of educators who'd like to exchange positions on a temporary basis. Each person draws his or her own salary while teaching classes at the swapee's institution. The Center doesn't arrange these switches. It merely prints the directory. Teachers can access the Faculty Exchange Center's home page on the WorldWideWeb at http://www.unca.edu/fec. Or write to Faculty Exchange Center, The University of North Carolina at Asheville, One University Heights, Asheville, NC 28804-3299. Phone: (704) 251-6476. Fax: (704) 251-6012. E-mail: fec@unca.edu.

Homelink International

Homelink is a pioneer among residence-swap organizations. Starting its life more than 40 years ago as Vacation Exchange Club, it's moved its headquarters from the East Coast to Arizona, then to Hawaii, and finally to Florida. The current proprietors publish five catalogs and supplements a year. The cost of belonging is that of one night in a nonluxury hotel. The club's membership is about 15,000 in 50 countries worldwide, with equal proportions in North America and in Europe. Contact Homelink International, P.O. Box 650, Key West, FL 33041. Phone: (800) 638-3841. Fax: (305) 294-1448. Phone outside U.S.: (305) 294-3720. E-mail: 72520.1414@compuserve.com.

In a recent Homelink catalog, we were enticed by the offer of a couple with a mammoth estate in Darien, Connecticut. And they were willing to throw in an apartment on Manhattan's Park Avenue. We also noted the offer from a businessman with a large lakeside vacation home near Orlando's Disney World; a legal officer with a home with pool near Honolulu and near beaches; a New Yorker with a deluxe condo on top of the Museum of Modern Art on Fifth Avenue; a retired couple with a "lovely" home in rural North Carolina; a Washington, D.C., lobbyist with a 6,000-square-foot mansion on acreage just outside the nation's capital; and a businessman with a luxury estate on Carmel, California's scenic 17-Mile Drive. The pictures that accompany the offers nearly knocked our socks off.

Overseas offers in that particular catalog featured homes in every country of Western Europe and a few in Eastern Europe, including Russia. In the Finland section we noted a "new house with beautiful lake view near small town, plus use of a summer cottage, plus a week's use of a flat in Helsinki." Africa was represented by several listings: In lush Kenya is a "long, low white bungalow, nestling beneath trees, only five miles from game preserve—cook, maids, groom, and gardener included." In addition to lots of houses made available in Britain, France, Belgium, and other obvious places, club members in the West Indies, Andorra, Liechtenstein, Iceland, Singapore, Hong Kong, South Africa, Canada, Australia, and New Zealand were well represented. In addition, members in Pacific islands such as Tahiti and the Cooks, Thailand, Morocco, Mexico, Tanzania, and the Persian Gulf states made offers.

We noted a number of houses and flats in excellent central London locations as well as large houses in wooded areas within a half-hour of Piccadilly. A titled lady living in a "luxury" flat on an exclusive square in Mayfair wanted to swap homes "anywhere," as a did a gentleman in the London suburbs whose residence boasts four living rooms and a library.

If you don't mind being five minutes from the beach in Cannes on the French Riviera, you could have stayed in a "modern luxury building"; amenities included extensive gardens, tennis courts, and pools, as well as the use of an automobile.

In southern Germany near Freiburg, and near the Black Forest, are houses available that Hansel and Gretel would be tempted to eat. Homelink International members in the Austrian Alps offer the use of houses with massive timbered roofs and geranium window boxes. In Italy are flats in the centers of historic cities such as Verona, Padua, and Venice as well as in the mountains near Bolzano, and on Lakes Como and Garda. In Portugal you can stay on the Algarve; in Australia on the Gold Coast; in Auckland, New Zealand, overlooking a yacht harbor; and in Capetown, South Africa, near Table Bay.

International Home Exchange Network

International Home Exchange network is an electronic club whose members meet on the Internet. E-mail address: linda@homexchange.com.

In addition to house swaps, club members are invited to arrange hospitality exchanges among themselves, to offer hospitality to other members for payment of money, and to offer property for short-term vacation rentals.

How well does the club achieve its purpose of facilitating residence trades? A member from California writes: "We exchanged our home in San Diego with a young couple from Tahoe who were looking for warmth to train for the Boston Marathon, while we were seeking great skiing. A win-win situation and it worked perfectly." Another satisfied member writes from Orlando, Florida: "To date we have received numerous e-mail inquiries from places such as Israel, Brussels, and Malaysia!!! The response has been so overwhelming, we are having trouble deciding where to go."

Surf on over and check it out. Website: http://www.homexchange.com.

Intervac

Intervac has helped facilitate worldwide accommodation exchanges since 1977. Intervac's listings include 10,000 members in more than 30 countries. It publishes three directories a year and is willing to sell directories to members who don't wish to be listed; thus, if you choose that option, you can offer your home to other members, but won't receive offers. Intervac publishes a "late" edition as well as a list of "last-minute" opportunities for those still looking for summer exchanges well into the season. In addition, they'll sell you an outdated catalog through which you can contact members who, presumably, have fulfilled their vacation dreams the previous season and may be open to your offer. Intervac offers a modest discount to seniors. Intervac US, P.O. Box 590504, San Francisco, CA 94159. Call them at (415) 435-3497. Or call toll-free:

(800) 756-4663. Fax: (415) 435-7440. E-mail: IntervacUS@aol. com.

The Invented City

For about the price of one night in the Fleabag Arms Motel, the Invented City will send you their three most recent directories of members, many of whom are willing to trade substantial houses. In addition, they'll print your listing in the next issue and send you that directory and the next two installments—a total of six directories. These books include addresses and phone numbers of Invented City's 1,600 members.

A majority of these far-flung swappers spend their nonvacation time at home in the U.S. and Canada, the United Kingdom, Australia, France, Italy, Spain, and Switzerland, but there are plenty of members in other countries worldwide. Contact the Invented City, 41 Sutter St., Suite 1090, San Francisco, CA 94194. Call them at (415) 673-0347. Or call toll-free: (800) 788-2489. Fax: (415) 673-6909. E-mail: invented@backdoor.com.

Loan-a-Home

Loan-a-Home is a venerable club that specializes in long-term swaps for sabbaticals. Professors and researchers, in particular, are invited to save a fortune in rent for a sabbatical residence by swapping with others during a semester or year-long leave. Thus, a writer and researcher near Vienna may want to live in Boston for the academic year; meanwhile a teacher from one of Boston's many colleges and universities needs to take courses in Vienna.

Some exchanges are arranged a year or more in advance. Educators who merely want to relax elsewhere swap during long spring, winter, and summer breaks as well. This service isn't restricted to savants on sabbatical or even to academics; anyone who wants to join may benefit. The fee is exceedingly modest. Contact Loan-a-Home, 7 McGregor Rd., Woods Hole, MA 02543. Phone: (914) 664-7640.

publishes three directories a year—in March, June, and November. The membership fee buys you all three directories and a listing in one. Homes are also featured on their website. Trading Homes is a member of the International Home Exchange Association, which shares listings among an extensive worldwide membership in 18 clubs. Contact Tradings Homes International at P.O. Box 787, Hermosa Beach, CA 90254. Phone: (800) 877-8723. Call (310) 798-3864 from outside the U.S. and Canada. Fax: (310) 798-3865. E-mail: info@trading-homes.com. Website: www.trading-homes.com.

The Travel Exchange Club

The Travel Exchange Club is an on-line service. In addition to home swapping, they also help members who want to offer or accept hospitality, exchange timeshares, or rent their property. Send e-mail to: solafson@travex.com. Website: www.horizon. bc.ca/travex/home.html. Phone them at (800) 549-9076.

> $$$—Cousin Thrifty McCheap says: "Go in with three friends or neighbors to join an exchange club. Only one of you can list a home, but you can all use the catalog to submit offers to exchange. Your vacation accommodations will end up costing the same as dinner for six in my favorite restaurant—about $15 without tip."

IMAGINATIVE ACCOMMODATION SWAPPING

Now that you've determined to trade with friends or relatives, advertise for an exchange partner, or list your home in a club directory, start thinking creatively. Home exchanging is, after all, a creative art. The possibilities are limited only by your ultimate vacation dreams. Let's look at several possibilities:

Get a (New) Life!

Randy is production manager in an electronics company. He worked in the company's New Hampshire branch. When he was in Las Vegas at a company convention, Randy met and befriended Sheila, the production manager of the company's plant in Kuala Lumpur, Malaysia. Sheila and her husband wanted to return to the states for a year, and Randy and his wife wanted the experience of living overseas. Randy and Sheila approached the company vice-president in charge of production and convinced him that both of their capabilities would be enhanced by taking each other's job for 12 months.

A few months later Randy and his wife packed suitcases and winged off to Southeast Asia and moved into Sheila's bungalow in the K.L. suburbs. Sheila and her husband now live in Randy's white Colonial in Manchester. Each is doing relatively the same job and remains happily married to the same partner, but as Randy wrote on his most recent postcard: "Malaysia is as different from New England as you can imagine. It's as if Sheila gave me her life and I gave her mine."

It seldom hurts to ask. If you have a counterpart in a branch of your company that's located in a desirable part of the world, and if your job and that person's job could be interchangeable, why not propose to trade duties for a limited period? If you can agree also to swap residences, you can move into a house and job and experience a different and perhaps exciting environment. Life will resemble a new adventure rather than a tired rerun. And you'll probably be a more knowledgeable and experienced employee when you return.

Swap That Sloop

Got a boat that will sleep one or more? Then you've got swappable accommodations. The advantages to boat or yacht trading are obvious: Instead of shipping your ship from the Atlantic to the Pacific, let another boat owner use yours out of its home berth while you use his or hers. Transporting a boat over long distances by land or sea is an expensive and time-consuming proposition, but exchanging boats gives sailors a chance to ply new and distant waters affordably. Swap your sloop in Sandusky, for example, for a catamaran in Catalina, or exchange your trimaran in Malaga for one in Malta.

Velma and Jim, whom we met in Vancouver, B.C., traded their house and small boat in Tampa, Florida, for the use of a cabin cruiser in Washington State's pristine San Juan Islands. Jim told us that their experience resulted in one of the best trips of their lives. Just about any home exchange club will list your boat; alternately or in addition, you might want to advertise in a boating magazine.

Recreational Vehicle Trading

Our friend Molly's parents wanted to use an RV for camping in and touring around Wisconsin and Minnesota in June and July, but they wanted to avoid driving their RV east from Nevada. Through an exchange club, they were able to find a Minnesota family willing to swap RVs. Molly's mom and dad drove their car to St. Paul and picked up the RV they were to use. They took a month's tour of northern Wisconsin and Minnesota; then they returned their borrowed RV and drove home in their own car. Meanwhile the Minnesota folks flew to Reno to pick up Molly's parents' RV. They made a leisurely trip though northern Nevada, Oregon, Washington, and part of Idaho, and then drove back to Reno and flew home. Both parties were completely satisfied with the arrangement, particularly because they didn't have to haul a home across country or pay to rent one on arrival. Most home exchange directories will list your RV offer.

A Free Second Home—Year After Year

Daphne and Herb live in rural western Massachusetts. Dan and Shirley live on Manhattan's Upper East Side. Dan and Shirley like to rusticate several times a year and Daphne and Herb salivate periodically for Big Apple activities. These smart couples have an ongoing arrangement to trade homes—for one week in the early autumn and for four or five long weekends year-round. They've been exchanging homes for three years now, and last summer each provided permanent closet space for the other couple; now it's no longer necessary for

Daphne and Herb to pack dress-up clothes for Manhattan, and Shirley and Dan can leave their jeans and cardigans in the Berkshires until their next visit. Their ongoing trade provides one couple with a quasi-permanent city residence and the other with a country house—all at no cost other than for transportation and for the groceries they'd buy anyway if they'd stayed home.

Three-Way Exchange

A three-way exchange can offer flexibility. Here's how it works. The Greens, who live in Asheville, North Carolina, want to spend Christmas week in Orlando and have contacted the Whites who've listed their home there to trade. But the Whites want to stay in Santa Fe, New Mexico, that week and have phoned the Browns, who are willing to give up their home for the same seven days. The Browns, however, want to go the Southeast. The three families coordinate their plans so the Greens can open gifts in Orlando, the Whites can carve their turkey in Santa Fe, and the Browns can sing carols in Asheville.

Mining Vacation Gold from "Outdated" Club Directories

After you've paid your fees to the home exchange club and—hopefully—arranged and enjoyed a great vacation in someone else's home, don't throw out last season's directory. Here's why: When members put their homes up for trade, they often have specific objectives, such as two weeks in Stockholm in August, three weeks in Melbourne in November, one week in Quebec in July, etc. It's sometimes a waste of postage to attempt to attract them to your area when they're bent on another specific destination. But by the following year they've probably satisfied that specific craving and become, whether they've realized it or not, open to unexpected offers. They may not even know they'd like to spend a week or two at your place—until your offer arrives.

Here's what a friend did with a previous season's directory.

He wrote 30 letters to people from Hawaii who had listed their residences in an "outdated" directory. Stephen's letter began: "Dear Home Exchanger: We hope you had a wonderful vacation on your exchange last year. I'd like to tell you about our area in southern Idaho and about our home in the hope that we might make an exchange for two to three weeks this coming June." Stephen and his family got exactly what they wanted— three weeks in a condo only yards from the beach in Kauai.

Can you use a directory that's two or three years out of date? Sure. You'll have a letter or two returned because the addressees have moved, but if you send enough offers, you have an excellent chance to make a reciprocal agreement.

> $$$—Cousin Thrifty McCheap says: "Talk a home-swapping friend into letting you borrow last year's directory. That way, you pay nothing for arranging your home exchange."

A String of Swaps During the Same Vacation

Not long ago we were spectacularly successful in using an outdated directory to set up a string of exchanges for a restful one-month vacation. We sent off 40 letters to people listed in the previous year's edition; all lived in or near Southern California beach communities. Our multi-swap adventure would probably not have worked as well had we contacted members who had advertised in a current directory; all but a few who had checked "anywhere, anytime" on their application had fairly focused destinations and time frames in mind for the previous summer, and none of them expressed a preference for vacationing anywhere near our house. But I assumed that having achieved their goals, one or two might consider a week or more in our home.

We received only three positive responses, but three were all we needed. The first caller was Bob from Marina Del Rey, the yacht harbor for Los Angeles. We agreed he could have our house the third week in July. The second respondent had a house on a beach directly across from the San Diego Yacht Club. Would we like it for two weeks? Of course! Would the first two weeks in August be all right? Maybe. The question then was where to spend the last week in July—the interim week between the two exchanges—without coming all the way home. Because I'm allergic to spending money on motel rooms, paying for staying wasn't an option. The third caller, who reached us two days later, offered a luxury condo in Newport Beach. He agreed to the last week in July.

Our plan seemed perfect. We would have a month on the beach, and we'd visit Southern California's considerable cultural attractions. After driving to Southern California, since the three communities were no more than two hours apart, we simply packed our bags on two successive Sundays and made our way from Marina Del Rey first to Newport Beach, and finally to San Diego.

Exchanging with three parties, none of whom knew one another and none of whom we'd met face to face—without coming home to check the house between exchanges—seemed like an adventure, if not a deliberate act of folly. It was easy enough to prepare the house for the first exchanger. We solved the problem of making sure the house was ready for the second and third exchangers by hiring a house cleaner to come in between exchanges to make certain all was spic and span.

When we arrived at the condo in Marina Del Rey, our first stop, around three on a brilliant Sunday afternoon, we found a note from Bob on a table in front of the corner window. The note read: "Welcome. I have ordered two hundred yachts to pass the window every half-hour for the rest of the day to greet you." And so it seemed he had. We looked out at the channel through the gigantic picture windows and saw a colorful parade of sailboats of every description returning to harbor at the end of a dazzling weekend. We saw skilled and graceful windsurfers wringing the last drops of Sunday out of the afternoon's remaining sunlight. The ocean was a sparkling backdrop. The magnificent nautical pageant for which Bob took credit was a visually sumptuous prelude for the month ahead.

Our swap with three families was an ambitious exchange vacation, but it was successful in every way. We still feel rested from leisure days. We learned that sending out a large number of exchange invitations is helpful, and that seemingly out-of-date directories are still valuable. We also learned that it pays to be creative when planning free travel.

Taking a String of Swaps a Step Further

Let's take the "string" concept and the merits of creativity a step further. Remember, homes are just one example of accommodation. Let's say you agree with a family in Bruges, Belgium, to exchange your apartment somewhere in North America for their flat for a week. When the exchange is over in Belgium, you go north to Copenhagen to pick up a cabin cruiser you agreed to use in trade for a Danish family's use of your apartment. After you've explored the Danish and Norwegian coasts by boat for several days, you travel by train to Cologne and pick up an RV that you've accepted from a German family for the use of your apartment back home. You and the RV are now off to an adventure in the Alps or the Rhineland, or both. Let your imagination soar.

Doubling Your Offer

Consider listing your home as well as that of friends or relatives who want to vacation with you. Let's say your home is near Philadelphia and your brother's condo is in Baltimore. List both and give your potential exchanger a choice of using one home for the entire period of, let's say, two weeks, or of spending a week each in Philadelphia and Baltimore. Your offer could be the most enticing in the directory.

Getting Maximum Benefits from Your Second Home

Jerry and Yvonne, semiretired business owners, live just outside St. Louis and summer in their second home in Tennessee's Smoky Mountains. When they weren't using the second home, it sat vacant—something else for them to worry about. After reading the first edition of *You Can Travel Free,* it occurred to Yvonne that they could *exchange* Shady Acres. Moreover, it didn't matter whether or not the exchange was simultaneous. The Steins from Munich could stay in the Smoky Mountains in June when Jerry and Yvonne were busy in St. Louis, and Yvonne and Jerry could use the Stein's apartment when the German couple were off on another trip in September. Jerry and Yvonne now enjoy free vacation accommodations without money changing hands, and someone occupies their second home from time to time when they're not there.

Three years ago Jerry and Yvonne exchanged their vacation home for a condo in the Bahamas, and last year for an apartment in Mexico City. If you have a second home, consider swapping it. Better yet, offer your principal home as well. Two for the price of one could be irresistible to someone who lives just where you want to vacation.

WRITING AN OFFER THEY CAN'T (OR WON'T WANT TO) REFUSE

Your most important task after joining a club is to send out offers that other members won't want to refuse. Here are some tips for writing winning proposals:

- Nine months prior to your vacation isn't too early to begin. Competition for the most sought-after residences is keen, and many summertime arrangements are already made by the preceding October or November. Your offer can be among the first they receive if you fax, phone, or e-mail it.

- Don't hesitate to offer your "convenience" apartment or "handy-man's fixer-upper" for a 20-room mansion. The swap isn't permanent, and your location can be far more important to a trader than room size or amenities.

- April in Paris? Even if a listee in Indianapolis states in the club catalog that they want to go to Paris, France, and if you want to be in Indiana, offer your home in Paris—

Texas. It makes little difference where your home is. It could be the only offer they get, they may see the advantage of saving money by not paying for a trans-Atlantic flight, or you may convince them how wonderful Texas really is in the spring.

- If you've exchanged before, offer to furnish names and phone numbers of your former exchangees. Many people feel more comfortable about lending their home to those who have references. If you're a novice, a lack of references needn't be a deterrent to swapping, but professional or association references could help cinch the deal.

- Be honest about your home and its location. Newark isn't "just steps" from Lincoln Center. The half-empty muscatel bottle in the coal bin doesn't make your basement a wine cellar. The acid rock music that blasts from the adjacent apartment shouldn't be referred to in your letter as "free all-night concerts nearby."

- *Sell* your home as though you were a creative rental agent. Our fliers include a very positive description of the features of the house, a list of all attractions located within a two-hour drive, the number of people who can be put up comfortably, and a few notes about the community and the climate.

- On a beautiful sunny day we take a roll of pictures of the exterior and interior of our home from the most attractive vantage points and have a couple of dozen copies made; we send two or three of these snapshots to prospective swappers. You and your family undoubtedly look honest and quite attractive, so send along your pictures as well.

- We run off maps of the area, showing distances to top attractions. We also send chamber of commerce brochures.

- Here's a sample letter for a hypothetical home. Ernest and Ima Swapper may not exist, but if they did, their home sounds mildly spectacular and it's in a great location. So, the odds are that if they were real people with the home we've described, they'd be able to negotiate a successful trade.

Dear Home Exchanger:

My wife and I were attracted by your listing in the [name of club] directory. We propose exchanging our home in Berkeley in Northern California's San Francisco Bay Area during all or part of July 23 to August 18. We hope the following information will be informative—and enticing.

The Immediate Area: We're about 20 minutes from downtown San Francisco, an hour south of the Napa Valley Wine Country, two hours from the Redwoods, and an hour and a half from Pacific surfing and swimming beaches at Santa Cruz. We're in the heart of a vibrant exciting metropolitan area. Our house is a 20-minute walk or five-minute bus ride from the renowned University of California, Berkeley campus. Public buses stop a block away and will take you to the Bay Area Rapid Transit station, from which you can access the entire East Bay including San Francisco.

Our Home: The contemporary two-story house is 25 years old. It is 2,600 square feet and sleeps four comfortably. It has three bedrooms and two baths. There is a marvelous view from the living-room picture window that looks over most of Berkeley and across the bay to the San Francisco skyline. At night, when lights are on everywhere, the effect is breathtaking. The two-story living room has a skylight that brings in generous amounts of natural light. The cluster of oaks and pines at the rear of the house reaches up to two spacious decks. The master bedroom has a Jacuzzi, dressing area, walk-in closet, and commodious bathroom. There is, of course, a laundry room with washer and dryer, three televisions (with cable plus two premium movie channels), radios, tape deck, CD player, phonograph, a room full of books and magazines, an all-electric kitchen, a two-car garage with automatic opener, and wall-to-wall carpeting.

The Neighborhood: This is an upscale residential neighborhood in the Berkeley hills. Neighbors include U.C. professors, physicians, businesspeople, attorneys, and retired professionals. Our next-door neighbors look forward to being of possible assistance to you should we agree to exchange. The nearest supermarket is nine blocks away, but there is a small convenience store three blocks from here. Berkeley has many fine restaurants, gourmet markets and delis, bookstores, craft and clothing stores, etc. Regional parks are close and offer possibilities for hiking and picnicking. There is a good French restaurant within easy walking distance from our house.

What Else to See and Do: The U.C. Berkeley campus is of great interest and beauty and offers public concerts, lectures, and other events. Sight-seeing across the Bay includes Golden Gate Bridge, Fisherman's Wharf, Telegraph Hill and Coit Tower, Ocean Beach and the Cliff House, Golden Gate Park, Japantown and Chinatown, Union Square with its elegant shops, the Embarcadero, Pier 39, Nob Hill, etc. San Francisco is known for its fine restaurants.

Just over the Golden Gate Bridge is Marin County, known for its elegant homes and also for Mount Tamalpais and Muir Woods. Oakland, which is next door to Berkeley, has beautiful Lake Merritt, Woodminster Amphitheater, and a great museum. Sports enthusiasts will enjoy games year-round at the U.C. campus, baseball at Candlestick Park in San Francisco, and easy access to the Oakland Coliseum. Lake Tahoe is a three-hour drive and Yosemite Valley a little farther. Los Angeles can be reached easily in a day.

A Word about Us: We're Ernest and Ima and we're in our early fifties. Ima is a software manufacturing executive and Ernest is a high-school principal. Our children are grown and living out of state, so there will be just the two of us exchanging. We are non-smokers, and ask that if you are a smoker, you confine your smoking to outside on one of the decks. We are experienced exchangers, having exchanged four times for a total period of six weeks in the last four years. We have no pets, but there are six indoor plants that will require periodic watering. We will be glad to furnish references.

We hope you have a marvelous vacation, whether it's at our home or elsewhere. We hope to hear from you.

Sincerely,
[signed] Ernest and Ima Swapper
[address, phone number, e-mail address]

Enclosed:—area map with points of tourist interest
        —Berkeley and San Francisco Chamber Commerce brochures
        —schedule for summer concert series

ARRANGING THE SWAP

If your letter is successful in "selling" potential exchangers on the merits of spending their vacation in your home, or if someone sends you an offer you can't (or don't want to) refuse, you must come to a general agreement with them about the exchange. The following points should be helpful:

• In a standard exchange, no money exchanges hands between the two parties.

• Agree on who will pay the phone bill. Usually anyone making long-distance calls on your phone will reimburse you for the costs if you send them a copy of the bill when it arrives after the exchange has been completed. Many swappers find it convenient to bypass settling phone accounts by charging calls on a calling card.

- Unless the exchange is for several months, the occupant whose home it is usually pays all other ongoing expenses such as utilities, rent, taxes, etc.

- Once you've committed your house, do everything you can to avoid backing out. If circumstances are such that at zero hour you can't fulfill this obligation, try to find a neighbor who's willing to exchange his home with the folks who've planned on a great free vacation in your town.

- Agree on the maximum number of people to stay in either home. Each club listing will indicate how many people want to exchange. We often invite a few guests to join us for a day or two of our exchange, but we always inform the home's owner at the time of making the exchange agreement and get their permission before allowing any friend to remain overnight.

- Empty nesters make up the bulk of exchangers. If you don't want children in your home, you can screen them out by looking carefully at the listing in the directory. You may also specify nonsmokers.

- On the day we switch residences, we try to arrange for the other party to arrive a couple of hours early, or remain a few hours after our return, so we can provide them with a meal and get to know them better. Some people do that for us.

Preparing Your Home

The list below of what to do to prepare your home for the exchangers may seem long, but when your free vacation is completed, you'll more than likely agree that any extra work you've had to do to make the trade a success has been worth the effort.

- If you're a renter, inform your landlord or manager of your intentions.

- Make certain the swappers have a key or know how to get a key to your place. Leave one with a neighbor, hide a key in a designated accessible spot, or mail them the key. Traveling all day only to find that they can't get in can get them off to a grumpy start.
- If you live in a gated community, make necessary arrangements so they can get in the gate. Tell the security patrol that they have your permission to live at your address.
- Tell your local police department who's going to occupy your residence and on what dates.
- If you belong to a home owners' association or country club, arrange for passes or identification cards so your guests can use the pool, tennis courts, rec room, gym, hobby room, marina, or golf course.
- Provide all the information your exchangees will need by leaving a note or video- or audiotape. Tell them where to find grocery stores, restaurants, public transportation, cleaners, hairdresser, barber, hospital, post office, etc.
- Let them know the quirks of your appliances, air conditioner, or furnace.
- Let them know the phone number of the fire department and police.
- If they're to use your garage, leave them your automatic door opener.
- Tell them how to deactivate the burglar alarm when they enter.
- Inform your home owner's insurance company of your plans. Ask if the company will pay if the Burnses incinerate your living room. If not, get a rider on your policy for the duration of the Burnses' visit. Or, agree with the Burnses about who will pay for any damages to property or belongings—and put it in writing.
- In our own experience, and according to every exchanger with whom we've spoken, exchangers are honest and will take good care of your place. Nevertheless, don't tempt anybody.

Put your Krugerrands, rare stamps, Rembrandts, Hemingway first editions, letters to Great-great Grandpa from President Lincoln, baseballs autographed by Babe Ruth, Fabergé eggs, etc., away for safe keeping.

- Some exchangers will declare a closed room "off limits" and store in that room any objects that are breakable, valuable, or too personal for the use of others. If the room has a lock, all the better.

- Ask a friend, neighbor, or relative to come around and say "Hi." Your guests will feel more at home, and they'll be able to ask questions they might have about their temporary vacation residence.

- Decide with the other party who will care for the yard and the pets. If they won't or can't, hire a gardener and put Poopsie in a kennel. Reluctant or sulky gardeners and pet sitters are sometimes neglectful.

- Be honest about your pet. We once spent a week being walked [and menaced] by Gargantua, an oversized great Dane that was represented as being a "sweet little mutt."

- If they agree to care for your pets, tell them when to feed Poopsie and when to let her out. Leave sufficient pet food. Leave the number of the vet.

- Give them a schedule for watering indoor plants and/or the garden.

- Tell them when and where to put out the garbage and recycling bins.

- Clear out a reasonable amount of closet and dresser drawer space for their use. Leave some clothes hangers for them.

- If your guests are to use your computers or fax machines, let them know the idiosyncrasies of those complex devices.

- Tell them where to find sheets, towels, soap, the vacuum cleaner, etc.

- Let them know the location of the emergency exits of your house, apartment, or condo complex.

- Make your home safe. If you can't repair all your booby traps, don't keep them a secret. You know about the broken step leading to the cellar, but they don't. Put a label on the rat poison you left in the mayonnaise jar in the refrigerator.
- We leave a recent weekend edition of the metropolitan-area newspaper so they can see what plays, concerts, art shows, and other events are available. Ask them to do as much for you.
- Stretch a banner across your entry hall proclaiming "Welcome Helmut and Irmegard," if, indeed, those are their names.
- We generally leave something for them—wine, cheese, cookies, or fruit—with a note inviting them to enjoy it.

  $$$—Cousin Thrifty McCheap says: "By the time they've flown 6,000 miles from Wiesbaden, they'll be grateful for ice water."

RETURNING THE BORROWED HOME

When you return to your own home, you'd like to move right in and find everything as immaculate and as orderly as you left it. They would too.

- Leave clean linens on all beds that you've used. Wash and dry their towels.
- Wash the dishes and put them away.
- Turn off appliances, heaters, or air conditioners and stifle the fire in the wood stove or fireplace.
- Vacuum the carpet.
- Leave sufficient food and water for Poopsie and Igor.
- Don't surprise them by using the last sheet of toilet tissue and not replacing at least one roll.
- Make certain you have all your stuff. Your stretch pants and dentures probably won't fit them.
- Leave a thank-you note and possibly a small gift.
- Lock up the place and leave their key where they asked you to.

IF YOU EXCHANGE CARS

- If you agree to exchange cars with the Bashams, exchange driver's license numbers of the persons who will be driving, and forward the numbers to your auto insurance company. Make certain your auto insurance covers the Bashams' use of your car; they could, after all, use your new Porsche to try to clear away congested traffic.

- Don't assume that your insurance will cover you in a foreign country, or that theirs will. Check with your agent.

- Leave tips for them about freeway access or arcane traffic or parking rules in your area. If they can't park in front of the house on Wednesday nights in order to accommodate street cleaning, let them know.

- Agree whether the gas tank should be filled by each party at the end of the vacation.

- Agree on the maximum number of miles the exchanger should put on your car. If you plan to drive their car only occasionally and in town, and they plan to drive yours from Walla Walla to Wally World, consider charging them a rate per mile to cover costs of wear and tear on your vehicle.

- Leave them the phone numbers of emergency road service, repair shops, and your insurance agent.

- If your car is quirky, let them know how to humor it so it performs well.

- Think twice about driving in areas where you may not have had driving experience. Examples of places you may wish to use public transportation are Britain, where driving is on the left and some rural roads are scarcely wide enough for two bicycles to pass; Rome, where painted traffic lanes signify that chaos is O.K.; or central Bangkok where jammed thoroughfares resemble parking lots.

A Good Home Exchange How-to Book

If after reading this chapter you feel you need to know still more, look at one book in particular: *Trading Places: The Wonderful World of Home Exchange,* by Bill and Mary Barbour (Rutledge Hill Press). The Barbours are veterans of more than 40 exchanges and their book details anecdotes from several. In addition, they've surveyed 643 experienced exchangers to pass tips on to their readers. It's in public libraries, or get ordering information from Vacation Home Exchange Services, 16956-4 S. McGregor Blvd., Ft Myers, FL 33908. Phone: (800) 532-4918.

HOUSE SITTING

Gwen, who's retired and is flexible in her travel plans, wanted to spend several weeks in Chicago to visit friends, shop, attend plays, and visit museums. She didn't want to pay exorbitant fees for hotels in attractive areas of the city. Gwen ran an ad for one week in March in the *Chicago Tribune,* in which she offered to house-sit during part of the late spring or early summer. She got a call from a family in Evanston who were going to Spain for a month. Gwen offered to take in their mail, forward certain messages to their Valencia, Spain address, water their numerous indoor plants, feed and walk Fluffie, and record phone messages. Moreover, Gwen's presence was a deterrent to burglars. For her efforts, Gwen had the run of a comfortable 10-room home and received a hundred dollars a week. The money covered her food bill quite nicely and there was a little left over for sight-seeing.

Tamara, a college junior, wanted to practice French during her summer break. She offered her services through a home exchange directory as a house-sitter. Because she was able to send photocopies of enthusiastic references from her college counselor and from a former employer, and because Tamara promised to take care of plants and pets at no cost to the owners, she became temporary mistress of a nine-room apartment near central Bordeaux during the month of August. Tamara was able to sight-see and practice French on a daily basis; moreover, she made a number of French friends and recently she received an invitation to sit the same apartment again next August. But Tamara has her sights on Avignon or Arles instead.

Just about any responsible person can offer to house-sit. You can advertise in newspapers, or make your offer through the home exchange clubs listed above and in the directory of the Affordable Travel Club, 6556 Snug Harbor Lane, Gig Harbor, WA 98335. Phone or fax: (206) 858-2172. Do either or both and you may live somewhere fun and scenic, free of charge. And perhaps you'll pocket a few bucks for your minimal efforts.

BOAT SITTING

Pleasure boats worth hundreds of thousands of dollars are often left unattended at marinas; these superb pleasure craft make attractive targets for thieves and vandals. Our friend Carly, who loves boats, advises, "Go down to a marina on a weekend—particularly early Saturday morning or late Sunday afternoon—when the boat owners are apt to be around. Offer to boat-sit for free, or even ask a small amount if you want. You need to bring references with you, and you need to appear to be a responsible person they'd entrust something valuable to, because that's what you're asking them to do. It worked for me. And I got some free trips when the owners took their boats to sea."

TAKING CARE TO GET FREE ACCOMMODATIONS

Like Gwen, Tamara, and Carly, 10,000 Americans are caretakers of other people's property. According to the *Caretaker Gazette,* they do chores around campgrounds and parks during off season, and take care of ranches or estates while the owners are away. Some sit by the pool in the summer in Scottsdale, Arizona, while the house's owner has gone back to his or her office in Detroit. Others sit by the fire in Grosse Point, Michigan, in the winter while the owner is dipping in his pool in Scottsdale.

Caretaking can amount to strenuous daily work such as

mending fences and clearing brush, for which a substantial salary is paid; or it can amount to merely inspecting fences for breaks and safeguarding property from intruders. When not much work is involved, caretaking can provide a welcome change of pace and scenery—a vacation.

Often caretakers do some work and are paid enough to vacation elsewhere when they're not caretaking. Numbers of these innovative folks save a bundle on not paying property taxes and utilities on a place of their own. Many take care of property for an owner for a stipulated period, let's say November through April, year after year. They might then do some seasonal summer work—as camp counselors or fire fighters, for example—and still have three months to vacation in the spring and fall, someplace where the sun feels good on their backs.

Find out more about this free-accommodation profession by contacting the *Caretaker Gazette*, 1845 N.W. Deane St., Pullman, WA 99163. Phone: (509) 332-0806. Want-ads in the gazette often lead to attractive caretaking positions. Ads in home exchange club catalogs and in newspapers can bring good results, too.

FREE RV SPACE

One of the most useful Internet sites is Cool Works. It lists jobs everywhere, and in addition it devotes a department to free RV sites. These sites are free in return for doing something, perhaps putting in a few hours of work in a park. You can earn free RV parking space at places such as Grand Teton, Colorado; Miami-Homestead KOA campground; the Florida state park system; Grand Canyon; Yellowstone National Park; Lake Powell; Mesa Verde National Park; Mount Ranier; Sequoia-Kings Canyon Parks, etc. Check it out on Cool Works' website: http://www.coolworks.com/showme.

BECOMING A TEMPORARY LANDLORD

According to the November 1997 issue of *Kiplinger's*, a quarter of vacation home owners rent their premises at one time or another. The concept is terribly simple, but it took an ad in the

Sunday edition of the *San Francisco Chronicle-Examiner* to bring it to our attention. Two families in San Francisco wanted to rent a home together for a vacation in our community. We phoned one of the couples and sent them a description and pictures of our house. After checking their references, we agreed on a rate for two weeks and started planning a vacation of our own. We were able to collect enough rent that we drove to Lake Tahoe for two glorious summer weeks; in fact, we returned home with a few bucks in our jeans. While we were gone, we felt confident that responsible people were looking after our house. Our instinct was correct: The house suffered no losses or damages as a result of having served as a vacation rental.

The advantages of renting your home during your vacation are several: You can collect the rent money, and since you have to leave your home while your renters are there, you're in the enviable position of planning the vacation of your choice. Or, you can descend on Aunt Wilda and put your money in the bank for next year's trip—or pay off last winter's cruise. If your renters enjoy living in your home, they may want to make it an annual event; in that case, your vacations for the next several years will be at least partially paid for.

Before you jump in with both feet, check with your home insurance carrier to make certain you're covered if you rent your place out; check with your landlord—if you're not the owner—to make certain you have the right to rent your home temporarily. Ask for references and check them carefully. Be aware, too, that if you rent a vacation home out for more than two weeks a year, the income is subject to federal taxes. Check with a tax consultant about your liability and about deductions to which you'll be entitled when renting the place out more than 14 days annually.

Buy a rental agreement form at your stationery store. They're cheap. Fill it in and get the renters to sign it. Don't tempt anyone: Put away your collection of diamond and sapphire tiaras. In addition, you'll find the suggestions listed in the home exchanging section of this chapter helpful for preparing your place for visitors. You can list your residence in the want-ads in a city that will most likely attract renters to your area, or you can list it through a home exchange club whose address you found earlier in this chapter. You can offer your home for rent on-line with the Travel Exchange Club. E-mail: solafson@ travex.com.

You can also advertise in the World Wide Home Rental Guide, 1112 San Pedro NE, Suite 105, Albuquerque, NM 87110. Phone: (505) 255-4271. Fax: (505) 255-0814. This organization publishes catalogs in which you can list your home for rent on a short-term basis. It's published twice yearly and features homes that go from $25 to $1,500 per night. Potential renters contact the owner.

LEASE A VACATION HOME AND SUBLET

When Steve and Laura rented a house in La Paz on Mexico's Baja Peninsula, several of their San Diego friends and neighbors made the drive south to visit. The neighbors must have loved it there, because they stayed several days each. Their neighbors Lou, Silvia, and the kids, for example, stayed 10 days, turning Steve and Laura's restful vacation into an intensive exercise in bed making, large-batch cooking, and kitchen cleanup.

At that point it occurred to Laura that if their friends enjoyed long Baja weekends and full weeks that much, they might be interested in renting a place of their own in La Paz. The next step in her thinking was to consider a long-term lease on the comfortable adobe house they'd been renting for two or three weeks at a time. She and Steve could then use the beach house when they felt like fishing, swimming, or sunning, and rent it out the rest of the season.

After sounding out a few friends, acquaintances, and neighbors, they found that they could rent out the house for several months. They took a six-month lease for $1,000 a month. Before long they were able to sublet it for 16 weeks to various people at $400 a week. In fact, Lou, Silvia, and the kids took the first three weeks in March. Steve and Laura collected $400 more in rent than they paid out, and still had the sole use of the place for the eight weeks of the lease when they hadn't sublet. During those eight weeks they were free to enjoy the house; in fact, they had many fewer house guests because their friends and neighbors had bought their own vacation weeks there.

Got money? Got a vacation? Have you found that perfect hideaway at a good price? Then consider leasing and subletting it. It could give you a rent-free vacation just where you want to be. And who knows? Like Laura and Steve, you could even turn a profit.

SCANDINAVIAN OVERNIGHTS WITHOUT USING MONEY

Empty farmhouses, fishermen's dwellings, and deserted boathouses are available for public use in Norway. Travelers can spend a night or two without paying. Contact the following Norwegian offices for information: For deserted farmhouses in Setesdal—Mandal Tourist Office, Tidermannsgate 2, N-4500 Mandal. For fishermen's dwellings in the Lofoten Islands— Bodø Tourist Office, Box 128, N-8001, Bodø. For Bjørnsund fishing huts—Molde Tourist Office, Box 125, N-6401, Molde. For information about 1,254 camping sites in Norway—N.A.F, Storgaten 2, Oslo 1.

The Swedes have enacted a law called *Allemansraten*—"every person's right." It's an entitlement to cross private farm or forest land anywhere in the country, so long as you don't cause damage or make excessive noise. Campers may camp on private land, but they must stay a respectable distance from buildings such as houses and barns and leave their campsites clean. For information about camping in Sweden, write to the Scandinavian National Tourist Office, 75 Rockefeller Plaza, New York, NY 10019.

STOP!

If you've been paying hotel and motel bills on your vacations, stop. It's an unnecessary drain on the pocketbook. Take time to plan ahead and save a bundle of cash. If you have a roof over your head, swap it or rent it. If you have no home to swap, offer your services as a house-sitter.

CHAPTER 3

Free at Sea: Cruising and Crewing

McCheap's Third Law of Travel:
When cruising for free, always order at least two desserts.

ANSWERING THAT INSISTENT CALL

There's a slight breeze brushing your cheek as you sit on deck anchored in picture-postcard perfect Cook's Bay on the Polynesian island of Moorea. How much better it is sitting here gazing toward the palm-fringed beach, you think to yourself, than commuting to work at 6:30 in the morning through ice storms to a dead-end job back home. No wonder you responded joyfully to the insistent call of the sea.

If you've heard that beckoning call but haven't responded, this chapter will help you formulate the proper answer. Plying the world's seas and oceans on cruise ships and finding passage in exchange for work on private vessels are this chapter's two principal subjects.

Good New, Bad News: First, the Bad News

Great-uncle Hugh says he worked his way to Shanghai, Singapore, and Southampton aboard a freighter during the Great Depression. Uncle Hugh says the trouble with young people today is that they expect everything to be given to them. Uncle Hugh says that kids today are lazy: "If they really want to see the great ports of the world, let them get a job on a freighter like I did."

Well, Uncle Hugh, it's not lack of ambition that prevents today's young men and women from getting to exotic places as able-bodied seapersons; it's the fact that labor unions and the Merchant Marine protect the jobs of thousands of officers and other workers aboard U.S.-flag merchant ships by making entry particularly difficult. Furthermore, in the computer age, jobs aboard cargo ships are far more technical than they were when you were swabbing decks and chipping paint during the Hoover administration, Uncle Hugh.

A former secretary-treasurer of the National Maritime Union of America replied to a question about working passage this way:

> Unless they have very special skills or have seniority, nobody can pick up a job on a U.S. ship to earn money during summer vacations. There are no opportunities for working your way just for transportation on an American-flag ship. Workaways, as they are called, are prohibited by union policy and company rules.

Today one needs a certificate from the U.S. Coast Guard showing his or her rating in order to get permanent shipboard employment on cargo vessels. Those interested in pursuing a seafaring career may write to:

• National Maritime Union of America, 346 W. Seventeenth St., New York, NY 10011, or

• National Maritime Administration, Washington, D.C. 20025.

And Now: The Good News

To travel free at sea without sticking thousand-dollar bills in the hands of travel agents or cruise line pursers isn't all that difficult. In fact, you don't really need a Coast Guard certificate. All many seaworthy travelers need is an up-to-date passport. Welcome aboard. Your presence is needed.

Aside from joining the navy or the merchant marines,

there are two viable ways to go sailing without paying: Provide a service on board a luxury cruise ship or provide a service for a private yacht or boat owner. Let's start with love boats and end the chapter with opportunities to navigate with the yachties.

SAILING FREE ABOARD FLOATING HOTELS

Forget the stereotypical retirees decked out in spanking new cruise clothes, whose oceangoing vacation is paid for by the capital gains from seven- or eight-digit brokerage accounts. Sure, they're out there filling deck chairs right now, but cruisers come in all ages and economic groups. Only 16 percent of those who have cruised in the last five years enjoy a household income of more than $100,000. Only 31 percent are age 60 or older. In fact, more than a third of cruisers were between 25 and 40; and 35 percent are 40 to 59 years of age.

Passengers sign up to sail with one or more of the 30-plus cruise lines because they want to eat, to be pampered, to shop in exotic ports, to learn about the world, to get warmed up in winter, to eat, to luxuriate aboard the plushest of all vacation options, to see something different, and/or because they have fallen in love with being at sea. And some folks cruise to find the Sweetie Pie of their dreams or to enjoy a honeymoon after they have succeeded. And to eat.

Are you among the 60 million passengers who have cruised for two days or more since 1970? If you were left on shore, perhaps it was because you didn't want to or couldn't cough up the whopping price of a luxury cruise. Then, take comfort in the fact that the shore was crowded with plenty of other reluctant land lubbers. Take comfort in the fact that if you qualify, you can be among the lucky few who sail the world's waters without paying, waddling off to overflowing shipboard feeding troughs with the paying passengers aboard these floating gourmet kitchens.

Five types of opportunities call to you to sail on cruise ships without paying.

Opportunity #1: Sailing with the Crew or Staff

Sailing As a Contract Crew Member

One way to sail without paying is to secure a contract for a full-time position with the ship's crew doing something to make the ship run smoothly to give the passengers what they've paid for—a diverting, safe, and enjoyable experience. Although they don't get to waddle off with the elite, women and men who avail themselves of the first opportunity sail— and get paid too. Unlike shrinking or nonexistent positions on freighters, the number of jobs aboard luxury passenger vessels should grow. The Cruise Lines International Association projects that seven million passengers will cruise annually during the infant years of the 21st century. The launchings of new megaships by the major lines are being announced several times a year.

Most ship's crew positions require a four-month to a year-long contract. Most positions require that applicants be at least 21, but some people ages 18 to 20 get hired.

Some berths require specialized knowledge. Ship's officers are on a nautical career path and have studied navigation or engineering in college; these individuals fill highly technical positions. They receive good salaries, wear handsome uniforms, and often dine with passengers. Head chefs and pursers too may have had years of higher education.

Other job titles include waiter, sous-chef, cocktail waitress, kitchen staff, cabin steward, deck hand, pool attendant, etc. Many people who fill these positions are foreign nationals. Many of these hard workers come from lesser developed countries. The tips and wages they send home enable their families to live fairly well by local standards. Many save every penny to open a shop back in the Philippines, to establish a small bed and breakfast in Greece, or to pay off the mortgage on a farm in Indonesia. Their jobs are anything but glamorous and the workers are to be admired for their perseverance.

Tamara, our cabin stewardess on our most recent cruise and

her husband, Rico, who was a barman, plan to work on ships together for three more years. They prefer short cruises—three to seven days—because the tips are better than on longer 11- to 21-day cruises. At the end of three years, they say they'll return to their native Philippines and open a restaurant. With their minimal salaries but substantial tips, there's no obvious reason they shouldn't achieve their admirable goal. Their board and room are free aboard ship, and they spend little money ashore. Like Tamara and Rico, a large percentage of ships' crews see their work as a temporary expedient to either see the world or amass an astounding savings balance. Because of the personnel turnover that results from people having achieved their dreams, many crew jobs become quite possible to get.

But being a crew member can be frustrating to those who want to explore every port on the itinerary. Below-deck workers, many of whom are largely unseen by passengers, may get off the ship only once or twice a month on a rotating basis. These employees live and work together for months at a time. Some sleep four to a room. Others, such as waiters, who actually are highly visible to passengers, are up before dawn and up until after the gargantuan midnight buffet has been consumed, cleaned up, and put away, with only a short afternoon nap to keep them going.

If you take a job such as waiter, cabin steward, or dishwasher and you can't leave the ship very often, you're hardly traveling free. You may be saving money, but you may as well be back home with all the window shades drawn and the door closed. Other detriments—for anyone who works aboard, from the junior pot-scrubber to the captain—are seeing good friends leave as part of the never-ending personnel turnover, living and working in a confined space, and seldom being alone.

Shipboard Services Staff Members

Other full-timers, often Americans, Canadians, and British, staff the shops and boutiques, work in the purser's office, or in the bars and casinos; still others work as cosmetologists, disc jockeys, massage therapists, fitness specialists, and so forth. Due to customs regulations and other local prohibitions, casinos and boutiques are usually closed while the ship's in port, so these employees can go ashore if all their work is completed. They enjoy a good opportunity to see what the passengers see. The disc jockey, fitness instructors, photographers, the port lecturer, and the sales manager may get into port more than most other employees. For them, round-the-world cruises, during which there are no repeat ports, offer the greatest sight-seeing opportunities. Weekly repetitious three- and four-island Caribbean cruises offer the least sight-seeing opportunities. In most ports, the shore excursion staff is fully engaged getting tour groups on their way or escorting them on tours. Although they get to look at what passengers come to view, if they get any free time, it's during days at sea.

Cruise Director's Staff

A supposedly more glamorous opportunity is to join the cruise director's staff. The cruise staff works hard at jobs that passengers perceive as being fun. One lady on a recent cruise marveled that the assistant cruise director "actually gets paid" to conduct the late-night trivia game. My own suspicion is that after conducting a couple of hundred trivia games, the staff member would have preferred to be elsewhere.

The staff may include the cruise director and assistant directors, social hostesses, children's activities director, teen activity director, and others. Although, they smile heroically and try to make passengers feel at home, their work is repetitious. Every cruise on large ships features swimming pool activities, lounge games, and social get-togethers for passengers. Several nights a week for years the cruise director asks rhetorically, "Didn't we have a great day?" For the right person, however, these could be dream jobs. It's these staffers audiences envy on "Love Boat" reruns. The cruise staff sometimes find enough time to get to shore when the ship's in port, but certainly not as much time as do the passengers.

Medical Staff

An important segment of any cruise ship's staff works in the dispensary. Ships' physicians and nurses are fully qualified and licensed. Some are on salary and some keep a portion of the fees they collect for services. Some are permanent full-time employees and others come aboard for a few weeks during their vacations.

When the seas are calm and the kitchen is sanitary, when passengers don't come aboard with contagious diseases, when passengers don't slip on wet decks or fall on untrustworthy gangplanks, when all aboard are hale and hearty, ships' doctors and nurses have a great time. One ship's doctor of our acquaintance had retired from a lucrative practice and spent half the year sailing with various lines, taking only those cruises that appealed particularly to him and to his wife; the other half of the year they returned to their home in La Jolla to watch warm, ocean waves kiss California.

Something More to Read

Those interested in working aboard cruise ships can read:

- *Working on Cruise Ships* by Sandra Bow, Vacation-Work Publications; distributed by Peterson's Guides, 202 Carnegie Center, Princeton, NJ 08543. Phone: (800) 338-3282.
- *Guide to Cruise Ship Jobs* by George Reilly; it's available from Pilot Books, 103 Cooper St., Babylon, NY 11702. Phone: (516) 422-2225.
- *How to Get a Job with a Cruise Line* by Mary Fallon Miller. This book is available from Ticket to Adventure, Inc., P.O. Box 41005, St. Petersburg, FL 33743. Phone: (800) 929-7447 or (813) 822-1515. It includes names and addresses of cruise line employment agencies.

Getting Hired

Before you pay an agency for a job or write directly to a cruise line, see what cruise jobs you can find on the Internet site Cool Works. It's at http://www.coolworks.com/showme. At the time of this writing, several cruise lines, including Delta Queen, Special Expeditions Marine, Philip's Cruises and Tours, and Alaska Sightseeing Cruise West, were advertising for employees. Cool Works gives lots of information, including about how to contact the line and whom to call or write.

These agencies can put you in line for a job in the hotel (food and housekeeping) divisions on cruise ships:

- Apollo Ship Chandlers, 1775 N.W. Seventieth Ave., Miami, FL 33126. Phone: (305) 592-8790.
- Blue Seas Cruise Services, 122 W. Twenty-sixth St., Suite 1202, New York, NY 10001. Phone: (212) 255-3326.
- Cruise Ship Catering Services, 100 S. Biscayne Blvd., Suite 700, Miami, FL 33131. Phone: (305) 377-4510.
- CTI Recruitment Agency, 1439 S.E. Seventeenth St., Fort Lauderdale, FL 33316-1709. Phone: (305) 728-9975.
- Global Ships Services, 141 N.E. Ave., Suite 203, Miami, FL 33132. Phone: (305) 374-8649.
- Marine and Mercantile, Inc., 6925 Biscayne Blvd., Miami, FL 33138. Phone: (305) 759-5900.
- Stellar Maritime Cruise Services, 333 Biscayne Blvd., Miami, FL 33132. Phone: (305) 358-7860.
- Trident International, 1040 Port Blvd., Suite 400, Miami, FL 33132. Phone: (305) 358-7860.
- Sunsail, The Port House, Port Solent, Portsmouth, Hampshire PO6 4TH, U.K. Phone: (011) 44-1705-214330. Hires deckhands, hostesses, clubhouse workers, cooks, and nannies for cruises in Greece, Corsica, and Turkey.

Some lines contract out to firms to staff concessions such as shops aboard ship. If you're going to sell perfume or shorts, it may be a lot more fun to do it on the SS *Jacuzzi* than back home in Humdrum Corners. Here are companies that hire boutique and/or photo staff to sail:

- Alders International, 1510 Seventeenth St., Ft. Lauderdale, FL 33316. Phone: (305) 763-8551.

- Apollo Ship Chandlers, 1775 N.W. Seventieth Ave., Miami, FL 33126. Phone: (305) 592-8790.

- Clerici Cruise Services, P.O. Box 121, Miami, FL 33172. Phone: (305) 763-8551.

- Greyhound Leisure Services, Inc., 8052 N.W. Fourteenth St., Miami, FL 33126. Phone: (305) 594-9358.

- International Cruise Shops, 8052 N.W. Fourteenth St., Miami, FL 33126. Phone: (305) 592-6460.

- Suncoast Cruise Services, 2335 N.W. 107th Ave., Miami, FL 33172. Phone: (305) 591-1763.

Many cruise lines contract with concessionaires to operate their casinos. The concessionaire hires casino staff. These include:

- Greater Atlantic Casinos, Ltd., 990 N.W. 166th St., Miami, FL 33169. Phone: (305) 359-0001.

- Shoreside Consultants, 1007 North America Way, Suite 305, Miami, FL 33132. Phone: (305) 381-9544.

- Zerbone Cruise Ship Catering Services, 100 S. Biscayne Blvd., Suite 700, Miami, FL 33131.

Ship's photographers are true professionals who have to charm their subjects into smiling poses, work quickly to shoot a maximum number of photos, and produce a desirable product. Passengers usually buy at least one professionally taken photo of themselves boarding the ship, waddling off to the feeding trough in their best clothes, looking gorgeous or debonair on costume night, or shaking hands with the captain. Some of the companies that supply services (and photographers) to ships are:

- Cruise Ship Picture Co., 1177 South America Way, Suite 200, Miami, FL 33132. Phone: (305) 539-1903.

- Transocean Photos, Berth One, New York Passenger Ship Terminal, 711 Twelfth St., New York, NY 10019. Phone: (212) 757-2707.

Opportunity #2: Enriching the Passengers

The second opportunity is short-term and presents an out-standing and most pleasurable free travel experience. A number of people, some of whom are well-known celebrities, serve as guest enrichment providers. You don't need to be a retired TV newscaster or ambassador to qualify, but you do have to have an area of expertise. Guest enrichment providers are experts. They come aboard to enlighten passengers on subjects as diverse as fauna and flora, marine biology, art, wine, cooking, astronomy, gastronomy, astrology, politics, economics, investing, or history.

Others put on seminars and workshops to show people how to rejuvenate their "minds, bodies, and souls," how to lose weight, or how to lose unwanted mental baggage. Lecture titles such as "My Thirty Years with the FBI," "Physician to the Stars," "Escape from Iran," "Raising Your I.Q.," or "How to Build a Pyramid and Embalm Your Mummy for Fun and Profit," draw shipboard crowds. Enrichment providers speak often for about 40 minutes and field questions for five or 10 minutes. They may be asked to make one to three presentations a week, usually on days at sea. They can spend the rest of their time enjoying the cruise.

What can *you* talk to passengers about? Passengers fill ships' theaters and lounges to listen to and watch and learn from financial planners, handwriting analysts, and arts-and-crafts instructors. Other providers have won themselves free cruises by talking about self-esteem, relationships, successful retirement, numerology, memory improvement, astrology, astronomy, speed reading, buying at auction, time management, or better photography. One lady we know vacations on luxury lines by reading tarot cards. Many ships engage bridge instructors to lecture and to monitor duplicate sessions.

Still others have instructed seaborne vacationers on how to write short stories and poetry or on how to sell their writing. Ornithologists gather large audiences of bird watchers. Can you discuss buying precious stones, putting together a family tree, planning plastic surgery, antique collecting, saving the environment, managing stress, or using herbs for better health? Can you draw caricatures, pastel portraits, or show passengers how to cut silhouettes? Can you tell people what colors look best on them, how to set attractive tables, how to shop more efficiently, or how to build their self-esteem? Are you an expert on Alaska, the Panama Canal, Caribbean islands, South America, the Baltic or Mediterranean, or any other part of the world visited by cruise ships?

Are you able to teach passengers a few necessary phrases in French, Spanish, German, Greek, Italian, Russian, Bahasa Indonesia, Chinese, or some other language that can be useful in a cruise port? Can you show people how to do the latest dance steps? Do you have a claim to fame such as being an author, artist, former cabinet member, 1950s singer, or TV star? Can you organize and instruct folk, line, or ballroom dancing?

How good is your knowledge of yoga or tai-chi? Can you demonstrate massage techniques? Can you lecture about computers or Buddhism or teach calligraphy? How about showing them some golf or tennis techniques? Can you teach scuba diving and organize snorkeling expeditions? Do you know the history of jazz? How about sharing knowledge of leading musicians from the days of the big bands? Some popular speakers help to motivate sales personnel and executives. Are you a sports figure who can discuss triumphant moments on the court or field? Are you a priest, minister, or rabbi? Clergy are invited to sail free on large ships in return for conducting sabbath services. Can you conduct an art auction?

Terms of temporary employment are nearly as diverse as are the topics covered. While several lines contract with enrichment providers directly, others require that speakers go through agencies. Agencies charge a fee, usually a dollar amount for each day the provider and his or her companion of choice is aboard the ship. Some lines will pay a stipend to the provider; others pay none. Some pay airfare in all cases, others when the provider does two cruises back to back, and others require the provider to pay transportation costs to and from his or her ports of embarkation and disembarkation. A few lines will give the provider free drinks, laundry service, and perhaps pay shipboard tips in the provider's name. Others give none of these extras.

But the vast majority of cruise lines do give the enrichment provider and his or companion of choice free cruise tickets. Enrichment providers almost always eat with the passengers and are given regular passenger cabins. These featured speakers enjoy the very same experience as paying passengers in every way except that they present an enrichment program of some sort one or more times during the cruise. We've seen some providers who've stayed on board for four months on round-the-world cruises, but it's more common for a provider to come on board for 10 to 24 days. Thus, speaking to passengers is an unparalleled vacation-time opportunity for the employed and a great diversion for retirees.

Retirees who serve as providers often cruise much of the year. A bridge instructor of our acquaintance sailed on one ship from Seville, Spain, to Barbados, and then boarded another vessel to Miami, only to sail from there on a third to Brazil and back again to Miami—a total of nine weeks at sea with only a night or two in hotels.

Let's hear what Belynda the arts-and-crafts instructor has to say, as we beat out the *Enquirer, Globe,* and *Star* for an exclusive *You Can Travel Free* interview:

Cruising with Belynda, Arts-and-Crafts Instructor

YCTF: How did you get started teaching arts and crafts on cruise ships?

Belynda: A friend was teaching crafts on the *Liberté,* which was owned by American Hawaii Cruises. It sailed once a week out of Papeete, Tahiti, and stopped at several of the Society Islands such as Moorea and Bora Bora. My friend Allison was supposed to fly to Papeete in July for three weeks as a crafts instructor on the *Liberté,* but she got engaged and her fiancé didn't want her to go without him. The cruise line said he could share Allison's cabin without paying, but he had to work. I was on vacation from teaching art in a junior high school. She got American Hawaii to agree for me to replace her.

YCTF: Then what? Did that lead to more cruises?

Belynda: I did three cruises on the *Liberté* in July and three at Christmastime. Then the company sold the ship. Then I sent applications to all the other cruise lines and got jobs with Royal Cruise Line.

YCTF: What do you have to do to get your free cruise?

Belynda: When we have days or partial days at sea I show passengers how to make collages, how to cut silhouettes, fold napkins, make baskets, make costume jewelry, wallets, how to draw, that sort of thing. I'd usually get about 20 people and 18 or 19 would be women. My cruise students are appreciative and fun to teach. I like it a lot.

YCTF: How many hours do you put in a week?

Belynda: Every cruise is different, but maybe five or six. Then there's the preparation before I leave home. I have to buy, assemble, and bring all the materials. You have to find something that's not going to fill your suitcase and empty your wallet. That's the hard part. And you don't want materials that will be too heavy to carry when you're traveling to the ship.

YCTF: Where did you cruise with Royal?

Belynda: The first time was to the North Cape of Norway; you look out of your porthole and it's sunny at three in the morning. Norway is probably the most beautiful country in Europe. The fjords are breathtaking. And we met some really neat people aboard. That was a great cruise.

YCTF: Then what?

Belynda: We—I always take my husband, Tom—did a Black Sea cruise for Royal. We started in Athens and went to Istanbul, Yalta, and Odessa, a port in Romania, Ephesus in Turkey, and then to Mykonos. The crew was all Greek and they were great. The next winter we got to go somewhere I'd always wanted to visit: Southeast Asia. We sailed from Singapore to Java, Bali,

North Borneo, Vietnam, Malaya, Hong Kong, Canton (now Kuangzchou), and back again. Vietnam was really interesting, but it's still a really poor country. The next year we went back to Vietnam, and to Thailand; also we went to Malaya and Singapore again. Right after that cruise something really sad happened. Royal got sold to another line. I sent out more resumés. Then I did a Transcanal cruise with another line and later a trans-Atlantic crossing. Next month I'm sailing in the Baltic.

YCTF: What about your friend who got you the job? Does she still teach crafts on board ships?

Belynda: Allison got married to her bossy fiancé and later got divorced, and now she's living with a guy who gets seasick. She hasn't cruised since. But I cruise about twice a year. The only problem is the food; I gain about three pounds every time I get on a ship.

YCTF: But you love it, don't you?

Belynda: Yeah.

YCTF: Thanks for talking about cruising with me.

Here are agencies that place enrichment providers. Some charge fees:

- International Voyager Media, 11900 Biscayne Blvd., Suite 300, Miami, FL 33181. Phone: (305) 892-6644.

- Karp Enterprises, Inc., 1999 University Dr., Suite 213, Coral Springs, FL 33071. Phone: (305) 341-9400. Fax: (305) 341-5592.

- Lectures International, P.O. Box 35446, Tucson, AZ 85740. Phone: (520) 297-1145.

- Lauretta Blake, The Working Vacation, 4277 Lake Santa Clara Dr., Santa Clara, CA 95054-1330. Phone: (408) 727-9665. Fax: (408) 980-1829.

- On Board Promotions, 777 Arthur Godfrey Blvd., Suite 320, Miami Beach, FL 33140. Phone: (305) 673-0400.

- Program Experts, Inc., P.O. Box 510, Cresskill, NJ 07626-0510. Phone: (201) 569-7950.

- Posh Talks, P.O. Box 5417, Palm Springs, CA 92263. Phone: (619) 323-3205.
- Sunworld Sailing Ltd., 120 St. George's Rd., Brighton, East Sussex BN2 1EA, U.K. Hires instructors and deckhands and other staff for sailing and windsurfing cruises in Spain, Greece, and Turkey.

If you're a professor who can get a semester off, you have a chance to sail around the world. Contact Semester at Sea, Institute for Shipboard Education, University of Pittsburgh, 811 William Pitt Union, Pittsburgh, PA 15260. Phone: (800) 854-0195. E-mail: shipboard@sas.ise.pitt.edu. SaS hires university professors for their round-the-world and Caribbean educational programs. They teach undergraduates and paying out-of-college passengers. Students, passengers, and instructors travel to Brazil, China, Egypt, Greece, Hong Kong, India, Israel, Japan, Kenya, Morocco, Philippines, South Africa, Turkey, Ukraine, Vietnam, and Venezuela.

Opportunity #3: Entertaining Passengers

The third category of free cruisers consists of entertainers. These include singers, dancers, magicians, orchestra members, jugglers, comedians, classical musicians, acrobats, cocktail-bar pianists, etc. Can you saw your girlfriend in half, play "Misty," or tell jokes that are only mildly offensive? If you can entertain, why do it Saturday nights at the Honky Tonk Corral for beers? Consider taking your act to sea.

Some shipboard entertainers are employed directly by large cruise lines but most are contract temporary employees. They get gigs through agencies. The agency takes a bite out of their salaries. Their contracts may be for a few days or a few months. They may work the same ship or rotate among the various ships of a single cruise line, or among the ships of several lines. Entertainers may stay aboard between two ports only—perhaps for three days total in order to do one show—and then fly 6,000 miles to board another ship. Or they may go home to wait for the next call.

But in any case, they visit exotic ports and, when not rehearsing, enjoy days ashore, just as the passengers do. Ship's lounge entertainers often eat with the passengers and have cabins the same as or similar to those of clientele who pay thousands for the experience.

The principal agencies through which entertainers get their bookings are

- Bramson Productions, 1501 Broadway, New York, NY 10036. Phone: (212) 354-9575.

- Fiesta Fantastica, 230 S.W. Eighth St., Miami, FL 33130. Phone: (305) 854-2221.

- Jean Anne Ryan Productions, 308 S.E. Fourteenth St., Ft. Lauderdale, FL 33316. Phone: (305) 523-6399.

- Peter Grey Terhune Productions, P.O. Box 715, Cape Canaveral, FL 32920. Phone: (407) 783-8745.

- Ray Kennedy Production Co., 244 S. Academy St., Mooresville, NC 28115. Phone: (704) 662-3501.

- Ship Services International, Inc., 370 W. Camino Gardens Blvd., 3rd Floor, Boca Raton, FL 33432. Phone: (407) 391-5500.

- Showmasters, 3038-D N. Federal Highway, Ft. Lauderdale, FL 33306. Phone: (305) 563-8028.

Opportunity #4: For Gentlemen Only

The fourth invitation is open only to unattached dashing gentlemen with at least a hint of gray in their hair. No hair? No problem if you're a great conversationalist and dancer. Gentlemen *escorts* or *hosts* are given free cruises in return for their promise to dance with, eat with, and chat with single ladies. Too good to be true? Not at all. Hundreds of men are dancing across the oceans of the world this very minute, and they pay little or nothing for the pleasure.

Why gentlemen escorts? Demographers tell us that women live longer than men, and because they do, ships have more widows as passengers than they do single male passengers older than age 50. Some single ladies who can afford to cruise, do so frequently. A number of these active ladies who sail chiefly to dance have told us that they choose a particular cruise line because the ship provides unattached men to dance with them. To keep their good female customers coming back, several cruise lines offer free passage to as many as 12 single gentlemen hosts at a time. Perhaps if you've cruised you've seen these dashing hosts dancing their hearts out in their white shoes, white trousers, and blue blazers. Perhaps you saw Walter Matthau and Jack Lemmon on the big screen doing the same thing, but with far less finesse.

Sought-after hosts have some common traits. They're trim, well groomed, outgoing, and they can mambo, foxtrot, waltz, and tango at afternoon teatime and far into the night. Nobody said Cary Grant. Nobody said seriously rich. But they are instinctively courteous, in good health, and they shave daily and keep their shoes shined. They're mostly sober. Moreover, they know how to keep a conversation alive and how to make a woman feel appreciated.

Cruise line officials counsel these gentlemen not to become attached to any of the ladies with whom they dance, drink, or dine. Rather, their assignment is to spread themselves around and to provide company for each of the single ladies present who would like to have totally noncommittal company off and on during the afternoon or evening. A host's contract may be for a single short cruise but is more often for two to four weeks. Many gentleman hosts are cruise-line repeaters.

The host's duties can be fun for the right man. It takes a certain kind of person to enjoy his obligations. He'll usually sit at a table with single ladies at lunch and at dinner. The ability to play bridge is a real plus; there's often the need for a fourth. He has to endure late nights. Sometimes he'll be assigned other light duties such as directing guests to tour buses in port or handing out landing cards.

But his most important duty is to get out there on the dance floor and help these ladies tear it up. We've spoken to a number of these gentlemen hosts and have yet to meet one who didn't enjoy his cruise and who didn't look forward to being invited back.

Contact cruise lines directly. Also contact these agencies:

- Lauretta Blake, 4277 Lake Santa Clara Dr., Santa Clara, CA 95054-1330. Phone: (408) 727-9665.

- Merry Widows Dance Tours and Cruises, 1515 N. Westshore Blvd., Tampa, FL 33607. Phone: (800) 374-2689 or (800) 313-7245.

Opportunity #5: Reservations for Fifteen, Please

The fifth chance to cruise free is to recruit and take a group and sail as the group organizer. Usually 15 paying passengers will get you a complimentary ticket. Chapter 5, "Hosting Group Tours," is full of valuable information on putting together a group.

CHOOSE YOUR CRUISE

To choose your cruise, find out specific cruise itineraries and when specific ships sail. Your travel agent will give you brochures from major lines; these slick booklets tell you all about the ship as well as cruise dates. Public libraries usually have recent editions of books written to help potential passengers select the right ship and itinerary. These books discuss shipboard etiquette, tipping, amenities, shore excursions, clothing, etc. They also indicate ships that require guest enrichment presenters, entertainers, child-care providers, scuba and snorkeling instructors, fitness directors, etc. These books include:

- *Berlitz Complete Guide to Cruising and Cruise Ships*, from Berlitz, 257 Park Ave. South, New York, NY 10010. Phone: (800) 257-5755.

- *Cruises and Ports of Call*, from Fodor Travel, 201 E. 50th St., New York, NY 10022. Phone: (800) 733-5515.

- *Fielding's Guide to Worldwide Cruises,* from Fielding Publications, 308 S. Catalina Ave., Redondo Beach, CA 90277. Phone: (800) 843-9389.
- *Frommer's Cruises,* from Macmillan Travel Books, 15 Columbus Circle, New York, NY 10023. Phone: (800) 257-5755.
- *Stern's Guide to the Cruise Vacation,* by Steven B. Stern. This big cruise compendium contains evalutions of more than 200 ships, as well as their history and statistics. Stern includes actual ships' menus and daily activity programs. He tells his reader how to make the most of a day in port and tells what major attractions not to miss in popular ports of call. This is a really comprehensive volume. Get it at your library, from your bookseller, or from Pelican Publishing Co., P.O. Box 3110, Gretna, LA 70054. E-mail: sales@pelicanpub.com. Phone: (800) 843-1724 or (888) 5-PELICAN.
- A popular magazine that chronicles and updates the cruise industry for potential passengers is *Cruise Travel,* from World Publishing Co., 990 Grove St., Evanston, IL 60201. Phone: (708) 491-6440.
- In addition, send a first-class stamp for the free pamphlet "Choose to Cruise...The Best Vacation Value" to Cruise Lines International Association, 500 Fifth Ave., Suite 1407, New York, NY 10110. Phone: (212) 921-0066. This free brochure explains why cruising is a good value and lists 101 reasons to get onboard.

Contacting the Cruise Lines

Whether you want a temporary full-time job, to get started on an oceangoing career, to lecture, to entertain, to be a gentleman host, or to take a group, you can start by contacting the major cruise lines. Here are a few basic pointers to keep in mind as you explore your options and go through the interview process:

- Make certain the line hires people to do the job you want. For example, lines that operate small expedition ships *do* use naturalists and historians, but they don't ordinarily employ a chorus line. Some large fun ships that hit an island a day in the Caribbean don't hire archeologists or bird experts, but they do hire a number of hoofers to dance on stage.

- When possible, phone first to find out the name of the person who hires people for the job you want. If you want to work in the kitchen or the restaurants, for example, ask who hires hotel staff. If you want to work in a technical position, such as radio operator, ask the name and title of the person in charge of hiring technical personnel. Always address correspondence directly to that person; if you address it to "To Whom it May Concern" or "Personnel Manager," your resumé or application could become lost. You may also find that nobody at the line does the hiring for the job you want; rather you'll be given the number of an agency. The agency will probably ask you to pay a fee if you get the job.

- When you contact the hiring official at the cruise line or at the agency, stress your interest in doing a superb job to contribute to the well-being and happiness of the passengers. Even if your chief reason for sailing is to get to balmy isles and pulsating foreign cities, don't tell your contact that you're applying to "get away," "have a blast," or "meet hunks." Remember the passengers!

- Before signing on be sure to find out who pays your airfare to the departure point. If you have to board the SS *Mealtime* in Capetown, South Africa, the airfare from North America alone could cut a big hole out of your first six months' pay. Ask who pays for your uniform, if you'll be required to wear one. Ask about insurance and other fringe benefits. Finally, ask if you'll have money deducted from your wages for your cabin and meals—an unlikely, but possible—event.

To get started, contact:

- America Hawaii Cruises, Two N. Riverside Plaza, Chicago, IL 60606. Phone: (312) 466-6000.

- Bergen Line, 405 Park Ave., New York, NY 10022. Phone: (212) 319-1300.
- Carnival Cruise Lines, 3655 N.W. Eighty-seventh Ave., Miami, FL 33178-2428. Phone: (305) 599-2600.
- Celebrity Cruises, 5200 Blue Lagoon Dr., Miami, FL 33126. Phone: (305) 262-6677.
- Costa Cruise Lines, 80 S.W. Eighth St., Miami, FL 33130-3097. Phone: (305) 358-7325.
- Crystal Cruises, 2121 Avenue of the Stars, Los Angeles, CA 90067. Phone: (310) 785-9300.
- Cunard Line, 555 Fifth Ave., New York, NY 10017. Phone: (212) 880-7500.
- Dolphin Cruise Line, P.O. Box 025420, Miami, FL 33102-5420. Phone: (305) 358-5420.
- Holland America Line—Westours, 300 Elliott Ave. West, Seattle, WA 98119. Phone: (206) 281-3535.
- Norwegian Cruise Line, 95 Merrick Way, Coral Gables, FL 33134. Phone: (305) 447-9660.
- Princess Cruises, 10100 Santa Monica Blvd., Los Angeles, CA 90067. Phone: (310) 553-1770.
- Radisson Diamond Cruises, 600 Corporate Dr., Suite 410, Ft. Lauderdale, FL 33344. Phone: (305) 776-6123.
- Regency Cruises, 260 Madison Ave., New York, NY 10016. Phone: (212) 972-4774.
- Renaissance Cruises, 1800 Eller Dr., Suite 300, P.O. Box 350307, Ft. Lauderdale, FL 33335-0307. Phone: (305) 463-0982.
- Royal Caribbean International, 1050 Caribbean Way, Miami, FL 33132-2096. Phone: (305) 539-6000. Call (305) 530-0471 for the employment hotline.
- Seabourn Cruise Line, 55 Francisco St., San Francisco, CA 94133. Phone: (415) 391-7444.
- Special Expeditions, 720 Fifth Ave., New York, NY 10019. Phone: (212) 765-7740.

- Windjammer Barefoot Cruises, P.O. Box 120, Miami Beach, FL 33139; Phone: (305) 672-6453.

Two-fer Cruise Freebies

Have you ever seen the cruise-line ads that state, "Second Person Goes Free?" There are plenty of such offers, particularly now that competition is acute among these oceangoing palaces. So how can you climb aboard without cost? You'll be off to the Caribbean for seven or 14 days of wintertime funning and sunning shortly after you've convinced your aunt Amanda that she needs to get out of Moose Mist, Montana, and float about where it's hot. Tell her you're willing to give up your projected February visit to her house so you can accompany her to the Antilles as her shipboard companion. Be sure to emphasize that your presence won't cost her a cent. Aunt Amanda pays full fare. Your passage, as the free second person in her cabin, is complimentary. See Aunt Amanda's travel agent for the latest array of cruise freebies.

CREWING ON BOATS

All kinds of people, whether they know port from starboard, crew on boats. If the boat owner is excruciatingly rich and needs extra hands, these vacation-time sailors walk up the gangplank and fall into the proverbial lap of luxury.

If you do know something about seamanship, you could have a fairly easy time getting a temporary shipboard job and you'll get to the next island or the mainland without paying. Those with navigational, culinary, or mechanical skills—cooks, carpenters, fiberglass repairers, engine mechanics, welders, painters, sail repairers, divers, radio and radar operators, and radio repair persons—are paid to crew on yachts, chartered boats, and boats that take day trippers sailing or fishing. Others are paid to deliver boats from one port to another.

Many yachtie wannabes—skilled and unskilled, with and without experience—go down to the marina and ask around. They often get passage on a yacht in return for some work.

They hang out at dockside bars and restaurants or supply shops. They check bulletin boards. And they often attach to bulletin boards fliers that advertise their expertise or eagerness to work.

The world of yachties is a surprisingly small world. Boat owners and their crews are able to meet and greet the same people in Fort Lauderdale; Bridgetown, Barbados; Minorca, Spain; Corfu, Greece; Mahe, Seychelles; Durban, South Africa; Rio; Auckland; Sydney; Honolulu; and Marina Del Rey. If you devote a few seasons to crewing and do a very good job, your face and reputation will get known and boat owners will seek you out for crewing positions. If you want to part company with the boat owner who's headed for Cartagena because you want to go to Guadeloupe, it won't be much of a problem. You're almost sure to find a yacht going to your dream port or to some place equally as enticing. And with your outstanding reputation, you'll probably be welcomed aboard.

Experienced yacht-hoppers know that Antigua, British West Indies, is the place to be in April, because crew members change boats there and other crew are taken aboard. They know that from the West Indies, boats make repositioning crossings to the Mediterranean, or they head for Hawaii or Tahiti through the Panama Canal. Experienced nautical hitch-hikers know that Fort Lauderdale is teeming with opportunities in the late fall and winter. They're well aware that in the summer, optimum places to position themselves for a free sail are the south of France and Spain's Costa Del Sol, including the British rock of Gibraltar. They know that in the winter St. Barts, St. Lucia, Martinique, and the Grenadines see lots of yachts.

Other yachties hang out in ports serving the Panama Canal; in Auckland and Bay of Islands, New Zealand; in Bermuda, Sydney, and San Diego. Still others haunt the waterfront in Suva, Fiji; Tenerife in the Canary Islands; Greece and its islands; and East Coast seaports in the United States. They know that in South Florida most boats sail by early May or early June. In New England it won't be until June or July.

Asia and Africa are most difficult for free-lance yacht casual crew because indigenous crew members work for little and experienced sailors among them are easy to find. We've noted in our own meanderings that that Pacific island ports are filled with sails: Moorea and Nuku Hiva in French Polynesia; Suva, Fiji; Noumea, New Caledonia; Port Vila, Vanuatu attract boats. St. Barts, St. Thomas, and St. Johns in the West Indies and California's San Francisco, Sausalito, and Marina Del Rey also offer good opportunities.

Do You Sincerely Want to Sail with Captain Bligh?

Before you sign on, take some precautions. Look over the boat and the captain. Is the vessel seaworthy? Is the captain seaworthy? Can he actually sail? Is he sober enough to do so? Is he smuggling illicit drugs? Does he have a cargo full of potential illegal aliens who want to come to the United States? Will you become part of his white slave cargo? Is a desperate gang of rival smugglers trying to kill him by blowing his boat out of the water? You must also determine, before you leave the relative safety of the dock area, if the yachtie is interested in your coming aboard to satisfy hormonal rather than navigational requirements. Boat hopping is extraordinarily similar to hitchhiking: Just as you wouldn't want to get into a car with a drunk, smuggler, or pervert, you don't want to be at sea with one either. Successful free travelers try never to put themselves in danger at any time.

When you do get passage on a boat, you may be asked to pay for your own food. You may even be asked to pay for your passage, or you could be offered money for working. There's no standard agreement; just about everything is negotiable. Before you sail, be certain you understand the financial conditions that the boat owner has set: If money is to change hands, who's paying whom? If possible, put your agreement in writing.

Understand too what type of work and how much of it is to be done. If you can't do the work, be honest; never jeopardize the lives of all the people aboard by boasting that you have skills essential to a safe voyage if you don't have those skills. Do you get too seasick to perform your duties? Gale-force winds can make plying the seas in relatively small pleasure craft a bilious nightmare for the faint of stomach. If you know you'll spend most of the day hanging over the side polluting the ocean with your breakfast, it's best to skip this chapter altogether.

Your personal traits are as important as a seaworthy stomach and honesty about your seagoing skills. Put yourself in a yacht owner's position: You're on vacation in a balmy bay, entertaining family, friends, and business associates aboard a vessel that commemorates your professional and financial success. You want rest, relaxation, and good conversation. Do you want a casual crew member who complains about food, choppy seas, confined sleeping areas, and his or her duties? What would you do with such a person when you reach the next harbor? Exactly.

On the Internet, punch in http://www.crewseekers.co.uk. moreinfo.htm for a list of safety tips for potential crew members. Two of these are 1) always give your itinerary to a friend or relative on shore before you sail away into the unknown; and 2) when you meet the owner on his yacht for the first time, take someone with you.

Crew Agencies

You can hang around the harbor and try to make friends and get invited to sail, or you can get help from an agency. Some marinas have employment agencies that find experienced crew for boat operators; usually the jobs are temporary. The agencies charge a fee. Some employment agencies are

- Antigua Yacht Services, P.O. Box 2242, St. John's, Antigua, West Indies. Phone: (809) 460-2711. Fax: (809) 460-3740.

- Captains and Crew, Route 5, #11, Long Bay, St. Thomas, U.S. Virgin Islands 00802. Phone: (809) 776-2395.

- Compass Yacht Delivery, P.O. Box 4283, Calabash, NC 28459. Phone: (919) 579-5241.

- Crewfinders International, Inc., 404 S.E. Seventeenth St., Ft. Lauderdale, FL 33316. Phone: (800) 438-2739 or (954) 522-CREW. Fax: (954) 761-7700.

- Crewseekers International, Hawthorne House, Hawthorne Lane, Sarisbury Green, Southampton SO31 7BD, U.K. Phone: (01) 489-578-319. E-mail: sailing@crewseekers.co.uk. This organization bills itself as a "high quality personal crew introduction service." Crewseekers specializes in introducing amateur crew for leisure cruising, racing, and delivery of boats. The potential crew members negotiate directly with the boat owners. Members are given details about yachts and their owners and three contacts to follow up on.

- Cruising Association, One Northey St., Limehouse Basin, London E14 8BT U.K. Phone: (01) 71-537-2828.

- Hassel Free, Inc., Crew Services, 1550 S.E. Seventeenth St., Suite 5, Ft. Lauderdale, FL 33316. Phone: (954) 763-1841. Fax: (954) 763-7421.

- Worldwide Yachting Services, Inc., 1053 S.E. Seventeenth St., Fort Lauderdale, FL 33316. Phone: (954) 467-9777. Fax: (954) 527-4083. Worldwide can help the captain, crew, and "even massage therapists" get hired. There's a registration fee.

- Yacht Crew Register, 1664 Philip Ave., North Vancouver, BC V7P 2W1. Phone/fax: (604) 990-9901. E-mail: yachtcrw@direct.ca. This organization places everyone from the steward to the captain on yachts. It's an employment register.

Look too for crew-wanted ads in magazines such as *Sail, Cruising World, Yachting,* and *Soundings.*

Reading More about Crewing

- *Born to Sail (On Other People's Boats)* by Jennifer P. Stuart; Sheridan House, 145 Palisades St., Dobbs Ferry, NY 10522. Phone: (914) 693-2410. This experienced sailor tells how to get crew positions.

- *The Seagoing Hitchhiker's Handbook: Roaming the Earth on Other People's Yachts* by Greg Becker; it's from High Adventure Publishing. Phone: (714) 643-3286.
- "Working on Boats" by Steve Wilson is in the January/February 1997 issue of *Transitions Abroad.*

SAILING ALL THE TIME

If you can't bear to get off the boat and want to sail all the time, you need to become a kazillionaire to have your own yacht and crew, or learn necessary navigational skills and earn a license. The best credential is a U.S. Coast Guard license. With it you can operate a boat with up to six passengers. The license is called a "six pac." To find out more, read Budd Gonder's, *The Coast Guard License: From Six Pac to Master—100 Tons.* It's from Charters West, P.O. Box 597, Summerland, CA 93067. Phone: (800) 732-8378. You could pass the license examination by studying Gonder's book. Or you can take a course from the U.S. Power Squadrons or from the Coast Guard Auxiliary. They have chapters on both coasts.

Bon voyage!

CHAPTER 4

"Thank You, Thank You": Accepting Hospitality

McCheap's Fourth Law of Travel:
The world is full of kind and generous people.
Never be so ungracious as to deny them the pleasure
of giving you a meal and a place to stay.

"SOUNDS TOO GOOD TO BE TRUE."

"Someone I never met is gonna put me up for the night and cook me meals? You gotta be kidding," a listener objected as I made a presentation about utilizing free travel strategies. I had been telling my audience about accepting generous invitations—extended not by old army buddies and distant cousins—but by friends you've yet to meet. In fact, I told the group of aspiring jet-setters that being a guest is one of today's premier strategies for free travelers.

Why People Offer Hospitality

When our free traveling friends return to tell all about their vacation trips, they usually tell us that meeting people and beginning to form friendships are the highlights of their journey. After all, visiting a foreign home is more conducive to forming clear perceptions about a culture than doing so on the basis of brief encounters with souvenir shop proprietors and taxi drivers.

Meeting people from other places is a principal reason lots of hosts nearly everywhere open their doors to travelers. Some invitations include room and board for several days; others for an overnight in a sleeping bag on the parlor floor. Some hospitality includes no more than coffee or a drink. If the coffee or drink session goes well, lots of hosts will drop what they're doing and show you the local and provincial sites, places you'd never get to visit on organized bus tours or ever find on your own. They may take you around and show you off to their friends and relatives, giving you a chance to widen your own circle of friends in the area you're visiting.

In some cases the guest has a reciprocal obligation to open his or her home to the host or to other members of a hospitality exchange organization. Surprisingly, in many other cases, the guest owes nothing tangible in exchange for the warm welcome. Due to health or financial setbacks or firm obligations, many gracious hosts can't travel as often and as far as they'd like. But they still want to learn about the world by meeting people; thus, they bring the world to them when they welcome sojourners into their homes. Because of their kindness and interest, there are plenty of opportunities—whether or not you plan to return the favor—to visit people you've yet to meet, both in your own country and abroad. The stimulating associations that result from being a guest are of far greater value than any amount of money you might save by accepting hospitality.

A Guest's Obligations

Whatever invitation you accept, you'll have an opportunity to make new friends and help cement international understanding. Although a guest is seldom asked to pay for food or lodging, nothing is absolutely free, even hospitality that comes without a need to reciprocate in kind. Yet a good guest always fulfills obligations: These include showing courtesy and respect for a host's culture or life-style, help in performing necessary household tasks if invited to do so, sincerity in expressions of gratitude, and good sense in limiting the length of the stay. Furthermore, a good guest will bring a thoughtful gift—a material token of friendship that needn't be expensive to be appreciated. Others hosts expect something more substantial in return for hosting you—a reciprocal visit to your place, for example.

Let's look at several ways to go about receiving, accepting, and enjoying an invitation for hospitality.

GETTING INVITED

STRATEGY #1: PUTTING THE WORD OUT

The first and often simplest way to get free accommodations is to get the word out. If you're planning a trip—let's say across the country—tell everyone you know and everyone you meet about your plans. Risk trying their patience by listing a fairly detailed itinerary. An astonishing number of your listeners will say something like, "My aunt Harriet lives in Birmingham. She'd probably put you up and show you around. Want me to tell her when you're coming?" And the nice part is that Harriet probably *will* put you up and will feed you an enormous breakfast, as will any number of old college dorm roomies, former teammates, pen pals, lodge brothers and sorority sisters, second cousins twice removed, service club members, former prison cellmates, and the retired couple your next-door neighbor met while fishing in the Gulf of Mexico last year.

And while you're helping Aunt Harriet dry the breakfast dishes, she may say something like, "You've got to stop to see my friend Yvonne in Savannah. She has a guest room. Here, you dry the pan while I call her."

STRATEGY #2: GETTING INVITED THROUGH LOCAL AND NATIONAL TOURIST BUREAUS

When Nyla and her friend Raine graduated from the University of California at Davis, their families bought them air tickets, a Eurail Pass, and gave them money for food and lodging for two summer months in Europe. The recent grads decided to meet as many Europeans as they could and to do so by making contact through tourist bureaus. The young women traveled in nine countries and contacted tourist bureaus in seven. Those bureaus arranged for them to visit in the homes of 37 European individuals and families during their travels. Although the two had little expectation of receiving anything more tangible from their hosts than tea and cakes, they were invited to spend a total of 10 nights in the guest rooms of host families and enjoyed 21 meals while visiting. Most importantly, they made a number of good friends, some of whom will look up Nyla and Raine when and if they come to the United States.

With nearly 200 countries in the world, the possibilities for meeting locals through local tourist offices are virtually unlimited. Bureaus in many cities and many towns will link you with locals who have signed up, hoping to host Americans and other foreigners. Start by writing to national tourist bureaus, which you will find listed in chapter 17, "A Wealth of Free Information." Tell them what places you intend to visit—for example, New Delhi from December 28 through January 2, Agra from January 3 through 5, Madras from January 10 to 15. National tourist bureaus will send the addresses of local bureaus. Write well in advance; it takes time for tourist bureaus to make arrangements and for residents to arrange their schedules to accommodate you. If you contact the bureaus after you've arrived, you may still get an invitation to visit.

Japan and Switzerland run model programs. Their hospitality services are good examples of the kind of royal treatment you can expect in many nations.

Meet the Japanese at Home

Travelers in Japan have an opportunity to get to know Japanese people who speak or are learning English. They welcome the opportunity to polish their language skills and to get to know all about your country. Volunteer host families who have joined the Home Visit System number about 1,000 and live in 14 cities.

The organization maintains offices where visitors are requested to apply in person. They're in cities such as:

- Tokyo—Phone: (03) 3201-3331
- Yokohama—Phone: (045) 641-4759

- Osaka—Phone: (06) 345-2189
- Narita—Phone: (0476) 34-6251)
- Kyoto—Phone: (075) 752-3010
- Kobe—Phone: (078) 303-1010
- Hiroshima—Phone: (082) 247-9715)

They are also in several smaller cities. After contacting the host families, the officials inform you of the host family's name and address and they'll help you set up a mutually agreeable time for a visit. They'll even give you directions. You can request to meet a family with a similar occupation or similar interests to yours. An overnight stay isn't implied in the invitation.

Japan's Good Will Guides

The Japanese and English languages are so utterly different that without having studied Japanese intensively, Westerners are often bewildered by signs and maps. Tokyo and other cities in Japan are so large and complex that it's easy to get lost. To help visitors untangle the mystery of getting around, more than 35 cities and districts will provide free "Good Will" guides. These guides want to meet foreigners and practice their English. And they want to show foreigners the city or rural area of which they're so proud.

Before you leave for Japan, contact the Japan National Tourist Organization, One Rockefeller Plaza, Suite 1250, New York, NY 10020. Phone: (212) 757-5641. Fax: (212) 307-6754. E-mail: jnto.nyc@interport.net. If you're in Japan, contact any local tourist office for details.

Meet the Swiss

Meet the Swiss, c/o Zurich Tourist Office, Bahnhofplatz 15, 8023 Zurich, Switzerland. Phone: (011) 41 1 211 4000. Fax: (011) 41 1 212 0141. The Meet the Swiss program is just what the name implies, an opportunity to receive an invitation to visit a Swiss home. At the least you might expect good conversation and a chance to plant the seeds of a valued friendship;

at the most, you might expect some guided local sight-seeing and a meal. The Swiss National Tourist Office information sheet states: "It should be emphasized that the Swiss hosts cannot be expected to provide accommodation."

STRATEGY #3: GETTING INVITED THROUGH MEMBERSHIP IN A HOSPITALITY EXCHANGE

Here's an idea so good that it's a wonder millions aren't participating. Members pay a small fee to join an exchange. Several exchanges publish directories that include names, addresses, e-mail addresses, and phone and fax numbers of people willing to offer free accommodations to other members for a night or two. Normally, each member can ask to stay with anyone who belongs to the exchange, whether or not they've met previously as host and guest. Whether they're passing through Butte or Bhutan, directory listees should be able to find a place to stay at no charge, an arrangement that, for many, is preferable to staying in an impersonal and costly hotel or motel. And it's preferable to freezing or perspiring in a bare-bones campground.

One principal benefit of membership is never having to pay for accommodations again while traveling, as long as you design your itinerary to take you to places club members live. The other principal benefit is obvious: making friends around the globe.

Everyone listed in exchange directories promises, when it's possible, to offer lodgings or at least refreshments or sight-seeing to members, and each host and guest is free to contact any other member to request a place to stay while passing through town.

The accommodations you're offered—or that you yourself could offer—might consist of the use of a comfortable guest room with private bath, a hideaway bed in the den, or simply sleeping bag space in the living room or in the yard when weather permits. Some hosts provide RV space and electricity for guests. Meals or kitchen privileges may or may not be included; it's up to the host.

Most directory members are extremely gracious to guests. When our friend Pauline stayed with a directory member in Quito, Ecuador, the host insisted that his guest sleep in the best bed in the family's modest house. The American visitor was entertained like a dignitary; in fact Pauline cut her stay a day short because she was afraid the Ecuadorean family was spending a disproportionate share of its small income on her food and entertainment.

Courtesy in informing your host of your arrival time is as important as not overstaying your welcome. The courteous traveler will call or write as far in advance as possible, requesting an invitation to stay a night or longer. The host will offer an invitation if the date is convenient. Well-organized members map out their trips to include places other members live so they can avoid hotels and to secure their invitations long before taking off.

After sending and receiving several letters, e-mailings, and/or phone calls, you should have a pretty good idea of whether or not you'll get along well with your host or guest. Most exchange club members, by definition, want to make friends and will therefore go out of their way to try to be compatible. But, if all of the vibes are negative, it may be best to cancel long enough before the visit so the other party can change plans. Causing someone to rearrange plans is preferable to going through with a dreadful visit.

Don't worry about imposing upon people or being imposed upon. Veteran exchange club members never hesitate to say "no" when a requested visit is inconvenient. Pauline, for instance, told a lady from Quebec she couldn't accept a visitor in late June because her company required her to work overtime that week taking inventory. Pauline never feels guilty telling people politely not to come to her home, which she must do several times a year. On the other hand, Pauline enjoys hosting exchange club members an average of three or four times a year—when she can give her full attention to making their visits worthwhile and pleasurable.

When you're planning a visit with total strangers, even if all signs say "go," you might still plan a fairly brief visit—let's say two to three days. What if your host's dogs bark all night, if the "plumbing" is a hundred yards from the house, if the guest bed is a converted torture rack, if your host can't stop talking? What if? If this brief encounter, for any reason, doesn't work out well, you haven't committed yourself to an uncomfortably long stay.

Always be sure to agree in advance on the final departure date. You wouldn't want the Leeches to stay and on and on, becoming your long-term roomies. Chances are, your charm notwithstanding, hospitality exchange members don't want you around forever either. If, however, you and your host or guest become inseparable friends, the stay can be extended for as long as you mutually agree.

Discuss with your host or guest whether both parties will perform household chores and what they'll be; although hosts and guests are usually equipped with a strong sense of ethics, prior agreements head off misunderstandings.

Inside the Clubs

To see why hospitality exchanging is a principal strategy used by thousands of savvy travelers, let's visit some of the clubs and see how one or more can help make your next vacation not only affordable but far more meaningful.

Educators' Bed and Breakfast Network

Educators Bed & Breakfast Network, P.O. Box 5279, Eugene, OR 97405. Phone: (800) 377-0301. E-mail: EduBabNet@aol.com.

It's not free, but it's quite cheap. More than 3,000 present, former, and retired educators in all U.S. states and in 50 foreign countries will rent you a room for the night at a very low rate. If you serve as a host and collect rent, you also accumulate credits that reduce your nightly fee when staying with other members. You never have to accept guests when it's inconvenient. It's an opportunity to travel at rock-bottom prices.

Headquartered in London, the club has branches in the United States and Canada.

The club started a half-century ago. At the end of World War II, world roamers Norman Ford and John Trenchord found themselves in Rangoon, Burma, and decided to sail around the world in a slightly leaky old vessel. When they advertised for two travel companions, they were astonished to receive 200 applications. Realizing as a result of this response that there really was a need for an organization that would allow adventurous travelers to exchange information and find travel companions, Ford and Trenchord founded Globetrotters. That body now counts several hundred members.

Members, most of whom search out unusual places that average tourists never see, exchange information among themselves and through their bimonthly journal, *The Globe*. The club's publication, *The Globetrotters Directory*, lists members' offers to show visiting GTs around their cities or to put them up for a night or two.

Nigel, a member from Blackpool, England, joined in 1979 and has since stayed with fellow members in 14 countries on three continents. "It's the people I meet that's the best part of it," Nigel told us. "And staying with members makes travel affordable. If I had to pay hotel bills I wouldn't be able to afford the airfare. I've been to Spain four times on Globetrotter stayovers, and to Greece twice and Australia once."

If you're in London you may attend Globetrotter meetings the second Saturday of each month at 3:30 P.M. at centrally located Friends Meeting House, 52 St. Martin's Lane, WC1. Featured speakers tell about their travels to places such as Thailand, Easter Island, Vietnam, the Peruvian jungle, the Sahara Desert, north Ghana, or South Island in New Zealand. Some talks are illustrated with slides. Nigel probably won't be there. He's off to South America for six months. Meetings are also held in Toronto, New York, and in California. See *The Globe* for details.

The Globe contains useful articles and snippets of information about how to travel safely and cheaply on your own. Between its covers, members advertise for travel companions and ask for information from those who have been to their next destinations.

When writing to Globetrotters London, be sure to enclose an international reply coupon. This address may seem odd, but it's guaranteed to work. Write to Globetrotters Club, c/o BMC Roving, London WCIN 3XX, UK. The unusual address is so that a volunteer staff, working out of various locations rather than permanent headquarters, can receive mail.

Home Exchange International

Home Exchange International is an exchange club for Internet users. You can contact potential swappers electronically. They're in 35 countries. Many will be willing to exchange hospitality. Website: www.west.net/~prince/he.

Homelink International

Homelink International-Vacation Exchange Club, P.O. Box 650, Key West, FL 33040. Phone: (800) 638-3841. Homelink International publishes directories that list mainly home-exchange offers, but also hospitality-exchange invitations. This is the largest of the home-swap organizations, and you'll find plenty of hospitality offers in the directory's pages. Recently a lady offered to exchange hospitality, inviting members to her home in a small town in Provence, an hour outside of Avignon, France. A gentleman in Cancun, Mexico, offered to host members in an apartment with a "great view, maid, pool, and tennis court." An engineer in the center of Florence, Italy, offered to host people in his flat near the city's great museums. Homelink's website is link@conch.net. E-mail: www.conch.net/~homelink.

HOSPEX

HOSPEX stands for Hospitality Exchange Service and Database. HOSPEX was founded in 1991 to aid traveling academics and students in contacting one another to find free or affordable accommodations in foreign countries. Today, you no longer have to be an academic to belong. But you do need to have access to e-mail in order to make use of HOSPEX's list of members and their offers of hospitality. To become a member of HOSPEX, you need to obtain an application and return it via e-mail. Your form will be stored in the club's database and accessed by other members in as many as 35 countries. E-mail HOSPEX at hospex@icm.edu.pl.

Hospitality Exchange

Hospitality Exchange, c/o Wayne and Kathie Philips, 704 Birch St., Helena, MT 59601. Phone: (406) 449-2103. E-mail: wphillips@mt.gov. The Hospitality Exchange goes back to 1965 when traveler John Wilcock established the *Traveler's Directory*, a compendium of people willing to host each other. Recently, the Hospitality Exchange reported members in 20 countries and 30 U.S. states and Canadian provinces.

As a member, you'd be listed in one of their two annual directories and receive both for a very small cost, far less than you'd pay for one night's lodging in the One-Night-Stand Motel. Members praise their experiences of having friendly hosts show them local attractions and the opportunity to make friends. What "jumps out" of the applications to this club, according to the Phillips, are the "members' passion for food, conversation, music, outdoor activities of every kind, and sharing local attractions with other travelers."

Members offer a place to sleep in their homes, at the hosts' convenience, for one or two nights. Members requesting hospitality are counseled to remember Ben Franklin's aphorism, "Fish and guests begin to smell in three days." Contact the club for an application.

International Home Exchange Network

International Home Exchange Network has a hospitality exchange option. For a modest fee, you can post on the Internet your offer of hospitality or your willingness to be someone's houseguest. Anyone can browse this organization's directory and make offers. The website is found at http://www. homexchange.com. Send e-mail to linda@homexchange.com for further information.

Intervac

Intervac US, P.O. Box 590504, San Francisco, CA 94119. Phone: (800) 756-4663 or (415) 435-3497. Fax: (415) 435-7440. Intervac US lists members who desire adult or family hospitality exchanges.

League of American Bicyclists

League of American Bicyclists, 6707 Whitestone Rd., Suite 209, Baltimore, MD 21207-4106. Phone: (301) 944-3399. Fax: (301) 944-4353. Join the bicycling advocacy organization and you qualify to participate in their hospitality exchange. *Hospitality Homes* is a directory of accommodations throughout the U.S. open only to LAB members as they cycle without cost from free accommodation to free accommodation.

Mi Casa Su Casa

Mi Casa Su Casa is a relatively new organization made up of gay and lesbian members who live in more than 20 countries and more than 20 states. This club facilitates home exchanges primarily, but it also provides contacts for hospitality exchanges.

Members, whose names and addresses need not be listed in the directory, agree to exchange hospitality for equal lengths of time. Thus, a Californian might provide room and meals for a New Zealander for five days in June, and then visit the New Zealander for five days in January. Exchanges may be agreed on between singles or couples. Gays or lesbians are invited to contact Mi Casa Su Casa, P.O. Box 10327, Oakland, CA 94610. Phone: (800) 215-CASA. Fax: 510-268-0299. E-mail: HomeSwap@aol.com. "Award-winning" website: http://www. well.com/user/homeswap.

People-to-People Directories

People-to-People series hospitality directories are books that you can find in your public library or order from your favorite bookseller. They are also available from Zephyr Press, 13 Robinson St., Somerville, MA 02145. Phone: (617) 628-9725. Fax: (617) 776-8246. This is a useful series of published directories for sale to the general public; it is not a club.

Russia: People to People is by Jim Haynes. Author Haynes counsels travelers to forget about getting off of tour buses, photographing monuments, and jumping back on. That's not really traveling, says Haynes; in fact, you're not really a traveler unless you meet the people, get to know their interests and concerns, and share their life-styles, however briefly. In an attempt to promote further understanding among people of diverse cultures, Haynes has compiled lists of individuals and families in Eastern Europe who would like to meet foreign visitors.

Just as if he or she were a member of a hospitality exchange club, the would-be visitor writes or phones ahead, at least several days in advance, and attempts to work a visit into what may be a busy schedule for the host. The host may provide tea, a snack, sight-seeing, a meal, or even accommodations. In fact, some willing hosts among a thousand or so in the Russia volume are willing or able to allow guests to stay over; there are enough willing hosts, in fact, that a traveler could stay in dozens of Russian cities or towns as a houseguest.

How free is free when it comes to being hosted in Russia? Haynes reminds us poignantly that a Russian schoolteacher might earn two hundred dollars a month, and a university student might live on two dollars a month! A gift of food, CDs, books, clothing, etc. would, under the circumstances, be more than appropriate. What might be nearly free to a North American—a no-longer-wanted CD, a jacket that's worn or out of style, or an inexpensive can of coffee—might represent more than a few days' earnings to a Russian.

Some of those who offer accommodations expect monetary

reimbursement, but the cost in most cases is far less than paying for a hotel room. Some potential hosts would like to return your visit by coming to your home in North America or in Western Europe, but the costs of passports, visas, and transportation from Russia often prohibit Russian citizens from leaving that dramatic land on vacations.

At the very least, by using the Russia book as a basis for visiting in homes, one could form friendships and gain a valuable insight into an altogether different way of life in a struggling economy. The thousand or so hosts are listed alphabetically under their towns or cities, which are also in alphabetical order. St. Petersburg, Peter the Great's "Window on the West," not surprisingly, boasts the greatest proportion of Russians who are eager to meet you. Each willing host has given his or her address, phone number, foreign language facility (if any), occupation, and perhaps a few words about interests and hobbies.

A 26-year-old librarian in St. Petersburg, who admits to speaking English "poorly," states: "I am very hospitable and like guests." Olga from Moscow says, "I love everything that could be loved." She offers bed and breakfast. Ludmilla from Moscow is an assistant professor who prefers opera and traveling, speaks English, and offers accommodations. She also enjoys folk songs and classical music. Elena from Murmansk says she enjoys life, the sun, skiing, and smiling people. Elena also offers accommodations.

Also in the People-to-People series, by the same author and available from the same publisher, is *The Baltic Republics,* which lists more than a thousand folks who want to meet you in Estonia, Latvia, and Lithuania. Other volumes feature hosts in Czecho-Slovakia, Hungary, and Bulgaria. All contain offers to meet Americans.

People-to-People International

People-to-People International, 501 E. Armour Blvd., Kansas City, MO 64109. Phone: (816) 531-4701. Fax (816) 561-7502.

E-mail: ptpi@cctr.umkc.edu. Website: http://www.umkc.edu/cctr/dept/ptpi/homepage.html.

I've seldom met better hosts than the family who took me in years ago on a People-to-People program in Fredrikshavn, Denmark, and the couple who hosted me in Støre Hardinge, Denmark. I learned more about Denmark in that week than in all my previous and subsequent visits. People-to-People is one of the best of all hospitality organizations.

Seniors Abroad

Seniors Abroad, 12533 Pacato Circle North, San Diego, CA 92128. Phone: (619) 485-1696. By joining Seniors Abroad, travelers who are 50 or better can be guests of seniors in other countries. They can also host foreign visitors who are in their age group. There's no cost to be a guest. Stays include a minimum of three homes for stays of six days in each. Six days may seem a trifle long, but the organizers' idea is to allow members to stay long enough to make friends. Members from these nations welcome Americans: Japan, Australia, New Zealand, Denmark, Sweden, and Norway.

Servas

Servas: For your application—to be a guest or host—write to U.S. Servas, Inc., 11 John St., Suite 407, New York, NY 10038-4009. Phone: (212) 267-0252. Fax: (212) 267-0292. E-mail: usservas@igc.apc.org.

Founded in 1948 in Denmark, the principal purpose of Servas is to further world peace and international understanding through promoting visits of citizens of one nation with those of other countries. *Servas* means, in Esperanto, "to serve," and 14,000 hospitable hosts in more than 100 countries are doing just that. Consequently, you have an ongoing, sincere invitation to stay with or visit members for two nights each, and your only monetary cost is a modest registration fee, payable to Servas.

How does Servas' visitor exchange program work? We know several people for whom it's worked exceedingly well. Our friends

Gail and Craig, for example, are an urban professional couple in their forties. Without children, they spend their annual vacations traveling, but Gail and Craig long ago tired of trying to understand foreign cultures through focusing only on museum and cathedral visits. They wanted to get to know the locals, to see what their life is really like, to exchange ideas and insights—"to see more than the outside of their homes," as Craig put it. They hoped, also, to participate in community activities in the places they visited.

Gail found out about Servas in the first edition of *You Can Travel Free* and wrote for an application. Gail made certain that she returned the form a couple of months before she and Craig planned to fly off to Europe. In addition to standard information such as name and address, Servas headquarters staff members wanted to know the languages she and Craig spoke. Gail truthfully wrote on the form that they spoke only English, but that was not a problem for them in enrolling, nor need being monolingual stop any American from participating.

Gail listed the countries they wanted to visit—Sweden and Finland—and their dates of travel. When they signed the application, they acknowledged that they understood "that the purposes of Servas are to promote peace, the unity of humankind, and mutual understanding of the cultures, outlooks, and problems of the people of the world"; and they promised to do their part to "further these purposes" through their visit. In addition, each submitted a letter of reference from a friend and from a business associate—people who knew them well.

Within a short time Servas notified Gail and Craig of an appointment with a volunteer interviewer. The interview took place in a nearby city. The interviewer confirmed that Gail and Craig were personable and sincere in their intentions and they'd represent the organization well abroad. Once Gail and Craig had jumped that minor hurdle, Servas sent them a list of hosts in Sweden from nearly 400 enrolled and a list of Finnish members from among more than 300 members there. The hosts' interests, professions, and other relevant details were included. It was then up to Gail and Craig to contact—by mail, phone, fax, or e-mail—the hosts and try to arrange a visit at a mutually agreeable time.

After a couple of weeks of e-mail correspondence, they had arranged to stay with people with their same professional and hobby interests in both countries—a physician's family in Malmo, Sweden, for two nights; a coin collector in Uppsala, Sweden, for two nights; and an accountant and her children just outside Helsinki, Finland. A "day host" in Stockholm invited Gail and Craig to afternoon coffee in her home, indicating she was unable to provide overnight accommodations.

Servas asks that guests show a genuine interest in the host family and their life-style, that they don't desert the host during the day to do independent sight-seeing unless the host family must be absent, but that they stay and converse and take part, to the extent they're invited to do so, in the life of the family and of the community. Fortunately, Gail and Craig were more than happy to answer questions about life in Colorado and to discuss mutual interests. They fully understood that to look at the host solely as the source of a free bed and meal would subvert Servas' purposes.

Having joined Servas and paid a year's dues, which, incidentally, amount to less than the tariff for a night in a hotel or motel, members are welcome to contact hosts in as many countries as they plan to visit in any year. When they returned from Europe, Gail and Craig stayed two nights with a couple in a Boston suburb, and last year two nights each with families in Sydney, Melbourne, and Brisbane, Australia. Next year they'll meet a family and stay with them for two nights in Bali, Indonesia.

Germany has the most hosts of any foreign country—about 1,600 listed in a recent year's directory—followed by Italy, France, Australia, the United Kingdom, New Zealand, Sweden, Switzerland, and India.

In addition to those popular destinations, hospitable Servas members could show you some out-of-the-way countries you may not have visited thus far. Botswana, Papua New Guinea, Fiji, Curacao, Paraguay, Bangladesh, Slovakia, Uzbekistan, Mauritius, Mali, Martinique, and Honduras are just a few. In fact, Servas' list of countries in which hosts are waiting is truly astonishing.

You don't have to leave North America to participate in a Servas program. The United States has the most hosts—about 2,000; Canada, more than 600; and Mexico, about 300. Thus, there's a host within driving distance of your place. Servas states that they need more hosts in North America and that need provides a great opportunity for the armchair traveler to meet people from anywhere or everywhere without leaving home. Contact Servas for details.

According to their prospectus, "U.S. Servas welcomes physically challenged travelers"; yet if stairs are an obstacle, it's always wise to inquire about access when contacting hosts.

Stayfree Travel Club

Stayfree Holiday Club, 12 Kissavou St., Athens, Greece 154 52. Phone: (+301) 67 78 709. Fax: (+301) 67 46 956. E-mail: stayfree@prometheus.hol.gr.

"Dedicated to the advancement of world peace by the development of greater understanding between peoples," Stayfree is a nonprofit club. Whatever money remains in the kitty after administrative expenses are met is donated to a registered charity of the member's choice.

Here's how the Stayfree club works: You e-mail club director Paul Gebhard for an application. In filling out the application, you'll answer questions about your age, religion, gender, marital status, family members, profession, hobbies, favorite sports, food preferences, and any physical disabilities or medical problems you or your traveling companion may have. You must indicate countries or specified cities you want to visit and the dates you plan to travel.

All of this information is "locked into Stayfree's secure data banks," and given out only when you authorize the club to send your application information to other members. You can then contact other members and arrange to share hospitality. No money exchanges hands between host and guest.

Teacher Swap

If you produce chalk dust in front of a group of pupils for a living, you're qualified to host and be hosted by other members of the educational profession. Contact Teacher Swap, P.O. Box 454, Oakdale, NY 11769-0454. Phone or fax: (516) 244-2845. E-mail: Tswap@aol.com.

With nearly 1,000 members in Western Europe, the U.S., Canada, and 36 additional foreign countries, Teacher Swap presents a great opportunity to get to know other instructors. Primarily a house-trading organization, a number of members prefer to exchange hospitality. There's a small membership fee, which includes receiving a directory in which members are listed.

Trading Homes International

Trading Homes International, P.O. Box 787, Hermosa Beach, CA 90254. Phone: (800) 877-8723, or (310) 798-3864 outside the U.S. and Canada. Fax: (310) 798-3865. E-mail: info@trading-homes.com. This is one of the large home-exchange clubs that invites members to list themselves as hospitality exchangers.

The Travel Exchange Club

The Travel Exchange Club is an on-line hospitality, time-share exchange, and home-exchange club. Send e-mail to solafson@travex.com.

Web Connection

Web Connection, an Internet site, links travelers at no cost. You can find travel companions at Web Connection, you can offer to host visitors, or you can connect with people willing to host you. You'll find it at http://www.molyvos.net:80/". You can add your own free message by e-mailing them at tili@molyvos.net.

The beautiful thing about Web Connection is the kindness and generosity of some of those who leave messages. "Hi, I'm Olov," announces a 34-year old Swede who invites anybody to come to his northern village to be shown around and offered a place to stay. Another party offers to help make visitors feel at home in Edmonton, Alberta—home of the world's biggest mall. Marcin, age 19, is from Lodz, Poland; she's delighted to show visitors her charming city. Anders, age 24, will do the same in Stockholm; and a kind Scottish couple will show visitors Glasgow and Central Scotland.

In addition, lots of interesting things are poised to occur through this site: A self-employed businessman is looking for a female between 25 and 40 to go on a trip with him; she's got to be "fun-loving and adventurous." Elsewhere, a single 36-year-old female, quite possibly fun-loving and adventurous, is looking for a self-employed businessman as a traveling companion. While that's going on, two "well off" men are looking for two "beautiful" female companions who want their vacation trip paid for. Across the ocean, a 19-year-old woman is fed up with bills and "the dreary English winter"; she's off to Florida and New Orleans and looking for someone to host her. If she's beautiful—and lacking further evidence one can only assume she is—does she have a beautiful friend? Will the businessman find Sweetie Pie? Is the 36-year-old woman actually Sweetie Pie? Will the well-off men find travelmates? Will the English woman see Miami Beach and Basin Street? You'll never find out if you don't log on to Web Connection.

If you're planning a trip, put your itinerary on Web Connection. Your e-mail box may fill up with offers of hospitality.

> $$$—Cousin Thrifty McCheap says: "Use the Internet without charge at your free public library and check out the hospitality-exchange websites to see if anyone wants you as a guest."

Women Welcome Women

Women Welcome Women, Betty Sobel, WWW USA Trustee, 10 Greenwood Ln., Westport, CT 06880. In the United Kingdom: WWW, 88 Easton St., High Wycombe, Bucks HP11 1LT, UK. UK phone or fax: (001) 44-1494-465441.

Women Welcome Women is a nonprofit organization that facilitates exchange of information and formation of friendships among 2,000 members in 70 countries. Although friendships may lead to invitations to stay for a maximum of three days, that's not WWW's primary purpose. Rather the purpose is to "extend the vision of women" as part of "the international community." A donation from those who use its services is suggested to help maintain this organization.

World for Free

World for Free, P.O. Box 137, Prince St. Station, New York, NY 10012. Fax: (212) 979-8167. E-mail: twff@juno.com. For a small membership charge, the World for Free will send you *The World for Free Address Book,* which will allow you to make arrangements with potential hosts all over North America and in more than 30 foreign countries.

After you've registered, the book will contain your address, phone number, and any hospitality message you wish to convey. Your job is to contact other members at least 10 days in advance and invite yourself to visit them. The club restricts stays to no more than four nights, but no member has to accept a guest for more than one night, or if a visit is at an inconvenient time, there's no compulsion to host at all.

The World for Free club really is free if you're the first enrollee from a state or country in which the club has no members. Also, if you enroll 20 new signups, you get a complimentary membership.

Variation on a Strategy

Join the Affordable Travel Club (6556 Snug Harbor Lane,

Gig Harbor, WA 98335; phone/fax: [206] 858-2172) and be both a host and a guest. Affordable Travel Club members, who must be over 40, have the same advantages of hospitality-swap club members, but must use cash rather than reciprocal kindness. However, if you work it right, you'll stop paying motel bills and you'll suffer no cash out of pocket.

Here's how it happens: Your dues buy you a membership directory of hosts who'll supply a comfortable bed with bathroom—and breakfast—for about a fourth or fifth of what you'd pay in a moderately priced motel or hotel.

You can add your name to the directory and prepare to host visitors and collect the nightly fee. The club's organizers feel you should serve as host about three times a year, although you're free to do so as many times as you wish. Let's say Doug and Dora call you from Frozenfish, Alaska. They want to spend two nights in your guest room. You'll probably get along well with them; you'll give them local sight-seeing tips, enjoy their company at breakfast, and then follow them out to the street and wave good-bye.

What to do with the money you've collected? Call Affordable Travel Club members Ed and Erma in Skijump, Colorado, and ask if you can come for two nights in the Rockies. Just as Doug and Dora have no obligation to host you in the future, you have no obligation to host Ed and Erma. All you need to do is give Ed and Erma the money you got from your Alaskan visitors.

A *nonhost* member either has no guest facilities or doesn't want guests. The nonhost pays a slightly higher membership fee and a somewhat higher nightly gratuity for hospitality; yet, what he or she pays is usually less than nightly motel rates.

Members tend to cluster in states that attract retirees: Arizona, California, and Florida. Washington and Illinois also have a number of members. Foreign members are found in Australia, Western Europe, Israel, Mexico, and New Zealand. Affordable Travel Club is truly affordable when it adds up to free lodging for you; but best of all, it's a terrific way to make new friends.

STRATEGY #3½: SWAP THAT KID!

What a great opportunity to send Trevor and Autumn out of the country—maybe for the whole summer. Think of the possibilities. Think of the peace and quiet. Get back your car, phone, and TV. These organizations will help you find unsuspecting hosts for your scions:

Holiday in Turkey Program

Holiday in Turkey Program, Interfon, Koroglu Cd. Kahrammankad in Sok. 18/3 Gaziosmanpasa, Ankara 06700 Turkey. Phone: (90) 4-446-1097. In exchange for the pleasure of conversation, young people are invited to spend one to three months, June through September, with a Turkish family. Conversations are held in English because Turks want to learn how to speak your language fluently. Hosts live in Ankara, Antalya, Istanbul, Izmir, Konya, and in various resort towns. There's a small registration fee.

The minimum age for a guest tutor is 12. Although we'd think long and hard before sending a 12- or 13-year-old off alone to teach English in any other country unless we knew the host family really well, this program can be a terrific education for an older American teen. With its thousands of years of history, Turkey has recorded the footprints of Alexander the Great, the Roman legions, St. Paul, Turkish sultans, and shiny-armored crusaders. Turkey has to be one of the most fascinating destinations in the world. Capadoccia alone, with its labyrinthine underground cities and carved-in-rock churches, is worth the trip.

Homelink International

Homelink International-Vacation Exchange Club, P.O. Box 650, Key West, FL 33040. Phone: (800) 638-3841. This mammoth home-exchange club lists names, addresses, and phone numbers of teenagers who would like to exchange with teens from other nations. Foreign members are mostly from Western Europe and Australia.

Lions Club Youth Exchange

Lions Club International Association Youth Exchange Program, 300 Twenty-second St., Oak Brook, IL 60521. Phone: (708) 571-5466. Here's a great chance to send your offspring abroad. You pay the transportation, but if that's a problem, the local Lions Club may be able to help. Lions in other countries welcome more than 3,000 American kids each year. The club members in your town will probably host foreign kids to reciprocate.

Rotary Club Youth Exchange

Rotary International Youth Exchange Program, 1560 Sherman Ave., Evanston, IL 60201-3698. People between ages 15 and 19, and not only sons and daughters of Rotarians, are eligible to live abroad with a host family arranged by a foreign Rotary Club. The student attends school during the year. The host family provides board and room, while the student takes care of air transportation. This Rotary program operates in 60 countries.

Web Connection

Web Connection is a free Internet service. Its website is at http://www.molyvos.net:80/". You can add your own offer to their bulletin boards at no charge. You can offer hospitality or post your proposed itinerary and hope someone invites you to stay.

Want to swap the little grabbers for some French kids? Awhile back, frequenters of the Web Connection's site had a golden opportunity to send the tribe off to the French Alps. A couple with a "big house" in a "superb park" wanted to send their four kids, ages ten, eight, six, and four off to someone's home to learn English. They were willing take English-speaking children in their place for the summer.

More to Read

- *Home from Home,* from Seven Hills Book Distributors. Phone: (800) 54s5-2005. Published by the Central Bureau for

Educational Visits and Exchanges, *Home from Home* lists organizations worldwide that facilitate not only hospitality swaps,
but home exchanges and homestays.

STRATEGY #4: MAKING FRIENDS BY MAIL

Pen pal clubs aren't only for children and teenagers. They allow
adults too to broaden their knowledge of other nations, increase
their understanding of foreign cultures and languages, and (best
of all) make friends. Since friends tend to extend and accept offers
of hospitality, correspondence can lead to an opportunity to see at
least a corner of the world you might not otherwise see by staying
with people you've come to know well but have never met.

Our former student, Gregorio, stayed at the homes of six former pen pals during his three-month grand tour of Europe following his college graduation. Gregorio brought gifts to his
hosts but paid nothing for his overnight stays and meals. The
highlight of his trip was falling in love with Anita, the sister of
his host, near Coimbra, Portugal.

Pen pal clubs have minimal fees and a whole wide world of
possibilities for travelers. In the age of e-mail, correspondence
and friendships move even faster.

International Pen Friends Club

For information on this 300,000-strong club, send an SASE
to International Pen Friends, 5 Appian Way, Allston, MA 02134.
For a modest fee this club will match you with pen pals in your
general age group and with people who have similar interests,
such as philately, golf, music, art, camping, chess, soccer, etc.
You may select "at least" eight countries in which you'd like to
have pen friends. Founded in 1967, the club, according to its
proprietors, is "now regarded as the oldest, biggest and best
penfriend organization in the world."

Transatlantic Pen Friends

Transatlantic Pen Friends, P.O. Box 2176, San Pedro, CA
90731. For a small amount, Transatlantic will enter your age,

gender, marital status, occupation, interests, hobbies, and activities into a computer and match you with 20 British members. You may write to as many of the 20 as you wish.

If you're searching far and wide for the perfect Sweetie Pie, you may specify that you want only the names of single people. Although it's not primarily a lonely hearts club, Transatlantic Pen Friends advises that several members have found marriage partners through corresponding. In fact, one harried member wrote the club's organizers: "Please take my name off your list for I am kept rather busy in answering to six ladies and one of them is very special to me, the first one I wrote to. . . . I am visiting her in May this year and she is coming over at the end of July. We are becoming very close." Could this lead to marriage—the ultimate hospitality exchange?

World Pen Pals

World Pen Pals, P.O. Box 337, Saugerties, NY 12477-0337. Phone/fax: (914) 246-7828. This club is for students, ages 12 to 20—more than 20,000 of them in 175 countries. You may request pen friends by continent and gender. The fee is modest. Send an SASE for further information.

STRATEGY #5: INSPECTING CONVENTION SITES

The next time you attend a meeting of the Loyal and Benevolent Order of Boars, and the Great Boar in the presiding officer's chair pleads for a volunteer to be chairperson of the convention site selection committee, leap to your feet and declare that you'll do it. Besides having the thrill of hearing the members' enthusiastic snorting and stomping, you'll have an opportunity to travel free.

Having taken on the onerous duty of arranging for the annual meeting, where Boars from every Sty in the land will assemble, you must contact hotels and resorts in desirable locations. Tell them you've been provided no funds by your club to visit their facilities but that the brotherhood has forbidden you to sign a contract without seeing what each has to offer.

Because hotel and resort sales executives will do just about anything necessary to get their share of the more than 200,000 annual meetings that attract 25 million delegates in the United States, and because they desperately want thousands of Boars to wallow in the luxury they offer, they'll give you first-class treatment. You may even get a pass to the first-class feeding trough. Nothing "boaring" about that.

STRATEGY #6: INSPECTING TIMESHARE CONDOS

Our friend Victoria, who has all the money she'll ever need, demands full value for her buck and is ever-ready to take full advantage of any opportunity for a free vacation that comes her way.

When Victoria went out to buy a timeshare condominium, she had to see just about every interval-ownership resort available in the area in which she was interested. Before she bought a one-week-a-year right to use a two-bedroom apartment in a resort in Cancun, Mexico, she inspected resorts in Cozumel, Manzanillo, and Acapulco. While searching for a unit to buy in the Caribbean, she visited the Bahamas, Jamaica, and the U.S. Virgin Islands, finally purchasing a timeshare apartment on St. Croix.

Victoria doesn't merely visit interval-ownership resorts to be whisked in and out of model units; she demands to live in them. She's often flown to resorts at the expense of the developers, chauffeured from the airport in a limousine, wined, dined, and comfortably housed. Victoria said, "Had I been the Queen of England, there's not a lot more they could have done for me."

Ted, whom we met while having a pub lunch in Winchester, England, came to the British Isles from Pittsfield, Massachusetts, with every intention of buying a timeshare unit in one of the many stately English homes that have been subdivided in recent years. Ted wrote ahead to timeshare managers that he was coming and that he hoped to stay in a unit before writing his check. He was housed in a well-appointed suite in a huge house near Lower Talley Ho and taken to dinner at an attractive restaurant by an attractive saleswoman.

"The flat is very nice," Ted said to the saleswoman the next morning, "but I think I'd like something a bit more posh, perhaps on the south coast." The sales representative phoned an affiliated resort near Payne Royal and reserved a suite for him there. After Ted was wined and dined within the sound of English Channel waves, he expressed an interest in seeing something still a bit more posh—perhaps on the coast between Duckwhistle and Lower Butterbread. Ted spent five nights in England and one in Scotland while testing timeshare condos.

"I still want to buy a timeshare, but the dampness in Britain turns me off," Ted told us. "I think I'll look for a unit in the Bahamas."

Victoria and Ted found interval-ownership sales representatives to be gracious hosts who are more than eager to please— and to sell. In fact, various resorts are willing to extend at least some of the same courtesies to anyone who qualifies as a potential buyer. Qualifying usually means being at least 25 years old, having good credit, having worked at the same job for at least three years, and (if married) bringing one's spouse to the sales pitch.

Developers extend invitations through newspaper ads, direct-mail campaigns, and telephone solicitations. One resort sales office in Mexico offered four days and three nights of sun and "five-star" luxury in Puerto Vallarta; the guest had to pay only for airfare, which was refundable if he or she bought a two-week annual right to use a unit. A Nevada developer offered a free "deluxe" room, a prime-rib dinner for two, and a few bucks to blow at a casino, all for listening to his slick sales routine. Another invitation included free airfare and a night's lodging in Palm Springs for anyone willing to listen to a long and determined presentation.

Now, what could possibly go wrong for the guests of a resort timeshare developer? For one thing, you could actually buy a week or two in a condo. That wouldn't be disastrous, particularly if you plan to timeshare swap so you'd have a variety of resort vacation experiences in the next several years. But a real danger is having to pay a bill for flight, room, and meals if you were to walk out on the sales session.

For free travelers who are genuinely, or even mildly, interested in having an interval ownership unit for years to come, timeshare shopping at the developer's expense can be an all-around good deal.

> $$$—Cousin Thrifty McCheap says: "Why buy a timeshare condo if you can get vacation accommodations for free? Try hospitality exchanging or house swapping before letting the moths out of your wallet."

STRATEGY #7: GAMBLING ON A FREE VACATION

Freebies for Big-Time Players

High rollers seldom pay for hotel rooms, food, drinks, or entertainment in Las Vegas, Reno, Atlantic City, the Bahamas, Aruba, Puerto Rico, Monte Carlo, or at any other major gambling mecca. Big-time wagerers are usually flown first-class to and from casinos at the expense of the management. Club operators, of course, are betting that high rollers will lose more than enough to pay for their "complimentaries," and leave the casino a nice profit. Champagne flights, multistar suites, and unlimited food and drink is the red-carpet treatment in spades, and anyone who intends to do some serious gaming ought to take advantage of this spectacular freebie.

Freddy, whom we met in Reno, is retired from the restaurant and bar business and is spending some of his leisure time trying to take a ton of money home from casinos. After he won $30,000 at blackjack and craps in Reno, he decided to use his winnings to fulfill his lifelong ambition: to gamble in Vegas in the plushest private lounges. Freddy had visions of standing elbow-to-tuxedoed-elbow at a gaming table with German steel magnates, Colombian coffee tycoons, rap music stars, and

Cupertino silicon-chip kings. Freddy phoned several casinos to arrange for his freebies. Freddy ordered credit applications. When his credit was approved, Freddy was flown to Las Vegas, ensconced in a large and well-appointed room, and pampered outrageously.

Poor Freddy lost a bundle at craps and blackjack and in *les machines automatiques,* but he had a great time and plans to go again, as soon as he wins another $30,000 in Reno. Clubs depend for their profits largely on the continued patronage of high rollers like Freddy. Nevada casinos ordinarily spend 15 percent of their expense money on complimentaries for preferred customers. To get preferred status, you must establish credit. To establish credit, you must furnish impressive bank references.

Alternately, when you sit down to play, tell the pit boss you want to be rated. Casino personnel will then note the size of your bets and how long you stay. They'll give you a rating of one to four. Those who bet $25 to $50 a throw for four hours are rated as *ones* and may be offered drinks and some food. But, if you're tossing $150 or more on the table at each play, you're rated a *four* and you may be offered a room, fine dining, a limousine ride, and tickets to a spectacular show. *Twos* and *threes* fall somewhere between and may get rooms or at least room upgrades and meals. If you do bet $150 or more and you're still putting room service on your charge card, speak to the manager or move your betting to a more generous club. If you stick around and bet for several hours, always ask for perks. Free travelers *always* ask for freebies.

A casino's profit may be approximately 20 percent, so if a customer loses $1,000, the casino gets $200. But if the club has picked up $500 of the customer's tabs, the club is out $300. In order to break even on handing out $500 in complimentaries, the casino must win $2,500 of the preferred customers' money, not on every one of the customer's visits, but on average for all preferred customers' visits. That's why casinos demand a large amount of front money and make their preferred customers sign an agreement to play a minimum amount per bet for a specified number of hours. That's why Freddy came home early.

Large casino hotels offer a lot more than gaming and sunshine. Las Vegas, Reno, and Atlantic City resorts offer lounge shows, golf, swimming, babysitting, sporting events, electronic games for the kids, first-rate restaurants, even circuses. Vegas hotel casinos are often so spectacular that even nongamblers go there to "ooh" and "aah."

For more information on gamblers' complimentaries, see this website: http://www.casinocomps.com.

Freebies for Small-Time Players

Small-time gamblers can also get in on the action. Travel agencies run frequent junkets to a growing number of casinos, including those in Reno, Las Vegas, and Atlantic City. These trips aren't totally free, but they're nearly free. A typical junket might cost the gambler $39 with $25 to $30 refundable on arrival at the club. A couple of free drinks are usually thrown in and usually a meal or two.

The Reno and Lake Tahoe Harrah's Clubs, for example, claim to be one of Greyhound Bus Lines' biggest customers. Since 1946, Harrah's has been busing hundreds of thousands of low-budget slot players to Nevada from more than 30 cities and at real bargain rates. Lots of other clubs also offer cheap transportation to attract people to Nevada.

One Reno club offered a deluxe room, unlimited food and drinks, and transportation from San Francisco for anyone who purchased $1,000 in house chips. A Las Vegas casino throws in a free long-distance call: "Hey, Mom—I won!" They even toss in a steak-and-eggs breakfast, a steak sandwich, and a chicken dinner—all for showing up to gamble and turning in a newspaper ad.

Harrah's has announced an interesting twist on getting freebies. Harrah's Total Gold card holders, which include just about any patron who wishes to join, earn points for slot play.

Redeemable in any Harrah's casino, the points can be turned in for food, lodging, show tickets, etc. They'll give you all the information you need when you phone (800) HARRAHS.

The final word on "free" gambling trips is *caution*. Whether they're really free depends on whether you win or lose. The best advice on betting is gamble only if you're prepared to lose, and gamble an amount that, if lost, won't cause your life-style to suffer in any way. The odds are always against casino patrons; if they weren't, casinos would go out of business. If you want to swim against the tide, defying the inescapable odds, here are some other ideas so you won't give away the family farm or Junior's milk money to a gaming club:

- Take stamped self-addressed envelopes with you. When you win, mail the winnings home. You'll be happy to open your mail when you get back.

- If you plan to gamble three days, and you've taken $3,000, gamble $1,000 a day—and no more. You could—and the laws of probability say you will—lose your entire amount in one or two days and have to spend day three in the Las Vegas Public Library.

- Blackjack and craps give the best odds. Slot machines use up dollars faster than a drunken sailor in San Diego.

- Don't gamble when you're exhausted, and go easy on the free drinks. You need to have good concentration.

- Leave your credit cards at home. Just imagine all the trouble you could get into.

- Good luck.

Ask your travel agent about gambling junkets. They are a good deal. You may also want to read *Casino Comps and Freebies for Low Rollers* by Tricolor Associates. There's a video version by Tapework, 1997. Both are available from Amazon: http://Amazon.com.

$$$—Cousin Thrifty McCheap says: "Save a few bucks by skipping two or three meals and then hitting the

all-you-can-eat buffets at the casino hotels. They'll hope you don't come back."

STRATEGY #8: STAYING WITH MONKS

Here's a unique opportunity to learn a wholly different way of life. Some monasteries welcome guests. For example, according to Mary K. Newborn, writing in *Transitions Abroad*, by tradition several Greek Orthodox monasteries in the Republic of Cyprus offer free lodging. The monks may not charge for hospitality, but they'll be more than happy to accept donations or to have visitors purchase what they produce: honey, wines, and liqueurs. The visitor must, of course, be courteous and quiet. Visitors are admonished not to display an excessive amount of skin within the sacred precincts.

One site is the Monastery of Aylos Neophytos, built in the 13th century in the Paphos district. It's open between mid-June and mid-September to visitors who wish to stay a night or two. A second possibility is Stravrovouni Monastery, which purportedly contains a piece of the True Cross, brought to the island by Saint Helena, mother of the Emperor Constantine the Great. It was founded in 327 C.E. Only men may stay, but not on Thursdays and Saturdays. A third location is Makheras Monastery, which is at an elevation of more than 2,000 feet above Nicosia. Call for reservations at (011) 357-02-312899.

Countless seekers of enlightenment travel to India, where they find thriving centers of spiritualism. One such is the ashram of Auroville. It's in Tamil Nadu near the former French town of Pondicherry. You may be asked for a monetary contribution to stay, or you may be asked to participate in work projects. For further information contact Auroville Greenwork Resource Centre, Isai Ambalam, Auroville, Irumbai Post, Tamil Nadu 605 101, India.

If you're planning to travel to Finland, you might want to work in an Eastern Orthodox Monastery in exchange for food and a bed. Contact Valamo Monastery, 79850 Uusi-Valamo, 72-570111, Finland.

BEWARE OF DISHONEST VACATION PROMOTERS

Everyone likes a free vacation. Nobody knows that better than dishonest promoters. They use the promise of free trips to take people for a ride. For example, a Washington State real estate broker was approached by a man selling "complimentary vacation packages" to Las Vegas. Each package was supposedly good for two nights in a big-name hotel, two dinners, four drinks, and $50 in casino chips. The package cost $25, or $200 for 10 packages. The broker bought 20 packages, writing a check for $400. He kept one package for himself and his wife and gave the rest to his sales staff and to preferred customers. Instead of building good employee and customer relations, the broker got taken.

The catch was that each vacation package recipient had to make reservations through the package salesman, not through the hotel. In order to make a reservation, the hopeful vacationer was required to put down a $50 deposit, payable to the salesman's organization, not to the hotel. Those who paid got neither a hotel room nor their deposit back. The promoter took off and was pushing his "product" in another state before the broker and other disgruntled customers alerted the sheriff.

A lady in Oklahoma City received a phone call from a man offering her two nights and three days at a Miami hotel for $50. Suspicious, she asked about the low price and was told, "The hotel wants you to have a great vacation on them so you'll come back again and tell all your friends. All our advertising is by word of mouth, and we put our advertising money into giving away nearly-free rooms." That sounded pretty good, so she bought the package. When she was ready to reserve her room a representative of the promoter's company, through whom she had to make her reservation, told her that she also had to buy her airline ticket from the promoter. She sent him a check and received what appeared to be a valid ticket from Oklahoma City to Miami. When it was time for her to leave, neither the airline nor the hotel had any record of her ticket or reservation, and the promoter was long gone.

Be suspicious of deals that seem too good to be true. The vast majority of junkets and familiarization trips are on the level, but check with the participating hotel, resort, or airline before reaching for your checkbook or credit card. Check with the Better Business Bureau or your state's attorney general's office. Make sure you're getting taken on a vacation, not just getting taken.

THE HOSPITABLE SCOTS: TEA FOR TWENTY-TWO

The Scots are possibly the most hospitable people in all Europe, or so we felt one bright July morning after being invited to an impromptu tea for 22. Taking a group of 17 students on a Mediterranean cruise and a bus tour of the British Isles was an enjoyable experience, but the highlight came when we persuaded the tour escort and driver to deviate from the route in the itinerary to find the Kirk ancestral home, actually a stone cottage in a small Scottish village.

There was no question of looking up long-lost relations; the last of the Kirks had left Scotland for America more than a century earlier. My wanting to find the house was a matter of natural curiosity. Having seen pictures of it taken some 30 years previously by a cousin, I immediately identified the house, which was set amid a spacious and well-tended yard. But during that 30 years a hedge that had grown parallel to the street made it difficult to get a good photo from the sidewalk. Luckily, a white-haired man stood before the gate. He stared incredulously at what was undoubtedly the first tour bus ever to have penetrated the peace of this small, out-of-the-way village.

"Good morning," I said. "I'm Bob Kirk and my great-grandfather built this house. My grandfather was born here. We've come from California. May we go into the garden to take a picture?"

"There's nothing to see," he replied without smiling, "but go ahead."

Five students, one tour escort, my wife, our daughter, and I entered the garden after swinging the gate wide. As our cameras clicked almost simultaneously, a middle-aged lady appeared at the door and when she saw the tour bus parked in front of her house, its engines purring, and the invasion that was in progress just outside her living-room window, her hands flew involuntarily to to her temples and she exclaimed: "Oh dear!"

"Your husband said we could come into the garden to take a picture," I said.

The lady looked even more apprehensive. "My husband is in the house doing exercises," she said.

"The man with the newspapers . . . ," I said in explanation.

"That's Charlie. He's allowed outside the mental hospital grounds every Sunday morning to deliver the papers. He's quite harmless but he'll agree to anything."

The great stone hospital that my great-grandfather John Kirk, a master stone mason, had completed before leaving for America in 1876 to build meat packing plants in Chicago, stood across the road, dominating the village. It was from there that Charlie had been temporarily liberated. My grandfather had been born in the house that this lady was defending and after the construction of the hospital was completed, it became the hospital's gatehouse. "I was born in a mental hospital," my grandfather had joked.

"It's alright," I told the mistress of the former gatehouse. "My name is Bob Kirk and my great-grandfather built this house and he was the contractor who built the hospital. My grandfather was born right here. I came all the way from California and these are some of my students and this is my wife, Barbara, and our daughter, Kathy," I said as I waved my finger at the small crowd. My explanation brought a brilliant smile of relief to the lady's face. I told her my grandfather's joke about being born in a mental hospital. That might have worried her, because her hands started the trip to her temples again, but she arrested them, flinging them back to her sides.

"Is it O.K. if we take a couple of pictures?" I asked.

"Yes, it's quite alright," she replied, re-entering the house that John Kirk built.

As we walked toward the bus, a man emerged from the stone house, waving an arm in the air. "Stop!" he said. "Come back."

"My name is Bob Kirk," I said and I ran through the abbreviated family history that I'd told Charlie from the hospital and that I'd told this man's wife, leaving out my grandfather's joke. And then I pointed in various directions, identifying the people with me.

"Oh, Bob," he said. "My name is also Bob. Don't leave yet. Please come back to the house. My lovely wife, Anne, and I will show you and your family around."

After the brief tour, Bob asked, "Will you stay for tea?"

"We really can't," I told him. "There are 17 students, a tour guide, and a bus driver waiting for us on the coach."

"Oh, I meant all of you," Bob said. "Anne, please make 22 cups of tea."

"Oh, dear," Anne said, her hands flying involuntarily to her temples.

We sat for two hours in Bob and Anne's pleasant garden, listening to stories about Scottish tradition and history, about Bob's experiences in the North African Campaign in World War II, and about his work as a therapist with patients in the hospital across the road. The students sat enthralled by this dynamic storyteller.

When it came time to leave, Bob and Anne invited us to visit them again on our next journey to Scotland.

When the bus left the village and we were once again on the road to St. Andrews, a student in the back of the bus called out, "Hey, Mr. Kirk, that was pretty neat. Why don't we stop in the next town and you can pick out a house and tell the people who live in it that your grandfather was born there?"

CHAPTER 5

Hosting Group Tours

McCheap's Fifth Law of Travel:
The most enjoyable way to travel free is
to find some pleasant companions to go with you.

WHY BECOME A GROUP TRAVEL HOST?

Recruiting a group to travel with you is the most direct strategy for getting a great vacation to destinations of *your* choice with *all* of your basic expenses paid. Like countless other tour and cruise group hosts, you may even come home with more money than you set out with.

Thousands of resourceful travelers find that taking others on tours, cruises, or outdoor adventures is an easy and pleasant way to visit any place in the world of interest to tourists, totally without cost. These travel hosts bring along friends, acquaintances, fellow club members, lodge brothers, sorority sisters, church congregations, members of professional associations, students—people in all types of groups and others who have never joined any group other than the line at the post office counter.

Because a portion of the trip's cost (known as the *prorate*) that each traveler pays is used to help defray the host's expense, the host enjoys a complimentary vacation for his or her efforts. If enough paying participants enroll, the host can bring Sweetie Pie along at no cost.

The purposes of this chapter are

• to help you decide if hosting group travel is right for you,

- to tell you about the wide variety of group travel possibilities available,
- to let you know how to contact organizations that can help you host travel,
- to offer tips on how to recruit travelers,
- and to share our own experience to help make your hosting job easy. Then, your group's vacation will be pleasantly memorable.

Is Group Travel Hosting Right for You?

Not everyone is equally comfortable recruiting people and taking them on a trip. Outgoing individuals who genuinely like others stand an excellent chance of success. If you enjoy organizing parties, chairing meetings, heading fund-raising drives, or selling just about anything, you'll probably love being a group host. Even a normally shy person with a genuine passion for traveling to exotic places without money can usually succeed in persuading enough people to sign up. But first . . .

A Brief Pause for Question Time

Question: I feel guilty about asking friends and acquaintances to pay part of my way.

Answer: You're really doing them a favor. In many cases they're people who probably otherwise would never travel were it not for your invitation to join your group. Widows whose husbands had never wanted to leave the backyard or their favorite trout streams during their marriages, teenagers whose parents are unsure of their kids' abilities to find their way across the street, people who feel they need assistance because they've traveled very little—all of these and millions like them are grateful for an invitation to accompany someone they know on a prearranged trip. For many, it will be the adventure of a lifetime and money well spent.

Question: I've traveled but I've never been to some of the places I'd like to take a group to visit. I don't think I'll have enough credibility to recruit people. For example, I want to see Rome but I've never been there.

Answer: Your travel experience and charm count for a lot. Most people want a chaperone and friend, and not an expert. Even if you were the world's greatest expert on Rome, some of your recruits don't want to hear much more about it than the fact that Romans live there and the food is tasty. Your travel companions will forgive you if you can't pinpoint the best restaurant on the Piazza Navona or explain in detail how to get to the top of the Aventine Hill by public transportation. In any event, you'll probably have expert tour escorts to make all you hear and see intelligible and to get your group from place to place without difficulty.

Question: What if the people I bring don't like the trip?

Answer: One of the most important points you must tell your potential travelers at orientation meetings is that things can and often do go wrong for travelers. There are transportation delays, days of pouring rain, unscheduled museum closures, hotel strikes, an occasional repetitious or even poor meal, and—on even the best planned five-star trips—someone is likely to catch cold or suffer a queasy stomach. Nothing is perfect and imperfection is an integral part of the travel experience.

You'll be surprised: Well-satisfied group members will probably sign up for your next trip as soon as you announce it. Others, including those who complained somewhat loudly about the air conditioning, the walking pace, the number of steps leading to the pagoda, or the fact that the guide's speech was unintelligible, will recommend your trips to their friends with great enthusiasm. When travels are completed, we tend to remember the marvelous moments, not the temporary tribulations.

Question: What if I don't get enough people to pay my way? What if I set out to get eight and I sign up only four?

Answer: In most cases, you can pay a supplement—perhaps

half of the trip's cost with four—and still go for far less than you would have paid for the same trip had you booked it on your own.

Question: I don't know.

Answer: Try it. It's probably the best chance you'll ever have to get the exact trip of your dreams entirely paid for. Remember, you *can* travel free.

Selecting from a Wide Variety of Travel Programs

CHOOSING THE RIGHT ITINERARY AND PRICE

There are hundreds of trips to choose from. Whether you go by sight-seeing bus, train, canal barge, or hot-air balloon, whether you soar around-the-world on a jet vacation, enjoy a luxury cruise, or opt for an adventure trek, you'll find plenty of people who are interested in joining you. Before you look for travelers, one of your most pleasant tasks is choosing an itinerary.

First, list the places that you really want to visit. If you simply want to return to Humdrum Corners where your old friends still live, where someone special waits for you, check out other chapters in this book and forget group hosting until you've satisfied that craving. If your passion for travel enables you to list a number of places you *really* want to go, you can probably find a suitable tour or write a good group itinerary with the help of a travel agent.

Next, get a general impression of what sort of travel program prospective participants in your community would write a deposit check for. This obviously entails talking with lots of people. In addition, sometimes you can make use of a sixth sense that will indicate what area of the world will command the attention of your would-be travelers. If you have a group of fellow workers, parishioners, friends, and neighbors at your disposal, try taking a poll. Give them a choice of two or three tours you'd like to take or of a few outdoor adventures you'd be willing to lead.

Not long ago, I polled several college classes by asking them to pretend they were to receive a free trip and to choose between visiting the British Isles; Spain, Portugal, and Morocco; and countries of Central Europe such as the Czech Republic, Poland, Hungary, Austria, and Romania. The British Isles won hands down. Unfortunately, I wanted to visit Central Europe that summer and as a result signed up a surprisingly small group. I ended up with the requisite number of travelers, but for a time success seemed uncertain. My advice is to listen to the consensus and act accordingly. Had I opted for Britain, I'm certain I would have signed up three times as many people and in a shorter time. The previous year I'd sensed, particularly after speaking with friends, students, and colleagues, that people in my community wanted to visit China. I was right. Twenty-five people gave me deposits seven months in advance of departure.

At the same time it's essential you get a general impression of what price people in your community are willing and able to pay for an exotic vacation. Price, of course, dictates the length, quality, and destination of the trip. Four days in Washington, D.C. will come in considerably cheaper than 30 days in southern Africa or four weeks in Australia and New Zealand.

Know your potential travelers. Many folks in upscale communities want a very comfortable trip and are willing to pay for business-class seating on planes, four- and five-star hotels, and small-group travel with private guides. To offer them less could result in your failure to form a group that would include them.

In less-affluent communities, the recruiter has to watch the bottom line—the trip's total cost. Through experience, asking around, and intuition, I know that if I price my tours above a certain amount, only a handful of people will be able to give my travel proposal serious attention. Were I to go a few hundred dollars above that price, I'd get few participants.

On the other hand, the price must be high enough to ensure quality accommodations, food, guides, sight-seeing, transportation, etc. The vast majority of adults won't sign up to walk down the hall in the Dumster Arms for a bath or to slurp cream-of-wallpaper soup at Chez Skidrow. They demand a certain degree of comfort and class for their hard-earned cash. The next step is to find an organization or travel agent that will put together a program that will provide the itinerary and price that's best for your purposes.

SERVING AS A PART-TIME TRAVEL REPRESENTATIVE

Some tour providers find it more profitable or just as profitable to engage part-time temporary travel representatives—you or someone like you—to sell their trips to people in local communities. Why would a company that publishes those glossy brochures with the stunning pictures of Irish meadows, Norwegian fjords, Japanese mountain peaks, and Polynesian palms give you a totally free trip and perhaps throw in a bucketful of cash? The tour company gets out of paying a hefty percentage of the tour price to a travel agent for reeling in paying participants. Because you propose the trip to people you know, the tour company sells tours to folks who wouldn't otherwise have written a deposit check.

The tour organizations give the representative a trip and perhaps a stipend. With enough additional signups, the representative can bring a companion, and if he or she has recruited an even larger group, the representative and Sweetie Pie go free and the company hands them a nice check. Depending on the travel provider, enough can be as few as five or six and as many as 20 or 25.

A package tour consists of air transportation and land arrangements at one all-inclusive price. Land arrangements include hotel rooms for each night of the stay, some or all meals, transportation between cities on the itinerary, admissions to places included in the program, and the services of a guide or conductor for the entire period from landing on foreign soil to takeoff to return home. The conductor (manager, guide, courier, or whatever) usually meets you at the airport, books you into your hotels, takes you to any lunches and dinners that are provided, offers road commentary, and answers questions about where to shop, where to eat, and which duke threw his nephew over the castle's parapet. The services of a bus driver are usually included in the overall price, as are tips for luggage handlers and for dining personnel when meals are provided. It's customary to tip your guide and driver when you say your final good-byes to them.

A cruise can be part of a tour. For instance, many tours of Greece include a four- or seven-day cruise to incredibly picturesque islands such as Santorini, Crete, Rhodes, Mykonos, etc. You can, of course, sign up people to take a cruise without a land tour that makes use of overnight accommodations. See your travel agent or contact cruise lines listed in chapter 3, "At Sea for Free."

You won't need a tour guide at sea. Just sit back and eat. On land tours, because the travel organizer provides an escort or tour manager, your main duty is to enjoy the trip on nearly the same basis as the people you brought along. Your other duty is to make certain that your group is happy with the arrangements and with one another. Sometimes it becomes necessary to smooth ruffled feathers when Lacie can't abide her roommate Pearl's snoring or when Henry can't understand why no one wants him to smoke his El Reeko on the bus.

Although your sales ability is essential to your success, no company expects you to have had prior sales experience. Nevertheless, the company values you as a recruiter more than as a host. Your group could take the tour without you, but they wouldn't have come at all had you not sold it to them.

All companies will allow you to bring a spouse or companion free if you bring double the number of paying travelers required for one trip. With fewer than the required number, say four out of five, you pay about a fifth of the advertised price. With more than the number required, most companies will give you a cash bonus. Some hosts do more than just cover incidental expenses; two, three, or four thousand dollars in cash for bringing in lots of people isn't unusual.

When people return with positive comments, their friends will want to go with you next time. You can make a seasonal career of taking groups. You probably won't get rich. You may not even make money. But eventually you'll see many of those parts of the world that draw tourists.

On a Roll: Free Trips Twice a Year

Some hosts travel as much as they want to. For example, a minister with a fairly affluent congregation can always get complimentary tours. Our friend Reverend Tyler does. Reverend Tyler's church members can easily afford to travel, so he hosts two programs a year for them. Last August he took people to Europe, landing in Zurich, and motoring by bus through Lucerne, Interlaken, and Bern in Switzerland before driving through Liechtenstein to Austria. From Innsbruck they ascended the Alps to visit Garmish, the fairy-tale castle at Neuschwanstein, Oberammergau, and Salzburg. From Salzburg they went sight-seeing in Vienna, Munich, Heidelberg, Rothenburg, and Dinkelsbuehl before returning to Switzerland for their return flight. Reverend Tyler and his wife, Brenda, paid nothing, not even for incidental expenses. And they returned $700 dollars richer. Reverend Tyler put his earnings in the church's Christmas food basket fund.

In the spring Reverend Tyler takes people to the Holy Land and either to Greece and the isles or on a Nile cruise in Egypt. When they arrive at the River Jordan, Reverend Tyler baptizes his flock, a memorable experience for all involved. He limits his groups to 18. That number provides air transportation and tour tickets for him and his wife and with cash for incidental travel costs and perhaps something for charity back home.

Reverend Tyler finds recruiting to be easy. His congregation is eager to visit the Church of the Holy Sepulchre in Jerusalem and Manger Square in Bethlehem. Reverend Tyler gives priority to his own parishioners and then takes nonparishioners on a first-come, first-served basis. He always has to turn away a few applicants, but he urges them to apply early to be included in the new group he's forming.

The company lends him travel films to show to prospective travelers, and they give him plenty of full-color brochures to spread around. When he recruited for his first tour, they showed him a step-by-step program to sign up travelers. When his groups don't fill up as fast as he'd like, he takes out a small newspaper ad or buys a few radio spots. He's adept at writing his own press releases about his trips for the local paper. While traveling, he sends back interesting stories and pictures of his group's progress though Europe or the eastern Mediterranean. Newspaper readers back home are glad to hear about what their friends are seeing and the editor is grateful to be furnished stories about what local people are doing abroad. Reverend Tyler sends postcards to parishioners who he would like to sign up for the next trip.

COMPANIES THAT WILL GIVE YOU A FREE TRIP

The organizations that follow recruit hosts and provide them with complimentary tours. Although they give away one out of five, six, or eight trips, they manage to keep prices competitive. There are itineraries on nearly every continent. If you've never been to Seville, Simla, or Siberia, here's your chance. Contact them.

ACIS

A large and venerable organization that specializes in student tours, ACIS offers a couple of dozen "adult recommended programs" on which adults travel separately from teenagers, who are the majority of ACIS clients. Student tour rates are fairly reasonable because youth travel organizations have the option of housing more than two high schoolers to a room. Adults demand more privacy than that, but adults can take advantage of the basic, low tour cost and when they pay a mandatory but modest supplement, ACIS guarantees double rather than multiple occupancy. An additional supplement buys single accommodations.

The group organizer travels free with six adults and may take a companion with double that number. Part-time representatives who recruit enough people get a trip for themselves, one for a companion, and hundreds or even thousands of dollars to play with abroad or to put in the bank. A sliding scale allows the organizer to pay a supplement if he or she has fewer than six and to reap financial awards with more than six. Recruiters who produce deposit checks for a requisite number of participants by mid-October are awarded abbreviated January vacations in Europe or Hawaii, or a cash bonus.

Trips recommended for adults include lots in Europe and one to Australia and New Zealand. "Sound of Music" is a 10-day trip with visits to Munich, Vienna, Salzburg, Innsbruck, and Lucerne. A Danube cruise is included. "Athens and the Aegean" consists mainly of a Greek Isle cruise with stops at Mykonos; Kusadasi, Turkey, for a tour to the ancient metropolis at Ephesus; Rhodes and its crusader citadels; Heraklion, Crete, and the Palace of Knossos; and towering Santorini. Of course, the Acropolis at Athens is the number-one attraction.

"Italian Serenade" is a 12-day trip made up of visits to Venice, Florence, Siena, San Gimignano, Pompeii, Sorrento, Capri, Paestum, Naples, and Rome. "London and the Emerald Isle" takes visitors to Ireland for the majority of its eight days and includes Dublin, the Rock of Cashel, Cork, Killarney, the Ring of Kerry, and Shannon. After extensive sight-seeing in the English capital, participants fly home from London. These are sample itineraries. The ACIS catalog has lots more.

If those sample programs look good, ask for a catalog and details about recruiting a group. ACIS, 19 Bay State Rd., Boston, MA 02215. Phone: (800) 888-ACIS. E-mail: edu_travel@acis.com. What does ACIS stand for? American Council for International Studies.

Ambassador Tours

Ambassador Tours, 717 Market St., San Fancisco, CA 94103. Phone: (800) 989-9000 or (415) 357-9876. Fax: (415) 357-9877. Website: www.ambassadortours.com.

Ambassador is an agency that sells tours and cruises. Because of their large volume, they are able to offer a free cruise to an organizer who brings in as few as 10 group members. Some cruises may require more than 10. Ambassador offers a big choice. They can put your group aboard ships of all the top cruise lines: American Hawaii, Carnival, Club Med, Crystal, Cunard, Holland America, Orient, Radisson, Royal Caribbean, Silversea/Windstar, and others. They also feature land tours by Globus and other firms.

To help you form your group, Ambassador Tours offers counseling by group specialists and marketing materials (including brochures, videos, and promotional mailings). The sooner you call Ambassador, the sooner you can set sail without any cost to you.

Bryan World Tours

Bryan World Tours, 1527 Fairlawn Rd., P.O. Box 4156, Topeka, KS 66604. Phone: (800) 255-3507. In a recent year Bryan offered a free trip with five paying guests. They offered cash for more than five; conversely, you pay around a fifth of the tour's price for every passenger fewer than five. Bryan tours invites you to take a companion free with 10. Bryan offers some cruises, but you need 10 paying travelers for one host to go free, and 20 for two free tickets. The company provides extensive notes on how to go about recruiting.

The itineraries are for connoisseurs who've been there and done that and are now looking for the unusual. In a recent year Bryan World Tours offered trips to places such as Albania (one of the first to do so); the Amazon rain forest; Bali and lesser known Sunda Islands such as Lombok, Sumba, Timor, Sumbawa, and Komodo—home of the foul-tempered dragons. Bryan travelers sail on canals and rivers in Russia, photograph wildlife in East African game parks, ride on camels and donkeys in Yemeni and Jordanian caravans, meet Tibetans and Nepalese at the roof of the world, ride trishaws in Saigon and Hanoi, and ooh and aah at the ruins of Angkor Wat. Every traveler, no matter how inveterate or intrepid, should find something to his or her liking in the Bryan catalog.

Globe Tours

Globe Tours, Inc., 369 E. Clearview, Worthington, OH 43085. Phone: (614) 846-4598. E-mail: travel@globetours. Website: www.globetours.com.

Globe's organizer, Dr. McElwee, a professor of classics, specializes in tours of the Eastern Mediterranean area. These education-oriented programs concentrate on classical civilizations. Tours go to Greece; Turkey; and Egypt, Cyprus, and Jordan. With eight travelers, the tour organizer goes free on scheduled programs. If you want to take a group on a date when a tour isn't scheduled, you need 10 to go free.

Let's look at one of Globe's offerings. The Jordan program starts with a visit of the capital, Amman. There travelers see the bazaar, citadel, Temple of Herakles, and other sights. At Jerash, an outstanding former Roman center, they visit the forum, temples, theaters, and baths. At Madaba they see the Church of St. George with its floor containing a reputed 2.3 million pieces of mosaic tile. At Mount Nebo is Kerak Castle, used by the crusaders. But Petra is the outstanding visit on this tour. After walking a mile down a narrow defile between 300-foot-high stone walls, you come out into an opening and there it is in front of you—The Treasury, a rose-red structure carved 2,000 years ago into the mountainside. The tour also visits Wadi Rum, Lawrence of Arabia's beautiful desert basin, and concludes in Aqaba on the Red Sea. There's an Israel extension available.

Sounds good. Your big chance to visit the Eastern Med. Globe will send full details on all their tours.

Go Ahead Vacations

Go Ahead Vacations, One Memorial Drive, Cambridge, MA 02142. Phone: (800) 242-4686. Recruiters receive a free trip from Go Ahead if they sign up seven and—on a few programs—eight travelers.

There are four considerations before deciding to recruit for Go Ahead. One, if the traveler you've rounded up has taken a previous trip with Go Ahead, they don't count him or her for your free trip.

Two, if the magic number is seven, and you recruit fewer, you get only a minuscule discount for each person credited to you. If you want to take a companion, you may need to try for 14 participants (two times the required seven), and if you take only 12 or 13, you get your free trip, but you pay for your companion's tour and flights, less a small discount. If you have participants begging to go and must screen some out, Go Ahead's rule presents no problem. You can stop recruiting after you sign up 14 and have a waiting list to assure you'll end up with 14, but not fewer. If you fall short, you must decide whether to pay almost all of the cost of the trip yourself.

The third quirk at Go Ahead is that you must estimate how many people you're going to sign up and put down your own money as deposits to reserve spaces on the trip for those people you've yet to recruit or perhaps haven't yet met.

Four, if you're trying to get eight paying passengers who haven't toured with Go Ahead in the past, you might want to put down 10 deposits and try to recruit 10, because any enrollee can get his or her deposit back without penalty up until the day the final payment is due. This bailing-out provision can cause major jitters to the recruiter who has the minimum number of travelers and no waiting list.

All this having been said, why sign up with Go Ahead? For one, they offer two free bonus days for early bookings, that is if the recruiter has put up the deposits by their published deadline date. Second, they offer some interesting itineraries. "Iberia to Africa," for example, includes visits during 18 days to Spain (Barcelona, Salamanca, Madrid, Granada, Seville), Gibraltar, Portugal (Lisbon and Coimbra), and to Morocco (Tangiers, Fes, Meknes, Marrakesh, and Casablanca). The tour appears to be rushed, but it's also a great introduction to a fascinating collision of cultures on two continents. "Eastern European Treasures" featured visits to Berlin, Warsaw and Krakow, Poland; Prague, Czech Republic; Vienna, Austria; and Budapest,

Hungary; with a six-night extension to Romania, including legendary Dracula country. "Scandinavian Heritage" (14 days) includes not only the capitals of Norway, Sweden, and Denmark, but visits to Helsinki, Finland; St. Petersburg, Russia; and Tallinn, Estonia.

If you've toured Albania, raise your hand. Go Ahead offered a 12-night tour of Albania and tempted travelers with a four-night extension to Rome and Sicily. For those who have "done" just about all of touristic Europe, Go Ahead offers cruises down the Nile and a tour of Israel and Jordan. Go Ahead includes three- and four-star hotels in its program package, as well as all breakfasts, but it usually doesn't include lunches and only some dinners.

A group I recruited for Eastern Europe felt most of their hotels and meals were great and they were unanimous in their praise of their guide. Most of all, they loved the Romania optional extension.

Go Ahead's prices are competitive and their staff is most helpful.

Grand Circle Travel

Grand Circle Travel, 347 Congress St., Boston, MA 02210. Phone: (800) 221-2610. Although it's barely past its own 40th birthday, Grand Circle's tours and vacation stays are for the age-50-and-better crowd. Retirees have the time to travel and more than any other age group, they can afford it. The problem for many retirees is that they don't want to travel alone. If you're over 50, consider doing a favor for people in your age group: Recruit 10 of them for a Grand Circle program and go free. Call the 800 number listed above and ask for a Free Group Leader/Vacation Ambassador kit.

Grand Circle offers a variety of itineraries for the first-time European visitor as well as for the well-traveled senior. The traveler who's been to all the well-trodden sites in Europe will probably enjoy sailing to the North Cape of Norway, following the recently forbidden Dalmatian Coast, and going on the

"All-Inclusive Sicily" tour or on the "Scandinavian Odyssey." Grand Circle produces an attractive and compelling catalog of itineraries and stay-in-one-place vacations, such as their 15-day "All-Inclusive Malta" resort package. If you're over 50, you probably know 10 people who've had the required number of birthdays to qualify.

HOSTING NATIONALLY ADVERTISED TOURS

A part-time college art history teacher's lectures were so popular that her students asked her to take them to look at major European art galleries. Because she didn't have enough time or experience to put together her own itinerary, she sat down with a travel agent, who gave her catalogs put together by well-known travel companies. Searching the catalogs, the instructor found the perfect tour for her and her group. It included visits to London, where she could take her art lovers to see the National Gallery and Tate Gallery; to Amsterdam to visit the Rijksmuseum; to Paris for the Louvre and the Musée d'Orsay to see works of Renoir, Manet, and Degas; to Vienna to tour the Kunsthistorische Museum; and to Madrid to enjoy Goyas, El Grecos, and Velasquezes in the Prado. She had no trouble selling this terrific itinerary. She got a slight price reduction for her group because they didn't participate in a few of the visits that were included in the company's comprehensive price. Instead, the professor spent extra time in the museums with her pupils. Her trip was free, and her students were grateful that she took the time to travel with them.

Most tour companies will give you a free, nationally advertised package tour from their catalog if you bring 15 or more paying passengers. They'll designate you a travel organizer and give you a whopping discount on your costs if you bring as few as four. Although they don't actively recruit part-time sales representatives, they certainly won't turn you away when you show up with a handful of deposit checks. Any good travel agent can give you a rundown of what companies operate tours and where. If you're interested in concentrating on a single country, that country's national tourist office can tell you what companies, domestic and North American, show tourists through their lands. See chapter 17, "A Wealth of Free Information" for addresses and numbers. If you wish to explore all the possibilities, ask your travel agent to let you see a copy of *OAG Worldwide Tour Guide,* a compendium of several thousand available escorted tours—your catalog of potential freebies.

LET YOUR TRAVEL AGENT ORGANIZE YOUR TOUR

The happiest hosts get the exact trips they want by getting them custom designed by travel professionals. A good travel agency can make up a group tour more or less to your specifications. If your favorite travel agent can make flight reservations, find you a guide and driver, and book you a hotel room in Kuching, Sarawak, he or she can certainly do the same thing for the eight, 10, or 12 people you've convinced to accompany you—enough for you to go to Sarawak, Samarkand, or Swaziland—nearly anywhere, actually—without paying. In addition, an agency can help you publicize your plans, produce tour brochures for you, and try to sell your trip to customers who want to visit your destination.

PUTTING YOUR TOUR TOGETHER: STEP BY STEP

At the outset, recruiting and leading a group on a tour abroad may seem like a formidable task. Like any complex project, it's much simpler when broken down into steps. Let me give you an example from my own experience. I satisfied a burning desire to see more of China when I took 25 terrific people on a two-week visit to the highlights of that vast nation. Our itinerary included Shanghai, Hangzhou, Souzhou, the Grand Canal, Nanjing, Guilin, and a Li River cruise. After that we went to Xian to see the terra-cotta warriors and Beijing to walk on the Great Wall and visit the Forbidden City. It was a superb trip and the moderate price included all meals, great hotels, and round-trip airfare as well as flights within China. I started recruiting at Halloween and had filled out my group by New Year's.

Step one was to visit my reliable travel agent. Anne Marie put together the best parts of two tours for us; the duration of the program was 14 days. She also arranged for us to have our own tour bus, drivers, and national guide, and a knowledgeable local guide in each city we visited.

Step two was to tell everyone I knew about my plans. "Everyone" included people I'd taken on previous summer trips. My enthusiasm was probably contagious because I soon had a core group pledged to go.

Step three was to write a press release for the local newspapers. Writing press releases is something I've been doing for years. I think I learned how initially by reading newspaper articles that were derived from press releases. Here's what I wrote and sent to several local papers. Following the release are comments to help you write your own. If you like this one about the China trip, you're welcome to use it as a pattern for your own publicity.

China Trip Planned

Local residents have the opportunity to travel to China May 30 to June 13. The 15-day program features extensive sight-seeing in China's most scenic areas, the services of English-speaking guides, as well as time for shopping and taking photos.

The tour's organizer is Dr. Bob Kirk of the [local] college history department. According to Kirk, "People wishing to participate do not have to be students. There are no classes to attend. The general public is welcome to join us."

The itinerary includes a nonstop flight from San Francisco to Shanghai aboard an Air China Boeing-747, followed by sight-seeing visits to Shanghai's Bund, built by European merchants in the last century, as well as to famous monuments and temples. The group will have the services of bilingual guides and an air-conditioned coach in Shanghai and throughout China.

Other highlights include Nanjing, a boat ride on the Grand Canal, and visits to the lovely canal cities of Wuxi and Souzhou. Further sights include Hangzhou and Guilin. Guilin lies in a region famous for the Li River and stunning mountains. The visitors will then fly to Xian to view the terra-cotta warriors, which are the larger than life-size guardians of the tomb of China's first emperor.

From Xian the group will travel to Beijing to visit the Great Wall, the Ming Tombs, the Beijing Zoo to see pandas, Temple of Heaven, the Forbidden City, and lastly, Tienanmen Square.

The cost is [amount], which includes round-trip air-fare, all transportation including flights within China, sight-seeing, admissions, all meals, and first-class and deluxe hotel accommodations (double occupancy).

Dr. Kirk has taught history at the [local] college since 1979 and has hosted 12 previous summer tours. For more information call Kirk at [phone number].

The following are comments on writing a successful press release.

- In order for an editor to give it his attention, it needs to be typed, double spaced, and on one side of the sheet only.
- Include your name, address, phone number, and the date in the upper left-hand corner.
- You may write "Press Release" or "For Immediate Release" in the other upper corner.
- Note that the most essential information—who, what, where, and when—appear immediately.

- Write your release in terms of the readers' interests: "Local residents have the opportunity . . ." rather than "Dr. Kirk is going to China and plans to take local residents." Nobody will care what the organizer wants to do; people are more attuned to opportunities that come their way.

- Shopping and photo opportunities appeal to many people and should probably be mentioned. We've noted in 30 years of travel that lots of North Americans may not know exactly where they are, but they do know what they want to bring back for their grandchildren or for themselves. And everyone wants pictures to show their friends on their return.

- Mention of bilingual guides and air conditioning gives people a sense of security and comfort, particularly in as exotic a place as China.

- After establishing my credentials as an educator I quickly dispel anyone's notion that they need to take a course or listen to me drone on about Sinological trivia. In other words, I tried to tell people I'd help them learn on this trip or they could have fun, or do a little of both.

- The itinerary includes all cities visited but mentions only those sights that are sufficiently famous that most readers will be familiar with them. Mention of too many visitation sites could overwhelm readers. That information is in the brochure I give potential enrollees.

- The cost appears after the itinerary. Everything that's included in the price is listed following that, so potential travelers will perceive value for their dollar.

- At the end, I tell a bit more about myself to add credibility and confidence.

- Finally, I let readers know exactly what to do next: Call for full information about the trip. I always include the phone number.

- The press release is relatively short. It's really all one needs. Most people won't complete reading a long tedious article in any case. The brochure, replete with fine print, will bombard them with enough details.

• It doesn't matter what headline you give your release; the editor will assign it a headline that conforms to his or her paper's space requirements.

> $$$—Cousin Thrifty McCheap says: "Unlike newspaper ads, press releases cost nothing."

All tour press releases don't have to conform to this pattern. But I must add that this is the only release I wrote. It was published once in three local papers, and it brought in 21 deposit checks. Within two and a half months I had deposit checks from 25 people. That seemed a sizable group so I closed the tour to new applicants.

Step four was to sustain interest from early January until late May, when the trip was to take place. I did that by mailing reading lists to each group member, lists that they could use or ignore as they wished. Some, incidentally, read extensively; one lady enrolled in a Chinese language course; others admitted to skipping the readings. In addition, I sent periodic letters to everyone about timely topics such as obtaining passports and visas, health precautions, getting into shape for lots of walking and some stair climbing, what to pack, etc.

Then, about a month before takeoff, I reserved a private dining room in a local restaurant for a no-host lunch to which all participants were invited. This was a time for the 25 folks to get acquainted and for them to ask me questions about what to expect. Most questions were about what clothing to take. It was easy to see friendships beginning to form. The get-together made us all feel positive about traveling with one another. As a result, the group got along exceedingly well in China and cooperated for two weeks so that we had no problems at all with personality clashes or lack of courtesy. The terrific group made my job easier and made the trip a success.

As your reputation as a tour host grows, it's possible to

negotiate with the travel agency so they'll share some of their commissions with you. Suppose, for example that you sell 20 tours of Europe at approximately $3,000 each. Your participants send in a total of $60,000 by the due date for full payment. The agency may get 10 to 15 percent commission on that amount. If the commission is let's say 12 percent, you can try to talk them into sharing some of their $7,200 with you. Ask for a third. They wouldn't have made it without you. Now, you can tour Europe, you can take a companion with you, and you have $2,400 (less income tax) to spend or bring home. It sounds like a nice summer!

LEAD A SPECIAL-INTEREST TOUR

What if you've never been more than 60 miles outside Macon, Georgia, or Grand Island, Nebraska? How can you recruit a group without travel credentials? You *can* do it and the best news is you don't have to be an experienced traveler. You don't have to have gone to all, or any, of the places on the itinerary. If you know all about a subject that many people are interested in, you can take a group to a place you've always wanted to see and focus on the topic of your field of expertise.

For example, if your interest is auto racing, take them to Le Mans in France. If your French in nonexistent, you can always hire a guide to interpret and take you around. If you love opera, take your fellow opera lovers to Milan to hear and watch Verdi at La Scala. If you're a budding thespian, take a group to attend theater performances in London. Your sincere interest in your avocation or vocation and your willingness to share your knowledge with others is far more important than your travel experience or linguistic ability.

A lawyer we know has long been interested in the British legal system. He convinced several colleagues, clients, friends, and their spouses to spend 10 days with him in London for a legal-eye view of the British capital. He took his group to listen to trials in Old Bailey and at the Royal Courts of Justice in the Strand. He made special arrangements to have his travelers visit the Inns of Court and to meet with powdered-wig-wearing barristers and solicitors. He asked a member of Parliament to get them admitted to the Strangers' Gallery in the House of Commons to watch MPs make laws. He also took his group on several excursions from London by train; they visited Bath, Winchester, Salisbury, Stonehenge, Oxford, Stratford-on-Avon, Canterbury, and Dover.

The attorney planned his trip with the help of a travel agent. The tour came off without a hitch, and it cost him and his wife nothing. Since his traveling companions were provided lots of free time to shop and explore, he and his wife had occasional free time by themselves to explore on their own.

There are five major advantages to leading a special-interest tour: 1) It can be free; 2) You probably have a built-in mailing list of potential travelers—members of clubs, subscribers to special interest periodicals, members of trade associations, etc. Or you may have met a number of people on the Internet who share your interests; 3) You can take them when and where *you* want to go and ask a travel agent to write the itinerary that you specify; 4) You spend time on the tour with people who share your fascination for your favorite subject; 5) You don't have to have been to the places you're planning to visit.

A Tour for Every Interest

Here are a few ideas from a virtually inexhaustible list:

- Religions of the Far East: Plan a trip to Bali (Hinduism); Java (Islam); Bangkok, Thailand (Buddhism); Singapore (Confucian, and a good sampling of all of the others); and Kyoto, Japan (Buddhism and Shintoism). Have local guides take your group to temples and explain the intricacies of these ancient belief systems.

- Photography: If you're a professional or advanced amateur, you can lead a photo safari. Where to? You name it. Snap wildlife in Kenya, Uganda, Tanzania, or South Africa. Shoot architecture in Kiev, Bergen, or New Orleans. Your drawing

card is your ability to advise your companions on photographing the places you're visiting. If you own a camera
shop, sell them the equipment they'll need. Throw in a couple of pre-departure class sessions and perhaps free film
developing when they return.

- Architecture and Interior Design: Lead a tour of English
manorhouses. Lots of them are open to the public. Include a
weekend in Paris and a drive to the French chateau country
in the Loire Valley. If you'd prefer to stay on this side of the
Atlantic, visit plantation houses in antebellum Savannah and
Charleston, or those European-style palaces that the Astors,
Belmonts, and Vanderbilts erected in Newport, Rhode Island,
and incongruously labeled *cottages*. Make your itinerary truly
unique by persuading the owners of particularly desirable private residences to open them especially for your group.

- Theater: Theater tours are fun and easy to arrange. Have
your travel agent reserve blocks of seats for popular plays or
musicals. Take the group to London or New York. Arrange
for them to go backstage to meet some of the actors, or get
someone who is involved in producing the play to meet with
you on the afternoon of the performance to furnish background information. Attend rehearsals. Read and discuss the
plays in advance so you can all be prepare for the evening's
entertainment.

- Gourmet Food: If your palate is educated and your tongue is
glib, conduct a gourmet tour. What a way to get a free lunch!
Take your fellow gourmets to Lyons, Paris, New York, New
Orleans, Hong Kong, or San Francisco. Visit cooking schools
and early morning vegetable markets. Have a chef give them
a lesson.

- Music: Take music lovers to one or more of the great European summer festivals. They're in spectacular settings such as
in the shadow of Edinburgh Castle, in Innsbruck, Montreux,
Lucerne, Athens, Bayreuth, and Spoleto. Visit three or four
festivals and you'll have a winning itinerary.

- Pilgrimages: The Holy Land, Fatima, Lourdes, Rome, Milan, Canterbury, Reims, Chartres, and Santiago de Compostela have attracted millions of the devout for ages. Tours to such places are a natural for the clergy and for interested laypersons.

- Golf: Arrange your itinerary around courses in the British Isles such as St. Andrews, Gleneagles, Royal Dublin, and Killarney. Top it off with a visit to the Manchester Open. Arrange for a well-known golfer to give your duffers a few pointers. Provide sight-seeing opportunities for nongolfing spouses during the day.

- Wine Tasting: Connoisseurs should consider taking people with similar tastes to France and Germany. Visit Burgundy, Bordeaux, the Rhine and Moselle valleys, and the famed cellars of the Champagne region. On this side of the ocean, Northern California's beautiful Napa-Sonoma-Lake Mendocino region produces wines second to none. Winery operators are delighted to give a tour and to allow your group to sample. Australia and South Africa also produce excellent vintages and are more than worth a visit.

The possibilities are nearly endless:
- taking elderly people to European spas for rejuvenation,
- leading a singles tour to a tropical paradise,
- taking nude-beach buffs to St. Martin in the French West Indies,
- visiting the Mayan ruins on Mexico's Yucatan Peninsula with amateur archeologists,
- visiting antique shows, antique stores, and flea markets in Europe,
- cruising the Amazon with wildlife enthusiasts.

ATTENTION COLLEGE STUDENTS

Jon is a junior at a large Midwestern university. He's majoring in biology and wanted to see the cloud forest in Costa Rica firsthand. But without extra money, he was unable to book a flight and hotel rooms. Ever resourceful, he talked 10 students into foregoing Florida beaches at spring break in favor of Costa Rica's fabulous Monte Verde Park. Their parents didn't mind shelling out money for a learning experience as opposed to a boozy frolic in the Atlantic surf. Jon traveled free.

Bettina is a senior at U.C. Berkeley. On weekends she wants to ski, but skiing is expensive. So she puts small ads in the *Daily Californian,* the campus newspaper, that offer ski packages put together by an agency. Group rates allow Bettina's skiers to pay less for hotel rooms and chairlifts than they normally would had they gone on their own. Off she goes on Friday afternoons with 12 fellow skiers to Dodge Ridge, Alpine Meadows, and other Sierra destinations.

The message is clear. Lack of money shouldn't be a deterrent to any smart student who wants to see more of the world, or to challenge the slopes.

THE CALL OF THE WILD: ADVENTURE TRAVEL

O.K., so you have zero interest in spending a sunny day in a museum. You feel that if you've seen one minaret, frieze, stupa, or fresco, you've seen them all. You're the outdoor type. Then you're in luck as a tour host, because adventure travel is the hottest item in today's tourist market. People who've seen everything now want to do everything, from climbing the mountains to hang-gliding. If you're an experienced outdoors enthusiast, you'll probably sign up enough rugged vacationers to be able to go where you choose and do what you choose, whether it's whitewater rafting on the Colorado or skiing at Zermatt.

As with any type of special-interest group tour, the services of a competent travel agent are invaluable. Hundreds of adventure travel companies vie to win the business of millions of Americans who will take adventurous vacations this year. Your travel agent knows their products and can pick from their vast array of offerings the best trip that will conform to your specifications.

Here are a few ideas from a vast pool of possibilities:

- Walk through dark German forests while singing robust *wandervogel* songs; quaff liters of dark beer and down hot white sausages at quaint inns;
- Deep-sea dive off Palau in Micronesia;
- Take a day hike just outside your own city;
- Backpack using llamas in California's Sierra Nevada or in the Peruvian Andes;
- Horseback ride through the Absaroka-Beartooth Wilderness and Yellowstone National Park in Montana and Wyoming;
- Hack your way through Brazilian jungles on the trail of the yellow-handed titi monkey;
- Take a camelback trek in the Lower Atlas Mountains in northwest Africa;
- Balloon over French vineyards and chateaus;
- Ski at Vail;
- Climb the Himalayas in Nepal with Sherpa guides;
- Photograph myriad wild animals in national parks in East Africa;
- Shoot the rapids on the Colorado River;
- Walk the Appalachian Trail.

You must make absolutely certain that your group members have passed physical exams before accompanying you on trips that call for more than normal exertion. Moreover, tell them to step up their exercise programs in the weeks before your trip begins; after all, some North Americans may be a tad out of shape after several years of doing potato imitations on the couch.

ATTENTION EDUCATORS

Teachers, counselors, administrators, professors, and others who deal with students—seventh grade through college level—

can travel totally free through the U.S. and Canada and to Europe, Mexico, the South Pacific, Far East, Africa, South and Central America, and the Caribbean. That's because several student travel companies want teachers to bring students with them and will give educators free trips for recruiting and chaperoning as few as five paying pupils.

Spending two to six weeks of a summer vacation with a group of adolescents may be a turn-off for some educators, but we thoroughly enjoyed the nine European trips we took with high-school students. In fact, I recommend without much reservation the experience of sharing young people's delight in discovering other cultures. When a teacher chooses the students carefully, prepares them sufficiently for their overseas experience, and makes the effort to show them the treasures of the Louvre or the Taj Mahal by moonlight, or whatever magnificent wonder is on the itinerary, there's very little problem keeping them out of mischief.

For some students, a trip to Europe—no matter how brief—arouses their natural curiosity. Even the adamantly ignorant show signs of wanting to know more. When you hear Derek and Samantha try out the Spanish, French, or German they've learned back at Elvis High, you'll realize that they actually have been paying some attention in class. And when they return, their interest in language, art, architecture, music, history, literature, drama, geography, and other subjects is heightened. For many, visiting Europe is a turning point in their lives, a mental catalyst.

Occasionally several teachers in a school want to take students overseas. When Mrs. Martinelli is recruiting for Italy, Mr. Perez for Spain, and Ms. Ling for Taiwan, unless the school is large and the students rich, there may be so much competition that none of the teachers will get a free trip. It's best to take turns, one taking a group each year. Without competition, you probably won't find it difficult to assemble a group of students.

When you announce your plans, your principal and superintendent will most likely be delighted at your demonstration of initiative and enthusiasm. Most parents are eager for their children to see Washington, D.C., or Europe's stellar capitals and other areas of cultural importance. These moms and pops are often willing and able to pay for most or all of their child's trip.

Paying for Student Trips through Fund Raising

When Mom and Dad don't want to, or can't, foot the entire bill, students can usually come up with some of the necessary funds through their own part-time work. In addition, some energetic teachers sponsor fund-raising activities such as cake sales, car washes, raffles, slave-for-a-day auctions, and similar activities. Even younger kids can raise a lot of cash.

Tameron, an 11-year-old boy in our community, is a super soccer player. He's so good, in fact, that his performance on his local team, the Hurricanes, won him a coveted invitation to help represent the U.S. at an international youth soccer tournament in Antwerp, Belgium, in the summer. Tameron needed to raise $2,500 to travel to Belgium, and he started his campaign as early as November. Tameron blanketed the local newspapers with articles requesting help. Promising to bring back a souvenir T-shirt for anyone sponsoring him for $100 or more, the player got pledges from a number of local businesses. "I would like to see all kids of the world, and adults too, just be able to play peacefully together and have fun," he stated diplomatically. After playing four games in the tournament, Tameron will get to do lots of sight-seeing. Tameron promised to get the names of his sponsors in the paper, which is good publicity for local business donors. Any student can follow Tameron's example and raise money through local donors.

Keeping Costs Down

Student tours usually cost less than an identical adult itinerary because tour companies have learned that teenagers will put up with inconveniences their parents won't tolerate: three or four people to a room and often crowded buses. Because competition for passengers is keen, many of these organizations have improved drastically since they began in the 1960s: No longer do most bed students down in hostels and remote university dorms, feed them fortified gruel in university cafeterias, and fly them to Europe on charters whose delays became legendary.

As a chaperone, you don't have to sleep in a cramped triple room with your students; chaperones are housed in doubles with the companion of their choice, with another chaperone of the same gender, or in singles.

Getting Started

The most obvious way to advertise your trip is to tell your classes, put notices in the school paper, and—by all means—in the daily bulletin. Keep your announcement short: "Students interested in traveling for two weeks in England, France, Italy, Austria, Germany, and Holland this summer should see Ms. Gulliver in Room B-12 for further information. This low-price tour is open to all students." Request that your succinct and inviting announcement be read over the school loudspeaker. Put attractive posters on school bulletin boards. Send a press release to the local newspaper.

Once you have a small core group, you'll find that students who have already committed themselves are your best salespeople. They give the all-necessary sanction that your trip requires when they term it "way cool" and then round up their friends for you. Sometimes two or three popular students can bring in all the sign-ups you need.

The next step is to invite all interested students and their families to a special evening meeting, preferably at the school. Explain the trip in some detail. Show a film if the student tour company provides one. Tell them about a typical day sight-seeing in Europe. Briefly discuss getting a passport, packing, and how much money to take. You'll have to go though details again about packing and foreign currency at a meeting nearer to departure. The most important thing you want to accomplish at this initial evening meeting is to build confidence so parents will willingly give you deposit checks. Don't push too hard. If you've excited them about your plans, you'll get the checks.

An educator usually needs five to eight students for a complimentary trip and a companion can go along with double the requisite number. Because teachers can also earn a stipend for bringing more than the required number, as well as experience bonuses for having taken similar trips in previous years, some make more money seeing the world than their colleagues make teaching summer classes back home. Some teachers come home with several thousand dollars as payment for having enjoyed a free tour or cruise for two.

On the Road with Your Students

Before you're scheduled to depart, you need to have meetings with students to establish rules such as curfews, to discuss foreign currency, to discuss packing, and to finalize a roommate list. Your young travelers and their parents will have a great number of questions that are guaranteed to make these meetings worthwhile.

When you take a group, the company designates you as a teacher counselor or by some similar title, but what you are is a successful sales representative and a traveling chaperone. A chaperone's duties overseas aren't particularly onerous if the students in the tour group have been selected for their interest in language and culture rather than their desire to escape parental supervision and experiment with inordinate amounts of wine and beer or—horror of all horrors—illicit drugs. Even the most resourceful of all chaperones can't get Timothy or Taylor out of the dungeon after they've been slapped with drug charges.

The chaperone sight-sees with the group, takes the students to a theater or concert in the evening, makes certain they spend the night angelically asleep in their own beds, helps them adjust to their surroundings, gets them to promise to budget their trip money, and makes sure they are getting as much as possible from their experience in another land.

Any veteran chaperone would be lying if he or she didn't admit having had some problems with students. On our nine trips, we've had to help Rebecca get a new passport after she lost hers in a Paris restaurant, help Dudley phone home for money every few days, and have a friendly chat with Morgan about holding up the bus 20 minutes every morning while drying her hair in her room. We've had to wean Brett from German lager. We've had to give a fast lesson in Anglicisms to Cherylie when she came to our London hotel room at midnight exclaiming, "A boy I met in a pub said he was going to come to my door to knock me up!"

All in all, however, our trips have been substantially trouble free. One reason is that student tour companies have trained multilingual staff all along the route and on the bus or cruise ship, so teachers never have to face problems without help.

SELECTING THE RIGHT PROGRAM

There's a program for every educator's taste and purpose. They range from week-long rush-rush spring vacation tours to summer programs of one to six weeks. There are winter-ski breaks, campus stays, language schools, marine biology dives, cycling trips, cruises, hiking vacations, and train journeys.

Below are some of the most important student travel companies and some samples of their offerings.

ACIS

ACIS, 19 Bay State Rd., Boston, MA 02215. Phone: (800) 888-ACIS. Homepage: http://www.acis.com. E-mail: edu_travel@acis.com. ACIS offers an astonishing number of itineraries and will make one up to suit you if you bring a busload of travelers. Teachers go free with six students. ACIS promises "3- and 4-star hotels in major cities, well located with private baths." ACIS advertises good couriers and professional guides in all major cities, scheduled flights on major carriers, liability protection, an escrow fund to protect deposits received, cancellation and health insurance, "balanced and nourishing" meals, and educational activities. The nicest hotel we've ever stayed at on a student tour—the Atrium in Prague—was on an ACIS tour.

Here are some sample itineraries, just to whet your peripatetic appetite: "Athens and the Aegean with Cruise"—nine days: Cruise to Mykonos, Kusadasi and Ephesus, Patmos, Rhodes, Crete, Santorini, and return to Athens for tours to the Acropolis, National Archaeological Museum, and a trip to Delphi. "Italian Serenade"—13 days. It includes a Venice walking tour; a visit to Florence to see Michelangelo's *David,* the Duomo and Bapistry, Santa Croce, Pitti Palace, and Ponte Vecchio. Featured too are visits to Siena, San Gimignano, Pompeii, Sorrento, Capri, Amalfi Coast, and—of course—Rome. In Rome students visit the National Archeological Museum, Colosseum, St Peter's, Vatican Museums, Sistine Chapel, and other sights. ACIS's sumptuous free catalog is full of these sorts of programs.

As a recruiting teacher you can take a companion with 12 enrolled students. If you're fresh out of companions, you can earn cash with more than six students, and if you have a companion, you and Sweetie Pie can return with a fist full of cash if you recruit and accompany more than 12 teens. As a result, you can easily earn enough to pay incidental costs on the trip.

ACIS offers lots of bonuses for super sales performance. Enroll pupils a year early and if your group is large enough, you get five nights in either Sydney or Buenos Aires as a reward. Other awards take you on long weekends to London, Paris, Prague, Dublin, or Costa Rica.

Since 1978, 25,000 teachers have gone abroad with ACIS. As a matter of interest, ACIS reports that 81 percent teach at public schools, the rest at private and parochial schools. Fifty-five percent teach foreign languages. Forty-one percent teach at schools with more than a thousand students.

College teachers take students on ACIS tours. In addition,

professors can accompany six paying students to summer courses abroad at no cost to themselves. Their stipend takes care of airfare, lodging, and whatever meals their students have arranged for. American Institute for Foreign Study, the sponsoring division of ACIS, calls it "Faculty Development" and it provides a great opportunity for academics to do research or see the sights while their pupils take classes. Some professors arrange to teach a class and are paid by their home institutions.

ACIS operates college-level summer programs in Buenos Aires, Argentina; Salzburg, Austria; Prague, the Czech Republic; Richmond (suburb of London); Cannes and Paris, France; Florence, Italy; Shizuoka, Japan; Mérida, Mexico; St. Petersburg, Russia; and Granada and Salamanca, Spain.

Contact ACIS, College Division, 102 Greenwich Ave., Greenwich, CT 06830. (800) 727-2437. Fax 203-869-9615. E-mail: info@aifs.org. Website: http//www.aifs.org.

AESU Travel

AESU Travel, 2 Hamill Rd., Suite 248, Baltimore, MD 21210-1807. Phone: (800) 638-7640 or (410) 323-4416. Fax: (410) 323-4498. Homepage: http://www.aesu.com. E-mail: res@aesu.com.

O.K., let's say you're at college, your name is Stu Dent, and you're sitting around the dorm thinking about a fabulous tour to Europe, but you can't afford a bus ride to the beach, much less a jet vacation. What to do? Recruit 15 people between the ages of 18 and 35 on an AESU tour and go free as a group organizer.

AESU has ambitious itineraries. You could see most of Western Europe—just about the Whole Pretzel—in 50 days with AESU. That would include Netherlands, Germany, Switzerland, Liechtenstein, Austria, Hungary, the Czech Republic, Greece and its islands, Italy, France, Spain, Belgium, and England. If 50 days is a bit too much bus-seat time, try the 20-day "European Discovery," which covers much the same area, minus Greece and the former Iron Curtain capitals.

Too many countries? Then take your fraternity brothers on

AESU's "Riviera Sun" vacation, centered in Cannes; or take the sorority on "Royal Isles," which covers the best of Britain. AESU has lots of offerings and if none appeals to you, make up your own itinerary and their staff will put it together for you as you set about recruiting your group.

Bravo Tours, Inc.

Bravo Tours, Inc., 70 Ridgewood Ave., Ridgewood, NJ 07450. Take six students and go free. Bravo specializes in trips to Spanish-speaking areas. These include programs to Madrid and Costa del Sol (eight days each); nine-day tours of Spain, which visit Madrid, Barcelona, Mallorca, Toledo, Avila, Segovia, Tenerife (Canaries), Santiago, Seville, Granada, etc. Closer to home you can spend seven days in Puerto Rico or at Cancun and the Maya ruins in Mexico. Bravo appeals mostly to Spanish teachers and their pupils. Website: www.bravotours.com.

CHA Educational Tours

CHA stands for Cultural Heritage Alliance. It's at 107-115 S. Second St., Philadelphia, PA 19106. Phone: (800) 323-4446 or (215) 923-7060. Fax: (215) 923-5583. Founded in 1969, CHA has taken more than half a million young Americans abroad. Tours range from eight to 23 days and include stays in Europe, Mexico, Costa Rica, Hawaii, Australia, and China. Or you can opt for a Caribbean cruise. CHA offers regularly scheduled flights, local guides, experienced tour directors, etc. Teachers travel free with six students.

Teachers can earn hundreds or even thousands of dollars with enough students. Enroll a requisite number by an early deadline and win bonus trips—in addition to your free trips with students—to London, Paris, Rome, Costa Rica, Egypt, Australia, Mexico, etc.

Most tours include breakfast and dinners. Sample itineraries: "Pride and Pageantry" hits the highlights in London, Windsor, Stonehenge, Bath, Bristol, and the Lake District (England); Waterford, Blarney, Killarney, Limerick, Bunratty,

Dublin (Ireland); and Edinburgh (Scotland). Fly home from Glasgow. "La Belle France" offers introductions to Paris, Versailles, Rouen, Caen, D-Day beaches, St. Malo, Mont St. Michel, Loire Valley, Poitiers, Limoges, Lascaux Caves, Toulouse, Carcassonne, Nîmes, Pont du Gard, Avignon, Aix, Nice, St. Paul, Vence, Cannes, Monaco, and Eze. "Sunny Spain" takes students to Barcelona, Montserrat Monastery, Zaragoza, Madrid, Toledo, Córdoba, Seville, Ronda, Mijas, Costa del Sol, and Granada—all of this in 10 days. "Along the Danube" gives you a preview of Geneva, Lausanne, Brig, St. Moritz, Neuschwanstein, Munich, Salzburg, Vienna, Budapest, Krakow, Prague, Dresden, and Berlin—17 days.

What do teachers and their students do on a typical day? In Vienna they visit the opulent Hofburg palace, from which the Habsburg emperors ruled a polyglot Central European empire; the Opera House on the Ringstrasse, one of the world's two or three most renowned venues for operatic performances; the Burg Theater, the University, Belvedere Palace, and Empress Maria Theresas's suburban Schönbrunn Palace. The evening may find them at a charming restaurant in the suburb of Grinzing.

CHA welcomes adult travelers but charges them extra for guaranteed double occupancy and a bit more for single occupancy.

CIEE

If you want to take a group of students abroad on your own itinerary, if you want arrangements made in advance, and if you want the total cost to be low, consider talking to representatives at CIEE. The Special Services Division of CIEE (The Council on International Educational Exchange) can arrange charter and other bargain flights; rooms in hostels, YMCAs, university dorms, or inexpensive hotels; and all-inclusive travel passes such as the Eurailpass. They can save you a bundle and make your trip affordable. They'll give you a quote if you plan to take a group. Write to CIEE, 205 E. Forty-second St., New York, NY 10017.

EF Educational Tours

EF Educational Tours, 1425 Chapala St., Santa Barbara, CA 93101-3000. Phone: (800) 637-8222. E-mail: edtours@ef.com. Also, One Memorial Drive, Cambridge, MA 02142-1346. EF teachers travel free with six students. Two people go free with 12. You can earn cash bonuses for more than six students.

EF offers another bonus: Teachers can accumulate points. You earn one point per day that a student travels with you, so if 10 people accompany you for 10 days you get 100 points. With these points, you can earn cameras, computers, TVs, and vacations in Canada, Mexico, Europe, Hawaii, Australia, on cruises, etc.

EF offers student-oriented trips to Europe, Mexico, Costa Rica, Australia, New Zealand, South Pacific, Egypt, South and East Africa, and China. Programs are five to 32 days. "Fifteen days in England, France, and Spain" includes visits to London, Windsor, Paris, Loire Valley chateaus, Biarritz, Barcelona, and Madrid. "Treasures of Central Europe"—14 days—takes groups to Berlin, Dresden, Prague, Budapest, Vienna, Munich, and Heidelberg. "Australian Adventure" offers a chance to see Sydney, Coffs Harbour, Surfers Paradise, Sunshine Coast, Fraser Island, Coopers Down Cattle Station, Whitsunday Islands, Great Barrier Reef (optional), Townsville, Magnetic Island, and Cairns.

EF Sport Tours

EF Sport Tours, address as above. Phone: (800) 577-6784. E-mail: sports@ef.com. Soccer teams play against foreign players while exploring parts of Europe or Mexico. America Football Tours matches U.S. players with players in London, Mexico City, Barcelona, and Dusseldorf. Ski programs are centered in popular European destinations.

EF Performing Arts Tours

The address of EF Performing Arts tours is listed above. Phone: (800) 332-7141. E-mail: perform@ef.com. Take a choir or orchestra, marching band, or tap dancers to Europe. EF performers have appeared in Venice's St. Mark's Basilica, Vienna's Schön-brunn Palace, the Duomo in Florence, the Vatican, Notre Dame Cathedral in Paris, Heidelberg Castle, and EuroDisney-land outside of Paris.

EF Explore America

EF Explore America programs address listed above. Phone: (800) 503-2323. E-mail: explore@ef.com. Take your students to Washington, D.C., to see the White House; Supreme Court; Capitol; National Archives; Lincoln, Jefferson, Holocaust, and Vietnam memorials; Smithsonian Institution museums; National Zoo; Mount Vernon, etc. Also EF has trips to New York City, Disney World's Magic Kingdom, Sea World, Epcot, Kennedy Space Center, and more. EF offers student trips to Quebec City and Montreal; Toronto and Niagara; Boston and Philadelphia; Chicago, Boston, and New England; Puerto Rico; California; Alaska; and Texas.

Passports

Passports, 389 Main St., Spencer, MA 01562-9968. Phone: (800) 332-PASS. Fax: (508) 885-0329. Website: http://www.passports.com. E-mail: info@passports.com.

Passports is a very major player in the student travel game. Founded by Dr. Gilbert Scott Markle, former professor of phi-losophy at Clark University, Passports has been sending stu-dents and teachers abroad since 1992. Markle was at one time president of American Leadership Study Groups, which he founded back in the mid-1960s, and thus has more than three decades of experience in school travel programs.

Passports rewards high school and college teachers well if they bring a group. Six students net the instructor a free trip, and more get him or her cash bonuses. Teachers who have taken groups in the past qualify for experience bonuses. Teachers who send in applications far enough in advance can have bonus trips—in addition to the trip with the students. Some of the des-tinations include Costa Rica for six days; Tobago in the West

Indies for a week; to a teachers' conference in Paris; from London to Paris through the Chunnel; to San Juan, Puerto Rico, for five days on the beach; or they may choose Yuletide in London.

Passports offers a full array of itineraries. These include all the usual fling-around-the-Continent tours of Western Europe. In fact, there's a European tour for every taste—from the Grand Tour to Alpine, Iberia, Greek islands, French countryside, Scandinavia, Russia, British Isles, etc. In addition, Passports takes groups to Costa Rica, Mexico, the Holy Land, China, Australia, New Zealand, Kenya for a safari—and for the absolutely laid back—to beaches in Tobago, Hawaii, and St. Martin in the Caribbean.

Passports has something for every teacher's taste and the generous recruiting materials and support from the staff make rounding up a group fairly simple.

One program that caught our eye is entitled "South Seas"; it's not your usual European capitals jaunt. Fly into Honolulu and stay on Waikiki; cruise out into Pearl Harbor to the *Arizona* Memorial that recalls the Japanese attack on December 7, 1941; tour the major sites of Honolulu and end the day with an "optional" luau. Fly off to Sydney, Australia, and see the Opera House, the historic Rocks district, Darling Harbour, and eat lunch on a Sydney Harbour cruise. An optional excursion goes to the Blue Mountains where the group sees koalas, kangaroos, and wombats. From Sydney, fly to Auckland, New Zealand. After sight-seeing in Auckland, the group goes to Rotorua, home of Maoris since the 14th century, when this wave of Polynesians reached North Island. After a cable-car ride up Mount Ngongotaha to see Maori Land from the peak, the group flies off to Tahiti (optional) for a couple of days in paradise. Who said teaching is inadequately rewarded?

To Help You Decide

• Read *Taking Students Abroad: A Complete Guide for Teachers,* by Maggie B. Cassidy. Pro Lingua Associates, 15 Elm St., Brattleboro, VT 05301. Phone: (802) 257-7779.

- Read *A Coach Full of Fun,* by Jeane S. Klender. Shoreline Creations, 143 Douglas St., Holland, MI 49424. Phone: (800) 730-3120.

YEAR AFTER YEAR

Whether you take your group on a tour, a cruise, or an adventure, your most pleasant surprise can occur after you've returned home. You'll be in a restaurant or the mall or the grocery store. A total stranger will approach you and say, "Aren't you the person who took my friend Sally to Europe last month? You are! Well, she loved it and I want to go with you on your trip next summer." And so it can go—year after year.

CHAPTER 6

Sight-seeing in the Land of the Free

McCheap's Sixth Law of Travel:
Never buy an admissions ticket when you can see or do
something equally as interesting without paying.

PRICELESS ATTRACTIONS IN UNCLE SAM'S AMERICA

Many more exciting sights, sounds, and events await the free traveler within a day or two of home than there's time for. Others, including world-class sights and experiences, are scattered all over the United States. The major type of free attraction is too large and spectacular for even the most intrepid entrepreneur to wall in and charge admission to visit.

Chicago's Sears Tower, New Orleans' Basin Street, San Francisco's Golden Gate Bridge, Oregon's Crater Lake, the Grand Tetons, New York's Greenwich Village, the Boston Common, Miami's Art Deco South Beach, San Antonio's River Walk, Washington State's Mount St. Helens, Southern California's golden beaches, Pike's Peak, and Waikiki's Diamond Head are only a few of these mammoth delights that people travel thousands of miles to experience.

If you want to see the best the nation has to offer, start here to get ideas and inspiration, and then contact tourist and convention bureaus. You'll find a few addresses and phone numbers in this chapter and all the rest in chapter 17, "A Wealth of Free Information." The glossy brochures and maps tourist bureaus will shower you with will cost you nothing.

Let's see how, with a little research and planning, the thrifty traveler can bypass budget-busting ticket booths and still have a fantastic time.

ATTENTION STUDENTS

Where admissions are charged, students can get free and reduced-priced tickets to cultural events of all kinds: theaters, lectures, ruins, concerts, museums, and more. These discounts and free admissions are to be found in the U.S. and Canada and abroad. You need an International Student Identity Card to prove you're enrolled. Full-time high school, college, and university enrollees, able to furnish proof by presenting student identification issued by an accredited institution, are eligible to apply for the card. Even teachers and professors can get in on this outstanding break by presenting proof of their employment as full-time educators. Students and instructors do, however, need to pay for the identification card, but not much. Get further information from the Council on International Educational Exchange (CIEE), 205 E. Forty-second St., New York, NY 10017.

ATTENTION SENIOR CITIZENS

State Parks, museums, theme parks—even restaurants, rental car firms, and motels—offer discounts or free admission to seniors. What's a senior? Usually it's a mature person 65 years or older, but depending on the admission or discount policy of the organization you're dealing with, a kid who's only 50 could qualify. If you're 50 or older, it costs nothing to ask. Free travelers always ask. If the answer's "yes," you get a break as a reward for celebrating so many birthdays.

Also see Caroline and Walter Weintz's *The Discount Guide for Travelers Over 55,* which should be available in your library. If it's not, order it from Pilot Books, 103 Cooper St., Babylon, NY 11702.

$$$—Cousin Thrifty McCheap says: "I can hardly wait 'til I'm a geezer so I can get all those discounts."

CHEAPSKATE-FRIENDLY SITES

Where should the impecunious or the admittedly cheap look for free attractions? Here are a few ideas for places to visit throughout North America.

Places of Worship

Churches, temples, mosques, and synagogues almost always offer free admission. Never walk past one, even if it looks unpromising from the outside. Some of the most breathtaking places of worship reveal themselves only after you've entered, particularly when a service or sacred concert is taking place. In Philadelphia, for example, visit the Society Hill Synagogue on Spruce Street. Go into St. Patrick's Cathedral in New York City.

Public Buildings

Visitors pay nothing to look around the most impressive parts of government edifices. The U.S. Capitol, the capitols of the fifty states, and metropolitan city halls are built to awe the visitor by their neoclassic permanence and majesty. These people's palaces are often richly detailed, incredibly formal, and pompously powerful—monuments to the administrations that conceived them and to the taxpayers who funded them. Some are of compelling historic interest.

Alabama's state capitol at Montgomery, for example, is the site where the Confederacy was proclaimed in 1861 and where Confederate President Jefferson Davis was inaugurated. Maryland's statehouse is the oldest capitol in use in the United States and has the room where George Washington resigned his general's commission at the end of the American Revolution. In the Boston State House you can find the Mayflower Compact, among other historic documents.

Louisiana's state capitol at Baton Rouge was designed to resemble a Norman castle, but Mark Twain called it the "Monstrosity of the Mississippi" and recommended dynamiting it as a corrective measure. Check it out. After all, what did Mark Twain know? See the United States Mint at Fifth and Arch streets in Philadelphia. Coins are made here and you can watch. In Washington, D.C., take the well-organized tour of FBI headquarters. In only an hour, you'll see state-of-the-art crime labs and other instructive exhibits.

Some edifices, such as the National Capitol and California's state capitol have opened to the public chambers painstakingly restored to evoke an earlier and more ornate era, the opulent 19th century. These museum-quality chambers are free to visit. The White House has brilliantly restored rooms that you can walk through.

And don't forget public libraries; they're not only full of friends waiting to be read, but some, such as the main branch of the New York City Public Library, are of immense architectural interest and are filled with fine art.

Museums

Governments, societies, and endowments maintain these repositories of mankind's past, of natural wonders, and human creativity so the public can enter free, be inspired, be dazzled, get wowed, and expand our minds. When there's an admission charge, students with student identification and children often enter free or at half-price, and senior citizens often receive hefty discounts.

The Wadsworth Athenaeum in Hartford, Connecticut, shouldn't be missed. Its collection of American paintings include works by John Trumbull and John Singleton Copley. The J. P. Morgan collection of Greek and Roman bronzes is here, as is an outstanding collection of European paintings. In Washington, D.C., the Air and Space Museum of the vast Smithsonian Institution is one of the most popular attractions in town. While in D.C., go to 1411 W St. SW and tour the Frederick Douglass National Historic Site. While there, you may learn more about Douglass, who was instrumental in getting the federal government to abolish slavery and later became the first African-American ambassador sent abroad from the United States. Your tour is free.

Aviation enthusiasts will also enjoy the free Naval Aviation Museum at the U.S. Naval Air Station in Pensacola, Florida. Old Town San Diego State Historic Park is a six-block area full of historic houses and museums, and several of them are free. It's here that San Diego, California's first settlement, began in 1769. See reconstructions of old adobes, which include period furnishings and relics of the romantic Spanish period of California's history.

The Honolulu Academy of the Arts on South Beretania Street houses the outstanding Kress Collection of Renaissance art as well as Oriental collections and local art. The New Orleans Museum of Art houses a superior representative collection that ranges from ancient to contemporary examples.

The exhibits at Chicago's Museum of Broadcast Communications (Michigan Avenue at Washington Street) explain the history of broadcasting. They allow you, for example, to get face to face with retired dummies Charlie McCarthy, Effie Klinger, and Mortimer Snerd. The St. Louis Missouri Art Museum contains one of the most representative collections of painting and sculpture in the country.

Small towns quite often offer museums that are well worth visiting. The next time you're in Glasgow, Montana, for instance, visit the Pioneer Museum, just a half-mile off U.S. Route 2; here you'll find displays that evoke the heroism of pioneer days, as well as outstanding Indian artifacts. Take the kids to the Davy Crockett Birthplace State Park to see a replica of Davy's log-cabin next time you find yourself in Greeneville, Tennessee.

And don't forget that Big Stone Gap, Virginia, is the home of the Southwest Virginia Museum and is full of pioneer tools and medical instruments. When you find yourself in Caribou, Maine, visit the Nylander Museum for its Indian and pioneer relics.

Nostalgic for a past that you've only read about or seen in movies? Visit the Greenwood Museum in Greenwood, South Carolina; the drug store, one-room school, and other buildings that line the reconstructed village street will take you back a century or more. Some towns are museums: Virginia City, Nevada, with its mining-era operahouse and saloons, comes readily to mind.

Colleges and Universities

University campuses offer verdant dales, inspiring groves, and ivy-covered walls to enchant visitors and attract students. From Tulane to Princeton, Harvard, Yale, Indiana at Bloomington, and Seattle's University of Washington to Texas at Austin, campuses are charming, and many evoke the academic aura of Cambridge and Oxford. Although you may have to mortgage your future to graduate from these gold-plated groves of academe, marveling at the ambience and enjoying free movies, symposia, concerts, sports contests, and lectures is an ever-present opportunity.

Cornell University in Ithaca, New York, for example commands an outstanding site overlooking sparkling Lake Cayuga. Landmark buildings include the McGraw Tower, Morrill Hall, and the Herbert F. Johnson Museum of Art, designed by the celebrated architect I. M. Pei. The University of Virginia at Charlottesville was designed by third president Thomas Jefferson. California State University at Chico boasts one of the most attractive campuses anywhere. The University of Wisconsin at Madison overlooks Lake Mendota, just west of the state capitol building, and is one of the prettiest campuses in the nation. Walk around Yale's historic grounds and hum the "Wiffenpoof Song," as you search for the place where Louie dwells.

Take a tour of West Point U.S. Military Academy, the Naval Academy at Annapolis, Maryland, or the Airforce Academy in Colorado Springs and see where the military gets its leaders.

Most universities offer free museums. The University of Illinois at Urbana, for example, boasts a comprehensive collection of Oriental and Pre-Columbian masterpieces in the Kannert Art Museum, lots of anthropological and botanic exhibits at its Museum of Natural History, and a great anthropological display at the World Heritage Museum. They're all free.

Moreover, if you want to stay overnight at bargain rates, inquire at college or university housing offices to see if dorm rooms are available, as they often are during vacation periods.

Small-town Ambience

Mere dots on the map that are proud of their heritage maintain history museums, the modest treasures of which include faded photos, worn plows, Indian baskets, outmoded fashions, and reconstructed rooms. In addition, small-town public gardens, beaches, statues, town squares, defunct defense works, battle sites, long-abandoned public buildings, libraries, antiquated fire trucks, statues of bearded soldiers, and historic homes are well worth a visitor's time.

Examples are the Shenandoah County Court House, designed by Thomas Jefferson, in Woodstock, Virginia; the displays honoring World War II's Admiral Chester Nimitz in the old Nimitz Hotel in Fredericksburg, Texas; the collection of Abe Lincoln artifacts in Duke Hall at the Lincoln Memorial University in Harrogate, Tennessee; over a hundred antebellum homes in Columbus, Mississippi; the eight-domed Byzantine monastery run by the Brotherhood of St. Francis in Hoosick Falls, New York; historic Front Street, whose buildings boast iron-lace grillwork in Natchitoches, Louisiana.

Stroll the streets of historic Coldwater, Michigan, and visit Tibbits Opera House for a tour. One seldom confronts crowds in these off-the-beaten-track Mayberrys, and it's a good chance to meet the locals.

Inviting Urban Neighborhoods

Take a walking tour of an inviting urban neighborhood. For example, from March through November, free walking tours are offered in Austin, Texas. Choose from a 60-minute Capitol Grounds Tour (Saturday at 2 P.M. and Sunday at 9 P.M.); the Bremond Block Tour (90 minutes beginning Saturday and Sunday at 11 P.M.); or the Congress Avenue and East 6th Street Tour, which is on Thursday, Friday, and Saturday at 9 and Sunday at

2; it also lasts an hour and a half. Report to the south entrance of the State Capitol for these tours—unless it's raining hard.

Many municipal tourist offices furnish free walking maps and explanatory guide sheets. Let the sights, sounds, and smells tell you the story of the neighborhood's inhabitants. Or find a quiet enclave amid the metropolitan din and bustle and listen to the message of the building's stones or of the birds in a wooded, big city sanctuary.

Count the nationalities that are represented by restaurants in Toronto. Enjoy the superb architecture in the area around the historic plaza in Santa Fe, New Mexico. Walk around Larimer Square and see the 19th-century buildings where Denver got its start. Look at the fine brick houses and paving on Boston's Beacon Hill. Drink in the beauty and history that permeates Mystic, Connecticut; Charleston, South Carolina; Savannah, Georgia; or Seattle's Pike Place Market. Go to Quebec City and pretend you're in France.

Memorial Parks

Cemeteries are fascinating and instructive. Visit the Old Spanish Cemetery in St. Augustine, Florida, and see the graves of some of very first European settlers on the North American continent. When you're in Boston, drop by the Granary Burying Ground to view the resting places of John Hancock, Samuel Adams, Paul Revere, the Boston Massacre's victims, and other Revolutionary-period figures. In the nation's capital is Arlington National Cemetery, where you'll find Pres. John F. Kennedy and the Unknown Soldier resting amid six hundred landscaped acres that contain the earthly remains of some of America's greatest unsung heroes.

Shopping Without Buying

Window shopping is fun when you get away from the hordes invading great department stores and malls. Visit street markets, craft exhibits, private art galleries, antique stores, used book shops, and perhaps best of all, auction galleries. There's always a chance that the $3 vase you can buy is easily worth $10,000, or that the $15 painting of a bowl of fruit has an El Greco under a thin layer of oils. If you spend nothing other than the afternoon, at least you've had an interesting adventure at no cost.

Public Outdoor Recreation Facilities

Public parks, forests, recreation areas, beaches, wildlife refuges, and other government-operated areas are often free to sightseers, picnickers, boaters, swimmers, and hikers. See the Etowah Mounds Archaeological Area in Cartersville, Georgia. Visit the State Historic Site at Fort Ransom, North Dakota; it contains Indian burial mounds and the remains of a U.S. military post.

Drop by Lyndon B. Johnson State Park in—where else?— Johnson City, Texas. Take the kids to San Antonio's HemisFair Park, the site of the 1968 World's Fair; here you'll find a playground for children that was designed by children. One of our outdoor favorite haunts is San Diego's Balboa Park, where you'll find subtropical growth within the otherwise closely manicured 1,074 acres.

National parks are an astonishingly good deal for folks older than 62, although they're not free for the first visit. If you're 62 or better, you can get a lifetime pass to all federal parks, forests, refuges, monuments, and recreation areas for a nominal fee. After the first visit, pile as many of the grandkids and their parents as will fit in the same car or van and they get in free. You probably look years younger than you actually are, so bring your driver's license as proof of age. The National Park Service, P.O. Box 37127, Washington, D.C. 20013, can tell you more about the Golden Age Passport or you can pick one up at any national park.

Festivals and Celebrations

Attend the free Fourth of July celebration in Lake Eola Park in Orlando, Florida, and enjoy free entertainment and fireworks.

Show up in Santa Fe, New Mexico, the weekend after Labor Day for Fiesta, when revelers celebrate the return in 1692 of the Spanish. In mid-April, attend the French Quarter Festival in New Orleans, where even more fun than usual can be had in and around Basin Street and on the Riverfront.

Parades, street fairs, lectures, ceremonies, mimes and buskers, religious services, acrobats, extremely minor league sports competitions, poetry readings, gallery openings, fashion shows, outdoor concerts, golf tournaments, air shows, grand openings, and a host of other performances and happenings attract nonpaying spectators in towns and cities all over the U.S. and Canada. To find out about these events, put in a little research. Ask at the local tourist office and look in local papers for happenings that will make your vacation not only free but memorable.

FREE TOURS AND FREE SAMPLES

Take a free plant tour and get free soup, free beer, free breakfast cereal, free dog food—in fact a bag or bowl of just about anything that eventually gets eaten or imbibed. If the factory doesn't produce edibles or potables, they'll load you down with brochures, key chains, postcards, balloons, bumper stickers, decals, calendars, pens and pencils, and product catalogs. According to a marvelous book, *Watch It Made in the U.S.A.* by Bruce Brumberg and Karen Axelrod (John Muir Publications, P.O. Box 613, Santa Fe, NM 87504), many companies will gift you generously with goodies just for showing up and looking as if you're paying attention. Even when they don't give you anything besides a tour, often with a video, you'll learn how someone's favorite product is produced.

Companies throw open their doors to the public to introduce them to their products, maintain goodwill, and reinforce product loyalty. A tourist can breakfast at a cereal mill, lunch at a bakery, snack at a creamery or jelly bean plant, and enjoy "happy hour" after a brewery or winery tour—all with management's compliments.

Among the hundreds of plants that will welcome you are these:

- Free: Herman Goelitz makes Jelly Belly jelly beans at 2400 N. Watney Way in Fairfield, CA 94533. Phone: (707) 428-2838. Pres. Ronald Reagan popped them while making major and minor decisions, and so can you. When you finish the tour you'll walk out with four ounces of Jelly Bellies. It's free Monday through Friday from 9 to 2 and takes about 40 minutes.

- Free: Whetstone Chocolates, 2 Coke Rd., St. Augustine, FL 32086. Phone (904) 825-1700 to set up a half-hour guided tour between 10 and 3 Monday through Friday. After that you'll have a shell-shaped chocolate sample as a reward for your stopping by.

- Free: Kathryn Reich, Inc. (Nestle Fundraising Co.) at 2501 Reich Rd., Bloomington, IL 61701. Phone: (309) 829-1031. You will receive a tour with video and the chance to browse their gift shop. When you've gotten past the Bit-O-Honey, Laffy Taffy, Golden Crumbles, and Katydids lines, you get . . . a candy bar.

- Free: At 5686 State Route 1 (in St. Joe, IN 46785; phone: [219] 337-5461)—is Sechler's, manufacturer of famous pickles. Watch these green wonders sorted into boxes that weigh a thousand pounds each. See them get cooked in the processing room. Watch them marinate. Get your very own free "samples of all varieties in the showroom." You can do this from April through Halloween from 9 to 11 in the morning and half-past noon to 3 in the afternoon, holidays excepted.

- Free: Binney and Smith makes Crayola crayons at 2000 Liquitex Ln., Winfield, KS 67156. Phone: (316) 221-4200. In fact they make more than two billion of these brilliant implements every year. You can watch them do it Mondays through Thursdays between 10:30 A.M. and 1 P.M., except November 15 through New Year's Eve. A coloring book and pack of 16 choice crayons await those who complete this tour. Think of the money you'll save taking Junior to Winfield, Kansas, instead of to see Mickey in Orlando.

- Free: Old Kentucky Candies, 450 Southland Dr., Lexington, KY 40503. Phone: (800) 786-0579. Here they make Bourbon Chocolates, Bourbon Cherries, Chocolate Thoroughbreds, and Kentucky Derby Mints. If you're the designated driver, better stick to the Thoroughbreds and the Mints. Tours and samples are to be had between 10:30 and 3:30 Mondays through Thursdays.

- Free: Moore's Candies at 3004 Pinewood Ave., Baltimore, MD 21214. Phone: (410) 426-2705. Moore's tour, during which you can watch the candies hand-dipped in bubbly caramel or watch them get that sugar coating, takes about 20 minutes. While all of this is going on, you can "sample chocolate right off the packing line." Moore's is open to visitors from 10 to noon and from 1 to 2 in the afternoon.

- Free: Franz Family Bakery, 340 N.E. Eleventh Ave., Portland, OR 97232. Phone: (503) 232-2191, ext. 365. Franz Family Bakery will give you donuts, coffee, milk, and a take-home sack with a miniloaf of Franz bread. All of that comes on top of an hour tour with a free 15-minute video. It's open to visitors from 9 to 4 Monday through Friday from September through June only. And it's warm inside.

Does that mean you can't get beer in Milwaukee, Coca-Cola® in Atlanta, or auto and truck samples in Detroit? Check out *Watch It Made in the U.S.A.* from the library and find out. The biggest disappointment among the 250 entries in *Watch It Made* is that the Bureau of Engraving and Printing—at Fourteenth and C Street SW, Washington, D.C. 20228; phone: (202) 874-3188—doesn't hand around samples of its highly touted hundred-dollar bills.

FREE IN EVERYONE'S FAVORITE CITY

There's no way that this chapter can alert you to all the free sites in thousands of small towns and in all major American cities. Therefore, we need an example. So let's concentrate on one city—everyone's favorite—San Francisco. "Baghdad by the Bay" isn't in the least unique in its number of free attractions. With minimal research you can find fascinating free places to visit wherever you want to travel.

This section will help you to leave your heart, but not your money in San Francisco. In the City by the Bay tourists may choose to spend their cash like drunken sailors (normally the case when the fleet was in) or to see the best of San Francisco while paying little or nothing.

San Francisco on a lovely day is a visual delight. It may well be the most beautiful city in America, if not the world. To enjoy it best, don't merely walk around, walk up. Walk to the top of Russian Hill, to the top of Nob Hill, to Coit Tower on Telegraph Hill and look down the streets that seem almost to slide into the bay. The views are incomparable.

While you're in the 210-foot Coit Tower, check out the Depression-era WPA-financed murals that illustrate the response of starving artists to the deprivations of the Great Depression. On top of Nob Hill, where the Big Four railroad tycoons and their imitators built palaces, walk through the monumental Fairmont, Mark Hopkins, and Stanford Court hotels. Shoes and shirt requirements are just for starters—look as if you belong there. Nearby is Grace Cathedral, huge and as subdued as pseudo-Gothic architecture can get.

What are some of the other most smashing tourist mustsees?

• Free: Union Square is the very heart of downtown, bordered by glitzy marble-facaded department stores and specialty shops. In the center is a towering monument to a nearly forgotten American footnote: Adm. George Dewey, who defeated the Spanish fleet in 1898 at Manila Bay, which led to the 48-year American domination of the Philippines. Dewey surprised the Spanish because nobody had bothered to tell them the United States had declared war. Nearby at Market and Powell, tourists line up for cable cars to take them to Fisherman's Wharf. Street musicians keep the scene lively and loud.

$$$—Cousin Thrifty McCheap says: "Even I paid to ride a cable car. But I saved money by walking back."

- Free: Fisherman's Wharf is San Francisco's quintessential tourist attraction. Here it's possible to buy souvenirs to bring home to Aunt Bertha for her upcoming garage sale. Near the Wharf you watch tourists visit a handful of "museums" designed to separate them from a lot of dollars. Skip the Wax Museum, the Museum of Guinness World Records, the Medieval Dungeon, et al. and head for the fascinating Maritime Museum at the foot of Polk Street. Phone: (415) 929-0202. You'll see ship models, steering wheels, old-time navigational equipment, etc., all against a stunning background of bay views. It's free. Go out back toward the water and you'll find yourself on a swimming beach known appropriately as Aquatic Park, for which there is no charge. Walk around Fisherman's Wharf and soak up the artificial atmosphere. When you get tired of the crowds, there's window shopping at three complexes that are very close: The Cannery, Ghiradelli Square, and Pier 39.

- Free: Chinatown. Save a small fortune by not going to Hong Kong. Chinatown will give the full flavor of the exciting and picturesque Orient. America's largest, oldest, and most highly defined Asian community was begun by immigrant workers during California's Gold Rush. This 16-square-block area is touristy, but it's also authentic. It's home to tens of thousands of Chinese who were born there and it's also the new home of more recent immigrants. The atmosphere is exotic. Check out the choices at the foodstalls for the flavor of another culture.

- Free: Visit Ocean Beach and stick your big toe in the Pacific. Have a look at the famous Cliff House.

- Free: Don't take your swim gear to North Beach. Every San Franciscan knows it's not a beach at all, but rather a sometimes raucous, sometimes reflective old Italian neighborhood full of trattorias, strip joints, and views of the bay. North Beach was the Beat capital of the West in the 1950s, California's Greenwich Village. Find Beat poet Lawrence Ferlinghetti's City Lights Book Store at 261 Columbus and you've found the epicenter of the Beat world Jack Kerouac, Ferlinghetti, Gary Snyder, Allen Ginsberg, and others made in this hilly and homey neighborhood.

- Free: San Franciscans love free events. The famous Bay to Breakers Race in May is fun to watch and there's no charge for spectators. If you decide to run in it, you'll see a lot of San Francisco without digging in your pocket for bus fare. San Francisco's *Carnaval* centers on a costume contest, street festivals, and a parade in the Mission District. Instead of passing around megabucks for concert tickets, attend a free concert. Look in the free *Bay Guardian* or stop at the tourist information office at Market and Powell to see what's on when you're in town.

- Free: Walk across the Golden Gate Bridge (and walk back). It can get chilly, so wear something over that Alcatraz inmate T-shirt you just bought. Pick a clear day and you'll see not only the famous island prison but the city lolling languidly on its hilly back between ocean and bay. Pick a foggy day and you'll be lucky to see the tourist in front of you.

- Free: Civic Center is more formal and imposing than a lot of state capitals. That's probably why the United Nations was chartered there in April 1945 in the War Memorial Opera House. Civic Center's United Nations Plaza commemorates the event. See City Hall, Herbst Theater, the Louise Davies Symphony Hall, and the recently erected Main Library at Larkin and McAllister. The library is an up-to-date example of what all big city libraries should be—wired to the rafters for the electronic data age.

- Free: The Palace of Fine Arts, in the elegant Marina District, is almost in the shadow of the Golden Gate Bridge. Here was the site in 1915 of a much-acclaimed international exposition.

- Free: Golden Gate Park is often foggy and cold because it's by the ocean, but when it's pleasant, it's a sylvan paradise. These thousand acres were set aside in the 1860s, when the city was getting over growing pains brought on by the Gold Rush of 1849. Here you'll find a windmill, gardens full of plants, and a stunning Shakespeare Garden that contains plants mentioned in the Bard's works. Just as free to visitors are the Rose Garden, Fuchsia Garden, Tulip Garden, and the Rhododendron Dell.

- Free: San Francisco's best art museum, the M. H. De Young Memorial Museum—alas—isn't as celebrated as other big-city collections, but it includes works by John Singer Sargent, Frederick Church, Grant Wood, Georgia O'Keefe, and other great artists. On the first Wednesday of every month, from 10 to 4:45 it's free.

- Free: The Haight-Ashbury District was the hectic scene where, in the summer of 1967, a collection of loose teens slid across the country to San Francisco. In the neighborhood near where Haight Street crosses Ashbury, they congregated and celebrated their precarious existence with music and drugs. Janis Joplin lived at 112 Lyon St., and the Manson family at 636 Cole St. Stand on the corner of Haight and Ashbury and try to imagine the way it was in the psychedelic tripped-out years.

There's lots more to see and do in San Francisco without opening your wallet. Contact the Convention and Visitors Bureau for free information. In fact, that works just about anywhere in the country.

SATISFYING YOUR THIRST

When you've had enough of San Franciscan delights for a while and want to go out into the countryside, pick Northern California's delicate and engagingly amusing Wine Country.

This world-class tourist mecca begins an hour north of San Francisco. The Napa and Sonoma valleys are the heart of the grape-growing region and Mendocino and Lake counties are peripheral Wineland, well worth visiting in themselves.

Anytime of year is likely to be great, but the best time to go is late summer or early autumn when the sun feels delicious against your skin and against the skin of the grapes, now ready for harvest. Spring, when the verdant valleys are blanketed with flowers, is equally as beautiful and summer is seldom disappointing. Winter is usually mild and the starkness of the fields and trees is lovely on a sunny day.

Follow the U.S. 101 highway up through Sonoma County and into Mendocino County; or slither up the ribbon-like California 29 highway that winds through the exquisite Napa Valley. The Napa Valley is the heart of Wineland, a densely planted area reminiscent of southern France or Italy's Tuscany. Here you see ivy-clad chateaus, acres of gleaming grapes, multistar restaurants with pretentious prices, stone bridges a hundred years old, giant oaks, protective mountain ranges—and all of this capped by colorful hot-air balloons that beckon visitors to view the scene silently from above.

What can possibly be free in this posh world of country clubs and $100 lunches? Wine, of course. The number of fine wineries has grown enormously in recent years and so has competition among them for the affluent imbiber's dollar. As a result, vintners invite the public to drop in for tastings. Some wineries charge a fee for tastings; of these, several throw in the glass as a souvenir, and most will refund the price of the sample when you buy a bottle or two.

Fortunately for free travelers, enough wineries still offer a few gratis gulps in the hope that day trippers will buy a bottle of the same or hopefully a case or more. To further protect their share of the market in the face of competition from dozens of other wineries that offer similar inducements, most give free conducted tours of their vats and presses. Many invite visitors to use their grounds for picnicking, and it's O.K. if you bring your own soda pop as an accompaniment to your picnic meal. You don't have to buy a thing to enjoy the ambience.

Concentrating on the Napa Valley, with its string of small towns that attract day-trippers and vacationers, here's a list of some wineries that will give you free tours, the use of picnic facilities, or even samples. The list is far from complete; the four-county region is studded with vintners ready and willing to pour for you without charge. This list, with addresses and phone numbers, should keep you busy enough:

- Beaulieu Vineyard, Visitors Center, 1960 S. St. Helena Highway, Rutherford, CA 94573. Phone: (707) 967-5230. Open 10 to 5 daily. Complimentary tastings and free tours.

- Beringer Vineyards, 2000 Main St., St Helena, CA 94574. Phone: (707) 963-7115. Free tastings and tours in a huge stone chateau. The chateau is well worth seeing.

- Chateau Potelle, 3875 Mt. Veede Rd., Napa, CA 94559. Phone: (707) 967-9440. Open 11 to 5 daily. Picnic facilities and free tastings are here.

- Dutch Henry Winery, 4310 Silverado Trail, Calistoga, CA 94515. Phone: (707) 942-5771. Open 10 to 4 daily. Dutch offers free tastings.

- Rombauer Winery, 3522 Silverado Trail, St. Helena, CA 94574. Phone: (707) 963-5170. Open 10 to 5 daily. Free tastings and picnic facilities.

- William Hill Winery, 1761 Atlas Peak Rd., Napa, CA 94559. Phone: (707) 224-4477. Free tastings.

- Silverado Vineyards, 6121 Silverado Trail, Napa, CA 94559. Phone: (707) 257-1770. Open 11 to 4:30 daily. Free tastings.

- Sutter Home Winery, 277 St. Helena Highway South, St. Helena, CA 94574. Phone: (707) 963-3104. Open 9:30 to 5 daily. Complimentary tasting and garden tours.

- V. Sattui Winery, 1111 White Ln., St. Helena, CA 94574. Phone: (707) 963-7774. In its beautiful grounds, enjoy the tree-shaded picnic grove. Complimentary tastings are offered. Open 9 to 5 daily.

- Vincent Arroyo Winery, 2361 Greenwood Ave., Calistoga, CA 94515. Phone: (707) 942-5924. Open Daily 10 to 4:30. They offer free picnicking, tours, and tastings.

You can get free maps showing winery locations from the Napa Valley Conference and Visitors Bureau, 1310 Napa Town Center, Napa, CA 94559. Phone: (707) 226-7459. Maps are also available at wineries.

POTPOURRI OF FREEBIES

What else is there to do in the Land of the Free? More than there's space within these covers to tell and more than any individual has time for. For instance:

- **Boston:** Hit Boston's museums at the right time and reduce your admission fee to nothing: To see the holdings of the Museum of Fine Arts, go on Wednesdays between 4 and 10; the Museum of Science is gratis on Wednesdays from 1 to 5 from November to April. The Gardner Museum is free Wednesdays from noon to 5; and you can see the Aquarium free between October and March on Thursdays from 4 to 8. The Children's Museum is without cost on Fridays from 5 to 9. The Harvard Museum is open to even the penniless on Saturday mornings.

  Walk the 3½-mile Freedom Trail past Boston's 16 venerated revolutionary sites. Pick up a free map at the Boston Common Information Kiosk at 146 Tremont St. or at the National Park Service Visitor Center at 15 State St. Starting at Boston Common, walk past the Old State House, Paul Revere's home, the U.S.S. *Constitution,* and much more. For further information, contact the Greater Boston Convention and Visitors Bureau, 800 Boylston St., Boston, MA 02199. Phone: (617) 536-4100.

- **Capitan, New Mexico.** Smokey Bear's Grave is in Smokey Bear State Park on U.S. 30. You can visit the site from 8 to 5 daily. Ask direction from there for the Smokey Bear Museum, 18 miles north of Ruidosa.

- **Chicago.** Try a free museum each day of the week: On Mondays go to the Chicago Academy of Sciences and/or the Chicago Historical Society; on Tuesday visit the incomparable Art Institute and the next Tuesday visit the Museum of Contemporary Art; on Wednesday or Friday you can see the Oriental Institute—it's free every day. Save Thursday for the John G. Shedd Aquarium and/or the Field Museum of Natural History.

  On any business day, visit the Chicago Mercantile Exchange's visitors' galleries. Here you'll watch as thousands of frenetic traders display super-human levels of energy as they buy and sell futures and options of currencies, interest rates, commodities, etc. See fortunes made and lost before your very eyes. It's open 7:30 A.M. to 3:15 P.M., Monday through Friday.

  Get more information about these and other free opportunities from the Chicago Office of Tourism, 806 N. Michigan Ave., Chicago, IL 60611. Phone: (312) 280-5740.

- **Columbus, Ohio.** When the kids want to go to Great America or Disneyland, save a lot of bucks. Get them prepared for the big day by saying, "Hey kids, guess what! We're going to do something really exciting today. We're going to—the Accounting Hall of Fame." Here they'll marvel at portraits of some of the greatest accountants in history. Explain to them how much fun they're having. You'll find memorabilia of accounting's megastars on the fourth floor of Hagerty Hall at Ohio State University. Don't let the kids get overly excited.

- **Crested Butte, Colorado.** Visit the two-story outhouse in the alley behind the Company Store in this Colorado Gold Rush town. It's probably best to spend most of the visit upstairs.

- **Cullowhee, North Carolina.** Visit Judaculla Rock. Travel south on State Route 107 and then east on a secondary road. Follow the signs, if any. Cherokees said a *giant* made the mysterious markings on the rock. See what you think.

- **Lakeview, Oregon.** Contrary to common belief, Washington, D.C., doesn't have the biggest faults in the country. Visit the Albert Rim, a 30-mile-long fault—the largest in North America.

- **Las Vegas.** Keep your hand out of your wallet and off the slot machine handle and that open-all-night extravaganza can be your huge free amusement park, filled with music and sights. Casino lounges are known for their free entertainment—live sound designed to keep you from wanting to leave.

  Visit the major casinos on the strip as if you were a sociologist intent on learning about casino culture, or an architectural critic examining the garish. Watch people. Assign them names to go with their faces. Decide for yourself which casinos and hotels are the most gaudy, the most exciting. Don't miss Caesar's Palace, the Mirage, Circus Circus—where you can see trapeze acts, Tropicana with its fantastic waterfalls, Excalibur—straight out of Arthurian legend, the Luxor with its shiny pyramid, and others. Try the shopping arcade at Caesar's Palace; it's like taking a trip to a Renaissance Italy that never was and should have been.

  When are these showcases open? Always. Contact the Las Vegas Convention and Visitors Authority, 3150 Paradise Rd., Las Vegas, NV 90109. Phone: (702) 737-2011.

- **Little Rock, Arkansas.** Visit the Governor's Mansion at Center and West 18th streets. Tours are by appointment. Call (501) 376-6884.

- **Missoula, MT.** The Smokejumpers Center is seven miles west of town on U.S. 10 next to the airport. Here from 9 to 5 you can take a tour of the important facility where Smokejumpers train.

- **Nashville.** Yes, you can have totally free admission to tapings of some TNN TV shows; you can have free entry to the Tennessee State Museum, State Capitol, and Fort Nashborough. Find out what free concerts are offered by the city park department and by Vanderbilt University. Get information from the Tennessee Department of Tourist Development, Room T, Box 23170, Nashville, TN 23170.

- **Norton, Kansas.** Visit the Gallery of Also Rans at 105 W. Main St. between 9 and 3 Monday through Friday. Here you'll see a picture of every losing candidate in U.S. presidential races.

- **Soda Springs, Idaho.** Beer Spring is one mile north of town. Pioneers said its natural soda water tasted like beer. Check it out.

- **Walnut Grove, Minnesota.** Visit the Laura Ingalls Wilder Museum. Who was Wilder? You remember: She authored the books from which the "Little House on the Prairie" television series was made. Her museum is at 330 Eighth St.

- **Washington, D.C.,** probably has more free attractions than any other American city. They are free because the tax payers fund the vast majority of them. Get your tax dollars' worth by visiting as many as you can: The Jefferson Memorial, Bureau of Engraving and Printing, Emancipation Statue in Lincoln Park, FBI Headquarters, Folger Shakespeare Library, and Ford's Theater (where Pres. Abraham Lincoln was assassinated by John Wilkes Booth). Have a look at the Jefferson Memorial, John F. Kennedy Center for the Performing Arts, Library of Congress, Lincoln Memorial, and National Gallery of Art.

  You can also check out all the "National" freebies: the National Arboretum, National Archives, National Building Museum, National Geographic Society, National Cathedral, National Law Enforcement Officers Memorial, and the National Museum of Health and Medicine. Other free admissions include the Navy Museum, Old Executive Office Building, Pavilion at the Old Post Office, Headquarters of the Society of the Cincinnati, Supreme Court Building, Textile Museum, U.S. Capitol (see your congressman or senator for tickets to the public galleries), Union Station, U.S. Botanic Gardens, Washington Design Center, Washington Monument, and of course, the White House itself.

Two of the newest sites are also among the most poignant: The U.S. Holocaust Memorial Museum and the Vietnam Veterans Memorial. See also the Vietnam Women's Memorial at Twenty-first and Constitution Avenue. All of that should keep anyone busy for weeks, but save time for the Smithsonian.

The Smithsonian is a complex of free museums that includes the Visitor Information Center, the Anacostia Museum (African-American culture), Arthur M. Sackler Gallery (Asian art), Arts and Industries Building (exhibits from the 1876 U.S. Centennial Exposition in Philadelphia), Freer Gallery of Art (Asian and American), Hirshhorn Museum and Sculpture Garden of 19th and 20th century art, National Air and Space Museum, National Museum of African Art, National Museum of American Art, National Museum of American History ("The Nation's Attic"), National Museum of Natural History, National Portrait Gallery, National Postal Museum, and the National Zoological Park. Whew!

HOMEWORK ASSIGNMENT

Contact the tourist bureaus in these terrific cities and find out what each has to offer.

- Anchorage Convention and Visitors Bureau, 1600 A St., Suite 200, Anchorage, AK 99501. Phone: (907) 276-4118. Fax: (907) 278-5559.
- Atlantic City Convention and Visitors Authority, 2314 Pacific Ave., Atlantic City, NJ 08401. Phone: (800) 262-7395.
- Austin Convention and Visitors Bureau, 201 E. Second St., Austin, TX 78701. Phone: (512) 474-5171.
- Branson Lakes Area Chamber of Commerce, P.O. Box 220, Branson, MO 65616. Phone: (800) 678-8766.
- Charlestown-Trident Visitors Bureau, P.O. Box 975, 375 Meeting St., Charleston, SC 29402. Phone: (803) 853-8000.
- Cincinnati Visitors Bureau, 300 W. Sixth St., Cincinnati, OH 45202. Phone: (800) 344-3445.

- Cleveland Visitors Information Center, Terminal Tower, Public Square, Cleveland, OH. Phone: (800) 344-3445.

- Fort Lauderdale Convention and Visitors Bureau, 200 E. Las Olas Blvd., Suite 1500, Ft. Lauderdale, FL 33301. Phone: (305) 765-4466.

- Hawaii Visitor Bureau, Waikiki Business Plaza, 8th Floor, 2270 Kalakaua Ave., Honolulu, HI 96815. Phone: (808) 923-1811.

- Little Rock Tourist Information, P.O. Box 3232, Little Rock, AR 72203. Phone: (800) 844-4781.

- Los Angeles: LA Convention and Visitors Bureau, 633 W. Fifth St., Los Angeles, CA 90071. Phone: (213) 624-7300.

- Miami: Greater Miami Convention and Visitors Bureau, 701 Brickell Ave., Suite 2700, Miami, FL 33131. Phone: (800) 283-2707 or (305) 539-3000.

- New Orleans: Greater New Orleans Tourist and Convention Commission, 1520 Sugar Bowl Dr. North; New Orleans, LA 80112. Phone: (504) 566-5011.

- Newport Convention and Visitors Bureau, 23 America's Cup Ave., Newport, RI 02840. Phone: (800) 326-6030.

- New York City Convention and Visitors Bureau, 2 Columbus Circle, New York, NY 10019. Phone: (212) 397-8222. Fax: (212) 484-1280.

- Oklahoma City Convention and Visitors Bureau, 123 Park Ave., Oklahoma City, OK 73102. Phone: (800) 225-5652.

- Orlando: Orlando Visitor Information Center, 8445 International Dr., Orlando, FL 32830. Phone: (407) 363-5800.

- Palm Beach County Visitors Bureau, 1555 Palm Beach Lakes Blvd., Suite 204, West Palm Beach, FL 33401. Phone: (407) 471-3995.

- Philadelphia Convention and Visitors Bureau, 1515 Market St., Suite 2020, Philadelphia, PA 19102. Phone: (215) 636-3300.

- Portland Visitors Association, World Trade Center, 26 S.W. Salmon St., Portland, OR 97204. Phone: (800) 345-3214.

- Salt Lake City Convention and Visitors Bureau, 180 S.W. Temple St., Salt Lake City, UT 84114. Phone: (801) 521-2822.

- San Antonio Convention and Visitors Bureau, 121 Alamo Plaza, Box 2277, San Antonio, TX 78298. Phone: (210) 270-8700 or (800) 447-3372.

- Santa Fe Convention and Visitors Bureau, 201 W. Mercy St., Box 909, Santa Fe, NM 87504. Phone: (505) 984-6760 or (800) 777-2489.

- Savannah Area Chamber of Commerce, 222 W. Oglethorpe Ave., Savannah, GA 31499. Phone: (912) 944-0456 or (800) 444-CHARM.

- Seattle Convention and Visitors Bureau, 800 Convention Place, Seattle, WA 98101. Phone: (206) 461-5840.

- Tucson Convention and Visitors Bureau, 130 S. Scott Ave., Tucson, AZ 85701. Phone: (800) 638-8350.

- Washington, D.C., Convention and Visitors Association, 1212 New York Ave. NW, Washington, D.C. 20005. Phone: (202) 789-7000.

- Williamsburg Convention and Visitors Bureau, 201 Penniman Rd., Williamsburg, VA 23185. Phone: (804) 220-7659.

WHAT ELSE?

Lots and lots of what's free has been left out, but much of it is covered in a huge book of free sites and sights: *Guide to Free Attractions,* compiled by Don and Pam Wright, Cottage Publications, 24396 Pleasant View Dr., Elkhart, IN 46517. The Wrights' compilation is where I found out about the two-story outhouse. I'm not brave enough to actually go into one.

CHAPTER 7

Europe's Free Sights and Sounds

McCheap's Seventh Law of Travel:
Whenever you encounter a ticket booth, run the other way.

The best places for tourists to visit aren't isolated by ticket booths. Take the sights and sounds of Europe for example. Europe's most outstanding attractions cost nothing. From Norway's North Cape to the Rock of Gibraltar, from Spain's Cabo de Finisterre where the Atlantic leaps against Iberian granite, to industrious Magnitogorsk in Russia's Ural Mountains at the "doorsteppe" of exotic Asia, Europe's absolutely free sights outclass in every way the majority of contrived tourist traps whose daunting ticket-takers keep away indigent and sagely thrifty travelers.

Free sites that inspire sheer enjoyment, not only in Europe but in the United States and nearly everywhere on this huge and complex planet, are virtually uncountable. There's no way this chapter—or any book—can catalog all the sunsets and mountain ranges, parish churches and jungle temples, flower-bedecked pedestrian streets, blinding white glaciers, municipal band concerts, Kodak-moment parades, verdant rice terraces, butterfly valleys, emerald lagoons, and kindergartens full of innocent laughter.

We can't list them all, but you can spend a lifetime enjoying them. World-wise free travelers will readily agree: If you're shelling out pounds or francs to traipse through someone's imaginative rendition of a medieval torture chamber or buying a ticket to snap pictures of some bozo in a clown outfit, you're probably missing the sights you should have come to see. So, rather than throw your rubles, guilders, and kroner away on costly attractions specifically developed by entrepreneurs to separate tourists from their foreign exchange, concentrate on seeing the best that each place has to offer—the totally free attractions that define the distinct character of cities, regions, and nations.

To get you primed and pumped to do just that, this chapter begins by highlighting examples in two of everyone's favorite metropolises, London and Paris. Of course, you'll find memorable street festivals in Bangkok, sculpted peaks in Nepal, scenic beaches in Montevideo, colorful temples in Bangalore, and dramatic vistas in Hong Kong, but no chapter—no single volume—can fully cover the world's free sights and sounds. Rather, these examples are an arbitrary selection, a delicious sample to whet your peripatetic appetite for what's available.

A TALE OF TWO FREEBIES

Year after year London and Paris shamelessly appear on lists of the world's most expensive cities. And rightly so. It's no trick to drop a thousand dollars or more for a night's rest in a posh hotel in Mayfair. And the price of dinner at a star-strangled Parisian restaurant could get you two or three months' worth of Leftover Helper back in Klammath Falls or Altoona.

Nonetheless, there's so much to do and see totally without cost in both these glittering capitals that it's amazing anyone would pay pounds to look at wax dummies in an overpriced museum or pay beaucoup francs to drive out of Paris to see Donald and Goofy.

First, let's do a leisurely tour of London's best attractions. We'll see how to enjoy the home of pomp and punks without reaching into our pockets. After that we'll have a very quick rundown on what's possible without a centime in the City of Light.

THE BEST OF LONDON WITHOUT CHARGE

An acquaintance of ours who crawled under circus tent flaps as a child and who still delights in slipping past ticket collectors has never been to London. Were he to go, he wouldn't like it. No challenge. Few of London's best attractions have ticket-takers to elude. A person determined to drop a few hundred pounds on hotels, meals, taxis, clothing, or jewelry won't be disappointed, but he'll have to keep his pounds in his pockets when visiting most of the major sights.

To get a breathtaking list of the full range of possible freebies, contact the British Tourist Authority (551 Fifth Ave., New York, NY 10110. Phone: [800] 462-2748. Fax: [212] 986-1188). Or when you arrive in London, visit a London Tourist Board Information Center. Information centers are conveniently located all over: Victoria Station Fourecort, in the basement of Harrod's at Knightsbridge, at Heathrow Airport Central Underground Concourse, at Selfridge's department store at 400 Oxford Street, or at the West Gate of the Tower of London. The telephone number is (01) 730-3488. Obtain as much information as you can about how to stay and eat relatively inexpensively and what there is to do for free. Among the freebies in the information packet they will give to you is the immensely well done London map for tourists.

Walk a bit each day and much of Central London will reveal itself to you. If you're like most of us, you'll come to love it by getting to know this contiguous set of big villages with some degree of intimacy. If you want to consummate your love affair with the metropolis as soon as possible, jump onto a double-decker red bus and tour as cheaply as possible through the center of the city. The route is emblazoned on the front of the bus and it's posted to bus stops.

Quite frankly there's more in London to do for free than a short-term tourist could possibly have time for. We worked away at our long list of freebies during 18 visits, the longest for three months. We ultimately had to admit defeat when we last left

London with dozens of parks, concerts, festivals, parades, and historic churches still to visit. What follows are some major attractions as well as some lesser known personal favorites:

- Free: Houses of Parliament. Burned to the ground in the 1840s, bombed by the Germans in World War II, both houses have been reconstructed and remain the "Mother of Parliaments." Parliament operates differently from the U.S. Congress. Unlike the American president who shoulders the symbolic and ceremonial duties of a monarch as well as executive duties, the prime minister is a member of the legislature and runs the government with the cabinet. The queen carries on by performing ceremonial duties and trying to control her family.

   Whereas the president may answer questions from the press if and when he chooses, the prime minister by tradition is questioned within Commons by the opposition party. You may have seen "Prime Minister's Question Time" on C-Span. Question time occurs around 2 P.M. Monday through Thursday and is sufficiently popular with the public that you need a ticket. You also need a ticket to attend Parliament at any other time it's in session. Watching Parliament in session is one of the most worthwhile ways a free traveler can spend an afternoon or evening.

   Tickets may be requested from your own embassy or from a member of Parliament. Contact the U.S. Embassy, Grosvenor Square, London W1A 1AE or the Canadian Embassy, Macdonald House, Grosvenor Square, London W1X 0AB. Otherwise, queue up at St. Stephen's entrance for a seat in the Stranger's Gallery. Depending on the crowd, your wait may be one to two hours. Around 6 P.M. you'll have a good chance of gaining entry. On Thursdays, however, Parliament may recess as early as 7 P.M. On most Fridays Parliament meets from 9:30 A.M. to 3 P.M.

   The halls of Westminster Palace, which is the name of the great neo-Gothic building in which Parliament meets, are filled with statues and carved wood and are a great sight in themselves. While most of the action takes place in Commons, the view from the Stranger's Gallery in the House of Lords after dark, when the chandeliers illuminate the red and gold wall coverings, makes Lords one of the great sights of Europe.

- Free: Westminster Abbey. The original church was built in 1065 by Edward the Confessor, but King Henry III rebuilt the abbey, beginning in 1245. Nearly all British monarchs have been crowned there and many monarchs and famous subjects are commemorated within by plaques or statues. Poet's Corner is a who's who of British and Irish letters. This primary repository of British history is a must see.

- Free: Oxford Street. For two miles between Marble Arch and Tottenham Court Road is an amazing array of world-famous department stores made for browsing: Selfridge's, Liberty, Harvey Nichols, Debenham's, John Lewis, Marks and Spencer. Work your way through the thick crowds that dominate Oxford Street's wide sidewalks and window shop in the incredible number of specialty stores. You'll soon agree that Oxford Street is the venue for world-class people watching. Here you'll see folks of every nationality, some in their national or regional dress. It may even seem to you that ethnic Brits are in the minority. Strolling Oxford is fun, and the sheer number of strollers make it a suitable challenge. Now get over to nearby Knightsbridge and check out Harrods, the world's largest department store.

- Free: Changing of the Guard at Buckingham Palace. Buckingham Palace was remodeled in 1913 but dates from 1705. It's the queen's principal London residence. Get as close as you can to the iron railings that keep the hordes of tourists who surround you out of the queen's home. Watch the guards' units go through their elaborate changing ceremony at 11 A.M.

- Free: St. Paul's Cathedral became a symbol of British invincibility in the Second World War when it withstood the bombing by Hitler's *Luftwaffe* that destroyed the surrounding heart of the City. Designed by Sir Christopher Wren after the Great Fire that destroyed much of London in 1666, St. Paul's was completed in 1710. Having arisen from the ashes and withstood the Blitzkrieg, this baroque cathedral was the scene of the royal wedding of Prince Charles and his tragic bride, Princess Diana.

- Free: The British Museum may be the jewel you'll return to time after time. So much is on display that there's scarcely ever enough time for this treasure chest of the world's past. Here you'll find Egypt's *Book of the Dead* as well as the Rosetta Stone. You'll find Gutenberg's Bible and Magna Carta. You'll ooh and aah at the Elgin Marbles, which is the frieze from Athens' Parthenon, and you'll find the Sutton Hoo Treasure along with the Portland Vase, and a gigantic winged bull from ancient Nineveh. The British Museum is arguably the most important repository of historical artifacts in the world. Many exhausted travelers have to come back another day, unable to see all of the highlights on the first. They find it overwhelming but worth every minute.

- Free: The National Gallery is centrally located on Trafalgar Square. It's the premier art museum of the British Isles and one of the finest in the world. Superb artists from Leonardo da Vinci to Rembrandt and El Greco to Turner to Van Gogh are represented here. The impressionist collection isn't as extensive as that in the Musée d'Orsay in Paris, but it's an exquisite representative collection and—unlike the French impressionist collection—without cost to you.

- Free: Go to the Horse Guards Parade near Buckingham Palace to see the changing of the Queen's Life Guard in their splendid scarlet and gold uniforms. Try to make them smile. The colorful ceremony takes place at 11 daily, but at 10 on Sunday.

- Free: Piccadilly Circus is the center of London, at least of London tourist life. Here you'll see the *Eros* statue poised to shoot an arrow into the ground, to bury the shaft, so to speak. That's only fitting, because it's a monument to Lord Shaftsbury, a 19th-century philanthropist. But forget Shaftsbury and the sculptor's intended pun and look around. If you stand there long enough you're bound to see someone you know from back home.

- Free: The National Portrait Gallery at St. Martin's Place just off Trafalgar Square outlines the history of Britain in paintings. Start with the earliest monarchs and work your way as you walk and view through the Tudors and Stuarts past a fistful of Georges right up to Elizabeth and Philip. Some of the stellar attractions in this art collection are commoners such as Lawrence of Arabia, Adm. Lord Horatio Nelson, John Stuart Mill, Charles Darwin, George Bernard Shaw, and W. S. Gilbert. And if Gilbert's there, Sullivan must be close by.

- Free: Speakers' Corner is in Hyde Park close to Marble Arch. This outdoor talkshow can provide one of the best series of performances in Europe. Go on Sunday to hear the totally unknown hold forth on the totally debatable. Want to give a speech? Go ahead, see if you draw a crowd.

- Free: Old Bailey is the Central Criminal Court. You can go in, sit down, and watch a trial. Trials can be boring or highly dramatic, depending on the case, but in any event, you'll see how the common law operates in England. Your experience will make you wish Perry Mason and Judge Judy would wear powdered wigs.

- Free: The Ceremony of the Keys. Most tourists aren't aware that every night at 9:40, a 700-year-old ceremony takes place in the Tower of London, as the Chief Warder and Escort of Guards lock the tower. For free passes to watch this colorful tradition, write in advance to The Yeoman Clerk, Queen's House, HM Tower of London, London EC3N 4AB. Include an international reply coupon if you're writing from abroad, or if you're already in Britain, a stamped (a United Kingdom stamp, please) envelope addressed to yourself.

- Free: Bank of England Museum on Threadneedle Street contains exhibits explaining the history and operations of the "Old Lady of Threadneedle Street."

- Free: Lloyds of London is on Lime Street in the City. The world's most famous insurance firm has been entrapped in a new building that resembles a transparent insect that's been the subject of intense radiation experiments. Visit it Mondays through Fridays from 10 to 2:30.

- Free: London Ecology Centre at 45 Shelton Street has an exhibition gallery, vegetarian restaurant, and events to promote a better environment.

- Free: The Geffrye Museum on Kingsland Road has a magnificent collection of woodwork and furniture dating from 1600.

- Free: The Museum of Garden History is next to the Church of St. Mary-at-Lambeth on Lambeth Palace Road, just across the Thames from Westminster Palace (Parliament). In the churchyard is the tomb of the very abrasive Adm. William Bligh who lost HMS *Bounty* to a gang of mutineers led by Mr. Christian.

- Free: Leighton House at 12 Holland Park Road was built for a 19th-century nobleman whose tastes ran to pre-Raphaelite and Middle Eastern art.

- Free: Keat's House commemorates the great Romantic poet. It's at Wentworth Place in Keats Grove near Hampstead.

- Free: The Commonwealth Institute on Kensington High Street features exhibits from dozens of Commonwealth countries, everywhere from Barbados to the Solomon Islands. The art exhibit from Papua New Guinea is in itself worth a visit, but there's plenty to learn in all parts of this well-planned exhibition hall.

- Free: The present buildings of Chelsea Royal Hospital, founded by King Charles II, were built in 1819. They serve as home for retired soldiers. Prints, drawings, uniforms, medals, etc. are on display. It's the scene of the annual Chelsea Flower Show. Have a walk down King's Road in Chelsea, window shop, and see what the modern British woman is being offered to wear.

- Free: Fascinating neighborhoods such as Belgravia are where the fictional "Upstairs, Downstairs" family of long-running PBS-TV fame lived; Belgravia is still occupied by the terminally wealthy. Set out in 1827 as an exclusive area for the well-to-do, Belgravia still is. Stroll around and look at the gleaming white facades of sumptuous homes in which the wealthy still live upstairs, although fewer servants than in the past occupy the nether areas. Also check out Chelsea Embankment, Kensington Square, Berkeley Square, Hampstead Heath, and St. John's Wood, among other posh districts.

- Free: The Inns of Court are the center of London legal life and date from the Middle Ages. See Gray's Inn on High Holborn; its gardens were laid out by Francis Bacon. Lincoln's Inn, at Lincoln's Inn Fields, has barristers' chambers and solicitors' offices. The chapel is by Inigo Jones (1623), and the Great Hall dates from 1845. See the Middle Temple and the Inner Temple.

- Free: The Museum of the City of London looks out at a portion of the ancient Roman London Wall and contains exhibits that highlight 2,000 years of city life. Reconstructed London shops and streets from various eras will lead you gently into the past.

- Free: The exterior of the Royal Naval College at Greenwich is a symmetrical masterpiece by Sir Christopher Wren.

- Free: The Wallace Collection at Manchester Square displays a prized private collection of art in a 19th-century mansion. Here are examples of the work of the fine 18th-century French painters Boucher, Watteau, and Fragonard. You'll find Canalettos, Titians, and Rubenses as well as furniture, firearms, and armor. Best of all, you'll enjoy a superb collection without the enormous crowds that suffocate the better-known National Gallery.

- Free: The Guildhall's Great Hall is used for ceremonies sponsored by the craft and merchants' guilds, which date from medieval times. It offers an interesting art gallery and library.

- Free: More churches than most tourists could possibly want to see. When they were built they were as ubiquitous as fast-food emporiums are today, but their arches were never golden and their beauty is lasting. Many, such as All Hollows, are ancient; it dates from 675 C.E. Others, such as St. Andrew-by-the-Wardrobe were designed by Sir Christopher Wren after the Great Fire of 1666. Many were bombed between 1940 and 1944 and later restored. St. Clement Danes in the Strand was rebuilt by Wren, destroyed in 1941, and rebuilt. Every four hours its bells peel out, as if to intone: "Oranges and lemons say the bells of St. Clement's."

  Westminster Roman Catholic Cathedral at Ashley Place is in Byzantine style and is worth visiting for its fine marble interior. You're bound to pass St. Martin-in-the-Fields, which is no longer in a field but near Trafalgar Square. Go in and marvel at the molded ceiling in white and gold. Listen to the free lunchtime music. This church, like so many others, is a heavenly place to rest.

- Free: Hyde Park is hard to miss, dominating central London as it does. It's fun to wander through to visit the Serpentine and have a stroll near Rotten Row. Best yet, watch the British enjoy themselves on a fine day, sunbathing, dog walking, picnicking, or playing ball. Nearby are Kensington Palace and Gardens, St. James's Park, and Green Park.

- Free: The Museum of Mankind at 6 Burlington Gardens has a rich collection of primitive art from Africa, Asia, America, and the Pacific.

- Free: Hampstead Village is an exquisite neighborhood to

wander in; it's on the edge of gigantic Hampstead Heath. Lots of architectural delights grace this quiet urban village. In the village you'll find Keat's House at Wentworth Place in Keat's Grove. On the periphery of the Heath, on Hampstead Lane, is the Iveagh Bequest, an art and furniture collection that fills Kenwood House. Kenwood House is a terrific destination for any tourist. The house was designed by Robert Adam and contains paintings of Reynolds, Gainsborough, and Rembrandt.

- Free: Highgate Cemetery. Not only does Highgate contain the remains of some of London's great and near-great (Karl Marx, George Eliot, Sir Ralph Richardson, etc.), but it's full of delicately carved funerary sculpture. Here we find cherubs galore, crypts dripping with rose petals and angels, and tombstones whose inscriptions make compelling reading. It's so enchanting, you may want to stay.

- Free: Covent Garden Market is where Eliza Doolittle sold flowers, but you knew that. Today it's full of shops and restaurants and in the square you can see and hear a host of entertainers, all for free.

- Free: Regent Street curves around on its way from busy Piccadilly Circus to calm and stately Regent's Park. Follow it. On the way you'll visit elegant shops. At the park you'll see more geometrically disciplined Regency architecture designed by John Nash.

- Free: Sir John Soane's Museum at 13 Lincoln's Inn Fields contains a Regency architect's collection of statuary, drawings, paintings, furniture, and valuable miscellany. The magnificent prize among this eclectic bunch of fabulous stuff is Hogarth's *Rake's Progress*.

- Free: Burlington Arcade has a narrow entry and if you are distracted by people watching, you will probably walk past without going in. *Do* go in when you walk down Piccadilly to see Fortnum and Mason's fabulous food hall, the Royal Academy, and the Ritz Hotel. This 1819 Regency-period shopping mall still looks out through its original shop windows. This part of London is pricey: Window shopping only is advised for free travelers!

- Free: The George Inn at 77 Borough High Street in Southwark is the last of the galleried coaching inns. It was built in 1677. It costs nothing to look at.

- Free: Cleopatra's Needle is an ancient Egyptian obelisk and can be found by the Thames on the Victoria Embankment. It predated Cleo by about 1,500 years. It's been a London landmark since 1878 when, in the period of high Victorian imperialism, the khedive of Egypt donated the monument to mollify the all-powerful British. Stroll through the lush Embankment Gardens nearby.

- Free: The National Postal Museum is a must-see for philatelists. It's on King Edward Street.

- Free: London Wall, or what little is left of it, dates from Roman times. It can be seen most easily from the Museum of the City of London, but it can also be seen at St. Giles Churchyard, Cripplegate; and Jewry Street off Trinity Square.

- Free: Paddington Station was built in 1850-52 and remains an engineering triumph of the early Victorian age. It's still very much in use, but it remains a "railway cathedral" as its designers meant it to be. Other railway stations such as Victoria Station are fun to visit for the bustle and excitement that bring these huge old caverns to life.

- Free: The Stock Exchange on Old Broad Street in the City has a public gallery from which you can watch the financial action.

- Free: Statues of the famous. You'll find Franklin D. Roosevelt on Grosvenor Square near the American Embassy, Winston Churchill at Parliament Square, and a magnificent statue to the Duke of Wellington near his house at Hyde Park Corner. Look for statues all over Central London. The loftiest is that to Admiral Nelson; it's what is atop that tall column in the center of Trafalgar Square.

- Free: The Percival David Foundation of Chinese Art is at 53 Gordon Square. Here you'll find priceless ceramics from the Sung dynasty to the Ching dynasty.

- Free: The Public Records Office on Chancery Lane displays letters and documents of English history. On show are a letter from George Washington to "his great and good friend" King George III, a letter from soon-to-be decapitated Anne Boleyn, the *Domesday Book,* and letters from Mary Queen of Scots and Queen Elizabeth I.

- Free: North Woolwich Station Museum on Pier Road houses a magnificent railroad locomotive built in 1876 and all sorts of photos and models of the Great Eastern Railway.

- Free: Those who read the detective novels and stories of Dorothy Sayers, Ngaio Marsh, Agatha Christie, or Sir Arthur Conan Doyle will want to follow in the footsteps of Sherlock Holmes and other sleuths as they tracked miscreants through the London fog. *Mystery Reader's Walking Guide: London* (Passport Books, 1987) takes sleuth fans on 11 scrupulously researched walks. Follow the footsteps of the incomparable Holmes from Marleybone to Baker Street and see all there is to see on the way. The walking maps are quite good.

When you've finished with all of this and still have no money for the wax dummy exhibit, Rock Circus, or to participate in Raging Hormone Night at a dance club, go look for the blue plaques that mark the homes where famous Londoners lived at one time or another. There are about 400. Those commemorated by blue plaques include Captain Bligh of the *Bounty,* Charles Dickens (the original author of *A Tale of Two Freebies*), Robinson Crusoe's chronicler Daniel Defoe, Prime Ministers Benjamin Disraeli and Winston Churchill, Charlie Chaplin, Benjamin Franklin (a long-term London resident), Sigmund Freud, economist John Maynard Keynes, Florence Nightingale, Oscar Wilde, and defunct French Emperor Napoleon III.

Time Out is a British periodical that announces activities such as concerts, plays, festivals, etc. Check out its website for free activities in London, Amsterdam, Paris, and Rome. Website: http://www.timeout.co.uk.

> $$$—Cousin Thrifty McCheap says: "My lady friends buy our theater tickets at the Half Price Ticket Booth at Leicester Square. They buy them on the afternoon of the performance."

PARIS FOR FREE? *MAI OUI!*

What can one do in Paris that doesn't cost a kazillion francs? Lots and lots of things. For free concerts and other free events in Paris, ask the Tourism Office, 127 Avenue des Champs-Elysées, Paris, 75008. Phone 47 20 94 94. The tourism experts will probably tell you about some of the following possibilities:

- Free: Visit the major flea market in Paris, Marche aux Puces at the Porte de Clignancourt, across from the metro station. It's huge and a great opportunity to see what ordinary Parisians buy and sell. It's at its best Saturday, Sunday, and Monday from 7:30 A.M. to 6 P.M. You can pick up CDs, clothes, antiques, and more at a good price. If you like flea markets, go also to Porte de Montreuil on Saturday, Sunday, and Monday from 6:30 A.M. to 1 P.M. Try also the antique market at Porte de Vavnes (av Georges Lafanestre and av Marc-Sangnier). It's open on weekends from 7 A.M. to 6 P.M.

- Free: Go to the Louvre without charge or to the Musée Picasso (5 rue de Thorigny) anytime they are open if you're under 18.

- The Musée Fondation Dapper, which has temporary exhibits of African art, is free on Wedesdays from 11 A.M. to 7 P.M. It's at 50 av Victor-Hugo.

- Free: Go to the Musée de Cristal to see . . . fine crystal glass. It's open Monday to Friday 9 to 5:30, and Saturday from 10 to noon and 2 to 5 in the afternoon.

- Visit Di Mauro Mini Musée du Bottier at 14 rue du Faubourg St. Honoré. It's full of boots and shoes that were created from the 1920s to the present. It's open Monday through Saturday from 10 to 6.

- Check out the Musée de la Préfecture de Polis, boulevard du Palais. It's open Monday to Friday from 9 to 5, and on Saturdays from 10 to 5.

- Get a guided tour (by appointment) of the Musée Edith Piaf. It's at 5 rue Crespin du Gast. Who's Piaf? A great French singer.

- Everything in the Musée de la Contrafaçon is fake: fake products, fake label, forgeries all. See it at 16 rue de la Faisanderie on Mondays and Wednesdays from 2 to 4:30, and on Fridays from 9:30 to noon.

- Free: Attend a court trial at the Palais du Justice, located right next to Sainte-Chapelle on the Ile de la Cité. Even if you can't understand the language, the drama of the courtroom is worth experiencing.

- Free: Go to an art gallery opening in the evening for wine and occasionally hors d'oeuvres. Find out about these gala events by picking up a listing called *Affiche Paris Rive Gauche/Paris Beaubourg* in any gallery. The listing is free, as are most of the events mentioned in it.

- Free: Attend a concert at the Eglise St. Merri on Saturday evenings or Sunday afternoons. Check the times of the concerts in the periodical *Pariscope*.

- Free: Go to Notre Dame Cathedral at 5:30 (sometimes 5) on Sunday afternoons for organ recitals. Notre Dame holds four masses on Sundays mornings and one at 6:30 on Sunday evenings.

- Free: Behind Notre Dame at the point of the Ile de la Cité is the dramatic Le Memorial de la Deportation. This monument has myriad tiny lights that represent the 200,000 French who were deported during the Second World War.

- Free: July 14 is Bastille Day. The French celebrate with a

mammoth parade down the Champs-Elysées. There are fireworks and dancing in the streets near the Place de la Bastille.

- Free: On summer solstice—June 21—the Parisians hold a
  Fête de la Musique de Paris. Visitors enjoy parades, live
  bands, and other amusements.

- Free: Visit the colorful flower markets. You'll find them at Place
  Lepine on Ile de la Cité (open daily 8 A.M. to 7:30 P.M.); Place
  de la Madeleine from Tuesday to Sunday (open 8 to 7:30); and
  Place des Temes, open Tuesday through Sunday from 8 to 7:30.

- Free: Visit the giant department stores such as Galeries
  LaFayette and Magasin du Printemps. Both are easy to find
  on Boulevard Haussman.

- Free: The Beauborg or Georges Pompidou Centre. Here you'll
  find the national art and culture centres full of art displays,
  libraries, as well as book and art shops. The museums con-
  tained within the centre cost francs to enter, but you can check
  out the centre itself without charge. It's open Monday, Wednesday, Thursday, and Friday from noon to 10 P.M., and Saturday
  and Sunday from 10 to 10. Out front in the square, you'll find
  jugglers, mimes, dancers, muscians, and other entertainers.

- Free: Go to see the historic Place des Voges in the colorful
  Marais District. This square was established by King Henri IV
  in the early 17th century.

- Free: Walk around the grand boulevards, the Ile-St.-Louis, Ile
  de la Cité, and around the Left Bank. Go up to Montmartre
  and drink in the views and watch artists work. Paris is full of
  things to do and see and hear, and many of the very best of
  those things are free.

Potpourri of European Freebies

IN THE LAND OF SPROUTS AND WAFFLES

Brussels, Belgium: What is there to do and see that will cost
nothing? Plenty.

- Free: By any standard, one of the top sites in all of Europe if not the world is the Grand Place, with its magnificent Town Hall and medieval guild halls. The square is crowded daily with tourists who have come to marvel at the architecture that constitutes what Victor Hugo aptly named "the most beautiful square in the world." After 10 P.M. there are light and sound shows at no charge.

- Free: In every direction from the Grand Place are other architectural delights, including the Musée des Beaux Arts, Eglise de la Chapelle, the Chapelle de la Madeleine, and more monumental structures.

- Free: A short walk from the Grand Place, on the rue de l'E-tuve (follow the crowds) is the *Mannekin-Pis*, the statue of a small boy who defused a bomb that was set to blow up the town hall during the troubles with Spain centuries ago. How did the small boy put out the fuse? The boy wasn't the least bit bashful, and you can still catch him in the act. The people of Brussels continually dress what a former student of mine labeled "The Little Pisser" in a great variety of costumes.

- Free: The Royal Palace is also within easy walking distance of the Grand Place. King Albert II doesn't live in the huge palace overlooking the Park of Brussels, but he does conduct audiences and ceremonies in its 150-foot-long throne room, illuminated by 11 elaborate chandeliers. You can see this room in August at no cost, when the palace is open to the public. You can also tour the Empire Room, two White Salons, the Mirror Room, the Music Salon, and the Blue Room. You'll also see the Goya Room, which has tapestries that are modeled on the Spanish painter's works.

- Free: Not far away is a renowned fine arts museum that's free—the Musée d'Art Ancien, at 3, rue de la Régence. Its mammoth collection includes incomparable works by Brueghel the Elder and Peter Paul Rubens. It's open 10 to noon and 1 to 5 from Tuesdays through Sundays.

- Free: Next door to the Musée d'Art Ancien is another free museum with the same opening hours. It's the Musée d'Art Moderne. It's full of Magrittes, Miros, Picassos, and Dalis.

- Free: A third no-cost museum in the city center is the Musée Royaux d'Art et d'Histoire, at 10, Parc du Cinquantenaire. Here we find Middle Eastern sculpture, early Egyptian caskets, and ancient Roman and Greek relics. It's open Tuesday through Fridays from 9:30 to 5, and on weekends from 10 to 5.

- Free: After you've overdosed on free art and relics, make your way to the free Botanical Gardens and rest among the shady trees and colorful flowers.

FREE BIKES

- In Copenhagen, bikes can be used without paying. One thousand "city bikes" are available. You leave a small deposit and get it back when you return the bike. Check with the tourist office across from the main train station.

- Free bikes can be had in Zurich, Switzerland, during the summer months. Fifty bikes are available at railway stations. Show your passport, leave a deposit, and pedal away.

FREE BREWERY TOURS IN BRITAIN

Perhaps the two most longed-for phrases in the English language are "I love you" and "free beer." There's no guarantee of free beer at the breweries listed below, and certainly no promise of falling in love, but according to the British Tourist Authority, all will give you a free tour of their facilities, and most—if not all—will reduce your thirst without charge before you leave. It's best to contact these breweries well in advance to get your name on the list for a tour:

- Carlesberg-Tetley Brewing Ltd., Plympton Brewery, Valley Road, Plympton, Plymouth, Devon, England PL7 3LQ. Phone or fax: (011) 44 1752 342385.

- Fuller, Smith and Turner Plc., Griffin Brewery, Chiswick Lane

South, Chiswick, London, England W4 2QB. Phone: (011) 44 181 996 2000. Fax: (011) 44 181 995 0230.

- Freeminer Brewery Ltd., The Laurels, Sling, Coleford, Gloucestershire, England GL16 8JJ. Phone: (011) 44 1594 810408.

- Samuel Smith Old Brewery, High Street, Tadcaster, North Yorkshire, England LS24 9SB. Phone: (011) 44 1937 832225. Fax: (011) 44 1937 834673.

- Scottish and Newcastle Beer Production, Ltd., Fountain Brewery, 159 Fountain Bridge, Edinburgh, EH3 9YY, Scotland. Phone: (011) 44 131 229 9377. Fax: (011) 44 131 229 1282.

- Traquair House Brewery, Innerleithen, Peebleshire, Borders, Scotland EH44 6PW. Phone: (011) 44 1896 830323. Fax: (011) 44 1896 830639.

- S.A. Brain and Co., Ltd., The Old Brewery, 49 St. Mary St., Cardiff, Wales CF1 1SP. Phone: (011) 44 1222 399022. Fax: (011) 44 1222 383127.

- Bragdy Dyffryn Clwyd Brewery, Chapel Place, Denbeigh, Clwyd, Wales LL16 3TJ. Phone: (011) 44 1745 815007.

- A further source of details on breweries offering tours in the United Kingdom is *The Good Beer Guide,* published by CAMRA (Campaign for Real Ale), 230 Hatfield Rd., St. Albans, Hertsfordshire, England AL1 4LW. Phone: (011) 44 1727 867201. Fax: (011) 44 1727 867670. *The Good Beer Guide* is also sold by Chautauqua, Inc., 1627 Marion Ave., Durham, NC 22705. Phone: (919) 490 0589. Fax: (919) 490 0865. This book explains different types of ale and where they're available.

Further Reading

Tens of thousands of other attractions are free in Europe. Your best sources of free information on free attractions are government tourist offices. See chapter 17, "A Wealth of Free Information" for addresses and numbers to contact. You may also want to check one or more of these books out of your free public library:

- *Europe for Free,* by Brian Butler, Mustang Publishing Co., Inc., P.O. Box 9327, New Haven, CT 06533. Butler treats towns and cities alphabetically in each country. He briefly describes the city and then lists free activities, which might range from cathedral visits to wine tasting to factory tours to festivals. He includes appropriate phone numbers, opening days, times, and locations.

- *London for Free,* by Brian Butler (Mustang). Butler lists free things to do in the metropolis on the shores of the River Thames.

- *Paris for Free (Or Extremely Cheap)* by Mark Beffart, Mustang Publishing Co., P.O. Box 3004, Memphis, TN 38173. Phone: (901) 521-1406.

- Ask for free *Heritage Cities Pack*—information on walking tours in Bath, York, Chester, and Edinburgh—as well as discounts on dining and shopping. Get it from British Tourist Authority, 551 Fifth Ave., Suite 701, New York, NY 10176-0799. Phone: (800) 462-2748.

THE EASIEST WAY TO SEE THE WORLD FOR FREE

Can one travel a few minutes across town to see the world? Sure. None of us, no matter how much and how far we travel, will ever see the Whole Grapefruit. There's just too much planet and too little time. But we can rely on the experiences of others to take us places, a few of which we'll visit and most of which we won't.

Travel agencies and many bookstores help us travel vicariously and without charge. They offer free slide presentations, motion pictures, or talks on exotic travels. Of course the travel agency would like to sign you up to go the destination that's the subject of the presentation, and the bookstore would like you to buy a guide, which is why their presentation is free. But there's no obligation to spend anything when you attend.

In a recent week in one metropolitan area, armchair travelers were invited to slide presentations or movies on Indonesia, Alaskan natural history, the Sahara Desert, Central Asia, and the pleasures of cruising in the Caribbean. Watch for announcements of free presentations. You'll find them in your Sunday metropolitan newspaper travel section.

CHAPTER 8

Free Land Transportation

McCheap's Eighth Law of Travel:
No free trip is worth putting yourself in danger.

HIGH COSTS VS. NO COSTS

Inflated fuel costs have raised the price of transportation, causing millions to limit the miles they travel on vacation and even on essential trips. As a result, many have given up recreational travel altogether. Yet smart globe roamers have always found a way to get from point A to point B without opening their wallets. Although getting free transportation has become increasingly difficult, this chapter presents a variety of strategies to help you get safely and legally where you want to go, when you want to go, at minimal—or better yet–no cost.

FROM HERE TO THERE ON FOUR WHEELS

Developed countries, particularly in North America and Europe, are strangling in traffic. With such an overabundance of motor vehicles, it's not too much of a trick to travel in one without paying or without paying much. Following are several strategies to do just that.

Auto Delivery

No car? Here's how to get one: Auto forwarding services need responsible drivers to bring vehicles to their owners a few hundred or a few thousand miles away. There's usually a minimum age requirement to become an auto deliverer—often 18, 19, or 21. Transportation services charge owners plenty, so more often than not, the car to be delivered is plush and powerful.

In addition to sending cars by truck, casual driveaway services contract with nonprofessional temporary drivers whom they find through newspaper ads. Typical notices read: "Cars shipped to all points; gas allowance"; or "Drive to Ariz., Utah, Texas, Iowa." Another way to find the names of the driveaway services is to look under "Auto Forwarding" in the yellow pages of the phone directory of your metropolitan area.

Auto forwarding services normally provide one free tank of gas; the driver pays for the rest, as well as oil, tolls (if any), accommodations, and meals. Furthermore, the driver puts up a security deposit, which is refunded by the car's owner when the vehicle is delivered unscathed.

Delivering a van or RV can save you even more: Sleep in it and save on motel costs. Prepare meals in the RV and save on restaurant bills.

Since gas and tolls for an RV, van, or even a subcompact car alone could mount to several hundred dollars on a cross-country drive, delivering cars is no guarantee of a free ride. There are, however, two strategies the delivery driver can use to get a free or nearly free trip.

Strategy One: Try negotiating. Sometimes these firms are so desperate at the last minute for drivers that they send recruiting agents into public places such as the New York Port Authority Bus Depot to find people with beating pulses and driver's licenses. In the spring, delivery recruiters comb Florida beaches looking for sober college students to drive cars north.

A delivery service's degree of desperation depends a lot on the season and the destination. If you have no plans other than to see as much of the country as possible while paying as little as possible, offer to drive to *any* destination and then negotiate for more gas than only the first tank. Try to get them to pay all the tolls. If that works, go for meals and motel rooms. Try to get the delivery firm to commit to giving you a car to drive for your trip back home—or to your next destination. Negotiating works, not always, but often enough to deserve a try.

Strategy Two is even easier and you can combine it with negotiating. If you do it right, you can get a free trip and pocket more money than you started with. Take riders with you. Locate riders through newspaper ads or with notes on cork or electronic bulletin boards. Walk around recruiting riders in the bus depot or on the beach. Find them at air terminals and railway stations. But before you invite them to take their places in the passenger seats, make sure you and they are compatible; you'll probably spend several days with them. Get those compatible riders to pay for *all* of the gas and tolls. Since your first tank is free, your riders will still be getting a bargain on transportation and if they're sharing costs two, three, or four ways, they'll be grateful for the low price of their transportation.

An even better possibility for a totally, or mostly, free trip is to bypass the middleman (auto delivery service) altogether. You'll need some good references, an honest face, and a squeaky-clean driving record. Start by advertising your services as a driver to deliver a car for a private party. An ad that appeared in a national magazine made this offer: "Responsible family will drive your RV from Northeast to the West this summer." If that family was successful in getting the use of an RV and negotiating a full gas allowance, their vacation transportation and accommodations more than likely cost them nothing.

Again, the more flexible your plans, the better your chances. The owner will save the whopping forwarding company fee, so he or she can give you all that money to pay your expenses to the vehicle's destination. In addition, try negotiating for return bus or airfare. Take a rider or two and turn the trip into a profit-making vacation.

Here are some major auto forwarding companies that offer toll-free numbers:

- AA Auto Transport—(800) 466-6935.

- All America Auto Transport with offices in Washington, D.C. and Los Angeles. They're as close as (800) 942-0001.

- All States Auto Delivery can be accessed at (800) 822-7447. Fax: (818) 865-0345.

- Auto Delivery (6304 Highway 10 NW, Anoka, MN 55303) is in business "to move vehicles of all kinds all over the world." They are at (800) 307-0013.

- Auto Driveaway Co., with offices in all major cities. Phone (800) 346-2277.

- Dependable Car Travel with offices in New York, Los Angeles, and Miami—(800) 826-1083.

- Worldwide Delivery Systems—(800) 822-SHIP.

Ride Sharing

When it comes to saving on travel expenses, college students are experts. When Alice attended Oregon State, she wanted to spend spring break on the beach at Malibu, about a thousand miles to the south. Because she didn't have enough money to pay for gas for her car and was reluctant to ask Daddy for a handout to hit the waves, she hit on the idea of taking paying passengers to the L.A. area.

Alice asked her friends to accompany her and she posted notices on the university bulletin boards. Soon she had four passengers eager to ride with her to Southern California. They not only divided the cost of gas and oil among them, but they also shared the driving. The result: Alice's transportation was essentially free.

If you have no car and no money but you do have a driver's license, chances are good that you'll get a free ride. That's because driving across North America is a grueling job and someone to share time behind the wheel is often welcome. A traveler wannabe might try placing an ad like this: "Charming, intelligent, good-looking 26-year-old male wants ride to Denver around Oct. 12. Will share *driving*." (But not—please note—costs.) Conclude the ad with your phone number.

Ride Exchanges

The cost-conscious practice of ride sharing probably dates from the time chariots dashed about in ancient Mesopotamia, but in recent years ride exchanges have sprouted and bloomed in most metropolitan areas. These exchanges advertise in the classified ad sections of newspapers, offering to match riders and drivers heading for the same destination on the same dates. If you want to go from, let's say Duluth to Pittsburgh on June 10, you phone the ride exchange. After arranging to pay a small service charge to the exchange, they will give you the names and phone numbers of drivers or would-be passengers with similar plans. The result is that you pay half, a third, a fourth, or even nothing for your operating costs.

Travel companion clubs also match riders and drivers, boat owners and passengers, pilots and fliers. In addition, by matching people of the same gender who are traveling alone, these clubs help to save their members the often exorbitant single supplement fees that are common for hotel rooms and cruise-ship cabins. And having company helps beat the loneliness that single travelers often experience.

Here are travel companion exchanges:

- Thorn Tree is the web bulletin board that's featured as a public service by the publishers of Lonely Planet Guides. Type out: www.lonelyplanet.com.

- Travel Companion Exchange, P.O. Box 833, Amityville, NY 11701. Phone (516) 454-0880. Fax: (516) 454-0170. There's a membership fee.

- The Web Connection, http://www.molyvos.net:80/" matches riders and drivers. It costs nothing. If you want a ride you can send your ad to their e-mail address: tili@molyvos.net. You need to tell them that the subject is 'Ride Sharing,' the dates you want the ad started and deleted, the message you want in the ad, and your e-mail address. You can also find a travel companion or make a home exchange through this free service.

If you belong to one of several home-exchange clubs listed in chapter 2, "Free Accommodations," look for offers to share transportation and look for requests for travel companions. Most catalogs include at least a few such listings. Put in an ad yourself or contact members whose plans are potentially compatible with yours.

Free Rides for Hospitality

When Charlie wanted a ride home from the University of Kentucky in Lexington at Christmas, he advertised on bulletin boards around campus and offered a free night's lodging and breakfast at his parents' house, 200 miles north, in exchange for transportation. Since Nancy, a University of Kentucky sophomore, had to pass through Charlie's hometown on her way home, 100 miles farther than where Charlie's parents live, she took Charlie up on his offer. Nancy paid for all the gas. After using the family's guest room for the night, Nancy continued her drive home. Charlie's trip was free. And when Nancy drove her car back to the university, she spent another night in the guest room and delivered Charlie to his dorm in Lexington.

Investing in Free Transportation

When Cynthia and Bud were married, Cynthia's parents offered them an all-expense-paid, 10-day honeymoon in Hawaii or $2,000. The newlyweds took the $2,000. For $1,500 of it, they found a decade-old, but mechanically-sound camper van and set off from Fort Wayne, Indiana, to see the western part of the United States. They stayed in a motel only twice, having set up housekeeping in the van. Bud and Cynthia stopped occasionally to work temporary jobs such as chefing and waitressing and they didn't return to Fort Wayne for seven months. When they did come home, their camper had an additional 18,000 miles of wear. They sold their roving honeymoon suite for $1,500 after putting in $150 worth of parts and giving it a coat of new paint. "We had the adventure of a lifetime," said Bud, "and because we worked along the way, we didn't go into debt."

Consider looking for a great vehicle deal and reselling your transportation when your trip is over. You might even make enough profit to offset some of your gas and oil expenses. Reselling a steal-on-wheels can work just as well in most countries abroad. In fact, thousands of Americans do that very thing in Europe.

HITCHHIKING

The very first rule of thumb for hitchhiking is *don't*—not if you have an alternate form of transportation. Decades ago when the hypnotic chirp of the bluebird of hippiness sent thousands of members of the tie-dyed generation on the road, hitchhiking was safer than it is today. Today our nation's highways are still bumper-to-bumper with vehicles whose drivers are good samaritans. It's even possible that the next person to pick you up may become the undying soulmate you've been traveling around looking for. Nevertheless, the brutal reality is that although the majority are samaritans, there are killers, rapists, robbers—a menagerie of miscreants and misanthropes—out there cruising around and prepared to prey on unwary ride-seekers. In fact, an expert on rape prevention advises that a female has a far greater chance of being raped while hitching than while engaged in almost any other activity. Unfortunately for free travelers in the United States, three times as many hitchhikers are assaulted by drivers as are drivers by hitchhikers.

And there are other hazards: The driver who stops for you could be drunk or under the influence of drugs; the driver could be exhausted and fall asleep at the wheel; or he or she could have illegal substances in the vehicle, making the hitchhiker a possible accessory to a crime.

Thus, hitchhiking is for the brave and/or desperate. Apparently Stephan Schlei of Ratingen, Germany, has been sufficiently brave and/or desperate to have hitched over 451,000 miles since 1960; his feat of getting more free rides than anyone has been celebrated in the *Guinness Book of World Records.*

If you're sufficiently brave and/or desperate, read on. The tips that follow, distilled from conversations with experts in the fine art of ride-thumbing, are designed to get you where you want to go as quickly and safely (under the circumstances) as possible.

Hitchhiking isn't a particularly fast form of transportation. Thirty-five miles an hour is the average speed for any given journey, taking into account the hours of waiting, or so says our acquaintance Angelo, who has thumbed widely in North America. Angelo's experience is that a male and female traveling together get rides without inordinate waits; somehow they seem less threatening as a pair. They have a reasonable chance of completing a trip in average or above-average time. A single, nicely groomed male has a good chance of getting lots of rides. Two males may have to wait quite a while. Angelo advises that three males who insist on hitching together should consider walking.

Good appearance is all-important. Hitchers have to dress for the climate, but in general experienced ride-seekers dress to look like people whom a driver would want to pick up. A military uniform, if you're authorized to wear one, identifies your profession and can be a basis for a conversation. If you have a high school or college letter-winner's sweater, athletic shirt, or jacket, wear it; it impresses others and serves to identify you and to establish your credentials. A neat and clean hitchhiker has a far better chance of success than the fellow who looks as if he's just been expelled from the Maniacal Marauders Motorcycle Club for gross untidiness. Leave your "Born to Kill" T-shirt at home. Cover your "Born To Loose" tattoo. Leave your three-piece Brooks Brothers suit in the closet as well; overdressing is out of character on the road, and arouses almost as much

suspicion as if you wore combat fatigues and a bandoleer
stuffed with grenades.

Female hitchhikers should wear attire that won't give any
would-be Lothario who comes barreling down the highway a
hormone attack. Attire that could cause a driver to misinter-
pret a hitchhiker's intentions can cause far more trouble than
any ride could possibly be worth. Above all, *women should avoid
hitchhiking alone.* It's flat out unsafe.

Our friend Danny, who's toured 37 states using his thumb,
believes that the morning, when motorists are setting out, is the
best time to get picked up. The afternoon is the second-best
time. Noon, when people are ready to stop for lunch, isn't
good for hitching. In countries where an afternoon siesta is the
custom, you have a better chance of getting a ride when people
return to work in the late afternoon. Night, just about everywhere, is the worst time, because drivers are more wary of
strangers after dark. Furthermore, it's hard to make yourself
visible at night by the side of the road.

Hitching is against the law in some states; that's understand-
able, because pedestrians on the shoulders of roads present a
safety hazard to themselves and to drivers who stop abruptly to
let them in. A ride isn't worth the danger of being hit by a vehicle or the inconvenience of being arrested. In states where
hitching *is* legal, never hitch on freeways, interstate highways,
or toll roads. It's against the law, as it is in most other countries.
Consider not smoking while you wait; nonsmokers are reluctant to pick up someone who's puffing away, and non-smokers
are now a majority in the United States and in many other
countries.

Make sure you carry identification in case you're picked up
by the authorities for hitching illegally. Danny also warns
against against carrying anything you wouldn't want the authorities to find in your possession.

Danny and Angelo both advise standing where drivers can
see you from a distance. Motorists need a few seconds to size you
up, slow down, and stop. Avoid standing where you're partially

concealed, such as the crest of a hill, around a blind curve, or behind foliage. Stand where a driver can stop safely. If you don't, you'll be there a long while. Experienced thumbers stand by a stop sign or traffic light, where vehicles are required to stop anyway. Moreover, it's easier to make eye contact with drivers who are waiting for traffic to move.

Angelo says, "Better yet, approach drivers in places such as gas stations, motel parking lots, or roadside diners to ask for a ride." The choice of whom to approach is then yours. "If you're a good judge of character, you'll have a greater chance for a safe trip," he advises.

If you stand by the side of the road to get a ride, carry a large sketch pad and a wide-tipped marking pen to write destination signs as you need them. Write in large letters, Some successful signs tell brief stories: "Job in NY"; "Home to Mom, Tulsa"; "Back to Wife—Memphis." These sign writers may have no job, not even a mom or wife who's willing to take them back, but their signs *do* get them rides. Our erstwhile friend Leo saw a driver screech to a halt before a young man whose creative sign read, "Hey! You forgot something—Me!"

Travel with as few possessions as you can get by with. You should be able to put everything in one backpack so you can hop in and out of vehicles easily and quickly. Most drivers would rather not take the time to get out, open the trunk, and help you load in your suitcase, guitar, portable tapedeck, surfboard, fishing gear, dog Slobber, camera tripod, martini shaker, skis, collapsible canoe, tent, sleeping bag, and porta-potty. If you insist on traveling with all these useful possessions, stack them neatly in front of you in as compact a pile as possible.

A car trunk is the worst place to allow a total stranger to lock up your valuables. Whenever possible, insist on keeping your possessions within reach inside the vehicle. It's too easy for a dishonest driver to stop, force you out, and drive off with your essential stuff in the trunk or even in the back seat. Furthermore, it's best to carry traveler's checks rather than cash; robbing hitchhikers is the local sport in some areas.

Before getting in any stranger's vehicle, it's a good idea to walk around to the driver's window and tell him or her where you're going, or ask his or her destination. You can even ask who won the ballgame. It doesn't much matter what you ask. The objective is not so much having your question answered as it is to size up the driver and see what's inside the vehicle. Does he reek of liquor? Is he fully dressed? Does he have a weapon showing? Does he have a pit bull in the back seat, avidly frothing at the mouth? Is his manner abusive? Is he coherent? Did he recently star on "America's Most Wanted"? Never get in unless you'd trust him with your life. That's exactly what you'll be doing.

Angelo insists that whenever you hitch, you should carry some food and water. You may get thirsty and hungry standing around for four hours, as Angelo once did in Ohio, before getting a ride. When he finally did get picked up, a rather famished Angelo discovered to his horror that the driver had just filled up with a huge meal and filled his gas tank at the same stop and had no intention of halting again for 200 miles.

Angelo and Danny know from experience that most drivers want one or more of the following from those to whom they give rides:

1) conversation, or at least company,
2) help staying awake,
3) someone to drive part of the way, and
4) gratitude in the form of a sincere "Thank you."

Giving them any or all of these intangibles costs nothing. Temporary friendships often form between driver and passenger and such friendships sometimes result in an invitation to share a meal, stay in the driver's guestroom overnight, or to visit a friend or relative of the driver en route to your destination.

So, be a good guest. Don't fidget with the car radio dial or demand that the driver play your tape of "All Hell is Breaking Loose" by the Dissonants. A smoker who lights up in a vehicle, without asking permission of a driver who isn't a smoker, may get a short ride.

The best advice on the road always comes from others on the road. Hitchhikers are valuable sources of information. Introduce yourself and ask questions. That's what Danny and Angelo do.

No Thumbing Required

Sarah hitched more than 5,000 miles in the United States over a few weeks right after her high school graduation. Yet she spent almost no time sticking her thumb into the slow lane of traffic. "I knew a trucker who was all set to go to Ogden, Utah, from California. He was a good friend of my brother and treated me like his kid sister," Sarah explained. "I didn't really care where I went so long as it was east, because I wanted to see as much of the country as I could. I'd never been east of Reno. I'd always wanted to travel and had joined a pen pal club. I had about 20 invitations to stay in various towns across the country, and I wanted to meet all the pen friends—mostly girls—I'd been writing to.

"When we got to Ogden, my brother's friend got on his CB radio and found me a ride with a driver he trusted. I actually had a pen pal in Ogden and stayed overnight with her.

"Very early the next morning, Gene, the next driver, took me to Cheyenne. In Cheyenne, Gene took me to eat at a truck stop. He knew a lot of drivers and all the waitresses there. He asked some of his buddies where they were going, and got me a ride as far as Grand Island, Nebraska, with an old high school buddy of his. From there I took a bus to Omaha where I spent three nights with the parents of a pen pal who, unfortunately, was away at college.

"Gene told me names of some drivers to look up in Omaha at a certain truck stop, and from there I got a lift with a guy named Alden to Chicago. Believe it or not [she laughs], I had a pen pal to stay with in Romeo, which is in the Chicago area. "By that time I knew enough to either get a ride from a truck driver I met in a diner or to ask one to arrange a ride for me with another trucker by using his CB.

"All the drivers I met treated me like a lady, actually more like a kid sister. I was gone four and a half weeks and I didn't have to spend much. I don't know if I'd recommend it to everyone. I had fun, though. I met my pen pals and I saw lots of states."

Hitching in Europe without Hassle

You can ride with drivers in Europe without begging at the side of the road, but it's not free. Eurostop is an organization that, for a small fee, matches drivers and riders. Riders share operating costs per kilometer with the driver. It's a good opportunity to get to know someone from another culture and perhaps improve your foreign language skills. Even better, you avoid lengthy waits among the litter at the edge of the road. You also avoid hitching, which is in some places illegal and occasionally dangerous.

Here are Eurostop addresses and phone numbers, where available:

- Amsterdam: ILC International Life Center, NZ Voorburgwal 256, 1012 RS.

- Belgium: Taxistop/Eurostop, 28 rue du Fosse aux Loups, 1000 Brussels.

- Cologne, Germany: Citynetz, Mitzfahrcentrale, Saarstr. 22, D-50677, Koln. Phone: 0221-19444.

- Florence: Alonsanfan, Via Guelfa 66 Rosso. Phone: 28-33-95.

- Granada, Spain: Iberstop Mitzfahrcentrale, 85 C/Elvira, 18010 Granada. Phone: 058 29 29 20.

- Madrid: A Dedo, Calle Estudios 9, 2nd Floor, 2801. Phone: 265-65-65.

- Newcastle, England: Freewheelers, 25 Low Friar St., Newcastle-upon-Tyne NE1 5UE. Phone: (01) 91-222-0900. Fax: (01) 91-221-0066. E-mail: freewheelers@freewheelers.co.uk.

- Paris: Allostop Provoya, Passage Brady 84, 75010. Phone: 42-40-00-66.

- Zurich: Impuls Mitfahrzentrale, Fiergasse 16, 8031. Phone: 271-23-00.

France, at least according to my own experience, is the hardest country in which to get a ride. Fortunately, there are driver-rider match-up organizations that will find transportation for you for a modest feel. They are:

- Grenoble: Centre d'Information Jeunesse, 8, rue Pierre Duclot, 38000.

- Lille: Allauto, 13 Faidherbe, 59000.

- Paris: AITITRA, 2 rue Rossini, 75009;
  or OTU, 137, boulevard St Michel, 75005;
  or Provoya, 14 rue Faubourg St Denis, 75010.

- Toulouse: Telestop, 7 Place des Hauts Murats, 31000.

For More Information on Hitching

A lot of people who have hitched extensively have written books about their experiences. Here's a partial list:

- Europe: *Manual for Hitch-hikers* and *Hitch-hikers' Manual: Britain* are two titles that can be ordered from Vacation Work Publications, 9 Park End St., Oxford OX1 1HJ, U.K. Phone: (01) 865-241978. Fax: (01) 865-790885.

- Robert Brown's *Europe: A Manual for Hitchhikers* contains maps showing the best places to stand to get rides out of over a hundred cities. These maps are an important contribution to the art of thumbing, because getting out of town is often the most difficult maneuver of all. The book is from Bradt Enterprises, 95 Harvey St., Apt. 8, Boston, MA 02140. Phone: (617) 492-8776.

- Inveterate wanderer and author Ed Buryn has written *Vagabonding in Europe and North Africa* and *Vagabonding in America: The People's Guide to the USA*. Check your local library or order from And/Or Press, P.O. Box 2246, Berkeley, CA 94702. Phone: (415) 548-2124.

- Ruth B. Davis's *The Hitchhiking Grandmother: The Adventures and Spiritual Journey of a Northwest Woman Who Hitchhiked Across America and Europe after 50* contains enough inspiration to sustain you as you endure the sensation of thousands of cars passing you by. It can be purchased from Pilgrim Way Press, RFD1, Box 398, Forest Grove, OR 97116. Phone: (503) 357-9738.

- Paul Coppersmith's *Rule of Thumb: A Hitchhiker's Handbook to Europe, North Africa and the East* is dated but contains good advice from an experienced traveler. Simon and Schuster published it. A copy may be sitting in your free public library.

- Don and Larry Evans' *Hey Now, Hitchhikers!*, which could be languishing on your public library's shelves or collecting dust in a Haight-Ashbury thrift shop, includes a survey taken among nearly a thousand thumbers to determine the best and worst stretches of highway in the United States for getting rides. Highway U.S. 101 through Northern California and Oregon proved easiest for getting rides; the highway approaching Salt Lake City came in last.

Hitchhiking is a form of free travel, but the wise free traveler will use it only as a last resort.

FREIGHT HOPPING

Riding the rails was big in the 1930s. It was how lots of people's grandpas got to Oregon or Florida to pick fruit during the Great Depression. To prove that you can still get from place to place reasonably safely in a railroad car, Daniel Leen has written the definitive guide. *The Freighthoppers' Manual for North America* can be purchased from Daniel Leen, P.O. Box 191, Seattle, WA 98111.

FROM HERE TO THERE ON TWO WHEELS

When you get there by pedal power, your means of transportation is nonpolluting, silent, invigorating, and—best of all—you don't need to stop every few hundred miles to give money to an oil company. Moreover, it's possible to see most of the world on a bicycle. According to the *Guinness Book of World Records,* a hardy pedaler named Walter Stolle covered 402,000 miles on his two-wheeler in 17 years, visiting 159 countries. Given fair weather, safe bike paths, and good health, two-wheel pedalers who don't have as much free time as Stolle did can still see part of this or any country without paying. And biking helps keep free travelers physically fit.

Getting Your Bike to the Starting Point

A major question confronting bicyclists is whether to take their own bikes abroad or to rent or buy bikes there. If you decide to take your bike with you on a plane, check with the airline's passenger representative to make sure they'll allow you to take it without extra cost as one of your two check-in pieces of luggage. Some airlines will ask you to take off the pedals and turn the handlebars until they're parallel with the frame. A few airlines will give you a free box for your cycle; otherwise, ask your friendly bike shop for a used box if the airline insists it be in a carton. If you've chosen a carrier that doesn't charge for your bike, your transportation abroad can be essentially free.

When you buy your ticket for intercity public transportation abroad, ask at the railroad station or bus depot about taking your bike with you to your destination. Look for a bicycle symbol on European train schedules to see if the particular train you hope to travel on accepts bicycles. Some railroads charge extra; others consider your vehicle to be baggage and allow you to load it on the train yourself without additional charge.

If you have to pay heavy fees to fly your bike, consider renting one at your destination. Alternately, you might try to buy a suitable used bike and resell it before you return home. If you can resell it for the amount you paid for it, your transportation will be essentially free.

Tuning Yourself Up

The first thing to tighten before you take your two-wheeler on a long trip is your muscles. Get into shape by taking progressively longer rides. Don't try to master mountains the first day out. Prepare for this vast project gradually. Stretch your lower back to strengthen the muscles; that's the part of the body that will ache the most after a day of pedaling.

PEDALING ACROSS THE U.S. WITH JONI AND DAVE
(An Exclusive *You Can Travel Free* Interview)

YCTF: About the time we first met you, you had just returned from a cross-continent bike ride, right?

Dave: Yea. We went 3,425 miles in 46 days. It's hard to forget numbers like that, even if it was 10 years ago.

YCTF: I don't have my calculator: How many miles was that a day?

Dave: We averaged 85 miles. During one five-day period we did 525 total.

YCTF:Wow! Where did you go?

Joni: We went from Seattle to Atlantic City.

YCTF: Did you get any days off?

Joni: A total of five out of the 46.

YCTF: Sounds pretty strenuous.

Dave: We were told to tone up and get in shape, so we biked every weekend for months before the trip. We did one 107-mile trip over Mt. St. Helena [2,500 feet above Napa Valley in Northern California] and through the Wine Country. After we completed half the ride of 107 miles, Joni went through a one-hour aerobics session.

YCTF: So you were in great shape for the trip?

Dave: Not really. No matter how much riding we did, it didn't prepare us for this trip. After the first six days we got to Sand Point, Idaho, and we couldn't walk. I mean we couldn't walk upstairs; well, barely. We had biked over the Cascade Mountain Range and our legs wouldn't work any more.

Joni: We had a hotel room on the second floor—no elevators—and I looked down to the first floor and saw a sauna. I really wanted to get in that sauna, but there was no way I could walk downstairs.

YCTF: Sounds punishing. What was the best part?

Dave: At 15 miles an hour, going into Gettysburg, I was really moved by the majesty of what Gettysburg is. On a bicycle when you get to a really special place like the Gettysburg Battlefield National Park, you have time to savor and understand, as opposed to driving through in a car.

Joni: Not only that but you can understand better. Your brain is clear. All that exercise really cleans out the cobwebs in your head.

Dave: After you've been riding 85 to 100 miles a day, what's interesting is that doing 50 to 75, which we did on a few easy days, is nothing. Fifty miles is a piece of cake.

YCTF: My book is for free travelers. Pedaling your bike is free, but is there any extra expense you incurred riding a bicycle across country?

Joni: We ate like you wouldn't believe. We had like two milk-shakes a day and two main courses at dinner.

Dave: We could eat anything we wanted and not put on weight.

YCTF: Do you recommend the trip you took to others?

Dave: Getting seven weeks off is a problem for lots of people. Shorter trips are more practical. Throw your bike in the car and bike around northern Wisconsin, Vermont, or California's Highway One. It's a gorgeous way to see the country.

YCTF: Joni, we've known you 10 years since your trip and I've never seen you on a bike.

Joni: After 46 days on a bicycle seat, you never will.

Getting the Best Information

Safe and pleasurable routes designated on accurate maps can keep you off dangerous main highways and make a long bike tour an inexpensive success. Fortunately, an explosion of information on bicycling and bike touring has made accurate guides and maps available to all. Here are a few books—from among a plethora—that contain suggested routes. Several have useful maps and bibliographies. Most have tips on wise bike selection, preparation, and touring:

- *Bicycle Tours of Great Britain and Ireland,* by Hendricks, is from Penguin Books, 375 Hudson St., New York, NY 10014. Phone: (800) 631-3577. Six tours are featured.

- *The Bike Book* is published by Meredith Books, 121 Regent Dr., Lido Beach, NY 11561. Phone: (516) 432-8120. *The Bike Book* tells all about how to choose the right bike, repair, and maintain it.

- *Biking through Europe* by Dennis and Tina Jaffe, Williamson Publishing, P.O. Box 185, Charlotte, VT 05445. Phone: (800) 234-8791. You can't a bike everywhere, but you can see the best of the continent on two wheels. Here are good tips for the first-timer.

- *The Best Bicycle Tours of Eastern Canada: Twelve Breathtaking Tours through Nova Scotia, Newfoundland, Prince Edward Island, New Brunswick, Quebec* is by Jerry Dennia and published by Henry Holt, 115 W. Eighteenth St., New York, NY 10011. Phone: (800) 247-3912.

- When you're in Boston, bike the 18-mile long Dr. Paul Dudley White Bikeway. Start at either Watertown Square or at the Museum of Science. Get your free bike route map from the Boston Area Bicycle Coalition. Write them at P.O. Box 1015, Cambridge, MA 02142.

- *Britain for Cyclists* can be had free from the British Tourist Authority by calling (800) 462-2748 or (212) 986-2200. This booklet details Great Britain's long-distance bicycling paths, which are along country roads, through forests, and generally out of the way of heavy traffic. As a result, you go where only cyclists, cows, and hikers go. You can visit England's lovely forests and glens and Scotland's crystal lochs. Cycle past dramatic granite mountains and coastal cliffs in Wales, and quiet lanes in the Channel Islands.

- Countryman Press, P.O. Box 175, Woodstock, VT 05091-0175. Phone: (802) 457-1049 publishes a great bike tour series. Dan Carlinsky and David Heim wrote *20 Bicycle Tours in and around New York City.* Other titles by other authors are *25 Bicycle Tours in and around Washington, D.C.,* and *25 Bicycle Tours in Eastern Pennsylvania.*

- Mountaineers Publishing produces a much-acclaimed cycle touring series.

  Order these from your free public library, bookstore, or from Mountaineers, 1011 S.W. Wickitat Way, Suite 107, Seattle, WA 98134. Phone: (800) 553-4453. Some titles include:

  Europe by Bike: 18 Tours Geared for Discovery by Karen and Terry Whitehill;

  Bicycle Tours of France by Hendricks. It contains five tours with day-by-day itineraries;

  France by Bike: 14 Tours Geared for Discovery by Karen and Terry Whitehall;

  England by Bike: 18 Tours Geared for Discovery by Les Woodland;

  Ireland by Bike: 21 Tours Geared for Discovery by Robyn Krause;

  New Zealand by Bike by Bruce Ringer;

  Bicycle Touring Australia by Leigh Hemmings.

- If you're serious about biking, consider joining The League of American Bicyclists (formerly League of American Wheelmen), 190 W. Ostend St., Suite 120, Baltimore, MD 21230-3755. Phone: (800) 288-BIKE. Fax: (301) 944-4353. This organization, founded in 1880, boasts 22,000 members who are united to protect the rights of cyclers and to promote bicycling. In addition, membership provides chances to meet other cyclists.

An outstanding freebie for members is free transportation for their bikes when they fly on American West, Continental, Northwest, TWA, U.S. Air, or Western Pacific Airlines; however, "some restrictions apply." Members receive the bimonthly *Bicycle*

USA magazine. In addition, the LAB operates a hospitality exchange, about which more is revealed in chapter 4, " 'Thank You Thank You'—Accepting Hospitality."

On Two Wheels in Japan

These bicycling clubs can give you information on cycling in Japan:

- Tokyo Cycling Association, c/o Nakamura, 7-15-11 Ginza, Gyuo-ku, Tokyo 104. Phone or fax: (011) 81-3-3541-6540;
- Japan Cycling Association, Jitensya Kaikan Building 3, 1-9-3, Akasaka, Minato-ku, Tokyo. Phone: (011) 81-3-3583-5628. Fax: (011) 81-3-3583-5987.

A Year on Wheels

The June 1997 issue of *Bicycling* magazine recommends a "cycling sabbatical." The author invites us to think about biking through an entire country. Brushing aside heavy considerations such as getting time off and costs, the writer stated (correctly for almost all of us) that if we wait for retirement to take 12 months for ourselves, we're not likely to cycle across a country; perhaps across town if we're lucky. The author suggests workers simply ask the boss for 12 months off, outlining how a year of relying on one's self against sometimes difficult odds would add to his or her value at the company. "If 'frugal cyclists' can get by on $10 to $35 a day, the year would cost as little as $3,500," says the article's optimistic author.

The optimistic author of *You Can Travel Free* says that if you combine strategies in this book—hosting group cycling tours, for example—with free pedal power, you can do it for $3,500, or maybe even for nothing.

CLEAN SHEETS AND THE AROMA OF COFFEE

Want to bike totally free? So you don't pay for food? So you sleep sandwiched by sheets that smell of Vermont breezes or northern Italian sunlight? Then, write an itinerary for a cycling tour and advertise it in *Bicycling*. Advertisers in a recent issue beckoned cyclers to join them pedaling in Crete, Vermont, Banff and Jasper (Alberta), Bryce Canyon, along the banks of the Mississippi, through Louisiana's Cajun Country, the Shenandoah Valley, New Zealand, Vietnam, and Australia. A combination biking and barging program in France caught our eye. For more ideas along these lines, see Chapter 5, "Hosting Group Tours."

WITHOUT WHEELS

Long-distance walking is a form of free transportation that can add years to the lives of participants. Increasing numbers of people with sufficient time, stamina, and willpower are proving to themselves that they can see a good part of North America or other continents under their own foot power.

As recently as the first quarter of the 19th century the chief mode of transport for most people was foot power. It's astonishing to read that our rural ancestors who'd gone 20 or 30 miles from their homes to a large town had done so by walking. Although 36 million Americans say that walking is their chief form of exercise, the sad truth is that too many North Americans rely on motor vehicles to get them home in time to hit the couch so they can snack out in front of the television screen. Most of us, however, are honest enough to admit that sitting life out is easier than walking, but far less healthy. If you're a life member of Exercise Anonymous, why not resign and learn more about the benefits of walking by reading Deena and David Balboa's *Walk for Life: The Lifetime Walking Program for a Healthy Body & Mind*. It's published by Putnam Publishing Group, 200 Madison Ave., New York, NY 10016. Phone: (800) 631-8571. Anyone who has read the Balboas' book will understand the health benefits of a good walking program. Perhaps you'll be motivated to use your feet to travel free, if not across country, at least through woods or meadows to a perfect picnic site.

Walking across the Country (Don't Laugh!)

Those who have traversed parks, counties, states, and continents suggest that the first step is to prepare yourself mentally, to psych yourself up for the sheer length of your contemplated journey. The second step is to prepare yourself physically. The third step is to select and plan your route.

Bill Steltzer, a retiree from Kennett Square, Pennsylvania, supplies an idea that will provide the satisfaction of having accomplished a significant walk, but it will prove less taxing than walking across a continent. Steltzer hiked across England from St. Bee's to Robin Hood's Bay in 12 days. He's also traversed some of Europe's smallest countries by foot: Liechtenstein, San Marino, Luxembourg, Monaco, Portugal, and the Isle of Man. Vatican City doesn't count; lots of university campuses are bigger. You can do a variation in the United States of what Steltzer did, which is to hike across counties, or to traverse smaller states, such as Delaware, Vermont, New Jersey, Rhode Island, Connecticut, New Hampshire, or Massachusetts.

A good way to start is by reading Peter Jenkins' inspiring *A Walk Across America* or *A Walk Across America II*. In 1973, when Jenkins graduated from college, he began a walk from New York State to the Oregon coast. In no particular hurry and seeking to "find" himself while walking, working, and thinking, he reached the Pacific six eventful years later. The height of his adventure was finding a walking companion while working on an oil rig in Louisiana. After he walked into her life, they were married. Both books were published by William Morrow and Company and are in good public libraries.

Books by Ffyona Campbell, a young Scottish woman, are equally inspiring. At age 16, Ffyona set off south from John O'Groats, the northern tip of Great Britain, and subsequently walked an estimated 20,000 miles on four continents. Her book, *The Whole Story: A Walk around the World*, chronicles her exciting adventures. After that she walked from the Cape of Good Hope at the southern tip of Africa to the Mediterranean in Morocco. *On Foot through Africa* details the real dangers and pleasures of her odyssey. Ffyona, incidentally, according to the *Guinness Book of World Records,* holds the title of the female who has walked the farthest. Ffyona's books should be an inspiration to anyone with a lust to see this country, or any country, by wearing out boots. According to *Guinness,* Steven Newman of Bethel, Ohio, beat Ffyona Campbell out as the individual to have walked the farthest, having hiked 22,500 miles through 20 countries on five continents in the mid-1980s.

Reading about Walking

Walkers, it would appear, get so tired that they go home, sit down for months at a time, and produce books about walking. There are lots of these tomes and most of their authors write about either the health benefits of exercise or specific walking trails. Probably British Isles trails are best documented in a number of books. The United States is exceedingly well mapped out by walk-book writers; titles feature paths in Connecticut, near Baltimore and Washington, in San Diego, the Adirondacks, Puget Sound—anywhere that walking is still a pleasant experience. Your public library's shelves will be heavy with these volumes.

Once you have finished some reading, start with a map, a pencil, and a sense of adventure, and then design your own route. For example, Eleonor, whom we met in England, walked her three children from London to Canterbury and read a chapter of Chaucer's *Canterbury Tales* to them at each stop. Other walkers follow the long path of the Franciscan fathers who left missions in their wake from San Diego to Sonoma in California. Still others follow the pilgrim route from Paris, France, to Santiago de Compostela in Spain.

A wealth of free information on walking routes through city and country is available from tourist bureaus just about everywhere. Chapter 17, "A Wealth of Free Information," contains addresses and numbers. In addition, these publications are of particular interest:

- *Walking Guide to the Caribbean* is by Leonard Adkins and is published by Johnson Books, P.O. Box 990, Boulder, CO 80306. Phone: (303) 443-1567.

- *Greece on Foot* by Marc Dubin is available from Mountaineers, 1001 S.W. Wickitat Way, Suite 201, Seattle, WA 98119. Phone: (800) 553-4453.

- *One Hundred Hikes in Colorado,* by Scott Warren, is published by Mountaineers, 1001 S.W. Wickitat Way, Suite 201, Seattle, WA 98119. Phone: (800) 553-4453.

- *Scenic Walking* is published four times a year by British Coastal Trails. For a free subscription, call (800) 473-1210.

- *Walking Easy in the Swiss Alps* by C. and C. Lipton can be ordered from Gateway Books, 13 Bedford Cove, San Rafael, CA 94901.

- *Walking in Switzerland the Swiss Way,* by Marcia and Philip Lieberman, is also from Mountaineers. Phone: (800) 553-4453.

- Consider joining The American Hiking Society, P.O. Box 20160, Washington, DC 20041-2160. Phone: (301) 565-6704. Fax: (303) 565-6714. E-mail: AHSMMBRSHP@aol.com. The AHS publishes detailed information such as *American Discovery Trail Maps*—1) through Indiana, Illinois, and Missouri; 2) through western West Virginia and Ohio; 3) Delaware, Maryland, and Eastern West Virginia; and 4) California. Members also receive the club's magazine, *American Hiker.*

WHERE TO SLEEP AFTER WALKING OR BIKING

Camping is cheap or free, depending on whether you select an inexpensive campground or ask the owner of bare land if you can camp and he or she says yes. Whether you're getting around by bike, public transportation, or motor vehicle, you should take the spend-the-night-outside basics with you: a lightweight sleeping bag (about two pounds), a lightweight tent (about four pounds), towel, washcloth, comb, soap, teeth-brushing stuff, and air mattress. You may want a collapsible camp stove to save money on restaurant meals. Local tourist offices can tell you where to find the free, least expensive, or most delightful places to camp.

In the winter you can camp near sunny beaches in the Caribbean. Some islands welcome campers: Jamaica, Martinique, Puerto Rico, and the U.S. Virgin Islands. Check with the tourist bureaus of each island to see about restrictions.

Major sources for the cheapest overnights for backpackers and tourists of all ages are

- American Youth Hostels, P.O. Box 37613, Washington DC 20013-7613. Phone: (202) 783-6161. Fax: (202) 783-6171. AYH, which isn't confined to youth and which has a special rate for senior citizens (over 54), boasts "the lowest prices anywhere." For a fraction of what they would pay in a hotel, travelers stay in dorm-style rooms, separated by gender.

  AYH accommodations aren't the Ritz, and you don't have the luxury of remaining in bed half the day; in fact, you check in at night and out you go after breakfast. Breakfast ordinarily means cooking and doing cleanup for yourself, but think of the friends you'll make over the morning dishes and think of the information you'll get about other hostels and the sights to see along your planned route.

  With 5,000 AYH hostels in 70 countries, including 150 in the United States, you should be able to find an inexpensive place to sleep just about anywhere tourists go. You'll find hostels in the obvious spots such as central London and New York and in out-of-the-way and unexpected lands such as New Caledonia, Saudi Arabia, Sudan, Greenland, and Zimbabwe. The membership is cheap, particularly for people under 18.

Reading More about Camping and Hiking

Everyone who ever spent more than one summer camping overseas seems to have written a book telling others how to have as marvelous a time as they had. Some of the better volumes are

- *Backpacking and Camping in the Developing World* by Scott Graham is distributed by Wilderness Press, 2440 Bancroft Way, Berkeley, CA 94704-1676. Phone: (800) 443-7227.

- *The Camper's Companion to Northern Europe: A Campground and Roadside Travel Guide,* Susan Williamson and Andrea Chesman, editors. This is a detailed book about seeing Germany, Scandinavia, and other northern lands from the vantage point of a pup-tent. Contact Williamson Publishing Co., P.O. Box 185, Charlotte, VA 05445. Phone: (800) 336-5666.

- *Budget Backpacker Hostels,* which lists cheap accommodations in New Zealand for backpackers only, can be requested from Budget Backpacker Hostels, 99 Titiraupenga, Taupa, New Zealand. Phone: (011) 64-7-377-1568.

- A list of more than 800 huts and shelters in New Zealand that cost hikers extremely little for an overnight stay can be requested from Back Country Huts, Department of Conservation Huts, Box 10-420, Wellington, New Zealand. Phone: (011) 7-4-471-0726.

- For a list of inexpensive youth hostels, write to New Zealand Youth Hostel Association, Box 68-149, Auckland, New Zealand. Phone: (011) 64-3-379-7970.

- Contact Bradt Enterprises, 93 Harvey St., Apt. 8, Cambridge, MA 02140. Phone: (617) 492-8776. Hillary and George Bradt publish an extensive backpacking series that includes essential information on hiking in Mexico, Central, and South America, Africa, and North America.

EXOTIC BACKPACKING TOTALLY WITHOUT COST

Develop your own backpacking trip and recruit people who'll pay their own way (and yours). Advertise your trip in *Backpacker: The Magazine of Wilderness Travel.* Announce your intention to take people on a trek in the foothills of the Himalayas, in East Africa, the Alps, through Provence, or New Zealand.

Remember, you're not General Patton and there's no hurry to arrive at your camp site hours early. There's no reason why your group can't do an easy six to nine miles a day over moderate terrain. Stop frequently for refreshments at convenient inns and restaurants. If you're hiking in a more remote area, refreshments can be brought along by a van that you've hired to meet your group and carry their equipment. The group pays your expenses, including airfare. Since an estimated 60 percent of walking tour clients are repeaters, you can offer your walking tours in different locales year after year and enjoy the company of some of the same clients.

Send for catalogs from one or more leading walking tour specialists; you'll get great ideas for itineraries. On the other hand, you could get so excited by their near-perfect itineraries that you might sign up for one of their tours:

- Butterfield and Robinson. Phone: (800) 678-1147. Website: http://www.butterfield.com. B&F offers 60 tours worldwide.
- Mountain Travel-Sobek (phone: [800] 227-2384; website: http://www.mtsobek.com) offers everything from whitewater rafting to safaris. Tours are in 60 countries.
- New England Hiking Holiday (phone: [800] 869-0949) has conducted tours in England, France, Switzerland, the New England states, Colorado, California, and Hawaii.
- Backroads (phone: [800] 462-2848; website: http://www.backroads.com) has 150 trips in the United States and abroad.

GETTING CREATIVE

Some creative travelers find unusual conveyances to transport them from place to place or they travel in conventional vehicles and publicize something about themselves that's unusual. For example, a few years back six young fellows wanted to bicycle from San Diego to Washington, D.C. Bicycling is conventional. What attracted the interest of the public was that the youngest fellow was 62; the oldest, 75. Because of the publicity, these enterprising retirees were able to talk a hotel chain into giving them free rooms everywhere they scheduled stops for a night. Taking a cue from these gentlemen, a creative traveler might try to get a hotel chain as well as a restaurant chain to help sponsor his or her travels. But, of course, to do so you must be an individual who has captured the imagination of the public either because there's something interesting about you as a person (age, physical disability, or other), because you're traveling to raise money for a good cause, or because your mode of travel is unusual.

One of the most creative travelers around is Lloyd Sumner of Riner, Virginia. He set off to travel around the world in 80 ways. Lloyd and his traveling companion announced plans to make their way through Latin America, Antarctica, Africa, Europe, the Middle East, South and East Asia, and the Pacific islands by 80 different modes of travel. These modes included a pogo stick, stilts, hot-air balloon, kayak, and so forth. They sent out brochures requesting donations, for which the contributors would receive periodic updates on their wanderings. And they promised to fill souvenir requests for foreign stamps, coins, postcards, and other inexpensive items.

Other innovative adventurers go from one place to another in bizarre manners to raise money for charity and to finance their trip at the same time. They skate across several counties, sail up a coast in a bathtub, paddle a surfboard from port to port, or soar in a glider. Donors pledge money for each mile the fund-raiser completes. All funds collected after expenses go to help a needy cause.

On the Road Less Traveled: Skateboarding to Malibu

Southern California beach communities are awash in skateboarders, but only one man, 22-year-old Troy Rodarmel, skateboarded from San Francisco to Malibu. His feat, in the spring of 1997, glided him through suburbs, town centers, along the shoulders of highways, and down country roads to the precipice of the Pacific. Rodarmel's fantastic journey calls

attention to the fact that skateboarding is fun, great exercise, and much faster than walking. And, once you've paid for your skateboard, your transportation is paid for.

The Right Place at the Right Time

Here's another strategy that works surprisingly well: On an April afternoon not long ago a truck pulled into a warehouse in Phoenix, Arizona. A temporary employee named Burt, about to be laid off for a few days, asked the driver casually, "Where to now?"

"Chicago," said the driver.

"I've always wanted to go to Chicago," said Burt.

"If you want to go now, be here in an hour."

So the temporarily superfluous employee went home, threw some necessities into a bag, and was off to Chicago before dinnertime. The driver brought Burt back a week later, the day before he was scheduled to go back to work at the warehouse.

Like Burt, stay alert. Free travel possibilities are all around; you merely have to recognize them.

CHAPTER 9

Flying: Bonuses, Bumps, and Other Freebies

McCheap's Ninth Law of Travel:
Anyone smart enough to buy You Can Travel Free *is smart*
enough to get a free flight.

FLYING FREE: THE FOUR PRINCIPAL STRATEGIES

The toughest aspect of getting free trips is getting free flights. You can recruit a group and get the entire trip, including the flight, paid for, as outlined in chapter 5, "Hosting Group Tours." Beyond that, four principal strategies prove useful. The first is to accumulate and use frequent-flyer miles. The second is to get bumped by an airline from an airline seat that's rightfully yours. The third is to win an airline ticket. But in order to do so, you need to know how to maximize your chances; this chapter explains how to do just that. The fourth is to go down to the airport and ask for a free flight; yes, it works! This chapter explains how these strategies have worked for hundreds of thousands of free travelers.

FLYING FREQUENTLY

Fly free across the United States and Canada, to Hawaii and the Caribbean, to Europe, Asia, the South Pacific—everywhere? Yes you can—if you accumulate enough paid-for miles with major airlines and their allies among hotel chains, auto rental firms, credit card providers, etc. It's a great opportunity, particularly if you're not the plane ticket purchaser handing

out hundred-dollar bills in order to rack up the miles. Let's see what it's all about.

Major airlines offer a free flight anywhere in the continental U.S. or Canada, for example, to passengers who have accumulated let's say 20,000 miles of paid travel. For 30,000 miles they earn passage to Mexico, Central America, or the Caribbean. Forty thousand gets them to Europe. For lots more points, flyers can land in Australia, South America, Asia, Africa, and other far-off destinations. And for megapoints (around 200,000), they lap up the luxury of first-class seating as they wing over half the world toward Montevideo, Capetown, Melbourne, Auckland, or elsewhere in the Southern Hemisphere.

Flying Free Since 1981

The first frequent flyers who began accumulating miles that led to free flights did so in 1981, when American Airlines (AAL) started it all off with their AAdvantage Travel Awards Program. Savvy passengers immediately saw American's generosity as an opportunity too good to be missed. They bought AAL tickets rather than those of American's competitors. Could United, TWA, et al. allow American to take their business away with this colossal bonus?

Of course not. Within a few months all the majors were advertising their own frequent-flyer programs, and now around 30 million passengers have their names on the airlines' membership rolls. Today, as Jay Stuller put it in *Across the Board*, consumers regard frequent-flyer programs as if they "were somehow written into the Bill of Rights." Since, according to *Frequent Flyer* magazine, a quarter of passengers say they buy tickets from an airline because of its frequent-flyer program, few companies are willing to abandon this gigantic freebie. In fact, when one airline allies with an auto rental company, hotel group, or another airline, others have to create similar tie-ins to guarantee additional opportunities for their passengers to pick up extra mileage points. Otherwise they could lose market share.

Getting the Most Out of Frequent-Flyer Freebies

Who gets the truly free flights? The answer is travelers whose tickets are bought for them by someone else, such as an employer or a tour group they've recruited. Most tickets are purchased by employers to send employees on business trips. As a matter of fact, seven out of 10 air miles are flown for business purposes.

Frequent business travelers who talk their employers into letting them keep their bonus points get lots of free trips to use in their free time for their pleasure and that of their families. Our former college classmate Cherylanne was dismayed when her employer told her she'd have to fly from San Francisco to Newark and to Dallas two or three times a month. But she made the best of the situation by convincing her boss that she be allowed to keep her mileage points. That's how Cherylanne and her husband Ross got a free trip to Aruba in the Dutch West Indies. That's how they flew to Fairbanks, Alaska, without paying. That's how they took a Florida vacation one January. Anyone whose job description includes flying should make it a priority to negotiate the right to retain mileage points.

No matter who is paying, no passenger should neglect to open a frequent-flyer account. You may think you won't fly again in the next several months, but life has twists and turns that could send you jetting off unexpectedly and perhaps more frequently than you imagine. Always claim credit for your miles.

Accumulating miles on your favorite airline is only one way to rake in points. Most airlines have reciprical agreements with other airlines and with non-air-carrier businesses. You accumulate additional mileage by patronizing the airline's partner businesses. The scope of these partnerships is staggering, and if you're a smart free flyer, you'll make yourself aware of them. For example, if you charge purchases on a Seafirst Bank Visa card, you ought to consider flying Alaska Air or one of Alaska's other flying affiliates such as Horizon, Northwest, Harbor,

British Air, TWA, or Quantas. And perhaps, as a Seafirst customer, you'll use Sprint for your long-distance phone service.
And when you join the Flower Club, still another partner, you
can accumulate points by sending flowers to Sweetie Pie while
you rack up Alaska Air miles.

American Airlines is fairly typical of large passenger carriers
in that it has extensive partnerships. Other AAL airline part-
ners include American Eagle, British Airways, British Midland,
Canadian, Cathay Pacific, Hawaiian, Japan Airlines, Quantas,
Reno Air, Singapore Airlines, South Africa Airways, and TACA
Group. When AAL Advantage members arrive at their destina-
tions, they might stay in a partner hotel and get more points.
These hotels include Crowne Plaza, Fairmont, Fiesta, Forte,
Forum, Hilton, Holiday Inn, Hyatt, Inter-Continental, Le Meri-
dien, Loews, Marriott, New Otani, Plaza, Radisson, Sandals
Resorts, Westin, and Wyndham.

AAL Advantage's rental car partners include Alamo, Avis,
Dollar, Hertz, Midway, National, and Thrifty. Members can accu-
mulate points every time they charge something using Citibank
MasterCard or Visa, or a Diners Club card. In addition, they can
add miles by phoning on MCI, using FTD Florists, and other
AAL services including the AAL Advantage mutual fund.

AAL's rival, United Airlines, boasts that its Mileage Plus frequent-flyer program has 19 airline partners, 15 hotel group tie-
ins, 6 rental car affiliated firms, Diners Club and First Chicago
Master and Visa cards, Bloomingdales, Crystal Cruises, Renaissance Cruises, Norwegian Cruises, GTE Airphone, and others.
If you spend enough, it's entirely possible to earn a free flight
without having climbed aboard a plane. The business person
who flies to France, Finland, or Belgium frequently will probably want to use Delta for domestic flights, because Delta
SkyMiles members accumulate points when they fly on Air
France, Finnair, and Sabena (Belgian airline).

But be aware that reciprocal agreements vary and some airlines may give miles only for specific routes or fares. For example, you might get miles only when you fly business or first class

on some partner airlines, on which you've accumulated only a sore neck from having spent long hours belted into a seat designed by the Marquis de Sade. Be aware that you may be asked to pay a membership fee; for example, American Express asks $25 per year to link an AmEx card holder to their "Membership Rewards" program, which in turn is linked to airline programs. Be aware of frequent-flyer miles' expiration dates. Several airlines' miles must be used or converted to certificates before three years of the date you acquired them. British Air has a five-year limitation. British Air, American, America West, Northwest, and United certificates expire December 31 of each year rather than on the three-year anniversary of the acquisition date. Free flyers always read the fine print.

Be aware that partnerships themselves change, so before paying too much for a car rental in order to accumulate points, or getting yourself pumped up to cruise on a line that's long since dead in the water, check with the airline to make certain that the partnership is still in place.

Getting Started in a Frequent-Flyer Program

Tell your travel agent when you book that you want to accumulate miles. Or, call the airline whose ticket you're about to acquire. Tell them you want to sign up:

- Alaska Airlines Mileage Plan: (800) 654-5669
- American West Airlines: (800) 247-5691
- American Airlines AAdvantage: (800) 882-8880
- Continental OnePass: (713) 952-1630
- Delta Air Lines SkyMiles: (800) 323-2323
- Midwest Express Frequent Flyer Program: (800) 452-2022
- Northwest WorldPerks: (800) 447-3757
- Southwest Rapid Rewards: (800) 445-5764
- TWA Frequent Flight Bonus Program: (800) 325-4815
- United Mileage Plus: (605) 399-2400

- U.S. Airways Dividend Miles: (800) 872-4738

American Express and Diners Club have extensive ties with airlines:

- American Express Membership Rewards: (800) 297-3276
- Diners Club Rewards Program: (800) 234-4034

Cashing in Your Frequent-Flyer Miles

For some mileage club members, it's easier to accumulate miles than to cash them in when they want to. Because airlines want to fill the most seats possible with paying passengers, they minimize the number of free tickets on fast-filling flights and make more available on runs that are empty. This practice is known as *yield management* or *capacity control*. Because few seats are available on busy flights, it's hard to use your frequent-flyer miles to get to super-popular spots such as the Caribbean in February or Europe in July. In addition, the most popular times—such as holidays and weekends during vacation periods—get blacked out so only paying passengers can fly. So, what should one to do to maximize air-mile freebies? Here's what the experts have to say:

- Plan your trip to a popular destination at a time other than the peak period.

- Book your flight as long in advance as possible.

- If you don't get the flight you want when you first call, call back a day or two later. Situations can change to your advantage.

- Don't try to accumulate a few miles on each of a lot of programs; concentrate on one or two by showing loyalty to your favorite airline so you'll have a good chance of earning sufficient points for a flight on one of their routes.

- Forget the upgrades. The big spenders in first class don't get there any faster than the folks who frugally fly peasant class and cram their legs into the standard 28 to 34 inches of space. Your purpose is to see the world, not to put your feet up.

- Be willing to give up extra miles for a flight on a peak date to a popular place.

What to Read to Learn More

- On your Internet, type in http://w1.itn.net/airlines. The FFP Site will give you comprehensive information on airlines, including frequent-flyer programs. In fact, it rates all frequent-flyer programs on a scale of one to 10. Few earn really poor ratings. British Airways, for example, gets 9.0, while Southwest Rapid Rewards gets 6.0.

- Read Sharon Tyler and Matthew Wunder's *Airfare Secrets Exposed,* published by Universal Information Corp., 2812 Santa Monica Blvd., Suite 203, Santa Monica, CA 90406. Tyler and Wunder cover air-courier flights, getting bargains through consolidators, and making the most of frequent-flyer bonuses.

- *The Miles Guide* lists businesses that offer frequent-flyer miles for purchase. For information on cost, call (800) 209-2810.

- *The Frequent Flyer Guidebook* is published by Airpress. Phone: (800) 209-2870. E-mail: flyers@usa.net; www.insideflyer.com.

- *Inside Flyer,* a monthly magazine, offers information about how to maximize frequent-flyer bonuses. *Inside Flyer,* 4715-C Town Center Dr., Colorado Springs, CO 80916. Phone: (800) 333-5937.

GETTING BUMPED: A BLESSING IN DISGUISE

Some travelers make reservations for flights and fail to show up at boarding time, so airlines (because they don't want empty seats) overbook by 10 to 30 percent. When nearly everyone does show up, the carriers have costly problems, problems that could be to your benefit as a free flyer. Airline passengers who know their rights can end up with free flights and cash to spend at their destinations.

Until consumer advocate Ralph Nader got bumped a few years back, irate passengers had little recourse against airlines that denied them their reserved and confirmed places. An irate Nader took his complaint to the U.S. Supreme Court. The Court ruled that under certain circumstances passengers with reservations who get bumped are entitled to compensation for their inconvenience. Because unfilled plane seats are particularly perishable products that lose all value when each partially filled plane takes off, the Supreme Court ruling didn't force the airlines to stop bumping paying customers. That's because it's too expensive for the air carriers to hold seats for no-shows. Instead, the Court allowed the Civil Aeronautics Board (CAB) to direct the airlines to compensate bumped flyers.

The Civil Aeronautics Board stipulates that compensation should include a free ticket and cash. The amount of compensation depends on how people are eliminated from the passenger list. While our longtime friends Ron and Betty were waiting in the check-in area to board a scheduled flight from Oakland, California, to Honolulu, an agent announced, "We've overbooked by two seats. Are there two passengers willing to take a later flight?" In no particular hurry to begin a long vacation, and being good Samaritans, Ron and Betty volunteered to stay behind and take the next flight. For their inconvenience, they were able to sell their tickets back to the airline for the amount they'd paid and were given two free tickets to Hawaii, this time in business class rather than in the tourist section. The airline also gave them $100 in cash and lunch vouchers for an airport restaurant. Thus, their flight to Honolulu was free, and the money they had been paid for their unused tickets covered the cost of their return flight.

When people don't volunteer, airline employees are authorized to offer an acceptable amount of money and a dollar-amount certificate for purchase of a flight, or a free flight, to get the necessary seats. Recently we heard this announcement at the boarding gate of a major airline: "Folks, we have a problem. We're overbooked by eight seats. If you're willing to take the next flight to San Francisco, four hours from now, we'll give you a pass for a flight to anywhere in North America that we fly, the Caribbean, Mexico, or Hawaii. It's good for one year."

Since the amount isn't stipulated in the regulations, free travelers can negotiate for whatever they can get. If they ask too much, the agent will find other passengers willing to stay behind for less. If there are enough volunteers willing to give up their sets for little or no compensation, that's exactly what they'll get—little or no compensation. If, however, other passengers cling desperately to their confirmed seats, volunteers are in a strong position to negotiate.

If the passenger agent has to up the ante for lack of volunteers, he or she may offer a voucher for two round trips or for a flight to Europe. Some of these vouchers have severe restrictions such as the recipient having to make reservations within a day or two of travel. Nonetheless, they are good for getting you without cost to some terrific destinations.

Involuntary Bumpings and Free Flights

When you're involuntarily bumped, the airline will give you a written statement describing your rights; that's a U.S. Department of Transportation requirement. The statement explains that if the airlines can't get you on your way in the prescribed time, you'll receive "denied boarding compensation," paid on the spot. The amount of your compensation depends on how much you paid for your ticket and how long you'll be delayed. Even if they can get you another plane within one to two hours, the airline pays you the price of your ticket, but not above a maximum set amount, $200 at the time of this writing. The reservation clerks then have to arrange another flight for you and give you a ticket. If they can't fly you out to your destination within two hours on a domestic flight, or within four hours on an international flight, you collect double compensation. For example, if your airfare is $156, you collect $312. If your airfare is $225, however, you collect $400—double the $200 maximum, not double the $225. You get to keep your original ticket to use on the flight they booked for you and you can stuff the money in your pocket and take it home or spend it on your trip. However, if the passenger agents get you another domestic flight to your destination within an hour, you collect no money.

Just because you get bumped and as a result, bummed, doesn't mean that tickets and dollars start to rain on you. There are catches. To be eligible for compensation, you must:

- have a confirmed reservation,

- have purchased your ticket within the airline's stipulated time after you made your reservation,

- have checked in on time for the flight from which you've been bumped. Turning up at the last minute as the plane's door is latched doesn't qualify. Airlines often want you to check in at least 30 minutes before departure for domestic flights and as much a three hours for international flights. If you haven't followed their rules, you could be denied compensation.

More snags: When the airline has to substitute a smaller plane, there's no compensation for getting bumped. Nor do compensation rules apply to international flights headed toward the United States or to flights between foreign cities— Tel Aviv to Athens, or Hong Kong to Bangkok, for example. If you're delayed due to a mechanical problem or because of weather—again, no freebies. You should know too that the compensation rules don't apply to commuter airlines or to charter flights.

Airline Goodwill Gestures

If your plane is delayed and you can't get a flight out the same day, most airlines, although they're not required to do so, will put you up for the night in a hotel, reimburse you for your transfer to and from the hotel, pay for a phone call to your destination, and give you meal vouchers. When we were delayed in

Rome for 48 hours because our charter carrier, Trepidation Air, was experiencing severe mechanical difficulties on its sole plane, we were at first irritated over what seemed an eternal delay. But when the airline gave us a posh hotel room for two nights and a fistful of lire to spend in the Eternal City, we decided our plight wasn't worth complaining about. No rule stipulated that the charter company had to pay to put us up; they compensated us to maintain customer goodwill. And because most of the passengers threatened to throw a fit.

When You Want to Get Bumped "Involuntarily"

Expert bumpees suggest that if you want to maximize your chances of getting bumped, ask when you make reservation whether the plane is nearly sold out. If it is, go ahead. If not, reserve on a flight that's filling rapidly. When you check in, be sure to show up early. Tell the agent you don't mind taking a later flight. The agent may be authorized to make a decision at that point and offer you a free later flight. Sometimes first or business class will be overbooked, and if you hold one of those tickets, you can volunteer to move to commoner class and possibly be given an aristocrat-class upgrade on another longer flight.

Book a ticket on a plane that's filling fast and bring up the end of the line. But be sure you check in at least 20 minutes before scheduled departure. Flights on Sunday afternoons and early weekday mornings are prime bump times. Friday evenings are also advantageous.

When you are bumped, make sure the airline gives you a free ticket that doesn't have so many restrictions as to be virtually unusable and that it books you on another flight. If you're bumped but they can put you on another flight to the same destination within an hour, there are no freebies. However, the airline is obliged to get you out on its next available flight to your destination.

Even when an airline isn't obligated to give you an overnight stay, a free flight, meals, or an upgrade, you should always ask.

Very often the answer is "yes." On a recent Chicago-to-London trip, our friend Roderick was delayed overnight in Chicago due to mechanical failure. After asking at the airline desk, he was given cab fare, a meal voucher, and a night in a hotel. Those who didn't ask spent the night at O'Hare or paid for a hotel room out of their own pockets.

If all of this sounds complex, order *Fly Rights: A Consumer's Guide to Air Travel* from Superintendent of Documents, U.S. Government Printing Office, Washington, D.C. 20402. This inexpensive booklet covers a lot more than bumps.

The free booklet *Air Travel Consumer Report* offers airline industry and individual airline statistics for delayed and canceled flights, overbookings, lost luggage, and consumer complaints. It can be had from the U.S. Department of Transportation, Office of Consumer Affairs, I-25, 400 Seventh St. SW, Washington, D.C. 20590.

GETTING THE AIRLINE TO PAY ATTENTION

If you've been inconvenienced by an airline and feel you deserve something more than what its personnel will give you on the spot, make note of the flight numbers, delay time, and the names of personnel you've dealt with. Most important, keep receipts for every expense you've incurred as a result of the delay. Write to the air carrier's consumer relations department or to the president of the company. By taking this approach, you'll usually get a legitimate grievance redressed out of court.

If the airline won't make things right, contact the airline industry's watchdog agency, the Aviation Consumer Protection Division, Department of Transportation, C-75 Room 4107, Washington, D.C. 20590. Phone: (202) 366-2220. E-mail: air-consumer@ost.dot.gov. They have a lot of clout and can pressure the airline to make things right.

Many weary passengers are turning to a private nonprofit group that's dedicated to making the air passenger industry more responsive to the needs of its customers. The Aviation Consumer Action Project doesn't have the CAB's authority of

law behind it, but it does lobby for flyers' rights. And it can give
you good advice about getting your grievances redressed.
When writing for advice, consider making a donation to the
project. The address is 1346 Connecticut Ave. NW, P.O. Box
19029, Washington, D.C. 20036.

If you're ever bumped against your will, don't get angry; get
a free ticket.

WIN THAT FLIGHT!

O.K., so the bill collector grabbed your air ticket money,
which leaves your chances of accumulating frequent-flyer miles
or getting bumped hovering precariously between zero and
zilch. Well, there's still lots of hope for getting you on a plane.
For years we've been opening magazines to see advertisements
depicting London's Tower Bridge, giraffes munching tree tops
in a Kenyan safari park, or the Leaning Tower of Pisa and pre-
dicting that we, the readers, will get to go to one of those world-
class sites without paying.

Why should someone send you off to some exotic destination?
Sales promoters and ad agencies offer millions of dollars in prizes
to tout their products. Many of these prizes are free round-trip
flights, some complete with hotel packages at top vacation destinations. We're tempted by contests and drawings that promise us
the hope of going to Bermuda, Rio, the Great Barrier Reef,
Orlando, Waikiki, Antarctica, Hong Kong, sunny West Indian
isles—nearly everywhere magazine readers would like to visit.

Winners of these fabulous trips have had their names drawn
from a gigantic drum, baked the best cake, written slogans,
guessed the correct number of beans in the bin, or answered
challenging questions correctly. Ads make winning seem easy. As
a result, the competition is swift. In fact, entering contests has
become a full-time job for many. Some people win thousands of
dollars a year in products and services by sending off entry forms.

Because you'll have lots of competition, if you really want to
win that trip, you can improve your chances by following a few
simple hints passed on by professional contest winners:

1. If the rules say the deadline is June 1, believe it. There are usually so many entries received before the deadline that the exhausted promotion agency staff takes grim pleasure in tossing all late entries.

2. If the rules state "25 words or less," don't write 26, even if that extra adjective jazzes up your entry. If the rules say "print," print.

3. Enter as many times as you're allowed. But make sure the prize is worth what it will cost you in postage, product purchases, and your time. If you spend $15 to buy some wretched cereal and end up with a $10 prize, you've really won nothing.

4. Whenever you can, enter a contest that requires skill or imagination; you'll have less competition and a far better chance when you use your brains to create a winning entry than you will having your name drawn from a huge drum full of the names and addresses of optimistic entrants.

5. If the rules say you can make your own entry form, or that you can write the product's name on a blank slip of paper instead of sending in the product wrapper or bar code, do so, and enter lots of times. That will multiply your chances.

6. Enter local contests that have worthwhile trips rather than highly publicized national competitions that everyone and his travel agent will enter. If the Lions, Elks, Moose, or Boars are raffling a trip to Raratonga, calculate the odds and buy lots of tickets. It may well be a good investment that will get you to that lovely Polynesian isle.

7. Enter contests only when the prize doesn't cost you more than it's worth. For example, our acquaintance Fred was informed he'd won a free flight to Florida, but in order to take it, he had to pay an exorbitant price for a week in a third-rate hotel. Fred passed it up and so should you.

ALL FOR LOVE

Inventing a unique strategy to get his airline ticket paid for was the superb work of a 34-year-old New Orleans man. He wanted to visit the woman of his dreams on Valentine's Day, but she was in London, England. So he sold raffle tickets to friends, relatives, and co-workers. The winner got all the money that was left over from the proceeds after he'd bought his air ticket from Louisiana to Gatwick Airport. Valentine's Day found the couple reunited, while a lucky ticket holder was left counting her winnings back home.

FLY FREE TO A CRUISE?

Boldface type screams from the ad in the Sunday paper's travel section: "Fly Free to Your Caribbean Cruise!!!" Before signing up, prospective passengers should ask themselves who actually pays for their "free" flight. In some cases, cruise ticket purchasers who live nearer the port of departure subsidize those who fly in from a distance. Florida residents, for example don't need a flight to the ship if the ship leaves from Miami or Ft. Lauderdale, so they should refuse to pay the same price as those winging in from Missoula, Portland, or Toronto on "free" tickets.

If you're planning a cruise vacation—and you should, because sailing on a posh ship is like going to heaven—see the free flight for what it is. It's a good deal for those with lots of miles to travel and not too good for those who can get to the ship cheaply on their own.

ASK THE RIGHT QUESTION

One day an unemployed bookkeeper was looking around a local airport. He soon got into conversation with a private pilot who was preparing for a flight. "Where you going?" the idle bookkeeper asked idly.

"Gulfport, Mississippi," said the pilot.

"Mmm," mused the bookkeeper. "I've got a sister in Biloxi."

"Hop in," offered the pilot. So the bookkeeper was flown 1,100 miles and back on a beautiful spring weekend and was reunited with a sister he hadn't seen in 4½ years.

Free flyers always know when to ask the right question.

CHAPTER 10

Free or (Really) Cheap
Courier Flights

McCheap's Tenth Law of Travel:
Leave your checkbook at home and prepare to negotiate.

"HAVE TRENCHCOAT, WILL TRAVEL"

If you're a halfway presentable, generally sober adult, have a passport, and can sit fairly still for a long time, you can be an air courier. International freight companies need you to sit in an airplane seat on an international flight so they can use your baggage allowance to ship priority parcels. Yes, it's legal. In the parcels are not illicit drugs or smuggled jewels, but legitimate stuff: blueprints, contracts, checks, securities, etc.

An estimated 25,000 to 35,000 courier flights originate in the United States each year. Couriers are professional people on vacation, retirees, students, housewives, the temporarily unemployed—anyone with the time and desire to fly overseas. They're usually experienced travelers, although that isn't a prerequisite. About all they have in common is that they save around half the price of an air ticket, and some fly free.

WHY COURIER TRAVEL IS SUCH A GOOD DEAL

Contrary to what many imagine a courier's image to be, nobody on your flight will know you're a courier unless you tell him. And you enjoy all the benefits that passengers who've paid full fare enjoy. Let's see why and how serving as an air courier works to your advantage.

The international delivery service will collect several thousand dollars for delivering the packages some client has assigned it. Let's say in this instance the packages are full of negotiable bonds. These bonds need to get from Vancouver, B.C., to Tokyo. Pretend you're in Vancouver. The courier firm buys a coach-class plane ticket in advance and sells it to you at a discount. They'll pay, let's say, $1,000 or so for the plane seat. If they sell it to you for $400, they'll still make a substantial profit.

Why does the customer spend so much to transport these documents and other items? Because some customers can't wait for their package to arrive at their doorstep after having been held up for days or weeks in a customs shed at a foreign airport. The luggage or parcels assigned to you come out of customs within a few minutes after landing. They come out when you exit the airport's arrival lounge, and the eager customer receives his shipment right away. That's why, like tens of thousands of others, as a courier you can save around half of the regular price for a round-trip flight or at least more than the cost of the most highly discounted ticket.

It's possible to get a free ticket if the international delivery service has had a courier they counted on cancel out on them at the last minute. For example, a retired physician happened to phone a courier dispatcher to inquire about a flight that was to take off several weeks later, when the dispatcher asked him if he could fly out that very afternoon. "I guess I could," said the ex-practitioner. He threw some necessities into his hand luggage and called a taxi to take him to the airport. He received his ticket from the company representative at the departure gate. As a result the doctor visited Hong Kong without charge. The disadvantage is that he had to take changes of clothes for his two-week overseas trip in no more than two bags that he could carry with him on the plane as hand luggage. That's because the company wanted his luggage allowance for its shipment. Because he packed clothing that he'd intended to give to a charity thrift shop, he was able to discard it in China and replace his wardrobe in Hong Kong department stores and tailor shops. He felt that packing light was to his advantage.

"Is That All I Have to Do?"

No. Air couriers have other restrictions and responsibilities as well. You may have to book your flight a month in advance. You may be asked to serve as a courier on a return flight and the return date is at the convenience of the customer, not you the courier-tourist. Sometimes your length of stay is as short as two to seven days or as long as several weeks or months. Often the length of stay abroad can be negotiated.

On a positive note, you don't have to lift or handle the courier company's luggage or parcels. Their agents will check their baggage in for you and claim it at the baggage carousel when you arrive. When you arrive the agent will give you your return flight information and instructions; these are particularly important if you should act as a return courier.

On your way out of the baggage area, you show the luggage manifest to the customs officer. Then you're free to go on to your hotel or other destination. You're free to enjoy your vacation.

Some companies may have more than one courier per flight. It's entirely possible then, that couples can fly together as couriers. Or you can book your partner on the same flight at full fare. If two couriers aren't required on the same day at the same destination, couples can leave a day or so apart if both are couriers and they can return home a day or two apart. Thus, you can have a free or cheap flight and the pleasure of your companion's company too.

At the start of your vacation or break between jobs or classes, when you have nothing to do but fly off to somewhere exotic, call around to courier companies and inquire if they have any "last minute specials." You may find yourself on the road to Caracas or Casablanca for a song . . . or less.

Keep your passport up to date. You may need a visa for some countries. The company will tell you how to get it.

Where Can an On-Board Courier Go?

Most flights to Europe leave from the East Coast, usually New York City or Washington, D.C. Latin American flights are from Miami. Most flights to East Asia are out of San Francisco, Los Angeles, or Vancouver, British Columbia. But there are plenty of exceptions—flights to Europe from the West Coast, for example.

Getting More Information Than You Probably Need

These publications will give you a full run-down on courier travel.

- *The Shoestring Traveler,* P.O. Box 1349, Lake Worth, FL 33460. Phone: (561) 582-8320. Fax: (561) 582-1581. *The Shoestring Traveler* is a 24-page bimonthly newsletter about courier flights. A sample is free.

- *The Air Courier's Handbook,* by Jennifer Bates, can be ordered from Big City Books, 7047 Hidden Lane, Loomis, CA 95650. Ask for the price.

- *The Courier Air Travel Handbook* by Mark I. Field gives an overview of the air courier industry as well as detailed instructions on how to use it to your advantage. Get it from Perpetual Press, P.O. Box 45628, Seattle, WA 98145. Phone: (800) 807-3030. Fax: (206) 971-3708.

- *Courier Flight Directory, Inside Track,* Box 28042, Harbour Centre Post Office, Vancouver, B.C. V6B 5L8, Canada. Information may be had by calling (604) 291-7294.

- *Insider's Guide to Air Courier Bargains: How to Travel Worldwide for Next to Nothing* by Kelly Monaghan can be had from The Intrepid Traveler, P.O. Box 438, New York, NY 10034. Inquire about the current price of this guide to domestic and international air courier opportunities.

- *A Simple Guide to Courier Travel* by Jesse L. Riddle. It's from Discount Travel, Carriage Group, P.O. Box 2394, Lake Oswego, OR 97035.

- *Worldwide Guide to Cheap Airfares* includes lots on courier flights; it's from Insider Publications, 2124 Kittredge St., 3rd Floor, Berkeley, CA 94074. Ask for the price.
- Pacific Data Sales Publishing (2554 Lincoln Blvd., Suite 275, Marina Del Rey, CA 90292) publishes a list of courier companies worldwide. According to Pacific Data, whether you're in Antigua, West Indies; Bahrain, Persian Gulf; Helsinki, Finland; or Mauritius, Indian Ocean, you can negotiate with a courier firm to get to where you want to go at rock-bottom rates or less.

AIR COURIER "CLUBS" AND "ASSOCIATIONS"

Courier agencies or "clubs" sell you the convenience of updated recent lists of all available flights. Knowing all your options can be worth the membership fee if you intend to serve as a courier several times during the course of a one-year membership. If you're going to fly once on your annual vacation, joining the club may be an unnecessary expense. Some clubs are

- Air Courier Association, Denver, CO. Call (303) 278-8810 (8 A.M. to 4 P.M. Mountain Standard Time) for an enrollment kit. This "association" advertises more than 600 weekly flights to the Persian Gulf, Egypt, Zimbabwe, Kenya, Israel, Honolulu, Tahiti, South Africa, Europe, major cities of East Asia, Mexico, and Central and South America, and elsewhere. One client claims to have saved an average of 60 percent on his six flights to South America by using the services of the Air Courier Association.
- International Association of Air Travel Couriers (P.O. Box 1349, Lake Worth, FL 33460) claims there are more and more opportunities to take advantage of cheap flights as couriers, particularly to China, Japan, Malaysia, Singapore, and Thailand. Call (561) 582-8320. Its bimonthly *Air Courier Bulletin* contains valuable information for saving money on flights, hotels, and other travel-related costs.

- Travel Unlimited (P.O. Box 1058, Boston, MA 02134) offers monthly updates on worldwide courier flights.

  $$$—Cousin Thrifty McCheap says: "Save courier club dues by calling the delivery service yourself. If you catch them at the right time, you can negotiate to fly free or at an unusually big discount."

CONTACTING COURIER DISPATCHERS DIRECTLY

If you're just about ready to take off, contact one or more of these international delivery firms by phoning to inquire about flights. You should be able to find one or more from major metropolitan airports to your preferred destination at the times you'd like to leave and to return home.

Flights Originating in New York

- Air Facility, 153-40 Rockaway Blvd., Jamaica, NY 11434. Phone: (718) 712-1769. Air Facility offers flights to Latin America: Buenos Aires, Caracas, Mexico City, Montevideo, Rio de Janeiro, Sao Paulo, and Santiago.

- Airhitch can get you departures from several U.S. cities to Europe. Phone: (212) 864-2000.

- Bridges Worldwide, Building #197, JFK International Airport, Jamaica, NY 11430. Phone: (718) 244-7244. The bridge leads to London.

- Courier Network, 295 Seventh Ave., New York, NY 10001. Phone: (212) 675-6876. They offer flights to Tel Aviv, Israel.

- East-West Express, Box 30849, JFK Airport Station, Jamaica, NY 11430. Phone: (718) 656-6246. Want to go to Africa? East-West goes to Johannesburg. Asia? They can send you to Bangkok, Hong Kong, Jakarta, Kuala Lumpur, Manila, Seoul, Taipei, and Tokyo. Australia? East-West will save you money on tickets to Brisbane, Cairns, Melbourne, or Sydney.

- Micom America (Jupiter Air), Building #14, JFK International Airport, Jamaica, NY 11430. Phone: (718) 656-6050. Fax: (718)

656-7263. Flights go to Hong Kong, Singapore, and London.

- Halbart Express, 147-05 176th St., Jamaica, NY 11434. Phone: (718) 656-8189 or (718) 656-8279 for information about cheap transportation to Europe: Brussels, Copenhagen, Dublin, Frankfurt, London, Madrid, Milan, Paris, Rome, Stockholm; and to the Far East: Tokyo, Seoul, Singapore, and Hong Kong.

- Now Voyager, 74 Varick St., #307, New York, NY 10013. Phone: (212) 431-1616. Now Voyager charges a special fee each year for the first flight you book through them. Now Voyager has lots of destinations—Europe: Copenhagen, Dublin, Frankfurt, London, Madrid, Milan, Rome, Paris, Stockholm; Latin America: Buenos Aires, Caracas, Mexico City, Montevideo, Rio, Sao Paulo, Santiago, San Juan; Asia: Bangkok, Beijing, Hong Kong, Seoul, Singapore, Taipei, Tokyo; the Pacific: Auckland, Sydney; Africa: just Johannesburg.

- Rush Courier, 481 Forty-ninth St., Brooklyn, NY 11220. Phone: (718) 439-8181. Rush sends couriers on flights to San Juan, Puerto Rico.

- World Courier, 137-42 Guy R. Brewer Blvd., Jamaica, NY 11434. Phone (800) 221-6600, (718) 978-9400, or (718) 978-9552, (718) 978-9408 for a recording of courier flights—recently to Milan and Mexico City.

From New York City try also:

- Able Travel & Tours, (Europe). Phone: (212) 779-8530.
- Travel Courier (Europe, Asia, South America). Phone: (516) 763-6898.
- Discount Travel International (Europe, South America, Asia). Phone (212) 362-3636 or (212) 362-8113.

Flights Originating in Houston

- Now Voyager sends Texan couriers to London after they phone (212) 431-1616.

Flights Out of Los Angeles

- Bridges Worldwide, Building #197, JFK International Airport, Jamaica, NY 11430. Phone: (718) 244-7244. This bridge stretches from L.A. to London.

- East-West Express, Box 30849, JFK Airport Station, Jamaica, NY 11430. Phone: (718) 656-6246. Flights (from L.A. in spite of the address) to Australia and New Zealand: Auckland, Brisbane, Cairns, Melbourne, and Sydney.

- Halbart Express, 1016 Hillcrest Blvd., Inglewood, CA 90301. Phone (310) 417-3048 if you want to fly LAX to London and Sydney.

- IBC Pacific, 1595 Segundo Blvd., El Segundo, CA 90245. Phone (310) 607-0125; or in Northern California, phone (415) 697-5985 for a recording of current flight schedules. IBC, which stands for International Bonded Couriers, has flights to Asia: Bangkok, Hong Kong, Manila, Singapore, Taipei, and Tokyo.

- Jupiter Air, 460 S. Hindry Ave., Unit D, Inglewood, CA 90301. Phone: (310) 670-1197. Flights go to Asia: to Bangkok, Hong Kong, Seoul, and Singapore.

- Now Voyager, 74 Varick St., Suite 307, New York, NY 10013. Phone: (212) 431-1616. Flights are from LAX to Sydney, Australia.

From Los Angeles, try also:

- Airhitch (Europe). Phone: (310) 458-1006.

- Midnight Express, 925 W. Hyde Park, Inglewood, CA 90302. Phone (310) 330-7096 for trips from LAX to London.

- Polo Express (Australia, Japan). Phone (415) 742-9613 for their San Francisco office.

- Way to Go Travel Club (Asia, Europe, Mexico, Australia, Tahiti). Phone: (213) 466-1126.

- SOS International Courier (Mexico City). Phone: (310) 649-6640.

Flights Out of San Francisco

- Bridges Worldwide, Building #197, JFK International Airport, Jamaica, NY 11430. Phone: (718) 244-7244. Flights are from SFO to London.

- IBC Pacific, 1595 El Segundo Blvd., El Segundo, CA 90245. Phone: (310) 607-0125. The address notwithstanding, flights are from SFO to Bangkok.

- Jupiter Air, 839 Hinkley Rd., #A, Burlingame, CA 94040. Phone: (415) 697-1773. Go to Asia: Bangkok, Manila, Singapore; and to London.

- TNT SKYPAK (Hong Kong). Phone: (415) 692-9600.

- UTL Travel, 320 Corey Way, South San Francisco, CA 94080. Phone (415) 583-5074 for information on flights to Bangkok, Manila, Singapore, and to London.

Also try:

- Way To Go Travel (Asian cities, London, and Mexico City). Phone: (415) 864-1995.

Flights Originating in Chicago

- Halbart Express, 1475 Elmhurst, Grove Village, IL 60009. Phone (847) 806-1250. Its couriers end up in London.

Flights Originating in Miami

- A-1 International (Caracas). Phone: (305) 594-1184.

- Travel Courier sends Floridian couriers to Europe after they call (516) 763-6898.

- Halbart Express, 7331 N.W. Thirty-fifth St., Miami, FL 33122. Phone (305) 593-0260 for flights to London.

- IBC, 8401 N.W. Seventeenth St., Miami, FL 33126. Phone: (305) 591-8080. Fly from Miami to Buenos Aires, Argentina; Freeport, Bahamas; Kingston, Jamaica; and Santo Domingo, Dominican Republic.

- International Business Couriers, 103 St. Vincent St., Port of Spain, Trinidad, West Indies. Phone: (809) 623-4231. You can fly from Miami to Port of Spain, Trinidad, and back again.

- Line Haul Services, 7859 N.W. Fifteenth St., Miami, FL 33126. Phone: (305) 477-0651. Routes take you to lots of Latin American destinations: Buenos Aires, Caracas, Guatemala City, Guayaquil, La Paz, Managua, Panama City, Quito, Rio de Janeiro, Sao Paulo, Salvador. On the other side of the Atlantic, flights are to Madrid, Spain.

- Martillo Express, 1520 W. Forty-first St., Hialeah, FL 33012. Phone: (305) 822-0880. Flights are from Miami to Guayaquil and Quito, Ecuador.

- Trans-Air Systems, 7264 N.W. Twenty-fifth St., Miami, FL 33122. Phone: (305) 592-1771. Fly from Miami to Latin America: Guatemala City; Buenos Aires and Mendoza, Argentina; Montevideo, Uruguay; and Quito, Ecuador.

From Miami, try also:

- Discount Travel International offers flights to Latin America, the Caribbean, London, and Madrid. Phone: (305) 583-1616 or (407) 483-8832.

- Now Voyager sends couriers to Latin America and London. Phone: (212) 431-1616.

- IMS Courier Service. Want to play in Jamaica? Phone them at (305) 771-7545.

Flights Originating in Toronto

- F.B. On-Board Courier Service sends Canadians to London, Paris, and Hong Kong. Phone: (416) 675-1820.

Flights Originating Overseas

Courier flights also originate in courier flight destination cities all over the world. For example, having arrived in Singapore from a U.S. or Canadian city, you could arrange to take a courier flight to Manila. From Manila, you could go to Hong

Kong or Bangkok, and then home, having spent several days in each capital and flown at half price or better.

AN INTERVIEW WITH NORA THE COURIER
(One More *You Can Travel Free* Exclusive Interview)

YCTF: How long have you been a courier?

Nora: Only three years, but I've taken eight trips.

YCTF: Where have you gone?

Nora: Australia, New Zealand, Russia, Singapore, Malaysia, Hong Kong, Tokyo, and Scotland.

YCTF: Where do you want to go?

Nora: South America, but that means I have to get to Miami, where most of those flights originate. I live in Illinois, so I have to plan ahead. I think I'll get to Rio and Buenos Aires eventually.

YCTF: What was your most recent trip?

Nora: I just got back from Singapore.

YCTF: Nora, what do you do if you get tired of waiting two or three weeks in Singapore or Glasgow for a return flight?

Nora: I never get bored waiting around. After I've done all the local sight-seeing I want, I arrange another courier flight. For example, when I took a courier trip to Australia, I got another courier flight out of Melbourne and visited Auckland, New Zealand. Then I returned on a courier flight to Australia and then flew back to the U.S. From Singapore, I did a courier flight to Bangkok and back again.

YCTF: Are you a professional full-time courier?

Nora: Heavens, no. I'm a school bus driver. I do courier flights during school vacations. Most couriers are free-lance. Some are paid full-timers, but they tend to do the same route and turn around at the airport to come back. I met a full-timer at O'Hare [Airport] in Chicago. He'd been to Caracas, Venezuela, so many times that he hadn't left the Caracas airport on his last 12 round-trips. He said he was sick of flying back and forth on the same route, but that it was an easy job and that jobs were scarce. He made flying seem really unglamorous.

YCTF: What airlines do you fly on?

Nora: TWA, Delta, American, United. I fly on major airlines on regularly scheduled flights. The downside is that I'm usually boarding late at night.

YCTF: Is it a hard job?

Nora [she laughs]: Gosh, no. There's little physical or mental exhaustion but you sit a lot. It's a lot easier than yelling at kids on a school bus. I pick up a package or envelope at the airport I leave from, and I give it to a representative at the baggage claim area in the airport where I arrive. That's it.

YCTF: Is living out of hand luggage a problem?

Nora: It's not a problem in hot areas where you don't need a lot of clothes; but I needed more and much heavier clothes when I went to Moscow last December. I couldn't pack winter clothes in a suitcase, but I got around it by wearing extra clothes on a flight. I probably looked like I weighed 300 pounds when I wore two sweaters, a wool scarf, and a heavy coat. Oh, and gloves. When I got to my seat, I put the winter clothes in a fold-up bag that I carried aboard in my pocket. I put the coat, sweaters, and scarves back on before I got off in Moscow.

YCTF: Do you need to plan long in advance for courier travel?

Nora: Yeah. I know when my vacations are going to be, so I make arrangements weeks or months in advance for overseas flights. A few times I've had to send my passport weeks in advance to foreign consulates to get visas put in. Otherwise I wouldn't get out of the foreign airport. Even Australia wants a visa.

YCTF: Are there any annoying restrictions during the flight that affect you as a courier?

Nora: Not really. As a courier you're not supposed to drink on the plane. You're not supposed to do anything that could cause you to be held up at passport check or customs at the airport when you arrive. I don't drink and I definitely don't do drugs.

YCTF: What's the biggest annoyance in a courier's life?

Nora: They change schedules or cancel altogether. The customer doesn't have the paperwork ready when you're ready so you get held up a couple of days. You go home and miss part of your vacation. My best advice to your readers is, "expect last minute changes and be flexible."

YCTF: Is there any benefit to courier travel we may not be aware of?

Nora: Yeah. Some companies let you keep your frequent-flyer miles. You'll probably get enough to take more free trips. That's how I took my boyfriend Rolly to Philadelphia.

Like Nora, plan ahead so you won't have to pay full airfare again.

CHAPTER 11

Volunteering to See the World

McCheap's Eleventh Law of Travel:
Giving—not money—but compassion,
help, and encouragement can take you places.

TRAVEL WITH A HELPFUL PURPOSE

Travelers of all ages, with or without job skills, have a stand-ing invitation to volunteer their services for short-term work at home and all over the world. A few recruiters of volunteers are able to offer transportation, room and board, and even stipends. But most unpaid helping positions are in areas of the world that have so little ready cash that they can't offer much of a material nature to helpful visitors. Although you'll find in the pages that follow some positions that require a cash outlay, this chapter singles out those few volunteer commitments that can enable you to help although you have little or no money to finance your stay. This chapter focuses on volunteer opportu-nities that will take you places.

Whether you go totally free or whether you choose a volun-teer program that requires you to raise some of your expenses, what you might accomplish could make your contribution the most important gift you'll give in your lifetime. One or more of these projects could enable you to help eradicate disease, hunger, and desperation. Your project could enable you to enjoy the camaraderie of workcamp volunteers as you aid in the restoration of historic buildings or assist visitors in their safe enjoyment of a wilderness area. Perhaps you'll dig to discover archaeological treasures.

OPENINGS NEARLY EVERYWHERE

What sort of opportunities exist? Right here at home you always have an invitation to dig in and work to help the less fortunate. In well-to-do industrial nations of North America and Europe you're invited to participate in work and conservation projects such as volunteering as a park docent, aiding the homeless, or serving as a camp counselor. Working in the Third World countries of Africa, Asia, and Latin America offers a superb chance to help people secure the necessities of life. Other projects can be fun, such as coaching baseball in Italy. And in a whole other aspect of volunteering, thousands of amateurs who are interested in archaeology and anthropology volunteer to help on digs at a variety of research sites all over.

Some volunteer service agencies recruit people for a long-term commitment. Two years of solving life-threatening problems in Chad, Lesotho, or Bangladesh is hardly a vacation, but it's certainly a practical education. These one- and two-year projects are included here because volunteers are desperately needed and because these programs do offer the chance to travel, even if you have little or no money.

WHY VOLUNTEER?

Your knowledgeable guide is driving you down a secondary road through parched countryside in Morocco, Malagasy, Mali, or Mauritania—or perhaps it's the well-worn road to Mandalay. It matters which country you're in. Of course it matters. But in these places and in similar forlorn areas beginning with your choice of alphabet letter, it's often essentially the same: squalid, bare-bones huts lean by the side of the road with the wind shifting dust or rain through their shameless gaps.

You ask a hopeful question: "These are shepherds' huts, places for people to get out of the sun or rain for a few minutes

during the day while they tend their animals? There's no running water. Nobody lives here full-time, do they?"

"They are the homes of our people," your guide answers.
"Our people are very poor."

They are poor indeed. Their poverty defies your imagination. Coming from the United States, where six percent of the
planet's people consume 40 percent of Earth's resources,
you're incredulous.

"We will stop," the guide tells you. You want to say no. These
houses are impossible for you to accept. Allotment garden
sheds on the periphery of Europe's meanest derelict industrial
cities compare favorably to these sorry abodes.

Like their hovels, the inhabitants seem to be made of sticks.
Their children, your guide says, suffer from diseases endemic
among the malnourished: measles, diphtheria, tetanus, polio,
tuberculosis, and whooping cough. These diseases kill tens of
thousands of children every day in underdeveloped countries.
You know that vaccinations against them cost little. You can't
understand why the children haven't been inoculated.

"Let's go back to the hotel," you hear yourself say. "The heat
here is stifling."

Like all of us, children need clean water, a sanitary environment, adequate and balanced nourishment, medical care, and
love in order to survive. Many exist on love, and too many others on not even that. These stick-limbed children, the progeny
of the stick-limbed people in the stick houses, have measles.
You had measles, a mildly uncomfortable childhood rite-of-pas-
sage, but you recovered quickly. You weren't an emaciated stick
person. According to UNICEF (United Nations Children's
Fund) officials, a malnourished child who contracts measles
has a 400 percent greater chance of dying from it than you did.

"I think I have to meet someone at the hotel—by the pool.
Can we start back now?" you ask, desperate to get out of this
place. Medical services can be brought to much of the underdeveloped world, as can water treatment techniques, better
agricultural methods, lifesaving inoculations, family planning,

irrigation, improved roads, adequate housing, parasite eradication, education, even peace. These necessities can be secured with the help of dedicated individuals who believe Third World people should look like strong structures rather than like bare-bones huts.

Fortunately for those in Third World Countries, and for those with needed energy and skills but no money to travel, charitable organizations are willing to support volunteers while they help the sick and the poor. Strength, love, expertise, and dedication to helping others can get you a trip across town or across the ocean; there's need nearly everywhere. These same qualities can help you save some of the tens of million who will die of disease or starvation every year. Millions of them are innocent children.

Just as it's better to light a candle than to curse the darkness, it's better for the flat-broke, would-be traveler to go out and help others than to feel sorry for being without the means to see the world. Helping others *is* a means of seeing the world.

Before you sign on, examine your motives. Never volunteer because you want to travel free; accept the opportunity of traveling free because you want to volunteer.

Every helping project may not give you the pulsating pleasure of saving lives. Many will require you to improve the environment, to pound nails, or to tell park visitors where to leave their vehicles and what not to feed the bears. Yet, even if you're not saving lives, you're bound to better your own life as a result of your volunteer vacation.

WHAT HAVE YOU TO OFFER?

Special skills or training aren't required for many positions, but if you have essential skills you can often get full support in the communities you want to help. A good water master who can turn the contents of Cholera Creek into potable tap water or a mechanic who can restore a sick generator to life are worth a community's support. Write to organizations in this chapter or to foreign embassies and offer your services in return for expenses. Similarly, health practitioners, agriculture experts, civil engineers, teachers, and others can often negotiate expenses around the world. This chapter is full of such opportunities. When negotiating for your expenses, remember that some communities have so little food that providing some for you will deprive others of proper nourishment. Let charity be your first concern and free travel an eager second.

OPPORTUNITIES WORLDWIDE

If you truly want to volunteer you should be able to find an organization from the list that follows that can use your help. When writing to volunteer organizations sponsored by churches or other nonprofit entities, consider enclosing return postage to help defray their costs. International reply coupons, available at post offices, enable overseas correspondents to reply to your inquiries without incurring costs.

American Volunteers for International Development

National Forum Foundation, 511 C St. NE, Washington, D.C. 20002. This foundation sponsors the AVID (American Volunteers for International Development) program. AVID volunteers are successful professionals with managerial experience in nongovernmental organizations, public administration, economic development, and journalism. They're needed primarily to work in the developing countries of Eastern Europe. Recent AVID volunteers have served in places such as Bratislava, Bucharest, Budapest, Kiev, Krakow, Lowicz, Moscow, Minsk, Nizhny Novgorod, Prague, Sofia, St. Petersburg, Tallinn, Vilnius, Warsaw, and Yekaterinburg.

AVID asks its volunteers for three months of their time and expects them to have some skills in the language of the host country to enable them to work smoothly with professionals there. AVID advisors aid in nonprofit management and development, budgeting and finance, development of local government, political communication, law, and legislative processes. They advise in areas such as business management, media management, economic development, and media production—including journalism, advertising, and public relations. AVID provides travel and basic living expenses to selected mentors. Here's an opportunity to live in Poland, Hungary, Russia, or another East European nation and have your expenses paid while helping change a fascinating part of the world for the better.

Brethren Volunteer Service

BVS places teachers in Poland, China, and a dozen other countries for two-year periods. It also has a program to help people in the United States. BVS looks for those rare individuals who can and are willing to assist in health care, child care, crisis intervention, peacekeeping, saving the environment, and other essential tasks. It provides room and board, insurance, and a stipend. Get further information from Brethren Volunteer Service, 1451 Dundee Ave., Elgin, IL 60120. Phone: (800) 323-8039 or (708) 742-5100. Fax: (708) 742-6103.

Catholic Medical Mission Board

Contact Catholic Medical Mission Board, 10 W. Seventeenth St., New York, NY 10011-5765. Phone: (212) 242-7757. If you're a health professional, you can provide medical assistance to needy people in Africa, Asia, Latin America, the Caribbean, and Eastern Europe. Short-term projects, for which board and room are offered, are in Guatemala, Guyana, Haiti, Kenya, and the Caribbean isle of St. Lucia.

This nonprofit organization treats victims of poverty regardless of creed or race. A surgeon, working with CMMB, writes from Cameroon: "The traditional culture, as reflected in the daily lives of the people, has the depth and richness of centuries. Everywhere we look in this culture we find overwhelming needs, but it takes so little from us to offer so much. This enhances our feeling of contribution. In return, we gain so much from these people who are culturally and spiritually alive."

CIEE International Voluntary Projects

You can find out all about current projects from CIEE International Workcamps, International Voluntary Projects (IVP), CIEE, 205 E. Forty-second St., New York, NY 10017. Phone: (888) COUNCIL or (212) 661-1414. E-mail: info@ciee.org. Website: www.ciee.org. This opportunity isn't entirely free, because participants must pay their own airfare and pay a registration fee, but room and board are provided by local communities that benefit from the services of volunteers.

Within the phrase *room and board,* the term *room* shouldn't be taken too literally. According to CIEE, "You'll live together as a group in a school, church, hostel, or tent, sleeping on cots or floor mats." The Ritz Hotel it's not, but volunteers earn the supreme satisfaction of having done a good deed, having lived among 10 to 20 volunteers from different countries, having had fun organizing their own group activities, and getting a firsthand education about another culture. Some colleges offer academic credit for participating.

CIEE volunteers, mostly in their early twenties, mostly students, work two to four weeks. Some projects won't accept people beyond their twenties, but Spain accepts volunteers as old as 30, and Turkey and Tunisia as old as 35.

Projects are generally scheduled for July, August, or September, but in India, fortunately, projects are scheduled in the more moderate and drier winter months. Programs are offered in Belgium, Canada, the Czech Republic, Denmark, Finland, France, Germany, Ghana, Greece, India, Italy, Japan, several countries among the Latin American nations, Lithuania, Morocco, the Netherlands, Poland, Russia, Slovakia, Spain, Tunisia, Turkey, Ukraine, United Kingdom, and in the United States. In the United States and Canada, airfare may not be a factor for you, depending on where the project is located; your travel costs could be minimal.

Volunteers work in nature conservation, construction, and archaeology. They work with children, and with the elderly. For example, you might help excavate ancient Roman ruins in the

Mediterranean basin, build playgrounds in Eastern Europe, plant grass to arrest soil erosion in Africa, or care for children in the United Kingdom.

A U.C.-Davis student wrote from France that she had worked with 10 volunteers (from the United States, Poland, France, Germany, Japan, Spain, and Canada) to restore a 10th-century castle. In her spare time she learned to play petanque, frequented pubs, visited other workcamps, attended festivals, shopped at flea markets, and learned outrageous phrases in the languages of the other participants. The writer felt that three weeks was just right. "I remember dreading the third week," she recalled, "hoping it wouldn't go by as quickly as the first two weeks had." Call or write CIEE for an application. There are moderate fees for these programs.

Citizens Democracy Corps

Citizens Democracy Corps needs experts to go to foreign nations to teach modern business methods. Managers in the emerging countries of Eastern Europe require a lot of training; they're getting the hang of capitalism, and American experts can help them make it work well. CDC pays for lodging and all economy-class travel, but volunteers pick up the bill for their own food. If you're a retired executive, here's your big chance to help. If you're still working, tell the boss that loaning you to CDC for a few weeks would be a great goodwill gesture for the company; all your employer has to pay is your regular salary and for your food while you're helping. Contact Citizens Democracy Corps, 1400 I St. NW, Suite 1125, Washington, D.C. 20005. Phone: (800) 394-1945. Fax: (202) 872-0923.

Coaching Baseball in Italy

Although soccer claims the attention of the vast majority of Italians, more than 200,000 residents of that nation play baseball. A legacy of America's military occupation during World War II, baseball is becoming increasingly popular. There's an opportunity for Americans to coach baseball in Italy as volunteers. If you're any good at all, you should be able to get players' families to give you room and board for the season. Contact Italian Federation of Baseball and Softball, Attn.: Segreteria Generale, Vial Tiziano No. 70, 00196 Roma, Italy. Phone: (011) 3906-36858376.

And if Americans can coach baseball in Italy, they can coach other sports anywhere sports are played. Write to the tourist bureaus of countries that interest you—see chapter 17, "A Wealth of Free Information," for addresses and phone numbers of sports and athletic associations.

Edinburgh Cyrenians

Edinburgh is indeed a lovely Scottish city, but not for the homeless. Winters can be amazingly cold and so can spring and fall. Would you like to work there helping homeless young men? Volunteers live in either the charity's city project or the farm project alongside the residents who have been saved from life in the streets. Placements of volunteers aged 18 to 30 are for six months. Contact the Project Manager, Edinburgh Cyrenians, 107A Ferry Rd., Edinburgh EH6 4ET, Scotland, U.K. Phone/fax: (011) 44-1-31-5553707.

Global Service Corps

Global Service Corps sends volunteers to work on projects in Kenya, Costa Rica, Guatemala, and Thailand. If you'd like to make a difference, call (415) 788-3666, ext. 128.

Global Volunteers

Global Volunteers, 376 E. Little Canada Rd., St. Paul, MN 55117. Phone: (800) 487-1074. This private alternative to the U.S. government-operated Peace Corps will send a catalog of short-term programs in the Unites States and abroad. No special experience or skills are required. Some volunteers teach English in Spain, southern Italy, and Greece. Many jobs consist of building homes, clearing roads in forests, etc. New programs are in Vietnam. This is not free, but the cut-rate expenses are tax deductible.

Habitat for Humanity

Habitat for Humanity International, 121 Habitat St., Americus, GA 31709. Phone: (800) HABITAT or (912) 924-6935. E-mail: meli_remeny@habitat.org. Most of us have seen Jimmy and Rosalynn Carter on our television screens pounding nails for Habitat. The former first couple are Global Village workers. Global Village workers build homes with nationals in Latin America, Asia, and Africa. This is also a good opportunity to learn construction skills while providing a home for a family who otherwise wouldn't have one.

Short-term Global Mission Trips, two to four weeks, take volunteers to build dwellings in Bolivia, Brazil, Central African Republic, England, Fiji, Ghana, Guatemala, Honduras, Hungary, India, Nicaragua, Papua New Guinea, Philippines, Poland, and Sri Lanka. Ask about your options for choosing a "Bike and Build" volunteer vacation. Ask for their free publication, *Habitat Global Adventure*. Volunteers usually pay for their own transportation and food but often receive free sleeping space.

Health Volunteers Overseas

Health Volunteers Overseas, c/o Washington Station, Box 65157, Washington, D.C. 20035. Phone: (202) 296-0928. Fax: (202) 296-8018. E-mail: hvo@aol.com. HVO is a private voluntary organization whose membership is comprised of physicians, physical therapists, dentists, nurses, and various other health professionals. Members pay dues and when possible volunteer to train indigenous health personnel.

Animated by the fact that more than half the world's population has no access to health care, these volunteers try to make a difference. While housing is usually provided, pay is seldom offered for short-term assignments. Thus working with Health Volunteers isn't so much a matter at all of traveling free, but of doing something even more important: saving and improving lives.

It's unlikely physicians need to read *You Can Travel Free* in order to take a trip, but it is likely they have the expertise and time to donate two to four weeks as anesthesiologists, internists, surgeons, orthopedists, and pediatricians. There's also a major need for dentists, physical therapists, and nurses.

Opportunities at the time of this writing exist in Guyana, India, St. Lucia, Tanzania, Uganda, Vietnam, Brazil, Mexico, Philippines, Bhutan, Ethiopia, Indonesia, Malawi, Peru, South Africa, and Jamaica. What a great opportunity to visit one or more of these countries and leave that country a better place.

Heimsonderschule

Work with mentally handicapped children in Germany. This is a superb chance to hone your German language skills and to gain experience in residential care. Volunteers receive food, accommodations, and pocket money. Contact the Heimsonderschule Brachenreuthe, 88662 Uberlingen, Germany. Phone: (011) 49-07551/8007-0.

Institute for International Cooperation & Development

Institute for International Cooperation and Development, P.O. Box 103, Williamstown, MA 01267. Phone: (413) 458-9828. Volunteers pay to travel overseas to help communities in Africa and Latin America. They teach and help build community facilities. They plant trees in Angola in order to arrest soil erosion.

To raise money for airfare, would-be participants stand on street corners in U.S. cities and "postcard" passersby. They carry open binders and show potential donors postcards and maps of their voluntary destinations. They explain that the organization is nonprofit and must be funded by volunteers. One sidewalk solicitor averaged more than $200 a day in a recent year and was able to finance her trip entirely through contributions.

International Executive Service Corps

International Executive Service Corps, 8 Stamford Forum, P.O. Box 10005, Stamford, CT 06904. Phone: (800) 243-4372 or 203-967-6000. IESC pays travel expenses and a per diem allowance but no salary to retired executive and technical volunteers in less-developed countries. Several hundred retirees are sent out on projects that last two or three months. They often take their spouses. Many of the projects are in the Caribbean and Latin America. Volunteers may advise manufacturers, help business people develop privatized companies in former Communist nations, organize curricula for schools, set up or reorganize food processing plants, advise bankers, etc. One spouse of a volunteer executive assisted in an orphanage in Sri Lanka, wrapped bandages in Panama, worked in a museum in Guatemala, and taught language skills in Honduras—all on a voluntary basis. Another helped set up an alligator farm.

International Network for University Volunteers

International Network for University Volunteers, c/o CIEE, Attn.: INFUV, 201 E. Forty-second St., New York, NY 10164. This program helps send retired North American academics to teach in Third World countries.

Kibbutzim

Many readers will already know a little about kibbutzim. They may know that a kibbutz is an Israeli settlement, urban or agricultural, in which the residents own in common the settlement and means of production. Residents share in the profits. If that concept sounds attractive, you may want to live and work temporarily at one or more of Israel's 270 kibbutzim. You'll need to pay your own way to Israel. Couples are accepted. A kibbutz volunteer can expect room and board and some pocket money. In addition, many kibbutzim organize sight-seeing for volunteers once a month or so.

Start by contacting Kibbutz Program Center, 110 E. Fifty-ninth St., 4th Floor, New York, NY 10022. Phone: (800) 247-7852. Fax:

(213) 318-6134. E-mail: ProjOren@aol.com. If you go to Israel before arranging a kibbutz stay, contact Kibbutz Program Center, Volunteers, 18 Frishman St., Box 3167, Tel Aviv 61030. They're closed Fridays and Saturdays and during religious holidays. Many returned volunteers recall having had a good experience and an active social life with other volunteers.

Learning through Service

Students and recent college graduates are invited to volunteer at one of 45 sites for a summer, semester, full school year, or longer. Stipends are available for some volunteers who aren't working for college credit. Contact Program Coordinator, Association of Episcopal Colleges, 815 Second Ave., Suite 315, New York, NY 10017-4594. Phone: (212) 986-0989. Fax: (212) 986-5039.

Loch Arthur Community

Here's a major chance to get to know and to help some of the friendliest people in Europe, the Scots. Contact the Loch Arthur Community, Stable Cottage, Loch Arthur, Beeswing, Dumfries DG2 8JQ, Scotland, U.K. Phone: 0387-76687. Work with handicapped adults and in gardens and workshops. Room, board, and pocket money are provided.

> $$$—Cousin Thrifty McCheap says: "You don't have to pay money out of your own pocket to volunteer, particularly if you don't have any. Get some of the philantropic folks and businesses in your community to pay your expenses. Start a fund-raising drive and tell people that you want to fly across the world to help the handicapped or the ill. Tell them you're going to get capitalism off the ground or cure measles in some sorry place. They'll feel mildly guilty about not joining you. They'll admire you and you'll be surprised at how much money starts rolling in. You'll probably have enough to go."

Malta Youth Hostels Association

Get in touch with Malta Youth Hostels Association, 17 Triq Tal-Borg, Pawla, PLA 06 Malta. Phone: (356) 239361. In Malta one finds the history of the Mediterranean: Stone-age cultures, Phoenicians, Carthaginians, Greeks, Romans, and the stalwart Knights of Malta. Later came Napoleon. Hitler tried to take Malta but the brave people held on.

Volunteers work three hours a day, seven days a week, and earn free accommodations with breakfast. You must be at least 16 and apply at least three months in advance. Work assignments (and accommodations) begin on the first and fifteenth of each month. Malta's a small island; in your free time you'll have time to see just about everything you came to see.

Mennonite Central Committee

Mennonite Central Committee, 21 S. Twelfth St., P.O. Box 500, Akron, PA 17501-0500. Fax: (717) 859-2171. This admirable charity seeks "active Christian church members committed to a lifestyle of nonviolence and peacemaking." They recruit skilled volunteers worldwide; it's an excellent chance for a professional to travel for free, do a lot of good, and see a developing corner of the world.

The Mennonites offer "round-trip transportation, full maintenance while in service, including room and board and a small monthly allowance." Recently they were looking for a person with administrative and business skills and experience to generate jobs for unemployed men and women in Kenya; a preschool teacher with a bachelor's degree for Swaziland; a clinical nurse-tutor for Zambia; and a librarian for Lesotho. During the same month they called for volunteers to go to Chad, Botswana, Sudan, Burkino Faso, Brazil, Bolivia, Honduras, and Guatemala.

Mother Theresa's Children's Home

Few people have been more admired than Mother Theresa, the self-sacrificing nun who dedicated herself to caring for the ill and destitute in Calcutta's teeming slums. Although the saintly caregiver has gone, volunteers are still needed to carry on her vital work. Because of the life-threatening poverty that surrounds Mother Theresa's hospitals, you can't expect remuneration, much less a place to stay. Still interested? Contact Missionaries of Charity, 54A Bose Rd., Calcutta 16, India. Their London office is at 177 Bravington Rd., London W9. Phone: (01) 81-960-2644.

National Civilian Community Corps

NCCC stands for the National Civilian Community Corps. For further information, contact AmeriCorps NCCC, 9th Floor, 1201 New York Ave. NW, Washington, D.C. 20525. Phone: (800) 942-2677. Website: http://www.cns.gov.

NCCC provides men and women between 18 and 24 an opportunity to help others and in so doing to help themselves. A major fringe benefit of joining up is the chance to get away from home and do some traveling within the United States. Applicants are asked to relocate to one of the five AmeriCorps NCCC campuses. These facilities are in Washington, D.C.; Charleston, South Carolina; Aurora, Colorado; San Diego, California; and Perry Point, Maryland.

Volunteers perform environmental work such as improving urban and rural parks. Other volunteers conduct environmental education programs in schools and community centers. Others might help renovate public housing or work with children who are in danger of slipping into delinquency. In Montana members helped develop a community radio station, and in Oregon Corps members provide English language training to immigrants. In Wyoming, AmeriCorps NCCC workers counsel young people about anger management, substance abuse, and life skills. In Hawaii, members help domestic violence victims obtain restraining orders.

If any of these projects sounds challenging and useful, consider volunteering for 10 months. In return, you'll be provided a "modest" living allowance, room and board, and a substantial award to be applied to your own education at the end of your service.

Peace Corps

Peace Corps, Room 8506, 1990 K St. NW, Washington, D.C. 20064. Phone: (800) 424-8580. E-mail: http//www.peacecorps.gov. The Peace Corps invites Americans to "make a world of difference" by helping people in nations with emerging economies. Established in 1961 by Pres. John F. Kennedy, the Corps claims 140,000 alumni.

Today 6,500 volunteers serve in 90 countries in Africa, the Middle East, Asia, the Pacific, Latin America, and Eastern Europe, including Russia. There's no upper age limit, but you must be at least 18. Volunteers are needed in education, business, skilled trades (mechanics, electricians, plumbers, refrigeration specialists, etc.), agriculture, the environment, and health.

The commitment is for 27 months. Apply nine to 12 months before you want to go. Not only is the Peace Corps an established and successful organization whose volunteers make a big difference, but these eager individuals travel free.

Among the benefits are round-trip transportation; a stipend for food, clothing, and incidentals; health care; and a substantial sum when they leave after two and a quarter years. In addition, alumni earn preference when applying for federal government jobs, career counseling, and a monthly list of job opportunities. More than 50 colleges and universities offer scholarships and assistantships for former volunteers under their Peace Corps Fellows Program. Some will give college credits to Corps vets.

If you want to explore this option, read *The Peace Corps and More: 120 Ways to Work, Study, and Travel in the Third World* by Medea Benjamin. It's published by Seven Locks Press and distributed by Global Exchange, 2017 Mission St., Room 303, San Francisco, CA 94110. Phone: (415) 255-7296.

Another opportunity to learn more about the Peace Corps is to access PCORPS-L, SUB Internet site: listserv@cmuvm.csv.

cmich.edu. This is a discussion group composed of former and potential Peace Corps volunteers.

Queen Elizabeth's Foundation for the Disabled

Stay just outside of London and do some good. Contact Queen Elizabeth's Foundation for the Disabled, Volunteer Organizer, Lulworth Ct. 25, Chalkwell Esplanade, Westcliff on Sea, Essex SSO 8JO, U.K. Work with severely disabled in a home 40 minutes from the metropolis. No experience is necessary. The charity provides board, accommodations, and a stipend. And there's always the chance the crowned lady from the palace will pop by to thank you.

The Simon Community

Write or phone The Simon Community, Box 1187, London NW5 4HW, U.K. Phone: (071) 485-6639. Here's an opportunity to help the homeless in a shelter in London. Board, accommodations, and allowance are provided.

VOCA/ACDI

VOCA/ACDI stands for Volunteers in Overseas Cooperative Development and Agricultural Cooperative Development International. This newly merged organization sends experts to exotic locales to offer advice and assistance to executives and farmers who are trying to improve their operations. For example, an American farmer might help farmers in Africa, and an executive might offer advice in Russia. VOCA pays all expenses. Contact VOCA/ACDI, 50 'F' St. NW, Suite 1100, Washington, D.C. 20001. Phone: (202) 638-4661. Fax: (202) 626-8726. E-mail: oalmog@acdi.org.

Volunteer Exchange International

Volunteer Exchange International offers opportunities for people ages 18-30 in 30 countries. There's no language requirement. Volunteers live with host families. E-mail this organization at leids@cyeus.igc.apc.org.

Volunteers for Peace, Inc.

Volunteers for Peace, Inc., International Workcamps, 43 Tiffany Rd., Belmont, VT 05730. Phone: (802) 259-2759. Fax: (802) 259-2922. E-mail: vfp@vfp.org. Website: http://www.vfp.org. Volunteers can provide an international workcamp directory that includes 800 listings in 50 countries; contact them for the current cost of the directory.

Volunteers for Peace isn't really free. Projects have a program fee, but that fee helps cover your room and board. They place 30 or more volunteers a year, and a quarter of them sign up for multiple workcamp experiences in one or more countries.

Even when you have to pay the program fee, you can live and work in a foreign country during the two- to three-week program inexpensively. If you choose to serve, you'll probably go abroad during the summer, when 95 percent of the camps are open. You'll probably arrive at the host camp with 10 to 20 people from four or more countries. Because workcamps are sponsored by an organization in the host nation, not solely by Volunteers for Peace, you can expect an eclectic collection of nationalities in the camps.

One of the first things you may notice is that the average age of volunteers is 21 to 25. Housing is in a school, church, private home, or community center. Workers coordinate food preparation and clean-up duties in the living areas. Work includes construction, restoration, environmental conservation, agriculture, archeological excavation, and maintenance.

The number of workcamps around the world is indeed impressive. They are nearly everywhere from Armenia to Zimbabwe. Thirty exist in the Netherlands, 60 in Italy, 20 in Ghana, 6 in Greece, and so on. Probably the best news is that "placements are made usually within 72 hours of receipt of your registration form," so you don't have to wait around until May 31 to find that you're going to the Philippines on June 4, when you've already packed clothing for Lappland.

When she returned home, participant Jennifer Lubkin

summed up her experience by saying: "The atmosphere and camaraderie we created gives me hope that one day we will all speak the same language, that of peace. . . . I feel warmed for I now have friends around the world."

Volunteers in Technical Assistance

Volunteers in Technical Assistance, 1600 Wilson Blvd., Suite 500, Arlington, VA 22209. Phone: (703)-276-1800. E-mail: QUERY@VITA.ORG. VITA, which is four decades old, looks for experts in small business development, agriculture, water and sanitation, housing, project planning, and other useful areas of knowledge. VITA's 5,000 volunteers, who live in 114 countries, usually provide support by correspondence; they'll write, fax, e-mail, or phone to help locals in developing countries solve technical problems.

Most of VITA's activities consist of giving long-distance advice, but when a volunteer needs to go abroad to render assistance on a *field consultancy,* he or she gets reimbursed for travel expenses. Depending on the complexity of the project, field consultancies can last a few days, several weeks, or even months or years. If you're a skilled professional, consider lending a hand.

Willing Workers on Organic Farms

Willing Workers on Organic Farms volunteer to help farmers overseas in return for room and board. WWOOFers might harvest bananas for Australian growers in Northern Queensland, plant and fertilize fruit trees in New South Wales, weed in New Zealand or Switzerland, or plant crops in Ireland. These willing workers stay a few days or as long as several weeks.

Write to WWOOF Australia, Lionel Pollard, Mount Murrindal Reserve, Buchan, Victoria 3885 for a worldwide WWOOFer directory. Write to The European Centre for Ecological Agriculture and Tourism, P.O. Box 10899, 1001 EW Amsterdam, Netherlands for WWOOF-like lists of opportunities in the Netherlands, Poland, the Czech Republic, Hungary, Slovakia, the Baltic States, and Portugal.

Winged Fellowship Volunteer Program

Winged Fellowship Volunteer Program provides an opportunity to do some good, extend your stay in Britain, and make some British friends. You can assist in providing care and companionship to severely physically disabled adults. Board and lodging are provided. Commitments are from one to two weeks. Contact Volunteer Bookings, Winged Fellowship Trust, Angel House, 20-32 Pentonville Rd., London N1 9XD, U.K.

Worldwide Internship & Service Education

WISE, which "rejects no genuine offer of service," stands for Worldwide Internship & Service Education. WISE provides opportunities to volunteer through the Community Service Volunteer Program in the United Kingdom. Volunteers work with the elderly, young offenders, homeless people, those with learning difficulties, or folks who have physical disabilities or who are mentally ill. Volunteers work in group homes, day centers, playgrounds, youth clubs, hospitals, and schools. It's really a chance to improve the lives of people who need your help. Applicants, ages 18 to 34, pay a stiff fee and must travel to either Spokane or Pittsburgh for an interview. In addition to the fee, volunteers pay for their airfare to the U.K. Once you've gotten past the fees and travel costs, the program provides an opportunity to live in the U.K. with only little personal expense. WISE provides transportation costs from the port of entry in the U.K. to the project site; accommodations with some utilities, food, or a food allowance; and pocket money for the duration of service. Service is for four to 12 months, with a week's vacation accruing for every four months of service. Contact WISE, 303 S. Craig St., Suite 202, Pittsburgh, PA 15213. Phone: (412) 681-8120. E-mail: wise+@pitt.edu.

WorldTeach

WorldTeach, c/o H11D, One Eliot St., Cambridge, MA 02138. Phone: (617) 495-5527. Billing itself as "an alternative to the Peace Corps for nonprofessionals who want to live and work overseas," WorldTeach asks volunteers to commit themselves for 10 to 12 months of teaching. If you need a shorter commitment, look into their six-month Nature Guide Training Program in Mexico and the eight-week Shanghai Summer Teaching Program.

Working in groups of five to 75 individuals, volunteers in the 10-month and year-long programs teach English in Costa Rica, Lithuania, Namibia, Ecuador, South Africa, Poland, Thailand, Russia, and China. Host schools provide housing, meals, and a small stipend. WorldTeach looks for college graduates who are flexible, interested in international development and education, and willing to help others. The teacher comes away with valuable experience and perhaps shining recommendations. There's a fee for processing, but it covers airfare, a four-week orientation, and insurance. WorldTeach has a fundraising guide written by past volunteers so you can raise the processing fee yourself. It's also possible that student loans can be deferred while you teach.

World Vision, Inc.

World Vision Inc., P.O. Box 9716, Federal Way, WA 98063-9716. Fax: (206) 815-3245. This international Christian relief and development agency looks for "qualified, self-sufficient personnel" to help improve the world. For example, not long ago World Vision needed an agricultural expert to travel to remote areas of Somalia to provide technical assistance to subsistence farmers to help them improve crop production. Conditions, World Vision warned, "are sometimes arduous."

If Somalia is too tame for you, they also required a project coordinator in Burundi; this coordinator must be a person who "demonstrates willingness to live and work in *war zone* conditions." This resourceful hero or heroine was given the essential task of coordinating relief and rehabilitation for unaccompanied children and "children in especially difficult circumstances." The admirable person they selected for this monumental task had an opportunity to save or improve lives far beyond that of most other volunteers.

In return for transportation, housing, insurance, and a stipend, volunteers are asked to tackle colossal projects that benefit enormous numbers of the world's more unfortunate victims. Other World Vision projects are in Mongolia, Mozambique, Liberia, Angola, Niger, and Cambodia.

FRESH AIR AND SQUIRRELS: HELPING IN THE GREAT OUTDOORS

Imagine sitting in front of a cabin on a mountain ridge while watching the blazing ball in the sky sink and atrophy into a faintly glowing vermilion cinder just off the western ridge. Your muscles ache from cutting back brush and extending hiking trails, but it's a good feeling because you know you're making the wilderness user-friendly. You love the outdoors. You love to help. You're a volunteer who is improving land to which the public has access.

Here are some possibilities to do just that sort of thing.

Alaska State Parks

Some of Alaska's 115 state parks have been looking for volunteer summertime trail crew members, ranger assistants, natural history interpreters, campground hosts, and others for related positions. A food allowance is provided for many of these jobs, housing and transportation for some. Let's look at specific opportunities:

Various project sites throughout the largest state need archaeological assistants to work with experts of the State Historic Preservation Office and the Archaeological Survey. These volunteers assist in excavation, mapping, photography, cataloging artifacts, and similar activities. Volunteers should have some course work in anthropology or archaeology. They need camping and hiking skills and some scientific experience. Food and housing are available for most projects as is transportation from Anchorage.

The Kenai Area State Parks recently called for aides to develop and present interpretive programs to tourists. These programs might include slides and/or videos. Volunteers need good public-speaking skills and an interest in natural history. Participants get housing. An expense allowance is "available."

If you enjoy remote areas such as Wood-Tikchik State Park, which is known for sport fishing, you might enjoy being a park researcher. The area is, according to the Alaska Department of Natural Resources, "characterized by spire-like granite peaks, spruce and deciduous upland forests, and hundreds of crystal clear lakes." Roaming the area are brown and black bear, moose, caribou; and the waters are home to huge numbers of sockeye salmon. Volunteers get "varied" living accommodations and food. There are normally lots of positions available. Ask for a *position openings* catalog from Volunteer Coordinator, 3601 "C" St., Suite 1200, Anchorage, AK 99503-5921. Phone: (907) 269-8708. E-mail: aathryn@dnr.state.ak.us.

American Hiking Society

American Hiking Society, P.O. Box 20160, Washington, D.C. 20041-2160. Phone: (301) 565-6704. Fax: (301) 565-6714. E-mail: AMHIKER@aol.com.

Here's an invitation to help maintain hiking trails such as the Natchez Trace, Pacific Crest, or Appalachian National Scenic Trail. Ask for the cost of their booklet, "Helping Out in the Outdoors." It's a directory of internships and volunteer jobs in state and national parks and forests and other lands open to the public. Opportunities are waiting in all 50 states. Funds are occasionally available to reimburse volunteers for expenses and to provide food. Sometimes housing is available.

Blueridge Parkway, North Carolina

Few places are prettier. Contact Blueridge Parkway, Department of the Interior, National Park Service, One Pack Square, 400 BB&T Bldg., Asheville, NC 28801. Phone: (704) 298-0398. Some unpaid helpers work in visitor centers. They demonstrate old-time crafts and musical instruments or assist in clerical work. Others work outside all day to maintain trails. Volunteers get to hook up their own travel trailers on park land at no cost, and if money's available they may be reimbursed for some lunches and commuter travel.

Chantiers de Travail Volontaire

Chantiers de Travail Volontaire consists of a number of volunteer projects in France to restore and maintain historic sites. Other projects safeguard the environment and improve rural areas. The average stay of a volunteer is a week, but some stretch their restoration work out to three or four.

Depending on the *chantier* (project), the minimum age is either 13, 16, or 18. Teenagers work only 20 to 30 hours a week, and adults as many as 35. For this work volunteers are provided lodging, meals, and special insurance. It's a great chance to extend your stay in France.

Contact French Cultural Services, c/o French Embassy, 972 Fifth Ave., New York, NY 10021-0144. Phone: (212) 439-1400. In France contact Centre d'Information et de Documentation Jeunesse (CIDJ), 101, quai Branly, 75740 Paris Cedex 15, France. Phone: (45) 67.35.85.

Colorado Trails Foundation

Colorado Trail Foundation, Trail Crew Program, P.O. Box 260876, Lakewood, CO 80226-0876. Volunteers perform sometimes physically challenging work to improve trails in the Colorado wilderness. In a recent summer, for example, a crew, working at 6,500 feet above sea level, waded across the South Platte River to construct a trail along the west bank and to construct bridge pylons to span the river. Some projects are accessible by car, some by jeep, and others are designated as "backpack" destinations—they are inaccessible by motor vehicle.

After paying a small registration fee, unpaid helpers turn up for the project at the beginning of the weekend. They're provided food and a camping site for the week. Wednesdays and several hours on Sundays are set aside for hiking, fishing, and enjoying the surroundings. Write for information.

Potomac Appalachian Trail Club

Potomac Appalachian Trail Club, 118 Park St. SE, Vienna, VA 22180. Phone: (703) 242-0693. Fax: (703) 242-0968. E-mail: patc@erols.com. Website: http://datasys.swri.edu.PATC/patc. html. This organization, which maintains sections of the Appalachian Trail, calls for volunteers for a variety of jobs. Those who help maintain a thousand miles of trails and cabins in Virginia, West Virginia, Pennsylvania, Maryland, and the District of Columbia enjoy camping privileges, "free grub," and crew shirts. Contact the club.

Student Conservation Association

The SCA recruits people age 18 and older for their Resource Assistant Program. Complete details can be had from the Student Conservation Association, P.O. Box 550, Charlestown, NH 03603. Phone: (603) 826-4301. E-mail: ra-program@sca-inc.org.

For 40 hours of work and a 12-week commitment, the SCA offers funds for travel to and from the site, free housing, a subsistence allowance to help offset food expenses, and a uniform allowance in some cases. Thus, a volunteer can have a potentially very happy experience at no cost to him- or herself.

Workers assist professionals in the National Park Service, U.S. Forest Service, Bureau of Land Management, U.S. Fish and Wildlife Service, the U.S. Geological Survey, the U.S. Navy and U.S. Army Natural Resource Program, as well as some state and local agencies and private organizations. Opportunities to serve abound at national monuments, wildlife refuges, national parks, research centers, recreation areas, national forests, historic sites, and nature conservancies. You can work at a number of sites, including the Grand Canyon, Mammoth Caves in Kentucky, or close to downtown San Francisco.

Let's examine two opportunities that are appealing examples of the full range of programs. Volunteers near Flagstaff,

Arizona, work among the 2,700 prehistoric Indian sites at Wupatki. These include Sunset Crater Volcano and Walnut Canyon, which has more than 300 such archaeological sites. Duties include staffing the visitor center, running trailhead contact stations, leading guided walks and hikes, preparing and presenting evening campfire talks, and assisting rangers in various projects. Applicants need an interest in Southwest Native American cultures. Sustaining interest is the easy part: Once exposed to the fantastic stone ruins that dot northern Arizona, it would be a truly apathetic person who would remain uninterested.

The second example is at the Haleakala National Park on Maui, Hawaii. The park reaches up from sea level to more than 10,000 feet and includes a rainforest in which live a number of endangered species. Volunteers assist with research whose purpose is to help endangered species survive and multiply. A helper might, for example, monitor endangered birds such as the Hawaiian dark-rumped petrel and Hawaiian goose. Applicants should have three years or more course work in wildlife, biology, zoology, or a related field. College graduates with degrees in those fields are particularly desired.

Traveler's Earth Repair Network

The Traveler's Earth Repair Network (TERN) gives temporary residents an opportunity to work in reforestation, sustainable agriculture, permaculture, and other ecology projects. Let's say you're going to Central America and want to make a contribution to agricultural production. For a registration fee, TERN provides you with names of hosts in the countries you'll visit; they are some of more than 250 hosts worldwide who are involved in this vital work. You contact the hosts and make arrangements for your stay. TERN advises that *most* hosts will provide food and lodgings. That may not always be a realistic assessment. The stark reality is that some are penniless and must charge for food or else see their own families go without.

What recent programs have TERN members contributed to?

Among them are tree planting in Ghana, reforestation in Uganda, the Women's Vegetable Project in Sierra Leone, tree planting at a beach camping area in Australia, cultivation of medicinal herbs in India, sustainable agriculture in Nepal, community education in Ecuador, and permaculture in Britain. This programs seems to combine the best of volunteerism with hospitality networking. Get more information from Friends of the Trees Society, P.O. Box 4469, Bellingham, WA 98227. Phone: (360) 738-4972. Check it out at http://www.pacificrim.net/-trees/tern/terno95.html.

U.S. Forest Service—Cordova, Alaska Ranger District

Cordova Ranger District maintains remote camping and day-use sites near the Gulf of Alaska. If you'd be interested in maintaining recreation cabins or 40 miles of trails, you could have a great summer in this campground with no running water, electricity, or telephones. Brown and black bears are among the 8,000 visitors each year. In return for your five-day workweek, you receive a place to stay, all necessary equipment and personal gear, and a stipend or food. If the volunteer works 60 days, the Forest Service will reimburse airfare from Seattle. Apply to Cordova Ranger District, P.O. Box 280, Cordova, AK 99574. Phone: (907) 424-7661. What about the bears? According to the Forest Service, they "have not been a major problem."

Volunteers in Parks

Many of the 374 "units" in the national park system in the United States require volunteers to answer visitors' questions, present living history demonstrations, serve as campground hosts, maintain trails, and so forth. You and your supervisor arrive at a schedule that's mutually convenient for you and for the park's administration.

As a VIP (Volunteer in Parks), you're eligible for reimbursement for local travel costs, meals, and uniforms, but, according to the Interior Department, "not all parks have the funds to defray these costs." In-park housing is rarely provided, but you should negotiate for free camping privileges. You may apply to the park at which you want to volunteer. A list of all parks, including addresses and phone numbers, is available from the National Park Service, U.S. Department of the Interior, Volunteers in Parks, Washington, D.C. 20240.

> $$$—Cousin Thrifty McCheap says: "I volunteered to tell Congress how to save money, but they didn't want to hear it."

SOURCES OF MORE INFORMATION

- On the Internet, look for Archaeological Fieldwork Opportunities. They are looking for paid and unpaid workers. Look at http://durendal.cit.cornel.edu.
- Church World Service will send you a free catalog of videos on hunger and multiculturalism in developing nations. The videos are also free; you pay only for return shipping. Church World Service Film and Video Library, P.O. Box 968, Elkhart, IN 46515. Phone: (219) 264-3102. Fax: (219) 262-0966. E-mail: cws.film.library.parti@ecunet.org.
- *Communities Directory: A Guide to Cooperative Living* includes a listing of more than 500 cooperative communities; they were at one time known as *communes*. Some of these accept temporary visitors who are willing to exchange work for room and board. This book can be purchased from Communities, 138 Twin Oaks Rd., Ouisa, VA 23093. Write for the current price.
- Cool Works is an outstanding Internet site. It's full of volunteer opportunities. Look for it at http://www.coolworks.com/showme.
- *Golden Opportunities: A Volunteer Guide for Americans Over 50,* by Andrew Carroll, is published by Peterson's Guides, P.O. Box 2123, Princeton, NJ 08543. Phone: (800) 338-3282. Carrol has a number of recommendations for professionals and for retirees.

- Kaye, Evelyn. *Free Vacations and Bargain Adventures in the USA,* Blue Penguin Publications, 3031 Fifth St., Boulder, CO 80304. Phone: (303) 449-8474. Published in 1995, this book lists and describes dozens of free and low-cost volunteer opportunities as well as you-pay-for-it-all educational vacations.
- High school students who would like to volunteer or work abroad should look at *The High School Student's Guide to Study, Travel, and Adventure Abroad,* Richard Hristiano, editor; St. Martin's Press. It's available from Council Publication Dept., 205 E. Forty-second St., New York, NY 10017. Phone: (888) COUNCIL.
- *The International Directory of Voluntary Work,* by David Woodworth, is from Peterson's Guides, P.O. Box 2123, Princeton, NJ 08543. Phone: (800) 338-3282. This book lists more than 500 agencies, particularly in Britain and Europe. It tells how to apply.
- *International Volunteer Program Guide: Peace through Deeds, Not Words.* Short-term volunteer opportunities are in Europe, Africa, and Asia. Contact IVS-SCI Route 2, Box 506, Crozet, VA 22932. Phone: (804) 823-1826.
- *International Workcamp Directory* has lists of volunteer projects in Europe, Africa, Asia, and the Americas. Write to Volunteers for Peace, 43 Tiffany Rd., Belmont, VT 05730. Phone: (802) 259-2759.
- *Invest Yourself: The Catalog of Volunteer Opportunities* is edited by Susan Angus and lists a couple of hundred projects in the United States and overseas. Some agencies provide room and board for workers; others cannot. A few organizations may spring for your transportation. It's available from Voluntary Service in Action, P.O. Box 117-G24, New York, NY 10009. Phone: (212) 974-2405.
- *Volunteer Vacations: Short-Term Adventures that Will Benefit You and Others* by Bill McMillan. Chicago Review Press, 814 N. Franklin St., Chicago, IL 60610. Phone: (312) 337-0747. Two hundred and fifty organizations sponsor volunteer projects. These programs are from one to six weeks.

- *Work, Study, Travel Abroad: The Whole World Handbook,* latest edition. Find it in libraries, in bookstores, and from Council on International Educational Exchange, 205 E. Forty-second St., New York, NY 10017. Phone: (212) 661-1450.

DONATING YOUR VACATION TO SCIENCE

There's seldom a shortage of volunteers for anthropological, archaeological, and other scientific expeditions. Because so many amateur scientists want the thrill of participating in a real discovery adventure, expedition leaders can afford to be choosy. So most volunteers are accepted only after making a financial contribution toward the work.

When you disgorge enough cash you'll most likely be appointed a *research assistant.* If your companion wants to go too, come up with double the fee. Your contribution will probably amount to just about the outlay for your trip. What a coincidence! The institution then gives you a "free" trip. Your entire contribution may well be tax deductible; double check with your accountant.

Helping scientists in their work might involve spending your vacation sifting sand at an archaeological site in Israel or Turkey, tape recording the music of Kanaks in New Caledonia, photographing landforms in Spain, attaching tags to birds in Brazil, or collecting plant samples in Borneo. There's a wide range of studies being done, of expeditions to choose from, and of destinations.

Contact your nearest university to find out what opportunities exist. In addition, *Archaeology* magazine publishes two annual guides to excavations, the organizers of which accept voluntary help. One issue listed opportunities at 110 ancient sites in 27 nations; another issue named 100 sites in North America. Write to Archaeology, 53 Park Place, New York, NY 10007. In addition, you can obtain information from these organizations:

- Archaeological Institute of America, Box 1901, Kenmore Station, Boston, MA 02215. Fax: (617) 353-6550. AIA publishes

Archaeological Fieldwork Opportunities, which lists volunteer and paid positions worldwide. There's a charge for this bulletin, which lists more than 200 projects all over the world. It's sold by Kendall-Hunt Publishing Co., P.O. Box 1840, Dubuque, IA 52004-1840. Write for the price.

- Service Archaeologique de Douai, 191 Rue St. Albin, F 59 000 Douai, France. Phone: 33-27-96-9060. Work on an archaeological dig for at least two weeks. Food and accommodation are provided.

- University Research Expedition Program is probably tax deductible. Sponsored by the University of California at Berkeley, UREP offers two- and three-week research programs. You can serve as a research assistant scraping out pre-Incan civilization in Peru or managing wildlife in East Africa, among other enticing programs.

Not long ago willing participants went to Florida to study bottlenose dolphins, sea turtles, ibises, eagles, and other barrier-reef wildlife. Others were off to Guatemalan tropical forests to find the largest and most ancient of the Mayan cities. Others collected tropical cancer-fighting sponges in the reefs off the coast of northern Papua New Guinea. A more party-oriented group flew off to Oruro, Bolivia, high in the Andes, to observe Carnival and to interview the costume makers, mask makers, dancers, musicians, and weavers.

Other UREP research programs exist in California, Ireland (studying medieval churches), Baja in Mexico, Thailand, Kenya, Brazil, and Belize. This is a great way to meet smart travelers, smart professors, and to save on taxes. It could be a most memorable vacation. Call (510) 642-6586.

Do a good deed. Volunteer to travel free.

CHAPTER 12

Traveling on Grants, Scholarships, and Awards

McCheap's Twelfth Law of Travel:
When people are eager to give you money to travel
and learn overseas, take it.

GETTING SHOWERED WITH TRAVEL MONEY

Showers are predicted—showers of money! Governments, foundations, philanthropists, businesses, fraternal and service organizations, schools, colleges, and universities give away millions of dollars every year to send individuals on trips just about everywhere. Representatives of these institutions actively seek out qualified recipients on whom to lavish their largess. Maybe they're looking for you.

In many cases, you don't even have to be a student. Although most trips that are funded involve some form of study, plenty of grants are out there strictly for travel and sight-seeing. A major purpose of travel grants is to increase the recipient's knowledge of a foreign culture or of his or her own nation. That's because traveling among people of other cultures teaches as it matures us. More than 1,200,000 students worldwide know this, as they pursue education outside their own countries. The 70,000 American students who study abroad know this truth, and lots of them also know how to get funding for their travels. In many cases, their travel is completely free.

If increasing your knowledge of the world is a purpose of your wandering, whether or not you want to go to school, you could get your next trip paid for. If the only grants you've ever heard of are Cary, Hugh, and Ulysses S., read on. There's real money out there waiting to be awarded to qualified people of all ages who want to roam the globe with a purpose.

FEDERALLY SUBSIDIZED STUDY ABROAD

The Advantages of Being a Student

College and university students have a number of sources of money available for study in the United States or abroad. Details are available from campus financial aid officers or study-abroad advisors. These opportunities include Pell (federal) Grants, SEOG (federal Supplementary Education Opportunity Grants), and federal loans—PLUS. Also available are federal Perkins Loans, federal subsidized Stafford Loans, federal unsubsidized Stafford loans, state aid, and merit awards or scholarships from your college. There are also merit awards or scholarships from community-based organizations, G.I. educational benefits, ROTC scholarships, and rehabilitation educational assistance. It takes some research and pen pushing to get money from any of these sources, but it can be well worth it in educational and travel benefits.

Getting Your Uncle Sam's Attention

When the federal government steps in with grants for needy individuals, study abroad can become—if not free—at least a lot easier. In a recent year, federal grants accounted for 20 percent of aid sources for American college students. In fact, Uncle Sam handed out $9 billion and said, in effect, "Study hard and don't worry about paying back the $9 billion. It's a gift to my nieces and nephews. And if you want to study overseas, go ahead. And good luck!" For he's a jolly generous fellow, our very own "Uncle" in the nation's capital!

Many smart students know that because costs are cheaper in a number of other countries, going to college abroad can be less expensive than staying home. If a student has rock-bottom expenses in an exotic locale and is subsidized by financial aid, travel and study become a happy and viable combination.

First the bad news: Uncle S. won't fund you to go to Bora Bora U. or Alma Ata J.C. As much fun as college in French Polynesia or Outer Mongolia may be, grants funded by the federal government may be used at colleges abroad only so long as they're overseas campuses of American institutions. Fortunate Stanford University students, for example, can study in Berlin, Vienna, Tours, Florence, and in the London suburbs, in addition to their main campus in Palo Alto, California. As is the case with a number of other American universities, all courses taken at the institution's overseas campuses are good for stateside college credit.

To get federal help you must demonstrate financial need. Waving your copy of *You Can Travel Free* in front of the loan officer could help, but you need to produce valid earnings records as well. In addition, you must have earned a high school diploma or GED certificate, enroll as a regular student working toward a degree, and continue to make satisfactory grades.

Students enrolled in and passing at least six semester units or their equivalent are eligible to receive Basic Educational Opportunity (Pell) Grants and supplementary grants, depending on the difference between their verifiable financial need and their ability to pay. These grants are for undergraduate students. In addition, they may be able to nail down a federal Supplemental Educational Opportunity Grant. Although the applicant has to make a full financial disclosure to prove he or she qualifies, the Pells and SEOGs need never be repaid. Thus they can be a source of free travel/study funds.

In addition to grants, government-guaranteed loans and work-study programs are available to the needy student. Colleges and universities also offer scholarships to offset the cost of tuition, textbooks, and living expenses. Individual states often supplement college costs through grants, loans, and work-study programs. It's all a marvelous conspiracy between government and school to make sure nobody who is qualified misses out on going to college because of lack of money.

The first step is to see your school's financial aid officer for current applications and information on eligibility. Ask for a free application for student aid. Or you can send for the most recent financial aid guide and application from the U.S. Department of Education, Federal Student Aid Information Center, P.O. Box 84, Washington, D.C. 20044. Website: www.ed.gov/offices/OPE/express.html. This department administers about two-thirds of all student financial aid.

Let's look at some specific programs.

Department of State Internships

The U.S. State Department has about a thousand paid and unpaid internships for college students. Perhaps you can work in a consulate or embassy. Contact Student Intern Program, U.S. Dept. of State, Recruitment Division, P.O. Box 9317, Arlington, VA 22219. Phone: (703) 875-7207.

Uncle Sam's Munificent Nephew, Senator Fulbright

Fulbright Grants allow American academics to travel and to exchange ideas with teachers and students abroad. The purpose is to "promote mutual understanding between the people of the United States and the peoples of other countries through educational exchange." Here's a rundown of the principal programs inspired by former Senator J. William Fulbright of Arkansas:

- Fulbright Teacher Exchange, USIA, 600 Maryland Ave. SW, Room 235, Washington, D.C. 20024. Phone: (800) 726-0479 or (202) 475-3095. In 1961 Senator Fulbright sponsored the Mutual Educational and Cultural Exchange Act. Because Congress passed it and President Kennedy signed it into law, educators and other academics can apply for a "Fulbright," a terrific addition to anyone's resumé. Teachers from U.S. elementary and secondary schools, colleges, and universities exchange places for an academic year or semester with their counterparts in foreign institutions.

Let's examine a couple of exchange opportunities. Four high-school teachers of Spanish, literature, world history, or geography in a recent year went to Argentina after getting leaves of absence with pay from their employers. Four Argentineans came to replace these teachers in the stateside schools. The U.S. teachers were given round-trip airfare and housing allowances through the U.S. Information Agency in Washington.

In the same year, five American high-school and community college faculty members winged their way to Denmark to teach various subjects for two semesters. They were given about $1,500, which should have covered all or almost all of their round-trip airfare. Their schools back home continued to pay them during their August-to-June assignment. Five Danes came to the United States to take their places. Since a knowledge of Danish wasn't required, the Americans were asked to teach their classes in English.

Fulbright exchange programs exist in Canada, Lithuania, Portugal, Senegal, United Kingdom, Cyprus, Denmark, Estonia, Latvia, Russia, Ukraine, Argentina, Bulgaria, Chile, Colombia, the Czech Republic, Denmark, Finland, France, Germany, Hungary, Mexico, Morocco, Netherlands, Norway, Romania, Slovakia, South Africa, Switzerland, Turkey, and Liechtenstein. Contact the USIA for an application. Deadlines are in the fall.

- Fulbright Grants are also U.S. government-funded. These grants support university teachers in temporary overseas assignments. These assignments include teaching, researching, or studying in one or more of 135 countries and regions. About a third of the grants are for research and the rest are for lecturing or lecturing combined with research or seminar participation.

    Grantees are covered for two to 12 months, depending on the country and the activity in which they're engaged. Congress has funded these grants for around a thousand Americans annually because a majority of Congresspersons believe these activities promote international understanding as well as professional development. About 30,000 U.S. academics have enjoyed these opportunities since 1947.

Most academics with Fulbrights have Ph.D.s, but people with outstanding professional records outside academia are also eligible. It's impossible to state a dollar amount for an "average" grant, because much depends on the cost of living in the country to be visited and the means of support the grantee has from other sources. Benefits, according to the Fulbright prospectus "may" include round-trip travel for the grantee and perhaps for a dependent, maintenance allowance, incidental allowances, housing supplement allowance, and tuition allowance in order to send the grantee's children to school in the country the recipient will work in.

What could a Fulbright grantee do in a multicultural society like India? Fifteen of them in a recent year lectured in colleges and universities. Two traveled. Ten did research for four to nine months. Lecturers had an opportunity to travel and exchange ideas with American and Indian faculty members. It wasn't essential that lecturers knew any of the subcontinent's 16 major languages.

Here's a sampling of other Fulbright freebies: Three Fulbrighters lectured on social science and humanities subjects in Malta, and six lectured or researched in Sri Lanka. Fulbrighters were found in Togo, Kazakhstan, Macedonia, Lesotho, and more than 120 other countries. Check it out. Even retired professors are eligible. Information is obtainable on request from Council for International Exchange of Scholars, 3007 Tilden St. NW, Suite 5M, Washington, D.C. 20008. Phone: (202) 686-4000. E-mail: info@ciesnet.cies.org. Website: http://www.cies.org.

• Fulbright-Hays Seminars Abroad program, c/o Center for International Education, U.S. Department of Education, 600 Independence Ave. SW, Washington, D.C. 20202-5332.

Teachers from the fourth grade through sixth, secondary-school teachers, curriculum specialists, faculty from colleges and universities, including community colleges, are eligible to attend government-funded seminars overseas. The purpose is to improve their understanding of foreign cultures. Each program consists of academic study and then a tour. Recent programs were conducted in Bulgaria and Romania, Chile, China, India, Indonesia, Japan, Mexico, and South Africa.

In the Bulgaria/Romania program, for example, held during summer vacation, 14 educators spent 12 days in Sofia attending lectures and meetings, taking day trips, and enjoying cultural performances. After that they traveled in Bulgaria for eight days. In Romania, they spent five days each in Bucharest and in Brasov, and then spent six days traveling in Romania. Uncle Sam picks up the tab. You need a minimum of a bachelor's degree.

- Fulbright U.S. Student Program is for recent college and university graduates, for master's and doctoral candidates, and young professionals and artists. These grants give young scholars a chance to meet people of other countries and to gain insights into other cultures. In the host country participants can take courses, do research, work on special projects, etc. Examples of recent projects are studying and participating in business in France, studying entomology in Madagascar, and learning about Chinese theater in Taiwan.

Most grants are for an academic year. Full grants provide round-trip transportation, language courses when needed, tuition, books and research materials, maintenance based on a country's living costs, and health insurance. Travel grants are available in Germany, Hungary, Italy, and Korea. You need to be a U.S. citizen, hold a B.A. or higher degree, and have studied primarily in the United States.

Fulbright funding will finance your trip along the beaten path to countries such as Canada (20 grants in a recent year) and Germany (91 grants). A few grantees can pursue the road less traveled and spend a year in Burkina Faso researching and teaching at the University of Ouagadougou. How about a year in Eritrea? Or Mauritius, Mozambique, or Nepal? These grants are administered by the Institute of International Education, 809 United Nations Plaza, New York, NY 10017-3580. Website: http://www.iie.org/fulbright. Fulbright scholarship and financial aid information is accessed on a website maintained by Institute of International Education. IIE's homepage is at www.iie.org.

Getting Your Humanities Endowed

NEH stands for National Endowment for the Humanities, and it's another program for which a generous federal government writes lots of good-sized checks. Most of these checks can be used by scholars, teachers, artists, and journalists to do advanced study or to work on projects. Those studies and projects may be done just about anywhere the recipient wants to go.

There are several NEH programs.

- National Endowment for the Humanities Fellowships and Summer Stipends. Contact NEH, Division of Research and Education Programs, 1100 Pennsylvania Ave. NW, Washington, D.C. 20506. Phone: (202) 606-8466. E-mail: fellowsuniv@neh.fed.us. For summer stipends, phone (202) 606-8551; e-mail: stipends@neh.fed.us.

   Educators, scholars, and writers may apply. The NEH looks for projects that will contribute to "thought and knowledge in the field of the project and to the humanities generally." You can study, write, research, or create for six to 12 months, or even for a short six weeks in the summer if you receive a summer stipend.

   The maximum amount in a recent year was $30,000. These grants are highly competitive, but you can do a good bit of traveling for $30,000.

- National Endowment for the Humanities Summer Seminars

for College Teachers. Write NEH, 1100 Pennsylvania Ave., Washington, D.C. 20506. Phone: (202) 606-8463. E-mail: education@neh.fed.us.

College teachers can spend six to eight weeks on major university campuses participating in seminars presented by directors who are known for their expertise in subjects such as philosophy, art history, sociology, political science, history, etc. While college teachers don't earn units to advance on the salary scale, they do interface with dynamic people in their field and perhaps spend a summer in another part of the country or abroad.

The program is open to full- and part-timers; as a result, a "freeway flyer"—a part-time instructor—who teaches choral singing on Monday nights at a local community college is theoretically as eligible to apply as is an assistant professor at a big-name university.

• National Endowment for the Humanities, Council for Basic Education Grant, supports summer study for elementary and secondary teachers who have completed five or more years of teaching. A generous grant allows six weeks of summer-time independent study in one of the humanities. Contact Independent Study in the Humanities, P.O. Box 135, Ashton, MD 20861. Phone: (202) 347-4171.

DO-IT-YOURSELF TRAVEL GRANTS

This idea works best for high school and college students and young professionals or businesspersons—the more sincere, avowedly needy, and wholesome appearing the better. To get money for your trip aboard, approach your chamber of commerce, veterans, service, church, local businesses, or fraternal organizations. The Future Farmers of America probably do it best. When an FFA member wants to go on one of the organization's worthy international programs, FFA's national office suggests: "With a little creative thought and initiative, you can find sponsors in your state and local community who are willing to fund a portion of your program." The national office recommends starting with the local chapter because some have scholarship funds. Then the Future Farmers fan out and visit local agribusinesses that want to promote the training of agricultural experts. In addition, the aspiring travelers contact local service clubs.

You don't have to be a future farmer to benefit from "a little creative thought." Let's say you want to visit gardens in Japan because you're a garden maintenance worker, a landscape architecture student, an amateur gardener, a flower shop employee, an art major, or whatever.

- Start with Japanese-American organizations and ask for their backing.

- Go to seed companies, garden supply companies, local nurseries, local service clubs, etc. Tell the clubs that you'll present a slide show at one of their meetings on your return.

- Tell the businesses that you'll include their logo in your slides that you're going to show to large audiences around town and that you'll get their names in the local paper as donors.

- Ask the local paper to include an article about your quest, complete with an address to which donors can send money.

- If you're going as a member of a club or other organization, schedule pancake breakfasts, rummage sales, door-to-door candy sales, car washes, spaghetti feeds, slave-for-the-day sales, etc. Get local businesses to donate goods and services to raffle off. Every time our local high school announces a trip to Europe, you can be sure they're out washing cars in the high-school parking lot several Saturdays in spring to raise money.

MORE SCHOLARSHIPS YOU CAN USE ABROAD

American Field Service

AFS offers semester or year-long exchanges in which U.S. students go abroad, live with host families, and attend local high schools. Foreign students come to the United States in exchange. If you're a needy high-school student, scholarship money is available.

Inquire from AFS Intercultural Programs/USA, 220 E. Forty-second St., 3rd Floor, New York, NY 10017. Phone: (800) AFS-INFO. Fax: (212) 949-9379.

American-Scandinavian Foundation

American-Scandinavian Foundation, 725 Park Ave., New York, NY 10021. Phone: (212) 879-9779. Fax: (212) 249-3444. This organization, founded in 1910 to encourage educational and cultural exchange between North Americans and Scandinavians, is responsible for enabling 23,000 people to work or study abroad. Each year they award more than $600,000 in fellowships and grants to students, scholars, and others in the Nordic countries and in America. Ask for the pamphlet, "Study in Scandinavia." It lists summer and academic-year study programs in Norway, Sweden, Denmark, Iceland, and Finland and specifies those programs for which financial assistance is available.

American Institute for Foreign Study

AIFS offers more than $100,000 in "merit" scholarships for study in Argentina, Australia, Austria, Britain, the Czech Republic, France, Italy, Japan, Mexico, Russia, and Spain. Write Dept TR, 102 Greenwich Ave., Greenwich, CT 06830. Phone: (800) 727-2437. E-mail: http://www.aifs.org.

AIFS operates schools abroad in England, Australia, Austria, Russia, Mexico, Hong Kong, Argentina, the Czech Republic, Japan, Italy, France, Spain, etc. AIFS offers a minority scholarship each semester and five runner-up awards.

American Society of Travel Agents

American Society of Travel Agents Scholarship Foundation, Inc., 1101 King St., Alexandria, VA 22314. Phone: (703) 739-2782. This major organization of travel professionals offers scholarships to students of travel and tourism.

Bailey Minority Scholarship for Education Abroad

The Bailey Minority Scholarship for Education Abroad helps fund travel costs for students "of color" participating in CIEE (Council for International Education Exchange) programs. Contact CIEE, 205 E. Forty-second St., New York, NY 10017-5706. Phone: (888)-COUNCIL or (212) 661-1414. E-mail: BaileyGrants@ciee.org. Website: HTTP://www.ciee.org. Those eligible include African-, Asian-, Arab-, Hispanic-, and Native-Americans. These applicants must be U.S. citizens or permanent residents.

CDS International

CDS International, 330 Seventh Ave., 19th Floor, New York, NY 10001. Phone: (212) 760-1400. Fax: (212) 268-1288. E-mail: info@cdsintl.org.

CDS, a nonprofit organization, sponsors several programs in which about a thousand Americans participate each year. These programs are centered in Germany:

- The CDS Internship Program is six months long and for college seniors or recent college graduates in business and technical fields. Participants work for the Bayer Corporation for three months and then find their own placements as trainees for three months.

- The Congress-Bundestag Youth Exchange for Young Professionals is a 12-month program for people ages 18 to 24. Successful applicants are German speakers who are high school graduates and have some work experience in business or vocational agriculture. They study German for two months, train for four months at a German technical school, and do six months of on-the-job training. Uncle Sam (America's gallant taxpayers) and the German Parliament pay for most of this incomparable experience.

- Study Tour Programs are one to four weeks in duration and allow Americans to pursue their particular interests and to attend seminars in Germany.

Camp Norway

Camp Norway is a four-week summer academic program that features Norwegian language studies and culture. It's for students ages 16 through 22. Scholarships and travel grants are available. Contact: Heritage Department, Sons of Norway, 1455 W. Lake St., Minneapolis, MN 55408. Phone: (800) 945-8851 or (612) 827-3611. Fax: (612) 827-0658.

Council on International Educational Exchange

CIEE, Council on International Educational Exchange, has financial aid available for some travel and study programs. These grants are to help high school and undergraduate college students who participate in educational programs in developing countries in Asia, Africa, and Latin America.

Get a free brochure from Travel Grants for Educational Programs in Developing Countries, c/o Council Student Services Department, 205 E. Forty-second St., New York, NY 10017-5706. Phone (888) COUNCIL. E-mail: ISICgrants@ciee.org.

Denmark's International Study Program

Since 1959, DiS, Denmark's International Study Program, has sponsored summer programs affiliated with the University of Copenhagen. College juniors and seniors who have chosen architecture and design majors are eligible. "Substantial" DiS grant and work-study scholarships are available.

DiS Arctic Biology Program in Iceland is a six-week course that examines arctic life and geology in the island republic. Students and faculty visit glaciers, geysers, and the volcanic Westmann Islands. Sound good? "Substantial" scholarships are available.

DiS Academic Year Programs in Denmark are taught in English. They are for college juniors and seniors. Students may enroll in fall or spring. These programs are in the arts, humanities, social sciences, international business, architecture and design, marine biology, ecology, and engineering. "Substantial" grants and work-study scholarships can be had. Contact DiS North American Office, 50 Nicholson Hall, 216 Pillsbury Dr. SE, University of Minnesota, Minneapolis, MN 55455. Phone: (800) 247-3477 or (612) 626-7679. Fax: (612) 626-8009. E-mail: dis@tc.umn.edu.

EF Travel Scholarships

If you're a high school student who wants to take an 11-day tour of Europe next summer, contact Ambassador Scholarship Program, EF Educational Tours, EF Center Boston, One Education St., Cambridge, MA 02141-1883. E-mail: scholarships@ef.com. This organization is in the business of taking great numbers of students abroad during school vacations—particularly to Europe. EF will fund a tour for 62 students, one from each U.S. state and one from each Canadian province and territory. Applicants will be asked to write about how they'd like to change the world; that shouldn't be too difficult for students who so readily change the world's history when taking exams.

Elderhostel

Yes, Virginia, believe it or not, there's life after 55! And one of the best reasons to hope fervently to become an older American is to join an organization called Elderhostel. Elderhostel schedules learning programs in every state and in 45 foreign countries. One can go to Mississippi to learn about antebellum plantation life or to Argentina to learn from gauchos about life on the Pampas. Members study everything from geology and astronomy to Shakespeare's plays and Alfred Hitchcock's films.

Elderhostel's affordable programs are one of the best reasons to take good care of your body and mind and hope for a long life. But for many, the body and mind outlast the savings account. As a result, Elderhostel offers "Hostelships," scholarships so that needy and deserving folks can attend their programs. For more information, contact Elderhostel, 75 Federal St., Boston, MA 02110-1941.

Explorers Club Youth Activity Fund

The Explorers Club consists of people who have made scientifically verifiable discoveries some place on the planet. The members have endowed a Youth Activity Fund to help students and other young people to advance "knowledge of the world by probing the unknown through field research." That means the club could give you several hundred to a thousand dollars as a funding source for your studies. What could you study? Your project might be on tribal customs in Papua New Guinea, plant life in the Amazon Basin, wildlife in Zaire, or the ozone layer over Antarctica. The amount the Explorers offer may not get you there and back, but supplemented by funds from other sources, it could be a valuable addition to your travel kitty. Needless to say, applicants need a clear and concise proposal to send in with their applications. Write to The Explorers Club, Youth Activity Fund, 46 E. Seventieth St., New York, NY 10021.

Future Farmers of America

Future Farmers of America (FFA), National Office, P.O. Box 15160, 5632 Mount Vernon Memorial Highway, Alexandria, VA 22309-0160. Future Farmers have an opportunity to take a variety of educational overseas trips. Members who are college students have interesting programs to choose among. "World Experience in Agriculture" is a three- to 12-month program available in Europe and Australia. "Agriculture Ambassadors to the United Kingdom," is a farm-stay with host families. High school students have several programs. They can spend three weeks with farm families in England or Australia. Others travel for 12 days in Belgium, Luxembourg, the Netherlands, and Germany learning about farming in those nations.

Some high school FFA members join the Dairy and Livestock Judging Teams' traveling seminar to England, France, Belgium, and Denmark. Others attend the "learn by doing" FFA Explorers Program in one of 25 countries. Every one of these programs has a substantial fee. To partially offset the fee, FFA can give several scholarships. In addition, local chapters can often help, and FFA members are urged to ask local businesses and service clubs for funding. We've never met a Future Farmer who wasn't sufficiently resourceful to make money on his or her own for such a commendable purpose.

Icelandic Ministry of Culture Awards

Iceland's Ministry of Culture and Education awards scholarships to foreign students to study Icelandic language, history, and literature at the national university at Reykjavik. Applicants must be at least in their third year of college. Inquire by contacting University of Iceland, Office of International Education, Neshaga 16, 107 Reykjavik, Iceland. Phone: (011) 354-525-4311. Fax: (011) 354-525-5850. E-mail: ask@rhi.hi.is. Website: http://www.rhi.is/HI/Stofn/ASK.

Lisle Summer Fellowships

Lisle Summer Programs Fellowships are for students "of racial or cultural diversity." Summer programs include stays on Bali or in Uganda. The program's objectives are service and cultural immersion. Contact Lisle Fellowship, 433 W. Stearns Rd., Temperance, MI 48182. Phone: (313) 847-7126. Bali or Uganda? It's a tossup decision between two paradises.

Lions Club Youth Exchange

Lions Youth Exchange is sponsored by Lions Clubs worldwide. Since 1961, more than 50,000 young people and their hosts have been united through this program that seeks to "foster a spirit of understanding among the peoples of the world."

All males and females between 15 and 21 are eligible so long as they want to learn about other cultures by sharing the lives of their host families. You don't have to be the offspring of a Lion. People with physical disabilities, including the blind and deaf, have been successful participants in the past and are as eligible as anyone to apply. Local clubs select the participants. "The costs of international travel and insurance are paid by the sponsoring local Lions Club or the youth's family, or a portion may be paid by each." Room and board are provided by the host family. Contact a member of your local Lions Club.

Rotary Club Scholarships

Rotary International, World Headquarters, One Rotary Center, 1560 Sherman Ave., Evanston, IL 60201. Phone: (847) 866-3000. Fax: (328) 8554. Website: http://www.rotary.org. The Rotary Foundation administers the Rotary Youth Exchange.

The Youth Exchange program sends about 7,000 young people abroad each year. American students, ages 15 through 19, have an opportunity to live for a year with a host family in one of 60 countries where Rotary Clubs are active. You don't have to be the son or daughter of a Rotarian; all applications are considered as long as they are submitted by students. Students submit a written application and essay and speak with a panel of Rotarians during an oral interview. Room and board is provided by the host family, but the students—sometimes with the help of local Rotarians—pay their round-trip air transportation. The Rotary Club sometimes pays or helps with tuition in the local school.

Armchair travelers, whether or not they're Rotarians, can visit other countries vicariously by welcoming foreign students into their homes. As the Rotary literature puts it, "Hosting a Youth Exchange student can be as rewarding as being one."

Norwegian-American Heritage Fund Awards

Sons of Norway Foundation, 1455 W. Lake St., Minneapolis, MN 55408. Phone: (800) 945-8851 or (612) 827-3611. Fax: (612) 827-0658. E-mail: fraternal@sofn.com.

The Sons of Norway offers the King Olav V Norwegian-American Heritage Fund award. Any North American, 18 or older, can apply for a grant that will help him or her travel in Norway to study subjects such as arts, crafts, literature, history, music, folklore, etc., at a recognized educational institution. More than 150 of these scholarships have been awarded to applicants, who must demonstrate an interest in Norwegian culture. In addition, other scholarship funds exist for members as well as for children and grandchildren of members. Write for details.

WHAT ARE YOUR CHANCES?

The sources and bibliographies mentioned in this chapter are only the beginning of the story. The next part of the tale consists of selecting the funding source that's most likely to send you a check, writing your application or proposal, and following through. You follow through by fulfilling your obligation to wing off somewhere exotic to do whatever it is you promised the granting authority you'd do.

The grant you're going after, located through meticulous research in this chapter of *You Can Travel Free*—in grant registers, on the Internet, or brought to your attention by a counselor or other person—should be tailor-made to your abilities, interests, and needs. You'll probably have a pretty good idea of your chances from the moment you read the grant announcement.

The moment I read about an eight-week study/travel grant to India, I knew I was a shoo-in. I had a strong feeling that if I were to spend a good part of a Saturday afternoon filling out forms and writing a "Why I Want to Go to India" essay, I wouldn't be wasting my time. It wasn't because I had any particular abilities that set me above other applicants. It was simply because I was certain I was the only applicant who was teaching world cultures in the American high school with the largest East Indian student enrollment in the United States. Moreover, I knew I could strengthen my cause with a handful of letters from school administrators, from an East Indian member of our schoolboard, and from East Indian community leaders who were personal friends. After reading the generous remarks that local Punjabi civic leaders wrote on my behalf, the selection committee would have been hard pressed to have turned down my application. It didn't.

Just as a travel grant appeared tailor-made for me, there's probably a grant or scholarship tailor-made for you. Don't waste your time. Search diligently until you've found the right grant, scholarship, or award. When you locate that funding source, write a proposal, and feel strongly you'll get the award, you probably will.

GETTING GRANTED

A few tips gleaned from personal experience and from the experiences of other successful applicants may help bring you a large check to be used for travel. Serious applicants should also read Virginia P. White's *How to Find Out About Grants and What to Do Next*. It's from Plenum Publishing Co., 233 Spring St., New York, NY 10013-1578. Phone: (800) 221-9369.

Your proposal should be well thought-out and well written. You must say exactly what you intend to do and detail a positive outcome, such as out how the results will help society or add to the existing scholarship in your area. You may be asked to explain how your travels through Arabia or Arkansas will make you a better architect, acrobat, or actor. Never try to fool the grant review board with a nebulous proposal; they're probably experts in your own field and can see through a poorly conceived travel plan: Somehow they know you want to frolic in the surf at Sydney's Bondi Beach, even though you clearly state you want to work from sun-up to sun-down in the cavernous Mitchell Library.

Don't waste your time or theirs. Apply only to those sources of funding that offer you a good chance of getting the money you want. Grant writing consumes hours, sometimes entire days, so don't pursue the improbable. Try to hit a bull's eye the first time out. Keep hunting until you honestly believe you have a sure thing—the grant that fits your interests and abilities and for which you can get enthusiastic letters of recommendation.

When writing the proposal, state the problem: "I have never been to Europe and will be a better music teacher for the experience because . . ." Be specific in your promises: "I will attend the Salzburg Festival on the 15th, 16th, and 17th, and will leave for Verona on the 18th"; "I intend to record Delius's 'In a Summer Garden' in Edinburgh on the 3rd, so I can play the tape for my Music 12 class during our discussion of . . ."

Estimate your costs reasonably. A good travel agent can help you in that department. Your proposal must convince the committee that its money will be well spent, so don't include caviar at Maxim's.

Convince the sponsor that you're the best candidate in the running by explaining how your training and experience make you qualified to carry through. Explain how your lack of travel opportunities has hampered your efforts in the past to study whatever it is you plan to study: "This institute will make me a better international relations teacher because I will come to understand Chinese agriculture firsthand." Applying for funding isn't unlike applying for a job: Eagerness counts.

Make copies of the forms and fill these in as a practice set. Once you're satisfied with what you've written, type out the real thing.

Universities, government agencies, school districts, and institutions hire people whose chief function is to write proposals for grants and other funding. If you know one of these experts, taking him or her to lunch could be a judicious investment. Ask for the benefit of his or her advice; it could get you a free trip or a free education abroad.

If the proposal application deadline is December 15, the proposal must be received by December 15. Don't leave anything for the last minute. Try to avoid asking the president of the Procrastinator's Club for a reference. It's absolutely essential all references be received by the cutoff date, or your application will probably be disqualified. When it's absolutely necessary to request a reference from the president of the Procrastinator's Club, tell him it's due a couple of weeks before it actually is due. He may get it in on time. Give him reminders until he does. If you, yourself, have been intending to start a club for procrastinators, but haven't quite gotten around to it, do things differently this time—start applying early. A last-minute rush job on your grant proposal (you know, the one with remnants of dinner on the cover sheet) looks exactly like what it is, a mess.

IN CHILE WITH ANANDA

Ananda, now a U.C. Berkeley graduate and mom, was a 17-year-old high school student when she decided she wanted to shake the small-town dust from her tennies and go off to see the world. She wanted to study abroad for a year before high school graduation.

Ananda started to investigate year-abroad study programs and found that the bottom line cash layout was more than she and her family felt comfortable about coming up with. Undaunted, Ananda wrote to every service club in the county, having found addresses in the phone directory. When Rotary replied, Ananda was ecstatic. If she could win a Rotary scholarship, she could have her year abroad.

Let's let Ananda tell the rest of her story:

YCTF: What did you have to do to get the Rotary scholarship?

Ananda: There was a long application to fill out and an interview with a committee of Rotarians. I was awarded a year-long home stay in Chile. I enrolled in high school there with the three girls in my host family.

YCTF: Did you have enough money for airfare?

Ananda: I still needed money so I applied to other service clubs. Veterans groups and the Rotary helped me out a lot, so I was able to go.

YCTF: What was your Chilean family like?

Ananda: They were great. There were three girls, ages 17, 15, and 10. They were like sisters to me.

YCTF: Do you still correspond?

Ananda: Maybe twice a year but it so happens I talked to them on the phone yesterday.

YCTF: Was the year in a Chilean school a challenge?

Ananda: I was really challenged. After two years of high school Spanish I thought I'd be O.K., but I could hardly communicate. People would ask me how I was and I'd tell them my name. But when you're immersed in a language you learn quickly. After three months I was dreaming in Spanish.

YCTF: Did you travel when you were there?

Ananda: Sure. My host family showed me a lot of Chile. One time—I only had around a hundred dollars—three other exchange students and I took a train to the Atlantic Coast. We sat in the last car of the train with chickens and stayed in inexpensive youth hostels. But I was able to see quite a bit of Argentina, and we went to Uruguay too.

YCTF: All in all, was your exchange year a good experience?

Ananda: If I could pick one experience out of my life I'd like to keep, that's probably it. It's the hardest thing I've ever done but the best. It was a challenge because I left everyone I knew and went to a strange country. You grow so much. It's such a big thing to meet so many people and to rely totally on yourself.

YCTF: Ananda, I think you're real success.

Ananda: Thanks.

YCTF: Thank you.

READING ABOUT GETTING FUNDED TO TRAVEL

A basic bookshelf of grant, scholarship, and award information will include some of these volumes. They're available at colleges and many can be found in public libraries. A couple are free pamphlets that can be requested. In addition, you'll find some interesting websites in this list:

- Attention artists: *Money for International Exchange in the Arts,* Jane Gulong and Noreen Tomassi, editors. It's from the Institute of International Education, P.O. Box 371, Annapolis Junction, MD 20701. Phone: (800) 445-0443.

- *Awards for Study in Canada* is a free booklet from Canadian Bureau for International Education, 220 Laurie Ave. West, Suite 1100, Ottawa, Ontario K1P 5Z9, Canada.

- *Chronicle Financial Aid Guide,* Chronicle Guidance Publishing, Inc., 66 Aurora St., P.O. Box 1190, Moravia, NY 13118. Phone: (800) 622-7284. This list is for college students.
- *Contests for Students,* Mary Ellen Snodgrass, editor. It's from Gale Research, Inc., 835 Penobscot Bldg., Detroit, MI 48226. Phone: (800) 347-4253.
- *The Directory of International Internships* is published by Michigan State University, International Placement Office. This guide lists intern openings sponsored by governments, schools, and universities. Ask for its current price from Michigan State University, East Lansing, MI 48824. Phone: (517) 355-9510. Fax: (517) 353-2597.
- *Don't Miss Out: The Ambitious Student's Guide to Financial Aid* is by Anna Leider and Robert Leider. It's from Octameron Associates, P.O. Box 2748, Alexandria, VA 22301. Phone: (703) 836-5480.
- *Fellowship Guide to Western Europe,* Gina Bria Vescovi, editor. It's available from the Council for European Studies, Columbia University, New York, NY 10027.
- *Fellowships and Grants for Training and Research* is a free booklet about money for social scientists. Get it from Social Science Research Council, 605 Third Ave., New York, NY 10158.
- *Fellowships, Scholarships, and Related Opportunities in International Education* may be requested from the Center for International Education, 201 Alumnus Hall, University of Tennessee, Knoxville, TN 37996.
- *Fellowships in International Affairs* is from Lynne Rienner, 1800 Thirtieth St., Suite 314, Boulder, CO 80301. Phone: (313) 444-6684.
- *Financial Aid for Study and Training Abroad,* edited by Gail Ann Schlachter and R. David Weber, is sold by Reference Service Press, 1100 Industrial Rd., Suite 9, San Carlos, CA 94070. Phone: (415) 594-0743. This book is a list of 1,000 sources of financial aid to support study, training, internships, workshops, and seminars overseas. This book is appropriate for high

school, college, and graduate students, and for some professionals. By the same authors and at the same address: *Financial Aid for Research and Creative Activities Abroad*. This volume has more than 1,300 listings.

- *Financial Resources for International Study: A Guide for U.S. Nationals*, edited by Sara Steen. It's available from IIE, 809 United Nations Plaza, New York, NY 10017. It lists funding possibilities for students and professionals who want to learn abroad.

- *Free Money for Study Abroad*, by Laurie Blum. Facts on File, Inc., 460 Park Ave. South, New York, NY 10016. Phone: (800) 322-8755. This book lists more than 1,000 grants and awards.

- *Grants for Study and Research in the Federal Republic of Germany* is free from the German Academic Exchange (DADD), 950 Third Ave., New York, NY 10022.

- *Guide to Financial Aid for Latin American Studies*. It's free from the Center for Latin American Studies, University of Pittsburgh, 4E04 Forbes Quad, Pittsburgh, PA 15260.

- *How to Find Out about Financial Aid: Guide to Over 700 Directories* is edited by Gail Ann Schlachter. It's from Reference Service Press, 1100 Industrial Rd., Suite 9, San Carlos, CA 94070. Phone: (415) 594-0743.

- *International Directory of Youth Internships* is from Council on International and Public Affairs, 777 United Nations Plaza, New York, NY 10017. Phone: (212) 953-6920. The directory contains mostly internship opportunities for high school students.

- *The International Scholarship Book* is by Daniel J. Cassidy. It's from Prentice Hall Publishers, 200 Old Tappan Rd., Old Tappan, NY 07675. Phone: (201) 767-5937.

- *International Scholarship Directory* is from National Scholarship Research Service, 2280 Airport Blvd., San Rafael, CA 95403. Phone: (707) 546-6777.

- *ISIC Travel Grants for Educational Programs in Developing Countries* tells how to get transportation paid in order to work, study, or volunteer in the Third World. Call (800) COUNCIL.

- National Association of Financial Aid Administrators provides information on financial aid and scholarhips for study in other countries. See its website: www.finald.org.

- *Princeton Review Student Access Guide to Paying for College,* by Kalman A. Chany with Geoff Martz, is from Random House, 201 E. Fiftieth St., 31st Floor, New York, NY 10022. Phone: (800) 733-3000. It's clear and practical.

- University of Minnesota's International Study and Travel Center maintains a website with lists of scholarships: http://www.ispacad.umn.edu/istc/istc.html.

- *Work, Study, and Travel Abroad: The Whole World Handbook,* latest edition, is probably the single best source of travel opportunities of all kinds for young people. While it doesn't list individual scholarships, the handbook includes a good bibliography of sources of grants and scholarships. It's available at bookstores and from CIEE, 205 E. Forty-second St., New York, NY 10017. Phone: (212) 822-2600. Fax: (212) 822-2679. You can access parts of the *Handbook* at http://www.tripod.com.

- *The Young American's Guide to Travel and Learning Abroad* is by Joseph Lurie. Get it from Intravco Press, 211 E. Forty-third St., Suite 1303, New York, NY 10017. Phone: (212) 972-1155.

SEEK AND YE SHALL BE FUNDED

Remember, the agencies, foundations, and governments that give grants for free travel (or for any purpose) are as interested in finding the right recipient as the applicants are in getting funded. By sending you checks, grant committees are merely fulfilling the functions for which they've been constituted.

Applying for lots of grants is counterproductive because each takes up so much of your time. Applying for the right grant will get you where you really want to go, and at little or no cost. Good luck.

CHAPTER 13

Working Vacations

McCheap's Thirteenth Law of Travel:
To earn money while traveling is commendable.
To not spend it all is a miracle.

EARNING AND LEARNING

The whole world is out there, an unlocked box full of surprise and promise. Don't let a lack of money keep you from savoring it. Hundreds of thousands of adventurous people seize the opportunity of getting to know other places on working vacations, paying for travel as they go. You may not save much, if any, money no matter how hard you work, but by taking temporary jobs, you may well be able to cover your expenses for a summer in the United States, in Europe, Australia and New Zealand, or elsewhere. And on the way, there's much to learn, much to see, and new friends to meet.

THE SAGA OF THE 50-STATE DISHWASHER

Dishwasher Pete (Peter Jensen) has become a legend in his own time. Pete is so well known that he merited a front-page story in the *Christian Science Monitor*. Dishwasher Pete's claim to fame is that he publishes a "zine" called *dishwasher*. Selling for 50 cents a copy, *dishwasher* (P.O. Box 8213, Portland, OR 97207) is the vehicle through which Pete philosophizes about working in restaurants while scrubbing away at his goal of washing dishes in all 50 states. If you happened to peek into the kitchen of the Black Cat Café in Seattle, or into the back room of any number of similar cafés across the country, you may have seen Pete with his head stuck in a cloud of steam.

This 20-something plate sudser has become so well known that the producers of "Late Night with David Letterman" were quite eager to have him do a face-to-face with Dave on nationwide television. But Dishwasher Pete isn't into fame or money, so he sent an impostor in his place, an acquaintance with nothing better to do. Letterman's producers were displeased, to say the least. That didn't upset Pete. He's still the nation's best-known dishwasher.

Pete's philosophy is that there will always be dishes to be washed, and since it's not hard to get hired, he's going to see the United States close up—200,000 dishes, spoons, and pots per state—one state at a time. Pete disclosed to a reporter from the newspaper *Out West* that he was in no hurry to move on: "I don't want to be 35 and have accomplished my life's dream. There'd be nothing left."

What you can learn from Pete is that if you're able and willing to work at temporary jobs during your vacation, be they dish washing or bed making, fruit picking or gardening, selling encyclopedias door to door, frolicking in a clown costume, or selling perfume over the counter, you may have a way to see the country. In fact, you can probably work your way through a number of countries without having a wad of cash to begin your journey. You may not get on a late-night talk show, but you'll certainly have lots to talk about.

SHORT-TERM VACATION EMPLOYMENT

Making lots of money isn't what a working vacation is about. If you regard short-term employment on an extended holiday as a chance to learn about places you're visiting, to work on foreign language skills, to make friends among the locals, or to get money to do more traveling, a job can be a culturally rewarding experience.

A working vacation isn't really a contradiction in terms.

Some temporary jobs, such as showing foreign visitors the United States and Canada, helping on an archaeological dig in Greece or Guatemala, taking care of children in Japan, or serving as a camp counselor in the French countryside, can be so stimulating that they're hardly work at all. Other jobs you might do overseas are seldom pleasant or stimulating, and they don't pay very well. Yet, picking grapes in the Moselle Valley, cleaning hotel rooms in Berne, or washing dishes in Hamburg may actually be the best opportunity many people will ever get to become partially assimilated into another culture.

WORKING-VACATION JOB HUNTING BASICS

A traveler can plan ahead and secure a job before leaving home or wait to run out of money overseas and then hunt for work. Most people opt for the latter, but planning ahead can take some of the frustration out of staying alive while traveling. If you're cautious, you'll do some job hunting by mail, phone, or e-mail long before your trip begins. Even if you're an adventurous type who likes to take chances and leave itineraries largely unplanned, this chapter will help you find work when you need it.

Nailing down a summer job overseas—in Europe, for example—is essentially the same as finding a summer position in North America, but several differences exist. Here are the basics on applying:

Before You Get There

- Tell everyone you know that you're looking for a job in Prague, Padua, or wherever you want to go. Don't be surprised if someone you know knows someone in Prague or Padua—perhaps someone who will hire you or who can help you find work.

- Write a letter to potential employers and include a resumé. In Europe, the resumé is called a *curriculum vitae* or *CV.* It's similar to an American resumé, but Europeans want information on age, marital status, and health in addition to being told how well you can do the job.

- Write directly to businesses overseas, even if they are branches of North American firms; writing to the U.S. or Canadian office of an international conglomerate—unless, of course, your Uncle Fenwick is the major stockholder—can hold up your search for an inordinate time.

- Any foreign language abilities you have are important. If you're applying for a job in a country whose language is other than English, and if you're fairly fluent, write your CV in that language. If you're applying for a job in Norway and you read and write Greek, don't assume that your facility with Greek is unimportant at the top end of the continent. A Norwegian company may be looking for someone with your linguistic skill.

- Include a photo of yourself. We've all seen photos of politicians that consistently lose them votes on election day. You need only the vote of the person hiring, so send a photo that shows you at your well-scrubbed, efficient, and dependable best.

- Ninety percent of French companies use handwriting analyses as one method of selecting employees. Armed with that knowledge, you can decide for yourself whether to write a cover letter in cursive or to type it. Elsewhere, cover letters may be typed.

After Your Plane Has Landed

- If you plan to look for a job after you get to Europe, take your resumés or CVs, letters of recommendation, and relevant academic transcripts with you.

- Find out everything you can about the company or organization that's going to interview you. Be familiar with their goals and major operations.

- Know the name and title of each person you're to meet in the interview process. Write down the names and titles.

- Punctuality in many societies overseas is of utmost importance. Arrive a few minutes early.
- Be prepared to discuss your strengths, experiences, and weaknesses.
- Look everyone, including the secretary who ushers you into the interview, in the eye, smile, and act as if you're confident about your abilities.
- Never say anything negative about a previous employer.
- If they take you to lunch and you've never used chopsticks, this may not be the best time to try. Stay away from foods that present a challenge to eat, such as cracked crab, huge sloppy sandwiches, yard-long spaghetti strands, etc.
- Unlike in the United States, an interviewer may ask you about your religious affiliations, or your marital status or living arrangement.
- Thank them for the interview.
- Write a thank-you note to each member of the interview committee.

Most of these simple tips will also work back home.

ORGANIZATIONS THAT WANT TO HELP STUDENTS

If you want to work in the United States, you don't need a permit if you're old enough. Like Dishwasher Pete, you can cross state lines as many times as you wish and get enough work to continue your North American odyssey. If you want to work overseas however, you'll soon find that jobs are scarce almost everywhere, so most governments protect their citizens by discouraging foreign workers from invading their employment markets. This protection takes the form of work permit requirements. To get a permit, you ordinarily need a letter from an employer in that nation stating that you have a job. Most employers, however, won't give you a job unless you have a work permit. Gotcha!

But there's lots of hope of getting a permit and a job if

you're a student. Foreign governments are caught between protecting jobs for their own nationals, fostering international understanding and education through allowing foreigners to live and work among them, and providing sufficient seasonal labor in areas and sectors where labor may be short. Many countries experience labor shortages in the seasonal tourist industry or in agricultural harvesting. Students benefit because the host country needs extra workers during the summer, for example, when students are on vacation.

If you're enrolled in, or recently graduated from, a high school, college, or university, you can apply for work permits in foreign countries through several organizations:

American-Scandinavian Foundation

American-Scandinavian Foundation, 725 Park Ave., New York, NY 10021. Phone: (212) 879-9779. Fax: (212) 249-3444. E-mail: training@amscan.org. The American-Scandinavian Foundation's Training Program: U.S. to Scandinavia enables Americans ages 21 to 30 to live and work in Nordic countries for periods of usually two to six months between late spring and autumn. The emphasis is on cultural understanding and training in areas such as engineering, computer science, and chemistry. Applicants need to have completed at least three years of undergraduate studies and be enrolled in programs that correspond to the type of training they want in Denmark, Finland, Norway, or Sweden. Applicants need to have had some work experience in their areas of training, but need not know a Scandinavian language or Finnish. There's an application fee.

In addition, the American-Scandinavian Foundation has agriculture and English teaching positions available in the summer in Finland. Again, there's an application fee.

Council on International Educational Exchange

The Council on International Educational Exchange, a non-profit educational consortium, helps more than 5,000 United

States students obtain permits to work in one of several countries. There's a small fee for the permit. To be eligible you must be a student or recent graduate age 18 or older. George, who worked in New Zealand during his vacation, characterized the CIEE Work Abroad experience as "the chance of a lifetime for students to travel abroad for a prolonged stay, before real life and its restrictions appear." Jeff, another traveling student, recalled that "of the whole experience, what I treasure most are the friendships that I made all over Europe." Contact CIEE, 205 E. Forty-second St., New York, NY 10017. Phone: (888) COUNCIL or (212) 661-1414. E-mail: info@ciee.org. Website: http://www.ciee.org. Ask for the free brochure, "Council Work Abroad."

CIEE has negotiated reciprocal agreements, with maximum time limits, so Americans can work temporarily in the following countries:

—Australia (up to one year)
—The United Kingdom (up to five months)
—Ireland (up to four months)
—France (up to three months)
—Canada (up to six months)
—Germany (up to three months, May 15 to October 15, and/or to do an internship any time of year for up to six months)
—Spain (up to three months between May 1 and October 31)
—Costa Rica (June 1 to Oct 1, up to three months)
—Jamaica (June 1 to October 1)
—New Zealand (April 1 to October 31)

Many young people, helped by CIEE, work in restaurants, hotels, offices, or shops. Kelly, an American student, found herself working at a vegetarian restaurant in Dublin, Ireland, only three days after her orientation meeting following her arrival. She found her work a great way to get to know lots of people. Sharing a flat with two Spanish women, she enjoyed her first experience out of the United States. Brandi, another American

CIEE participant, worked as an editorial assistant in London, where she proofread medical articles and books. Marissa helped staff the information desk at the Louvre museum in Paris. When Jeff got home from having sold computers in Britain, telling job interviewers about his experience in England worked for him as an easy ice breaker; he had five job offers in the first three weeks after his return.

The Council on International Educational Exchange will provide:

- work permits
- an opportunity to obtain discounts on airfares
- a program handbook to help you get ready
- lists of potential employers
- group orientation on arrival and a chance to meet other participants
- support from CIEE Work Abroad personnel in case you need advice
- assistance locating suitable and affordable housing

There's a program fee, you must pay for your own round-trip transportation, and you need enough money to get started until you get your first paycheck abroad. However, CIEE offers scholarships to minority applicants and to those applying to work in developing countries such as Jamaica.

CIEE calculates that a nearly unanimous 98 percent of applicants find work abroad and 86 percent do so within a week to 10 days. Sixty-two percent find jobs within one to five days. One of the luckiest of that 98 percent is Darlene, who found a job working as a receptionist at a beach hotel in Costa Rica. So she could tell American guests about optional day excursions, the hotel management sent Darlene into the rain forest, whitewater rafting, volcano spotting, and deep-sea fishing. "I constantly saw monkeys, sloths, lizards, toucans, parrots, and parakeets," Darlene recalled happily.

If you're interested in working in a country that's not on

CIEE's agreements list, you may write directly to the embassy of the country in Washington, D.C., or Ottawa if you're Canadian. Ask about work permits, visas, availability of work, working conditions, and wages.

WISE

Worldwide Internships and Service Education (WISE), 303 S. Craig St., Suite 202, Pittsburgh, PA 15213. Phone: (412) 681-8120. E-mail: wise+@pitt.edu. Website: http://www.pitt.edu/-wise.

WISE is a nonprofit organization that can help arrange for community service work in the United Kingdom; au pair placements in France, Germany, the Netherlands, or Austria; and WISE also helps place 18- to 30-year-olds with farm families in Norway to help with chores. There are application and program fees, but workers receive stipends as well as room and board. WISE provides internship opportunities abroad too.

THESE ORGANIZATIONS CAN HELP YOU GET VACATION-TIME JOBS

Some of these organizations are agencies that charge a fee to help you find work:

- Alda Luxembourg, 70 Grand'rue 1660 Luxembourg City, Luxembourg. If you're already there, stop by for information on temporary work.
- Alliances Abroad, 2830 Alameda, San Francisco, CA 94103. Phone: (415) 487-0691. Fax: (415) 621-1609. For a modest program fee, Alliances Abroad will help you get a job in a hotel and a work permit for short-term work in England. The hotel provides full room and board to its workers, and pocket money and tips are possible. If you're 18 or older and have been enrolled full-time at an accredited American university within six months of the starting date, you can start work any time of the year. Participants work no more than 40 hours a week in four- and five-star hotels, country mansions, and seaside resorts in Great Britain. Send for particulars.

- The Center for Interim Programs, Western Branch Office, 45640 Peak-to-Peak Highway, Ward, CO 80481. Phone (303) 459-3552. Or contact Interim Programs, P.O. Box 2347, Cambridge, MA 02238. Phone (617) 547-0980. This organization matches applicants to more than 2,000 opportunities, including paid work, worldwide according to the applicant's interests and abilities.

- Continental Waterways, 76 rue Balard, 75015, Paris, France. Phone: (011) 33.1.40.60.11.23. Work as a deckhand on barges on canals and rivers in France during spring, summer, and fall tourist seasons.

- Council of International Programs, 1101 Wilson Blvd., Suite 1708, Arlington, VA 22209. Phone: (703) 527-1160. In cooperation with the French Ministry of Foreign Affairs, the CIP sponsors exchanges for social workers, youth leaders, and special teachers. You need to be 25 to 40 and fluent in French, and you must have some professional experience. Contact CIP for details.

- Disney Paris: Want to work for a summer near Paris? Europe's Disneyland hires 12,000 people to serve food, work in hotels, take tickets, and to parade around in a mouse outfit. You'll need a good command of French. Contact Service du Recruitement-Casting, Disneyland Paris, BP 110 77777 Marne-la-Vallee Cedex 4, France. Phone: (1) 49.31.19.99.

- French hotel, restaurant, and resort jobs: Ever wanted to be a French waiter or waitress? A *chambre* maid? If you're fluent in French, here's your chance. Keeping in mind that you need to apply for a work visa once you have the job, you can get lists of hotels and restaurants from English-language travel guide books, such as Maverick Guides, Frommer, Fielding, Fodor, Blue Guide, Insight series, etc. Write (in French) to your prospective employer. In France, write to the Syndicat d'Initiative in the area where you want to work, and include the name of the town and the zip code. You can also research ads in the French magazine *L'Hôtelerie*, 79, avenue des Champs-Elysées, 75008, Paris, France. Phone: (1) 47.83.66.72.

- Inside Paris: you can find job announcements in *France USA Contacts* and *J'Announce.* Also look at the bulletin boards at the American Church, 65 Quai d'Orsay, Paris 7. Still another source for jobs in and near Paris is the FUSAC, 3 rue Larochelle, 75014 Paris (Metro Gaité or Edgar Quintet). Phone: 45.38.56.57. FUSAC's magazine, *France USA Contacts,* lists employment opportunities as well as events of interest, housing information, and news about how to make contact with other expatriates.

  If you're a foreign student who has completed a year of studies in France, you can request a work permit from the Direction Départementale du Travail et de l'Emploi pour la Main-d'oeuvre Etrangère (DDTMOE), 80, rue de la Croix-Nivert, 75015 Paris. Phone: (1) 45.31.10.03. Summer employment is performed between June 1 and October 31 and can't exceed three months in one year. During the school year, foreign students can work up to 20 hours a week. Apply also to DDTMOE.

- InterExchange, Inc., 161 Sixth Ave., New York, NY 10013. Phone: (212) 924-0446. Fax: (212) 924-0575. E-mail: interex@ earthlink.net. This 20-year-old nonprofit organization operates several programs. They place teachers in the Czech Republic, Hungary, and Finland and are working on establishing similar programs in Spain and Poland. They help young people find summer resort jobs in Germany and Switzerland. In addition, you can tutor English and help with chores while staying with a family in Finland. "All positions are paid and most include housing," states a recent InterExchange announcement. Ask for *Work Abroad,* a free booklet.

- L'Administration de l'Emploi, 38a rue Philippe II, 3rd Floor, L-2340, Luxembourg. Phone: (011) 352-47-68-55. Visit the office in person and ask about temporary summer jobs in warehouses, restaurants, tourist facilities, etc.

- Taiwan: Contact the Cultural Division of the Taipei Economic and Cultural Representative Office in the United States to subscribe to *Culture and Education News,* which is an electronic news bulletin that describes job openings in Taiwan. Contact Dr. Chenching Li by e-mail: moeusa@pop. erols.com. Or call (202) 895-1918. Fax: (202) 895-1922.
- Travelbound/Skibound, Olivier House, 18 Marine Parade, Brighton, East Sussex BN2 1TL, U.K. Phone: (011) 44-1273-677777. Travelbound/Skibound hires domestic and kitchen help in Alpine resorts in Austria and France.

OTHER OPTIONS FOR SHORT-TERM WORK ABROAD

The balance of this chapter is full of suggestions for various kinds of vacation-time work you can do while traveling. Hopefully, there's something here for every reader: everything from child care to travel writing. If none of these ideas appeals to you, this section is followed by suggestions for further reading and research.

LIVING WITH A FOREIGN FAMILY AS AN AU PAIR

Our dictionary defines *au pair* as a foreign girl or young woman living with and working for a family in England in order to learn English. This rather narrow definition can be broadened to include young people of either gender living with families abroad in exchange for their performing child care or household chores. Literally, *au pair* translates as "on par," or on a basis of equality. It means that the caretaker of the children lives as a family member. Living with a family gives you a chance to immerse yourself in the country's culture. Many au pairs do, indeed, learn the language of the host family, but their reasons for living abroad will be as many and varied as your own reasons are. The advantage of being an au pair is obvious: Your room and board are provided, and your duties allow you time to learn and meet people, see the sights, and have some fun.

Au pair work often provides excellent opportunities for

additional travel. For example, if you're au pairing in Paris and you must accompany little Yvette and Alain to Cannes or Biarritz for the annual August holiday, or to Tahiti or Martinique to check out the colonies, the family is obligated to pay transportation, food, and lodging.

Many agencies offer part-time au pair work—ten to fifteen hours a week. Normally part-timers receive free lodging but not meals. Often cooking facilities are available in the home.

But first, a word of warning. In France, and other countries as well, although the law may clearly stipulate that au pairs must have their own room and be given board as well as pocket money for five hours of daily work, some families exploit au pairs by working them much longer and denying them pocket money. For these parents, au pairs are a bargain, because families pay these temporary workers less than they'd pay maids. Before you sign a contract, come to an agreement with the employer about your hours and exact duties; ask to see the room you'll be assigned, and be certain you know what pay you'll receive. Au pair situations should provide a pleasurable opportunity to learn, not an excuse to reinstitute slavery into the Western world.

These agencies and organizations promise to help settle you into what ought to be a comfortable au pair situation:

- AIFS Au Pair in Europe program. E-mail: Info@aifs.org or www.aifs.org. Live with a European family. Work five hours a day caring for children and attend language or other courses in your free time. Programs are available in the United Kingdom (London), France, Germany, and Spain.

- Alliances Abroad, 2830 Alameda, San Francisco, CA 94103. Phone: (800) 266-8047 or (415) 487-0691. Fax (415) 621-1609. Website: www.studyabroad.com/alliances. Alliances Abroad helps arrange au pair work and work permits in Europe. "The main point and the best," states the Alliances Abroad brochure, "is that you'll be treated as a member of the family." There's a program fee, which rises with the length of your stay. It covers your insurance, screening, and your international student ID card. You get room and meals and an opportunity to attend six classes a week. In addition, you earn a stipend. Stays vary from three to 12 months. Opportunities exist in France, Germany, Italy, Spain, England, and Australia.

- Atlantis Youth Exchange, Rolf Hofmusgat 18, N-0655, Oslo, Norway. Phone: (011) 47-22-67-00-43. Fax: 011.47.2268.68.08. The au pair positions in Norway are for a minimum of six months.

- Au Pair Activities, Box 76080, 17110 Nea Smyrni, Athens, Greece. Phone/fax: (011) 30-1-932-6016. This is a fee placement service.

- Au Pair and Activity International, Box 7097, 9701 JB Groningen, Netherlands. Phone: (011) 31-50-3130666. This organization arranges au pair appointments in the Netherlands.

- Au Pair Australia, 6 Wilford St., Corrimal, NSW 2518, Australia. Young women are employed for at least three months as live-in child care providers.

- Au Pair in Europe, Box 68056, Blakely Postal Outlet, Hamilton, ON L8M 3M7, Canada. Phone: (905) 545-6305. This organization arranges positions in 16 countries, mostly in Europe but also in South Africa.

- Au Pair Homestay Abroad places 18- to 29-year-olds with families overseas to care for children. There's a program fee. They're at 1015 Fifteenth St. NW, Washington, D.C. 20005. Phone: (202) 408-5380. Fax: (202) 408-5397. E-mail: imelda.farrell@worldlearning.org.

- Au Pair in Germany, Ubierstrasse 94, 53173 Bonn, Germany. Phone: (011) 49-228-95-73-00. If you're under age 24, you can apply for an au pair job.

- *Au Pair Work in France* is a fact sheet that French Cultural Services (972 Fifth Ave., New York, NY 10021) will send you on request. To be an au pair in the land of the Gauls, you need at least high-school-level French, to be between 18 and 26, willing to stay at least three or six months (with a maximum of 18 months), and willing to enroll in French language classes during your stay. If you're there for only three months in the summer, you don't have to take the classes. Au pairs receive a private bedroom, meals, a monthly allowance, and (in Paris) a transportation pass. Although they're required by law to get a free day off every week, many au pairs enjoy the entire weekend off. To obtain a position, write to one or more of the agencies listed in the fact sheet *Au Pair Work in France*. When you've been hired, the agency will help you secure your work visa.

- Avalon 92 Agency, Erzsebet rrt. 15, 1st Floor, #19 Budapest 1073, Hungary. Phone: (011) 36-1-351 3010. They place child-care providers in private Hungarian homes.

- Dogan International Organization (Au Pair and Employment Agency), Sehitmuhtar Caddesi 37/7, Taskim 80090. Istanbul, Turkey. Phone: (011) 90 216-235-1599. Dogan helps au pairs find jobs with Turkish families.

- Exis-Europair, Skeldevigvej 12, 6310 Broager, Denmark. It places au pairs in Denmark, Norway, and Iceland.

- Eurojob Au Pair, Jarpgatan 11, S-58237 Linkoping, Sweden. Eurojob places au pairs in Sweden.

- Galentina's European Child care Consultancy, Box 51181GR, 145.10 Kifissia, Athens, Greece. Fax: (30) 1808-1005. This agency has a number of openings. Here's one: "Seeking a nanny who loves to pack her bag and travel with this family of 2 children aged 2 and 3 years. They absolutely love to seek out all sorts of interesting European cities, and they have a second residence in Switzerland. Candidates must be experienced, love children, and enjoy travel." Here's another: "Ship owner requires a cracker-jack summer au pair for 4- and 5-year-old children. Lots of travel, lots of sun, and lots of fun. Must have experience and ability to entertain children.

Nonsmoker, excellent swimmer, and must be able to cope with yachting." You can at least *try* to cope with yachting.

- International Au Pair Intercambio P-1/4 de Gracia 86, 67-1/4-7-1/4, 08008 Barcelona, Spain. You can work in Catalonia as an au pair.

- Interexchange, Inc., 161 Sixth Ave., New York, NY 10013. Phone: (212) 924-0446. Fax: (212) 924-0575. E-mail: interex@earthlink.net. Interexchange arranges au pair placements in Austria, Finland, France, Italy, Netherlands, Norway, and Spain. To be considered, you must be a female between 18 and 25 for most programs, or as old as 27 to apply in France. If you want to work in Austria, France, Italy, or Spain, you need to have some language courses behind you, or at least an ability to communicate verbally in the language of the country. Commitments are six to 12 months, generally.

- Stufam V.Z.W., Vierwindenlaan 7, 1780 Wemmel, Belgium (011) 32-2-460-3395. This is a fee employment agency that arranges au pair positions in Belgium.

- WISE stands for Worldwide Internships & Service Education. They offer six-month to one-year au pair placements in France, Germany, the Netherlands, Norway, and Iceland. If you speak French or German, you may apply for two- to three-month placements in France and Austria. Language classes are required of au pairs in this program in France, Germany, and Switzerland. Maximum ages for working as an au pair in Germany are 24; in France and the Netherlands, 25; and 30 in Finland, Norway, and Switzerland. In France and Germany, families will pay for your transportation to your language classes. Contact WISE, 303 S. Craig St., Suite 202, Pittsburgh, PA 15213. Phone: (412) 681-8120. Fax: (412) 681-8187. E-mail: wise+@pitt.

- World learning, Inc. 1015 Fifteenth St. NW, Suite 750, Washington, D.C. 20005. Phone: (202) 408-5380. World Learning organizes placements for au pairs in Argentina, France, Finland,

Germany, Great Britain, Iceland, the Netherlands, Norway, and Switzerland. There are application, administrative, and insurance fees.

Reading about Au Pairing

For further information about what you could be getting into, read *The Au Pair & Nanny's Guide to Working Abroad* by Susan Griffith and Sharon Legg. It's available from Southern Hills Book Distributors, 49 Central Ave., Cincinnati, OH 45202. Phone: (800) 545-2005. Website: www.southernhillsbooks.com. This volume tells how to find a child-care job and what to expect. A list of agencies all over the world is included.

TRAVELING WITH JUNIOR

Many affluent families don't want to leave Caleb or Nicole at home and want a reliable, mature person to accompany the family and look after their kids while Mom and Pop enjoy their vacations. Since maturity is a matter of attitude and emotional security rather than age, traveling babysitters come in all ages, 13 to 80-something. The job may not pay much, but it can win you that dream trip totally without cost.

Your trip may be only a far as the nearest mountain or lake, or it may be to Montego Bay, Jamaica, or to the Greek isles as it was for Jill, the New York art student we met in Paris. "It's the most fabulous experience I've ever had," Jill told us. "The children have been super, and taking them to the beach every day on Mykonos isn't even remotely related to work. I got to see a fabulous archeological museum in Athens and fascinating ruins at Delphi and Olympia, and here I am in Paris on my way to the Louvre!"

You don't need to pay an au pair agency to be a free-lance traveling babysitter for American families. Advertise yourself. Here are a few ideas:

- Send fliers around to the heads of expensive private schools; they probably know the names of parents who want to take their children abroad and who'd appreciate readily available child care.

Get to know the proprietors of preschools in your area. Tell them you're a reliable child sitter who loves to travel.

Leave your name and number with travel agents located within a hundred miles or so of your home.

Put ads in weekend editions of big-city newspapers.

Announce your availability in the catalog of one of the home-exchange clubs listed in chapter 2, "Free Accommodations." If Junior is a good kid, you're bound to have a good trip.

A FREE TRIP FOR BEING COMPANIONABLE

Marilyn is a fortyish young widow. Her husband provided her with enough money to maintain a modest life-style in the family home in Bloomington, Indiana. Her only daughter is happily married and living in another state. Marilyn has a quiet and most pleasant personality. She's a good listener and she seems reliable—someone to talk to and even to lean on. She speaks some French, Italian, and German. Her language abilities don't come even close to fluency, but she can ask for the check, find the ladies' room, and buy a train ticket in Western Europe.

Edith is seventyish and is a recent widow. She lives near Central Park in New York City. Her husband Willard, an investment banker, left Edith with a six-figure annual income, substantial property, and a formidable stock portfolio. Edith's husband hated to travel, and Edith, who spent hours looking at travel brochures during her long married life, was ready to take off within a few months after Willard's death. But Edith had never been farther than Bermuda (on her and Willard's honeymoon) and she didn't want to travel alone.

Marilyn had spent her junior year and a year after college graduation in Europe, and she wanted to return, but there was no money in her widow's budget for foreign travel. So Marilyn put an ad in the *New York Times* offering to serve as a travel companion in exchange for her trip and spending money. Edith answered the ad and hired Marilyn.

Marilyn was recently seen dining with Edith at the Excelsior Palace Hotel in Venice. They always stay at the Excelsior, unless they stay at the Danieli, as they did on their fourth European trip. Next year Marilyn and Edith are off to Brazil to cruise the Amazon.

Some companions get trips every year with the same employer and more often than not, lasting friendships form on these trips. Others travel several times a year with different employers. If you're sincerely interested in this type of vacation, leave several copies of your resumé, including solid references, with travel agencies located within a hundred miles or so of your home. Also try an ad in a big city newspaper. It might read something like this:

> Traveling companion available June 5 to Sept 30. Educated female, mid-40s. Fluent English, French, German, Italian. Experienced European traveler. Call (phone number).

In addition, you may want to advertise your services in a home-exchange club directory. These clubs are listed in chapter 2, "Free Accommodations."

WORKING VACATION/SKIING VACATION

Yes, it's possible to hit the trails, make money while doing it, and to live at some beautiful sloping white place—all by getting a ski resort job. Of course, they are temporary, but some employees return every winter for more of the same, so these jobs must be either fun, lucrative, or both.

Village Camps S.A., a Swiss camping and skiing vacation organization, hires instructors to teach skiing. You must be a qualified ski instructor. Contact Village Camps S.A., Dept. 820, 1854 Leysin, Switzerland. The best book on the topic is *Working in Ski Resorts—Europe and North America*. It's by Victoria Pybus and it's available from Seven Hills Book Distributors, 49 Central Ave., Cincinnati, OH 45202. Phone: (800) 545-2005.

CAMP COUNSELING

A colleague's son, Bradley, was 17 when he got a job in Normandy as a camp counselor. Four years of getting A's in French in high school readied him for his assignment with French eight-, nine-, and ten-year-olds. At first *les enfants terribles* laughed when he spoke their language, but weeks before Bradley returned home to start college in the fall, he could say, "Shut up and go to bed" in French with no trace of an American accent.

Like Bradley, you can probably get a job as a summer-time camp counselor, perhaps in a beautiful spot such as the coast of Normandy or the Swiss Alps. Contact one or more of these organizations:

- Village Camps S.A., Dept. 820, Village Camps, 1854 Leysin, Switzerland. Phone: (025) 776-20-59. This organization hires counselors to work at children's camps in Swiss and Austrian resorts.

- YMCA International Camp Counselor Program/Abroad, 356 W. Thirty-fourth St., 3rd Floor, New York, NY 10001. Phone: (212) 563-3441. The Y makes available positions for applicants between 18 and 25 in camps in several countries. You must have completed at least a year of college and have camp counseling or other group leading experience. There's an application fee that covers insurance and placement. Counselors get their room and board and some pocket money, but they pay their transportation to and from the camp.

- *Backpacker: The Magazine of Wilderness Travel* has classified ads for camp counselors, resort personnel, outdoor adventure directors, and other bucolic-types. Many offer salary plus room and board. This could be a good way to spend the summer. They work in Yellowstone, Alaska, and other lovely wilderness areas.

Camp Counseling for Big People

- Club Med can make you a G.O. (Gentile Coordinateur) at one of their 115 vacation villages all over the world. G.O.s are

hired for six months and many are able to renew their contracts beyond a half-year. American G.O.s usually start their
G.O. careers at a camp in North America, the Caribbean, or
Bahamas, and may later get to work elsewhere, such as
Europe, Africa, and balmy Pacific islands. Club Med provides
health insurance, salary, room, board, and sunshine. You
must be at least 19 and must love water and fun. Call their
employment hotline at (407) 337-6660.

EATING YOUR WAY AROUND NORTH AMERICA

If you owned a restaurant, it's a pretty sure thing that every
time you came in, sat down at a table, and looked hungry, the
waiter or waitress whose paychecks you write would rush over
with a menu. The biggest tipper in town couldn't get better service in your own place than they would give you. But wouldn't
you wonder if other customers were also getting good service?
A lot of owners and corporate managers of chains do wonder.
That's why they hire anonymous diners.

An anonymous diner orders a good dinner, eats it, and pays for
it. The diner keeps a receipt or puts the meal on a credit card.
Then he or she writes a report on the service, atmosphere, and
food. The service that hires the anonymous diner reimburses him
or her for the price of the meal. The biggest challenge is having
to eat too much. The diner must order and at least try an appe-
tizer or two, a main course, and (needless to say) dessert. Gettting
free food for reports is a great sideline for travelers. They keep
moving and don't often eat at the same place twice. After eating
their way through Chicago, they might move on to Cleveland,
Pittsburgh, Baltimore, and on and on to more great meals.

If you think you can handle lots of good food without paying
for it, contact Restaurant and Hotel Services at (800) 296-7368.
Also try Service Evaluation Concepts at (800) 695-4746.

DIVING INTO YOUR WORK

Want an outdoor job with lots of water activity, surrounded
by bikini babes and/or hunks, and other adoring pupils? Want

to get away from it all and hang out with pastel-colored marine life? Writing in *Transitions Abroad* (March/April 1997), divemaster Steve Wilson states that "lots" of jobs exist for divers in resorts in the Caribbean and South Pacific. Whether you want a short-term seasonal job or something year-round, working your way around the world teaching diving to vacationers can be a pleasant way to spend a year or three. Vacationers at resorts need and will pay well for diving courses. Twenty-five to 40 hours of underwater and classroom instruction are needed before a person is certified to dive alone.

Diving is a big business (nearly $2 billion a year). Six million Americans are certified as divers and 2½ million of them dove within the last year. They traveled to the Caribbean islands, Belize, Costa Rica, Honduras, Hawaii, Fiji, Papua New Guinea, Micronesia, Indonesia, the Red Sea, and elsewhere. This is truly a popular sport, energized by better equipment and more flights to remote islands. Dive enthusiasts float on water-borne hotels called liveaboards and cruise to remote reefs.

Diving enthusiasts need instruction and support. That's where you could dive in. Give them the instruction they need and then take them to view submerged vessels and exotic aquatic life. Steve Wilson advises that instructors should get certified by PADI (Professional Association of Diving Instructors), NAUI (National Association of Underwater Instructors), or SSI (Scuba School International). PADI has a list of affiliated schools and both PADI and NAUI have websites that list schools.

- PADI International, 2151 E. Dyer Rd., #100, Santa Ana, CA 92705. Phone: (800) 729-7234 or (714) 540-7234. Website: www.padi.com.

- NAUI, 9942 Currie Davis Dr., Suite H, Tampa, FL 33619. Phone: (800) 553-6284 or (813) 628-6284. Website: www.naui.org.

- Scuba School International, 2619 Canyon Ct., Fort Collins, CO 80525-4498. Phone: (303) 482-0883. Instructors complete at least 150 hours of training. Inquire about location of schools and cost. Schools usually will help place instructors.

WORKING AT THE WORLD'S BEST RESORTS

Ever look at a brochure from a resort? The weather's always perfect. The sky is a brilliant blue. And these places are filled from the entryway to the broad sand beach with swimming pools. All the patrons are gorgeous. All the food is gourmet. Sound good? While you may not be ready to spring $500 or more per night to stay there, you can probably work there. But don't settle for any resort, work only at the best.

How do you locate the best? Get a hold of *Stern's Guide to the Greatest Resorts of the World,* by Steven B. Stern, Pelican Publishing Company, P.O. Box 3110, Gretna, LA 70054-3110. Phone: (800) 843-1724 or (888) 5-PELICAN. Stern has inspected more than 100 top resorts in all locations. Decide which you want to work at and send your resumés to these watering holes of the rich and famous. Offer to bus tables, bartend, do bookkeeping, or do housekeeping. Offer to do dish washing, cleaning, or whatever. It could land you in a luscious spot where you can earn enough big tips to keep traveling.

SHORT-TERM WORK DOWN ON THE FARM

Just as the United States invites foreign nationals to come in to help with harvests and other heavy-duty farm work, some foreign countries invite Americans get a taste of another culture by doing seasonal farm work. These organizations can help you get started:

- Centre for International Mobility, International Trainee Exchanges Unit, Box 343, 00531, Helsinki, Finland. CFIM arranges for 17- to 23-year-olds to work on Finnish farms in the summer.

- Farm Helpers in New Zealand, Kumeroa Lodge, RD1, Woodville 5473, New Zealand. Phone or fax: (011) 64-6-376-4582. Farm Helpers charges a small membership fee to help arrange temporary jobs working with farmers in exchange for room and board.

- Grape harvesting in France is done in September and October and generally lasts two to four weeks at each site. Although pay is minimal, room and board are generally provided. For information, contact Centre de Documentation et d'Information Rurale (CDIR), 92, rue due Dessous des Berges, 75013, Paris, France. Phone: (1) 45.83.04.92.

- Interexchange, Inc., 161 Sixth Ave., New York, NY 10013. Phone: (212) 924-0446. Fax: (212) 924-0575. E-mail: interex@earthlink.net. They can help arrange for you to get paid for doing farm work in Norway, Switzerland, or Finland. In Norway, an American can live as a "working guest" on a farm, picking fruit, caring for animals, and performing other chores. The average stay is three months.

- Northern Victoria Fruitgrowers' Association, Box 394, Shepparton, Victoria 3630, Australia. It recruits pickers in February and March. Contact also the Victoria Peach and Apricot Growers' Association, 30A Bank St., Cobram, VIC 3644, Australia.

- Norway: Atlantis Youth Exchange. Contact Atlantis, Rolf Hofmosgat 18, N-0655, Oslo, Norway. Phone: (011) 47-22-67-00-43. Fax: (011) 47-22-68-68-08. Atlantis arranges for people from age 18 to 30 to work on Norwegian farms for one to three months. Workers receive room, board, and pocket money.

- Stablemate (156 Pitt Town Rd., Kenthurst, NSW 2156, Australia) can help you get a job working with horses Down Under.

- World Experience in Agriculture, National FFA Center, 5632 Mt. Vernon Memorial Highway, P.O. Box 15160, Alexandria, VA 22309-0160. Phone: (703) 360-3600. Fax: (703) 360-5524. This organization facilitates long- and short-term agricultural exchange programs with farmers abroad. Write for full information.

Spending the Summer with Your Uncle Sam

Our most generous Uncle Sam not only gives out buckets of money to deserving nieces and nephews (see chapter 12, "Traveling on Grants, Scholarships, and Awards"), but he also provides short-term summer employment. Here's how to find out about Sam's summer specials: Contact the U.S. Office of Personnel Management. Phone Career America Connection, the Federal Job Opportunities Bulletin Board: (912) 757-3100.

The federal government offers opportunities to students, ages 16 and older, to work for its agencies full-time during the summer. After finding out what jobs are open by calling the numbers above, applicants apply directly to the agency that requires workers. In addition, you can open your phone directory to the government pages and ask agencies that interest you about job possibilities. When the job takes you away from where you live, you're able to combine an interesting work experience with travel.

BUSKING

Instead of depending on someone to hand you a paycheck or feed you, why not strike out on your own? This idea is for the mildly adventuresome individual who has talent. Play your musical instrument, sing, swallow fire (don't really), dance, manipulate puppets, pretend to saw your girlfriend in half, mime, lift trucks in the air, act, tell stories, juggle, etc. With any luck, and if you have some true talent—or at least look hungry—passersby will throw enough money in your hat or violin case to keep you touring. Find out first if it's legal in the city or town where you want to rake in money.

ADVANCING AS AN INTERN

Here's an opportunity to live abroad, advance in your profession, develop your skills, and pay your way as you go. Working as an intern also allows you to enjoy the great sights of Europe during your days off. To get involved, contact one or more of these organizations:

AIPT/IAEST

AIPT/IAESTE: All those initials stand for Association for International Practical Training (AIPT)/International Association for the Exchange of Students for Technical Experience (IAESTE). This tongue-twisting organization places interns in paying programs in engineering, math, science, tourism, and with the hospitality industry. Contact them at 10400 Little Patuxent Parkway, Suite 250, Columbia, MD 21044. Phone: (410) 997-2200. Fax: (410) 992-3924. E-mail: aipt@aipt.org or http://www.aipt.org.

AIPT arranges visas for students to obtain practical training abroad. Applicants need to be between 18 and 35, have a degree in the field they want to pursue as an intern, and have a year's practical work experience in that field. In addition, applicants need a "working knowledge" of the language of the country they want to visit.

AIPT can assist you in finding an assignment or in getting a visa for a job you've already secured. While the participant covers his or her travel costs, the employer is expected to cover maintenance expenses by paying a decent wage. Programs vary in length from three to 18 months. Countries that host interns are Austria, Finland, France, Germany, Ireland, Japan, Malaysia, the Slovak Republic, Switzerland, and the United Kingdom. There are application fees.

FACC/ACTIM

FACC/ACTIM Internship Program, c/o French-American Chamber of Commerce, 509 Madison Ave., Suite 1900, New York, NY 10022. Phone: (212) 374-4466. Young people entering the professions of banking, advertising, marketing, computer science, engineering, or telecommunication, and who can ply their trade in French, can apply for a paid internship that lasts from a month to a year. It's for college seniors, graduate students, or otherwise qualified individuals.

Interexchange, Inc.

Interexchange, Inc., 161 Sixth Ave., New York, NY 10013.

Phone: (212) 924-0446. Fax: (212) 924-0575. E-mail: interex@ earthlink.net. They have internships in Finland in commerce, marketing, hotel and restaurant management, and environmental protection. These placements are for three months. You must be between 18 and 30 and pay a modest program fee.

International Cooperative Education Program

International Cooperative Education Program, 15 Spiros Way, Menlo Park, CA 94025. Phone: (415) 323-4944. Fax: (415) 323-1104. ICEP has placed more than 12,000 students in paid internships in Austria, Belgium, Finland, France, Germany, Japan, Hong Kong, Singapore, South Africa, and Switzerland. Participants must have completed at least a year of a college-level courses in German, French, Dutch, Italian, or Japanese before leaving for the assignment. The objective is to immerse students in language and culture while they gain practical experience through working.

Programs include retail sales, teaching, hotel and restaurant work, farming, office duties, work in hospitals and banks, and in computer sciences, etc. For eight to 12 weeks in the summer, participants work 30 to 40 hours a week and earn a modest salary. Accommodations are provided by local host families or by the employer. International Cooperative Education arranges work permits. Due to labor regulations in the countries involved, applicants have to be under age 30. This organizations inquires: "Why work at home when you can work abroad?" There's a fee and the participants cover their airfare costs.

Internships in Francophone Europe

Internships in Francophone Europe, Reid Hall, 4, rue Chevreuse, 75006 Paris, France. Phone: (1) 43.21.78.07 or (1) 43.63.97.15. If you've managed to complete four years of French in school with no grade under B+, and if you're a college junior, senior, or graduate student, you can apply for an internship working in an office of the French government.

Reading about Getting Internships

Read *Directory of International Internships: A World of Opportunities* by Charles Cliozzo et al. It's published by Michigan State University and obtainable from Career Development and Placement Services, Attn.: International Placement, MSU, 113 Student Services Bldg., East Lansing, MI 48824. Phone: (517) 355-9510, extension 371. This book describes opportunities for academic and nonacademic internships.

TRAVEL WRITING

Consider doing some part-time travel writing on your vacation. It's a good way to pay for all or part of your trip. Anywhere you go for the first time, whether it's Timbuktu or the zoo, will be interesting. Because you're seeing it with a sense of wonder, your excitement will find its way into your writing; and your readers will share your delight in your new discovery. Laptop computers, e-mail, and fax machines make it entirely possible for writers to keep moving from place to place while they work.

If you haven't written for publication but have always wanted to, enroll in a creative writing course at your local community college or adult school. No matter how good your instructor is, more than likely the greatest benefit of taking a writing course is networking with like-minded classmates who are talented and who may encourage you in pursuit of your new vocation.

No matter how good your instructor is and how much encouragement you get from your fellow students, your best source of education as a writer is reading. Read authors whose words sing in your ears and try to reach their pitch as you create your own works. See how they string words together to weave the exact tapestry they've sketched in their outlines.

No matter how good a creative writing course is, how stimulating your new writing friends are, and no matter how much you're learning from the printed page, there's no substitute for writing. It's the one essential task you must perform in order to learn the craft.

Once you start getting entire articles down on paper and they seem to be coherent and compelling, get them published in your local weekly newspaper, in your club's bulletin, or in the college literary magazine. After that, graduate to writing for the travel section of your daily paper and for *International Travel News*. *ITN* is not only must-reading for anyone who loves exotic travel, but it provides an entry to new writers because the vast majority of every issue is written by its readers. Readers tell others about their adventures and advise what hotels to book in Katmandu, what restaurants to patronize in Tangier, and what tours to avoid in Guadalcanal. Your free sample copy will arrive after you've contacted the monthly magazine at 1901 Royal Oaks Dr., Suite 190, Sacramento, CA 95815. Phone: (800) 486-4968. If you're ready to submit an article, it goes to 2120 Twenty-eighth St., Sacramento, CA 95818. Phone: (916) 457-3643.

Once you've chosen a publication to write for, become downright intimate with it. Read lots of back issues. Send an SASE for writers' guidelines; they're always free. Don't be intimidated by editors. Remember, they need you as much as you need them; without writers, they'd be looking for jobs in another line of work.

Find out what sort of articles, what length, what style the editor prefers. Here's a formula worth the price of this book: Spread out three or more articles from the same magazine. All three articles ought to have the same general intent: to tell about a visit to an exotic destination, to explain how to save money on travel, or to give historic background about different places, and so on. Now, underline all anecdotes with a red pen, all facts with a yellow pen, all descriptions with a blue pen, and all dialogue or quotes with a black pen. This way, you'll know what the editor likes; for example, you learn that the editor prefers one fifth of each article to be anecdotes. The editor may not know that, but you will; and your knowledge of his or her preferences will give you a terrific advantage in selling your articles to that particular editor. In fact, you may well sell every article you submit over time to that same buyer.

Before you spend much time going beyond basic research, write a query letter to the editor. Briefly tell about the article you plan to do. Send the editor a sample of your writing, either some published work or a part of the proposed piece. You may get an assignment on speculation, which means that the editor wants an article on the subject you've proposed and will buy it from you if you meet the editor's expectations. If it's not good, he or she will get it from someone else or go without it.

If you get a definite assignment, you can take some or all of your travel expenses off your income tax. Write Internal Revenue Service, Department of the Treasury, Washington, D.C., and ask for publication 463, "Travel, Entertainment and Gift Expenses." It states: "Travel expenses are your ordinary and necessary expenses while traveling away from home for your business, profession, or job. You may deduct these expenses if you prove them." These necessary expenses are transportation, baggage charges, meals and lodging, cleaning and laundry while traveling, telephone calls, tips, and "other similar expenses related to qualifying travel." Let's say you go to Hawaii for a week to write an article about secluded beaches. You're paid $3,000 for the article, but your expenses are $2,000. If you've stuck to business for the entire trip, you can deduct the $2,000. You pay taxes on $1,000, and you've paid for your trip.

> $$$—Cousin Thrifty McCheap says: "Bob Kirk may know a lot about free travel, but he isn't a tax adviser. Check with an expert before taking any deductions."

Unless you're a real pro, you probably won't get an advance to take that travel-writing trip. In fact, you may not get paid until the article is published, which could be six to nine months after you've submitted the final draft, and perhaps a year or more after you've proposed it. So how do you keep traveling while waiting to get paid? The trick is to write and sell lots of articles so you'll have a steady stream of checks coming in.

Here's a way just about anyone can get published: Although they don't pay much, hometown newspapers love articles about local people who are out traveling. However, your article is more likely to get on the society page than in the travel section because the editor is more interested in the fact that *you* went to Pisa than in being told how far the precarious Tower has been leaning lately.

Here's a twist on names-in-the-local-paper articles. We met Miranda, a 30-something American in Avignon, France. Miranda told us she was low on money but that she was able to prolong her stay in Europe by meeting Americans, finding out where they'd been touring, and sending articles about them back to their hometown papers. When an editor paid her for the short articles she wrote, the newspaper sent the check to her sister's home in Bangor, Maine. Her sister forwarded the checks every two weeks to Miranda in Europe. Every time she collected $20 or $30, Miranda was able to pay for a night in a hostel, eat well enough, and buy a train ticket.

Miranda told us she had been inspired by Norman Ford's book, *How to Travel and Get Paid for It* (Harrian Press, Greenlawn, NY 11740; distributed by Grosset & Dunlap, Inc.). Miranda recalled word for word that Ford had stated: "So great is the demand for foreign reporting by smaller American magazines and newspapers that any American who can sell nonfiction should be able to go overseas and set himself up in his own territory with a good chance of success."

Many travelers are unable to contain the raging enthusiasm and sense of wide-eyed wonder that are the exciting rewards of discovering world-class places; as a a result, they get pretty serious about travel writing. Those who master their craft are often able to pay for their entire trips by writing articles or books. Others illustrate their articles and books with first-rate photography. A rarefied few are able to support themselves entirely as traveling journalists.

IN COPENHAGEN WITH GARY, THE ROVING PHOTOGRAPHER

We met Gary, from Duluth, Minnesota, when he snapped our pictures in Copenhagen. We had just hopped out of a canal tour boat in Nyhavn. We'd boarded at the *Mermaid* statue and intended to have lunch and then wander off to the Strøget for people watching. But Gary had been watching us. When the picture developed a few seconds later, Gary offered it to us for $2. Although we knew it had cost him just pennies to take and develop, we accepted. It was a good picture of two people happy to be in the Danish capital on a sunny afternoon and anticipating a good meal. Wherever you travel, you might take a Polaroid instant camera and get good pictures of tourists to sell to them. Photograph enough tourists and pay for your trip.

MAKING MONEY BY DRAWING PORTRAITS

Similarly, if you're a good artist, you might consider drawing people's pictures. Set up an easel in a public place such as the town square, if you're permitted by the authorities to do so. If no customers want to pay, offer to draw the face of a particularly attractive passerby for free. Display your work and if it's good, it'll attract customers. Some artists make a reasonable living during good weather, particularly in tourist season.

MORE STUFF TO READ

Here are a few sources to help you explore the travel writing and travel photography option:

- *Free Money for Travel Writers* is a 185-page guide that's available from DeBillot Publishing, 2022 Cliff Dr., #101, Santa Barbara, CA 93109. Phone: (805) 563-2795.

- *A Guide to Travel Writing and Photography,* by Ann and Carl Purcell, is available from Writer's Digest Books, 1507 Dana Ave., Cincinnati, OH 45207. Phone: (800) 289-0963.

- *Sell Your Photos: The Photographer's Market,* edited by Michael Willins, Writer's Digest Books, 1507 Dana Ave., Cincinnati, OH 45207. Phone: (800) 289-0963 or (513) 531-2222. This book lists names and addresses of editors who buy photos, including travel pictures. The editors explain submission requirements, payments, etc.

- *The Travel Writer's Handbook,* by Louise P. Zobel, is published by Surrey Books and can be ordered from Publishers Group West, 4065 Hollis St., Emeryville, CA 94608. Phone: (800) 365-3453.

- *Travel Writing: A Guide to Research, Writing & Selling* is available from Writer's Digest Books, 1507 Dana Ave., Cincinnati, OH 42507. Phone: (800) 289-0963.

- *Writer's Market,* latest edition, is published by Writer's Digest Books, 1507 Dana Ave., Cincinnati, OH 42507. Phone: (800) 289-0963. Look in the section that lists travel periodicals. Here you'll find addresses, phone numbers, names of editors, requirements, and rates of pay of magazines that purchase travel articles and photos. You'll be surprised at how many there are.

- *Writing Jobs Abroad* is a guide published by *Transitions Abroad,* P.O. Box 1300, Amherst, MA 01004-1300. Phone: (800) 293-0373. E-mail: trabroad@aol.com. It includes tips on making money travel writing and writing for overseas markets.

- *Working Writer* is a monthly newsletter for nonfiction—including travel—writers. WW has information on press trips, travel discounts for writers, and international and domestic markets for your work. Ask for a free sample copy: *Working Writer,* 130 W. Eightieth St., Suite 2F, New York, NY 10024. Phone: (212) 874-3367.

These organizations have membership rosters that are filled with the names of travel writers. Contact the associations for membership information and tips to help you get started:

- International Association of Travel Journalists, P.O. Box D, Hurleyville, NY 12747. Phone: (914) 434-1529.

- International Food, Wine, and Travel Writers Association, P.O. Box 13110, Long Beach, CA 90803. Phone: (310) 433-5969.

- North American Ski Journalists Association, P.O. Box 5334, Takoma Park, MD 20913. Phone: (301) 864-8428.

- Outdoor Writers Association of America, 2017 Cato Ave., Suite 101, State College, PA 16801. Phone: (814) 234-1011.
- Society of American Travel Writers, 4101 Lake Boone Trail, Suite 201, Raleigh, NC 27607. Phone: (919) 787-5181.
- Travel Journalists Guild, P.O. Box 10643, Chicago, IL 60610. Phone: (312) 664-9279.

VACATION-TIME IMPORTING

It's possible to pay for your travels by importing goods to sell to retailers in the United States. For example, were you to go to Bali or Java in Indonesia, you'd find extraordinarily inexpensive but beautiful hand puppets and model sailboats that you could bring back and consign to gift shops. In Kenya, you'll find exquisite handcarved statues of people and of animals; they make extraordinary ornaments in homes and offices. Mexican, Guatemalan, Peruvian, and Ecuadorean markets are full of fascinating goods that could be profitably resold in the States. Primitive carvings from Cameroon or dolls from the Ukraine cost little on the spot but are marked up considerably in American shops. Wherever you go, you're sure to find items that you instinctively know people back home will want.

In *How to Be an Importer and Pay for Your World Travels,* Mary Green and Stanley Gillmar explain how they started an importing business by buying some scarves in North Africa and selling them to a shop in San Francisco. In a chatty volume, they recall how their subsequent trips centered around buying goods abroad that would appeal to the American public. They were successful enough to pay for their travels and even make a profit. Green and Gillmar explain where to go, what to buy, what questions to ask yourself before buying, how to haggle, how to sell to shop owners, how to get around language barriers, and how to get your goods through U.S. customs. Start by reading:

- *How to be an Importer and Pay for Your World Travels,* by Mary Green and Stanley Gilmar. Ten Speed Press, P.O. Box 7123, Berkeley, CA 94707. Phone: (800) 841-BOOK.

- *Building an Import/Export Business* is by Kenneth D. Weill. It is available from John Wiley and Sons, One Wiley Dr., Somerset, NJ 08873. Phone: (201) 469-4400.

MORE INFORMATION ON SHORT-TERM WORK ABROAD

If there's a job for you in another country, you'll either find it or find out how to get it from one or more of these sources.

- Cool Works is a comprehensive Internet site that has excellent information on jobs that are available. Separate categories include working in summer camps, national parks, resorts, on ranches, in ski areas, on cruise ships, etc. Check out this website: http://www.coolworks.com/showme.

- *Directory of American Firms Operating in Foreign Countries* lists 3,000 companies with overseas subsidiaries and affiliates worldwide. The publisher, Uniworld, lists this compendium at $220, so try your library first.

- See *The Complete Guide to International Jobs and Careers* by Ronald L. Krannich and Caryl R. Krannich, from Impact Publications, 9104-N Manassas Dr., Manassas Park, VA 22111. Phone: (703) 361-7300. Website: http://www.impact. It's full of strategies for getting hired overseas. Also see the Krannichs' *The Almanac of International Jobs and Careers: A Guide to Over 1001 Employers*. The Almanac's from Impact too.

- *Directory of Jobs and Careers Abroad* by Andre DeVries, Vacation Work Publications, from Peterson's Guides, P.O. Box 2123, Princeton, NJ 08543. Phone: (800) 338-3282. It includes short-term unskilled and volunteer possibilities as well as professional opportunities, country by country.

- *Directory of International Internships: A World of Opportunities* by Charles Gliozzo et al. It can be had from Career Development and Placement Services, Attn.: International Placement, Michigan State University, 113 Student Services Bldg., East Lansing, MI 48824. Phone: (517) 335-9510. Write for the price. Some of the opportunities are for pay. The book contains both academic and nonacademic internships.

- *The Directory of Overseas Summer Jobs* is edited by David Woodworth and is published each January by Vacation Work and available from Peterson's Guides, P.O. Box 2123, Princeton, NJ 08543. Phone: (800) 338-3282. This book starts applicants on their way to accessing information about more than 30,000 paid and unpaid temporary positions in more than 50 countries. It includes details about work permits, compensation, the application process, etc.

- *Directory of Summer Jobs in Britain,* Emily Hatchwell, ed. From Vacation Work, it lists 30,000 jobs including on farms, performing child care, and in the hospitality industry, etc.

- French Cultural Services, 972 Fifth Ave., New York, NY 10021. Phone: (212) 439-1400. Ask for *Employment in France for Students,* which summarizes employment opportunities and work regulations.

- Global Alternatives, Professional Development Resource Center, School for International Training, P.O. Box 676, Kipling Rd., Brattleboro, VT 05302-0676. Phone: (802) 258-3397. Fax: (802) 258-3248. GA publishes monthly job bulletins listing around a hundred openings for educators, consultants, administrators, etc.

- *Guide to Employment Abroad,* Michigan State University, Career Development Services, International Placement, 113 Student Services Bldg., East Lansing, MI 48824-1113.

- *How to Find an Overseas Job with the U.S. Government* by Will Cantrell and Francine Modderno. It's from Worldwise Books, P.O. Box 3030, Oakton, VA 22124.

- *How to Get a Job in Europe: The Insider's Guide* by Robert Sanborn. By the same author is *How to Get a Job in the Pacific Rim.* Either or both can be bought from Surrey Books, Inc., 230 E. Ohio St., Suite 120, Chicago, IL 60611. Phone: (800) 326-4430. Addresses are listed for businesses in several countries and the authors make good suggestions.

- Impact Publications will furnish a free catalog of books on international jobs and careers. Website: http://www.impact-publications.com.

- ICEN-L. Sub request to listserv@iubvm.indiana.edu. You can access a list of international job openings.

- *International Career Employment Opportunities,* Route 2, Box 305, Stanardsville, VA 22973. Phone: (804) 985-6444. Fax: (804) 985-6828. E-mail: intlcareers@internetmci.com. This biweekly list of five to six hundred openings, mostly overseas, is largely for professionals with two or more years of experience.

- *International Employment Gazette,* 220 N. Main St., Suite 100, Greenville, SC 29601. Phone: (800) 882-9188. Fax: (803) 235-3369. Four hundred or more current job listings worldwide in all occupations are published every two weeks. They're listed by geographical area and by field of preparation. Call for the subscription price.

- *International Employment Hotline,* P.O. Box 3030, Oakton,VA 22124. This monthly newsletter lists foreign jobs in health care, international development, civil engineering, small business, information management, computers, and teaching English. Write for the current subscription cost.

- *International Job, Career, and Travel Resources for the 1990s* is a free catalog of books on jobs and careers. Order it from Impact Publications, 9104-N Manassas Dr., Manassas Park, VA 22111. Phone: (703) 361-7300.

- *Jobs for People Who Love Travel* is by Ron and Caryl Krannich. The book's from Impact Publications, P.O. Box 1896, Evanston, IL 60204. Phone: (312) 475-5748. It includes myths about jobs that involve travel. See also *Jobs Worldwide* by David Lay and Benedict Leerburger, also from Impact Publications. The second book focuses on key employers and job opportunities.

- *Passport to Overseas Employment,* by Dale Chambers, Arco/ Prentice Hall, 15 Columbus Circle, New York, NY 10023.

Phone: (800) 223-2336. It covers work permits, how to find jobs, etc.

- *Special Career Opportunities for Linguists/Translators/Interpreters.* It's free from the U.S. State Dept., Language Services Division, Room 2212, Washington, D.C. 20520. Phone: (202) 647-1528.

- University of California Irvine International Opportunities Program has comprehensive information on working overseas. Website: www.cie.uci.edu/-cie.

- *Work Abroad: $70,000 Exemption,* published by *Transitions Abroad,* P.O. Box 1300, Amherst, MA 01004-1300. Phone: (800) 293-0373. E-mail: trabroad@aol.com. The book explains another advantage to overseas employment, which is an exemption on U.S. taxes as long as you're not earning your money in the United States.

- "Work Abroad," CIEE Work Abroad, 205 E. Forty-second St., New York, NY 10017. Phone: (212) 661-1414, ext. 1126. It's a free description of work abroad programs administered by CIEE.

- *Work-Study-Travel Abroad Guidelines* are free from U.S. Information Agency, Office of Public Liaison, 301 Fourth St. SW, Washington, D.C. 20547.

- *Work, Study, Travel Abroad: The Whole World Handbook,* CIEE, St. Martin's Press, 175 Fifth Ave., New York, NY 10010. This is a comprehensive guide that deserves an honored place in your library of books on free and reduced-cost travel.

- *Work Your Way Around the World,* by Susan Griffith, is from Vacation Work Publications, 9 Park End St., Oxford OX1 1HJ, U.K. Phone: 011-44-1865-241978. This admirable, exhaustively researched volume contains extensive firsthand information. It's also available from Peterson's Guides, P.O. Box 2123, Princeton, NJ 08543. Phone: (800) EDU-DATA. If you're serious about working abroad, you'll read Griffith's terrific volume. I recommend it most highly.

- Write to Zink's 119 (P.O. Box 587, Marshall, MI 49068-0587) for a list of publications telling you how to get overseas jobs. Among these are *Travel Industry Jobs, Resumes for Overseas and Stateside Jobs, Cruise Ships,* and *Airline Jobs.* Zink's publications emphasize opportunities for free travel. *Overseas Exotic Jobs* offers tips and lists of positions available through the federal government, on cruise ships, and through American and foreign firms overseas. These include work for unskilled, skilled, and professional workers.

BARTERING TO TRAVEL

And now, for all of those well-established readers who are already ensconced in a marvelous profession or business and who have no intention of closing up the firm in order to pick peaches in Paraguay or play an accordion in Acapulco, here's an idea for earning vacation travel without reaching into your pocket.

Imagine for a moment that you're a dentist (unless, of course, you are), and business has been a bit slow lately. You have more hours than teeth to fill, vacation time is approaching, and your family is pressuring you to rent a beach house for $2,000 for the month of August. You even tell your patients about your problem. Since parting with two big ones at this point in your career would be tougher than pulling teeth, you decide to put off the trip to the shore for another year. Then, one morning when you pull your hand out of a patient's mouth, she says to you: "You can fix teeth for the key to the beach house. It's called bartering."

Probably the first two cave people invented bartering and it has never gone away. In fact it has grown and become institutionalized. Bartering networks now operate in most urban areas and are listed in the yellow pages under either "Bartering Organizations" or "Trade Exchanges." Network members, who are mostly small-business people, skilled craftspersons, and self-employed professionals, can trade surplus goods and work time for what they want.

Typical trades might be a year's garden maintenance in exchange for a boat, accounting services for a trip from a travel agent, or new appliances for use of a rental car. Boat charters, restaurant meals, hotel rooms, flights in private planes, airline tickets, use of a vehicle, admissions to theaters and tourist attractions—all that's necessary for a real red-carpet vacation is available through barter.

Most barter networks work pretty much the same. Each charges either an initiation fee or 10 to 15 percent commissions on trades—or both. Once in, a member offers his or her skills, expertise, or superfluous goods at retail or at a standard hourly fee. Offers aren't made in terms of dollars. Money is out of the picture. Members use trade units to keep track.

Assume Dr. Green, an optometrist, wants new carpeting for her office. She "buys" it from member Brown, who owns a floor-covering store. Green pays 1,500 trade units. Brown has no need for an optometric exam at this time, but he does need close to 1,500 trade units' worth of accounting, which he gets from member White, the CPA. This makes White happy because he owes 1,500 units to a caterer who provided sustenance for his daughter June's wedding.

All of this would be a bookkeeping nightmare for the entrepreneurs who set up the club were it not for a computer, which sends members monthly statements. Dr. Green is billed 1,500 units for her carpet, but she doesn't have much in her account, so she'll eventually have to do more optometric work for members.

Because of this transaction, Dr. Green will attract new patients, members who otherwise may not have engaged the services of that particular professional. Brown makes a sale he wouldn't have made had it not been for the club; Dr. Green probably wouldn't have put out cash for a carpet at a time when her practice was slow. Accountant White pays off one more wedding debt. Everyone benefits.

Bartering is also profitable for the entrepreneur who manages the network. The network rakes off its sizable percentage.

Bartering is profitable, too, for the IRS. Would our own Uncle Sam let this creative type of business transaction go untaxed? Silly question. According to the IRS, whatever changes hands in a barter exchange—an airline seat for chiropractic services, for example—is taxable and must be assessed at fair market value. The good news is that there's nothing illegal or undercover about making an exchange in a legitimate barter network. Today something like 500 barter networks facilitate the transactions of 350,000 members. These members do substantially more than a billion dollars' worth of business annually.

Look for two important items when you sign up with a barter club. One: If you intend to travel, make sure there are travel agents, restaurateurs, tour operators, hotel owners, people with planes or boats, etc. among the membership. If there are none, there will be no one to offer you travel in return for your goods or services.

Two: Make sure there aren't already too many people in the club offering the goods and services you're dispensing. If you're a poodle groomer and the club has a pack of poodle groomers, the competition will be so keen that you'll have to lower your price to make a deal.

Set a realistic retail price or a reasonable professional charge, but be aware that some members may be setting their prices or charges too high, and others may try to fob off otherwise unusable goods on you. Let your slogan be *caveat emptor,* or perhaps *caveat swapper.* Remember, even though you're not dealing in real money, the taxes on the exchange are in Uncle Sam's official currency.

For more information, send large SASEs to the two largest barter organizations:

- International Reciprocal Trade Association, 6305 Hawaii Ct., Alexandria, VA 22312.

- National Association of Trade Exchanges, 27801 Euclid Ave., Suite 610, Euclid, OH 44132.

Subscribe to *Barter News,* P.O. Box 3024, Mission Viejo, CA 92690.

WHAT IT'S ALL ABOUT

The message of this chapter is simple: Instead of working at a dead-end job back in Humdrum Corners to fund your trip, work at a dead-end job in Palermo, Penang, San Juan, Yokohama, Cairns—wherever you want to visit. You may not make a fortune, but you'll earn a fortune in new friends, memories, and knowledge.

CHAPTER 14

Travel Careers and Their Perks

McCheap's Fourteenth Law of Travel:
If you've got to work for a living, you may as well do it
in a job that gets you free vacation trips.

LONG-TERM JOBS THAT ALLOW YOU TO TRAVEL

This chapter is about choosing a career that allows you to travel at little or no cost. The first part concerns working in the travel and tourism industries. It gives valuable information on some high visibility careers such as those in travel agencies and in airlines. Whatever travel career path you choose, your job can help you travel inexpensively or free for pleasure during your vacations, on long weekends, as an occasional and nonobligatory part of your duties, and during retirement.

The second part of the chapter is about working abroad full-time, for long periods of time—becoming an expatriate worker. Such jobs can allow you to get to know other parts of the world intimately and to use your overseas home as a base for wider explorations during leaves, long weekends, and vacations.

TRAVEL AND TOURISM CAREERS

Millions of employees and self-employed individuals in the travel and tourism industry enjoy free vacation perquisites ("perks"). When you've finished reading this chapter, you'll know how they do it and how you can enjoy the same perks.

AN INDUSTRY ON THE MOVE

Travel and tourism is big. It brings in a tremendous amount of foreign exchange to the United States and employs about a tenth of American workers. These workers not only facilitate the travel of foreign visitors, but they also help make possible the one billion vacation and business trips Americans make each year. Moreover, the industry is predicted to boom and bloom even more in the future. For anyone looking for a career for the 21st century, travel and tourism might be a good field to look at in some depth.

Railways, cruise ship lines, freighter operators, bus companies, hotels, inns and bed and breakfasts, restaurants, campgrounds, amusement parks, marinas, airlines, airports, charter boats, tour organizers, resorts, motel chains, and a host of other travel industry components hire people with a variety of skills and training.

Tour wholesalers, for example—those largely invisible organizers who arrange for hundreds of hotel rooms, entire buses, blocks of jetliner seats, and whole sections of restaurants—all to sell to retail agencies or tour operators—hire lots of people. They need secretaries, reservation clerks, salespeople, managers, and tour escorts. In addition to drivers, bus lines need ticket clerks, baggage handlers, sales representatives, supervisors, attorneys, personnel managers, computer programmers, mechanics, office clerks, custodians, dispatchers, and others. Opportunities working for hotels and resorts aren't limited to the more obvious positions as desk clerks and bell captains; hotels and resorts employ executives, housekeepers, accountants, maintenance personnel, gardeners, attorneys, salespeople, food preparers, and more.

Lonni is one of 10 million Americans employed in the hospitality and tourism industry; by 2005, if the U.S. Bureau of Statistics prediction is correct, she'll be one of 12.4 million. She's a conference center manager for a hotel chain. It's her job to rent her firm's facilities and hotel rooms to conference and convention organizers. Lonni has one of the more interesting jobs in an industry that includes food service, hotel maintenance, transportation, and just about any service that facilitates travel. Many of the 10 million work in places that have less to do with moving people than with recreation: theme parks, marinas, campgrounds, parks, and other attractions. Yet, all of these people, like Lonni, serve travelers in one capacity or another.

The hospitality industry shares a large portion of the 2½ *trillion* dollars in annual revenues from travel and tourism, the largest industry in the world. Where do all of these travelers and tourists come from? Between 85 and 90 percent, not surprisingly, come from the 25 percent of the world's industrially developed nations. Since a number of other nations are developing rapidly, the basis of tourism is sure to expand, making it an even greater source of employment.

The good news for young people between ages 18 and 24 is that workers in their age group are highly sought after, especially in the service sectors of hospitality and tourism. Those who get some of the better jobs have graduated from hospitality and tourism programs in colleges and universities. Not only do they receive generous travel perks, but their managerial salaries compare favorably to those with similar responsibilities in other industries. Like Lonni, people who choose these hospitality and tourism jobs enjoy working with people and are service oriented.

The hospitality industry lives up to its name by extending deep discounts at hotels, resorts, and other facilities to people within the industry. Often these employees receive discounts on rental cars, cruises, tours, etc. That's why Lonni pays less than half what most people pay when she vacations in Hawaii every June.

Unless you're easily satisfied with an entry-level job that requires minimal skills, you may need some training that will make your travel career even more interesting and rewarding.

TRAINING FOR A TRAVEL CAREER

Many community colleges offer certificates, diplomas, and associate degrees in travel and tourism. This training might be for travel agency operations, hotel or restaurant management, corporate travel planning, various airline careers, travel wholesaling, auto rental management, tour operations, or some related field. Let's look at two such programs:

West Los Angeles College (94800 Freshman Dr., Culver City, CA 90230-3500), for example, boasts that a quarter of all travel professionals in the greater L.A. area have taken its courses. This college is one of a few around the country that can set you on your travel career path in a hurry. If you take four classes in any one semester, including the introductory course, you can earn a basic certificate in travel at West L.A. Take four more and you'll earn your advanced certificate. With 36 units (approximately 12 courses) as a major, you can work toward a 60-unit associate in arts degree—in travel.

And you can choose the travel classes that will best suit your needs. Those courses might be elementary and advanced APOLLO and SABRE reservations; you need that knowledge to book airline tickets. You might take two travel-related geography courses, so if your client wants to see the Alhambra, you'll send him to Granada, Spain, and not to the balmy island of Grenada in the West Indies. And you'll know that Djibouti isn't a shoe store. You could take introduction to the airline industry or introduction to the hospitality industry; or you might pick up a marketing and sales class or a course on how to escort groups and plan tour operations. Any of these classes could lead to a career. Needless to say, West L.A. provides job opportunity listings, foreign language classes, and counseling, among other services.

Miami-Dade Community College (11380 N.W. Twenty-seventh Ave., Miami, FL 33167) turns out professionals with associate degrees in travel and industry management and in travel and tourism management. Their courses are similar to those of West L.A. College, but they also offer classes such as psychology of leisure travel, narrative presentations, and tour guide field study.

A good way to start travel career training is to phone community colleges in your area and see what programs they have to offer. If you're willing to relocate to take courses, look in the latest edition of *Lovejoy's* or *Peterson's* college guides; these volumes are in the reference sections of nearly all public and college libraries, and they should also be in the hands of high-school guidance counselors. They are quite up to date and will give you a good description of the programs currently being offered by various schools. Most states have community college programs in travel and tourism areas.

A number of universities offer bachelor's degree programs in travel and tourism, hotel administration, restaurant management, business administration with an emphasis on the travel industry, and similar fields. A few universities grant master's and doctorate degrees in travel-related fields; some states have only one such university graduate program, while several states have none. Most graduate degree seekers will have to relocate. Again *Lovejoy's* or *Peterson's* guides will give you a full list of what's available at travel-degree-granting institutions.

The University of Hawaii and the University of New Haven in Connecticut offer such programs. George Washington University in the nation's capital has an MBA program in tourism management. How necessary are these advanced degrees? "They're immensely helpful, but not essential," admits the dean of the travel and tourism department in a large university. "Many travel managers are trained in general business management and find themselves in the travel business only after receiving their bachelor's or master's degrees, without having taken *any* travel-related courses," she said.

In addition to considering college and university training, look under "Schools" in your phone book's yellow pages. When you've located a travel academy or private college that offers courses leading to travel careers, don't assume without investigating that they'll give you the training necessary to find a good job easily. Ask the school for the names and phone numbers of graduates; phone these alumni and ask if they got the jobs they had trained for and if their training was relevant to the work they do. Ask them if they'd attend the school if they had their lives to live over, knowing what they know now. Ask the school what percentage of their graduates get jobs in the areas for which they've prepared. Your list should include questions about costs, financial assistance, qualifications of faculty, application deadline dates, courses offered, placement services, and accreditation. If the school's not accredited, skip it.

A CAREER AS A TRAVEL AGENT

Let's explore some career options that can lead to free travel and to trips at radically-reduced prices. We'll start with travel agency positions. Millions of travelers put their precious vacation days and dollars into the hands of travel counselors. Airlines, tour companies, cruise lines, bus services, railroads, hotel chains, and rental car firms can't maintain ticket and reservation offices in every neighborhood, small town, or shopping center, so travel agencies do much of their work for them. Agencies make money from the commissions paid by travel providers when they sell the providers' tickets and services. Unless an agent has to work out a particularly complex itinerary or perform chores for the customer that net little or no commission, the customer pays nothing for the agency's services.

Commissions from airlines are the agency's lifeblood. Agencies are licensed by the Air Traffic Conference (ATC) to sell tickets within the United States and by the International Air Transport Association (IATA) to sell tickets for foreign flights. In order to go into business, an agency's owner must prove to both the ATC and the IATA that there's a competent manager at the helm—someone with at least two years' sales experience in an established agency.

Beyond the stipulated two years' experience, there's no specific training required of managers or of other agency employees; they're not certified like teachers or even licensed like cosmetologists. Yet, they need a host of skills and specific training, learning that can be had either on the job or in the classroom. They need to know about the products of a bewildering number of tour companies, airlines, hotel chains, rental car companies, and cruise lines. In addition they need to be able to understand train schedules in many places of the world and to advise on which travel insurance policy is best for their customers. They need a good grasp of geography.

Getting Agency Travel Perks

Pam and Monica graduated from a community college business skills program three years ago and now work in busy downtown offices. From nine to five, Pam is either on the phone explaining why an errant pump part didn't arrive in Pasadena or she's writing parts numbers on order forms. Last year she saved enough for her vacation to spend six nights in a budget motel at a beach 130 miles from her home. When she ran out of money before she ran out of vacation, Pam drove home and sunned herself in her backyard.

Monica also spends her nine-to-five hours on the phone, taking and writing orders and answering questions. As a travel counselor Monica makes about the same salary as Pam. But that's where the similarity ends. Monica has taken trips to Puerto Rico, Montreal, Miami, Bermuda, Hawaii, and Las Vegas in the three years since she went to work for the travel agency. Next year she'll spend her two weeks' vacation in Jamaica while Pam's soaking up rays back home. Pam's fringe benefits include a 15 percent discount on pump parts. Monica's include free and nearly free travel.

Monica soon learned that agency employees must be organized, personable, and able to handle a tremendous amount of detailed work conscientiously and accurately. During her first week on the job Monica was astonished at her own ignorance when she tried to reply to some of the questions customers asked her: "Can I wear shorts in downtown Santiago, Chile?" "What's the most direct air route to Sri Lanka?" "Do we need shots to visit Turkey?" "Is the express bus ever late arriving in

Arbuckle?" Others tried Monica's patience: "I don't want to buy a ticket from you, but how much does it cost to fly to Belize?"

Because her manager and fellow employees helped train her, Monica was able to keep her sanity during her first few months on the job and she learned to complete intricate routing tickets while juggling phones. Now that she's over the first hurdle, Monica decided she'd like to be a manager some day, but she realizes she needs more experience and training in this complex business. As a result, Monica headed back to college to take evening courses such as principles of travel and tourism, travel geography, destination Europe, introduction to travel agency operations, domestic airline ticketing, international airline ticketing, and travel marketing.

Booking Travel Agency Freebies for Yourself

When Monica becomes a manager, she'll realize the most pleasant duty the head of a well-producing agency has is allocating free and nearly free trips among the staff. For example, ATC and IATA will allocate passes when the agency is generating lots of business for the airlines. It's up to the owner or agency manager to decide who gets the passes. Before taking an agency job, ask the interviewer about the company's policy on distributing these complimentary plane tickets. If people employed there under five or 10 years never get them, keep looking.

Airline passes allow employees to travel at a considerable discount. An employee must work for an agency for one year before becoming eligible for airline passes; that's the airline association's rule, not the agency's. Each employee is limited to two domestic and two international flight passes a year, usually at around 75 percent off the published airfare. However, they must observe black-out periods around major holidays and during other peak travel times such as July and August in Europe or February in the Caribbean.

Airlines are glad to fly agents nearly free as a goodwill gesture, because agents bring in a substantial amount of airline business. When they fly agents during periods when business is dismal, airlines are also able to fill seats that might otherwise have gone empty. When the plane is full of paying passengers, airlines bump bargain-ticketed agents and the agent gets no free flights or monetary compensation for getting bumped.

Agents and their families are also awarded as much as 50 to 75 percent off some tours. Agents usually get somewhere around half off the hotel rack (published) rate for rooms, but those rates aren't always the best, because some promotional rates for which the general public qualifies can be even less. Rates vary on car rental discounts. Cruise lines give agents variable discounts, some of which can be quite attractive. In addition, theme parks and other tourist attractions often admit travel counselors without charge, so they'll tell their clients how exciting the experience is.

Hosting tours and cruises is the manager's prerogative, but experienced employees are often invited to escort tours or even to design, sell, and lead these trips on their own. A tour conducted by an agency clerk might be a visit to two nearby ghost towns or to a gambling casino, or it could be a sumptuous around-the-world cruise. Agency personnel may host cocktail parties and act as social mentor for agency clients during a cruise. That can be quite pleasant work.

More Agency Freebies

Travel agencies and their employees are invited to take part in familiarization ("fam") trips. Fam trips are provided at little or no charge by government tourist bureaus, airlines, resorts, hotel chains, and cruise lines to show the product to those who sell it. Agents and their clerks find out about fam trips when they're invited directly by a travel provider or when they read an announcement such as: "We want to encourage agents to see for themselves that Kauai is one of Hawaii's most spectacular destinations." These ads, in industry periodicals such as *ASTA Travel News, Travel Agent,* and *Travel Weekly,* go on to invite agents to stay at a posh hotel for a couple of nights absolutely or nearly free. Hotel management encourages them to enjoy amenities such as free use of a golf course, tennis courts, saunas, pools, and rental car. The invitation concludes by disclosing a toll-free number to reserve the fam trip. The agent's companion of choice travels too, but at a higher, although substantially discounted, rate.

Fam trips aren't always fun trips. When Monica was in Puerto Rico for three days, she inspected five beachfront hotels, toured Old San Juan in a minivan packed with other agents, and attended two meetings and two business-related cocktail parties. At a compulsory breakfast meeting Pam saw a travelogue on Puerto Rico and read lots of brochures on the island commonwealth and its touristic delights. The hour and forty-five minutes she spent at a hotel pool was between 8:45 and 10:30 A.M., precious free time between a business breakfast and a hotel tour. But Monica didn't mind at all. She'd never been to San Juan and she still had her two-week vacation to look forward to later in the year. This trip had been on company time.

The best fam trip is "by invitation only" and the invitations usually go to the most valuable industry players, agents who generate lots of business and whose good relations the provider wants to cultivate. These trips may include all meals in posh restaurants, plush suites, and stretch limos. The agent's companion comes along at no extra charge.

Seminars at sea, offered to agency personnel by cruise lines, serve the same purpose as fam trips but are usually more relaxed. Presentations take place during days at sea, leaving plenty of time for the pool and for port tours. An agent may get a free trip or deep discount if he or she is seen as a valuable salesperson by cruise ship executives. The agent's spouse may go free or pay a few hundred dollars—but however it's calculated, the seminar at sea is a good deal.

If the product is a sunny resort, a fresh ski slope, or the maiden voyage of the SS *Deckchair,* a fam trip or seaborne seminar can be a welcome break in the office routine. The greater the agency's sales volume, the more invitations its employees get. Some nonproductive agencies get few invitations; avoid working for them.

One of Monica's instructors warned her students about being the inept agency clerk who sends a businessperson to the airport with a ticket to the wrong destination or sends someone off to New Delhi with the mistaken belief that hotel reservations exist in his or her name. "That clerk," said the instructor, "will soon be in another line of work. But the successful trainee can work up to the position of general agent, and many successful general agents eventually open their own agencies. That's where the bucks and the free trips are."

GETTING FULL PERKS FOR FREE-LANCING AS AN AGENT

You say you're perfectly happy as a computer programmer, dental hygienist, or loan officer? You don't want to quit your $50,000-per-year job to start all over again? You don't want to take the vows of poverty often necessary to start as a travel agency clerk just so you can get discounts on trips? Well, there's good news. You can keep your $50,000 and be a travel agent as well, working out of your own home in your spare time. And you can get fam trips, seminars at sea, discounts, and other freebies just as the full-time agents do. Moreover, you'll have a chance to rake in commissions.

Why would a travel agency hire you as a free-lance representative? They are looking for "bird dogs" to round up more customers. Perhaps you live in a suburb or small town several miles away from the agency and can serve customers who prefer not to travel into the city to the agency's office. Perhaps you've developed a base of potential travel customers through an organization you belong to, such as a luncheon or civic club, a senior citizens community in which you live, a university you attend or at which you teach, your church, or your place of work.

Perhaps you're an expert on a certain type of trip such as horseback treks, cruising, scuba diving, attending music festivals, deep-sea fishing, or a whole variety of other purposeful travel activities. Maybe you can sell trips or even lead them to a particular popular area; the Caribbean, Mexico, Europe, or China are good examples. Our local agency relies on a retired banker, born in Turin and fluent in Italian, to lead one tour a year to the hill towns of northern Italy. Carlo always travels free because he's able to put together groups of 15. By selling and leading trips to a specific country, Carlo complements the knowledge and experience of the agency's staff. His slice of the agency's commissions complements the money in Carlo's bank account.

If you're particularly resourceful and have the proper connections, perhaps you can haul in that mammoth corporate account—you know, the company whose executives are always flinging themselves back and forth by commercial airline across the country, renting cars on arrival, and staying at top hotels.

The advantages of being a part-time representative are simple: It's a low investment profession that you can pursue without commuting; and you can work as many hours a week as you please. If you don't feel like working Monday morning, you don't have to. It's ideal for retired people, teachers, sales personnel, students, housewives, consultants, and small-business persons.

To serve as a part-time representative, you need a good knowledge of geography and some travel experience. A pleasing personality, neat appearance, a head for details, and the patience to do paperwork are also assets. To work for some agencies you'll need a diploma from a travel academy or community college travel program. Other agencies require no formal training. It also helps to have had some sales or customer relations experience, or at least to possess innate sales sense.

The part-timer with a good sales sense will send newsletters of offers to clients, phone them about upcoming tours or cruises, advise them about their travel needs, and arrange air flights for them. Instead of receiving a salary, representatives' earnings are based on sales; the free-lancer is working totally on commissions. Outside agents make somewhere between 10 to 80 percent of the commissions they bring in. That's quite a wide range and requires some explanation: If you become indispensable to the agency by bringing in some large accounts and as they come to depend on you for a significant part of their income, you'll find yourself in a good negotiating position. When you're indispensable, you'll be paid at a rate closer to the high end. If you bring in only an occasional sale, you'll have to take what they give you—something closer to the bottom of the scale. It's all negotiable.

As an agent, you are, of course, eligible for fam trips, reduced rates on hotels and transportation, reduced prices on cruises, etc. In addition, your position could enable you to take groups on tours or on cruises, which could result in a no-cost or substantially free trip for yourself.

Before you apply with a travel agency, come up with a plan to market travel to a wide base of clients; the soundness of that plan will probably get you a great part-time job.

BECOMING AN *INSTANT* PART-TIME AGENT

Several large national agencies create instant independent agents with the flourish of a pen. The pen that's flourishing is yours, as you sign a check for several hundred bucks to receive your credentials and independent agent kit. The cost may or may not be less than taking travel agent courses through a college or academy. Presumably, one can travel free by a combination of generating enough business for the firm to earn commissions and by paying substantially reduced costs for travel as an agent. Another source of income is collecting commissions on your own personal travel. These companies may hire you:

GTI

GTI—Global Travel International, 2300 Maitland Center Parkway, Suite 140, Maitland, FL 32751. Phone: (800) 716-4440. GTI's independent agents don't have to take college courses and pass tests to show that they understand airline ticket codes or making hotel reservations—GTI's home office agents do the intricate computer reservation work for them.

The part-timer's job is to do some "bird dogging" by bringing in clients. For his or her efforts, the independent agent gets full travel perks. Perks may be a substantial reduction in hotel rates, 75 percent off on "selected" Intercontinental Hotel rooms in Europe, for example. They receive about a quarter off at Disney resorts, reductions and/or first-class upgrades on some airlines, reductions on selected cruises, free nights in Reno hotels, etc. GTI states its agents also get free or discounted admissions to theme parks and attractions. Fam trips are fabulously discounted and take agents to fabulous destinations such as London and Copenhagen.

GTI literature emphasizes travel discounts and freebies, but more than that, agents can write tickets for themselves or their family, friends, or employees and receive a commission from those tickets. In addition, GTI rewards agents with checks when they refer people who will sign up as agents. Do you qualify? A *Wall Street Journal* article answered that question when it stated, "Virtually anyone over the age of 18 can obtain the credentials." The biggest requirement is having a checking account or credit card.

InteleTravel International

InteleTravel International, 4225 Executive Square, Suite 1550, La Jolla, CA 92037. Phone: (800) 873-5353 or (619) 625-5000. Fax: (619) 625-5130. InteleTravel also creates instant "independent travel agents" at the stroke of your pen. Once you've registered, your spouse or companion can be a "Secondary Agent" for much less than you'll pay; as a result, you can both enjoy travel discounts.

InteleTravel promises a book of "agent passes" that translates into upgrades, discounts, and free days in hotels and resorts. In addition, flash your travel agent's credentials at appropriate personnel and get discounts on hotels car rentals, cruises, hotels, resorts, theme park and show admissions, and complimentary upgrades at hotels. "Independent" agents receive a commission on all travel they book through InteleTravel, including trips they book for themselves. They receive a bonus for bringing in more "independent" agents and bonuses on any commissions the "independents" whom they recruit generate for the firm. And, of course, agents are eligible to participate in fam trips.

Independent agents rely on the professional staff at the office to book the actual travel, so it's not necessary to be able to actually write plane or cruise tickets. Your training is through a home course provided by the International Travel Academy, which "helps you develop the simple skills you need to tap the contacts and resources you already have."

Reading about Outside Agenting

For more information on being an outside part-time agent, read *Part-Time Travel Agent: How to Cash in on the Exciting New World of Travel Marketing*. It's from The Intrepid Traveler, P.O. Box 438, New York, NY 10034. This is probably the best single book on the subject. It covers all aspects of outside agenting, including selection of office machines, accounting, advertising, sales techniques, etc.

READING ABOUT TRAVEL AND TOURISM CAREERS

- *A Guide to College Programs in Hospitality and Tourism* published by John Wiley and Sons. It provides details on more than 400 schools around the world that offer tourism and/or hospitality programs. In addition, the authors explain career ladders and salaries within the industry. Order it from Council on Hotel, Restaurant and Institutional Education (CHRIE), 1200 Seventeenth St. NW, Washington, D.C. 20036-3097. Write to CHRIE for a list of sources of financial aid and scholarships for students pursuing hospitality and tourism careers.

- *Career Opportunities in Travel and Tourism* by John K. Hawks explains requirements, duties, and compensation for a great number of jobs. Hawks also tells how to break into 70 specific jobs in the travel industry. It's available from Facts on File, 460 Park Ave., New York, NY 10016. Phone: (800) 322-8755.

- *First Class: An Introduction to Travel and Tourism* by Dennis L. Foster. Glencoe Publishing Co., 15319 Chatsworth St., Mission Hills, CA 91345. Phone: (800) 257-5755.

- *Flying High in Travel,* by Karen Rubin, is from John Wiley and Sons, 605 Third Ave., New York, NY 10158. Phone: (800) 225-5945. This is an extensive guide to entering a travel career.

- *Travel and Hospitality Career Directory,* Ron Fry, ed., can be had from Gale Research Co., 835 Penobscot Bldg., Detroit, MI 48226-4094. Phone: (800) 877-4253. It supplies details on working for airlines, cruise ships, hotels, resorts, travel agencies, etc.

- *Tourism and the Travel Industry: An Information Sourcebook* by Peter M. Enggass. Order it from Oryx Press, 2214 N. Central Ave., Phoenix, AZ 85004-1483. Phone: (800) 457-6799 or (602) 254-6156.

- *Travel Selling Skills,* by Carl Bryant et al., is available through Southwestern Publishing Co., Madison Rd., Cincinnati, OH 45227. Phone: (800) 543-0487 or (513) 271-8811.

Write to one or more of these professional organizations, tell them you're considering a career in travel, and ask for information on training, jobs, and free travel perks:

- American Culinary Federation, 10 San Bartolla Rd., St. Augustine, FL 32084-3466. Phone (904) 824-4468.

- American Hotel and Motel Association, 1201 New York Ave. NW, Washington, D.C. 20005-3931. Phone: (202) 289-3100.

- American Society of Travel Agents, 1101 King St., Alexandria, VA 22314.

- Association of Retail Travel Agents, 1845 Sir Thomas Court, Suite 3, Harrisburg, PA 17109.

- Council on Hotel, Restaurant, and Institutional Education,

1200 Seventeenth St. NW, Washington, D.C. 20036-3097. Phone: (202) 331-5990.

- Cruise Line International Association, 500 Fifth Ave., New York, NY 10110. Phone: (212) 921-0066.
- Institute of Certified Travel Agents, 148 Lindon St., P.O. Box 56, Wellesley, MA 02181.
- Travel and Tourism Research Association, 10200 W. Forty-fourth Ave., #304, Wheat Ridge, CO 80033.

GOING PLACES WITH THE AIRLINES

Looking for a lifetime career that will send you places? A job in the airline industry can do it for you. Since the first commercial passengers took off in 1926, the industry has grown astronomically: Today 400 million passengers each year are served by airline personnel. Although airline jobs are often seen as exciting and glamorous, flying back and forth week after week as a pilot, flight attendant, engineer, or navigator is no vacation. It's hard work, even if it can land you on runways in exotic airports.

Repetitive job-related travel isn't the suggestion here. The suggestion is that if you're going to be a physician, mechanic, security guard, instructor, secretary, personnel director, public relations specialist, compartment cleaner, computer programmer, salesperson, or member of any number of trades or professions, why not perform that task for an airline? When an airport restaurant is a wholly owned subsidiary of an airline, that restaurant's waitresses, cooks, dishwashers, and managers are eligible for free and reduced-cost flights. The question is fundamental: If you want to travel and if you're going to work as a waitress, why not do it at the airport?

Most people know someone who works for an airline. They're administrators, pilots, flight attendants, passenger agents, and station attendants. Station attendants are those unsung heroes and heroines who brave the elements to service the plane on the field, handle luggage, clean the toilets, and load cargo. Yet many people are envious of their airline-employee friends, even those with the most demanding jobs. When they ask folks who work in the air transport industry how things are going, the answer's often that the airline worker has just returned from Prague for no reason except to buy crystal glassware, from London to see plays before they open on Broadway, from Hong Kong to pick up custom-tailored clothing. These enviable workers sport tans from Mazatlan or Montego Bay.

Airline Employee Perks

Airline employees usually get two weeks off after the first year on the job, with a maximum of five weeks at the end of 20 years with the same company. They can spend these weeks anywhere in the world at a fraction of what it costs others to get there. Our friend Mark, for example, takes great vacations, and he doesn't have to save money to take them. When we first met Mark, he was an accountant for a major oil company, but since he loves to travel, he kept his antennae pointed toward the airlines and waited for a suitable job opening. Five years ago he went to work for United's accounting department.

Mark does work that's similar to what he did for the oil company, but now he gets free and nearly free flights. He flies free to Miami several times a year to see his mother, and last year he flew to Rio de Janeiro for a little more than $100. In Rio, he got a 20 percent discount on his hotel, 25 percent off on his rental car, and discounts on local sight-seeing—all because of his airline employee status.

The previous year found Mark in the British Virgin Islands, on vacation, and the year before that in Italy and France, all at very little cost for transportation. "I enjoyed working for the oil company," Mark told us, "but they never handed out free plane tickets like I'm getting now."

After an employee has passed a probationary period, the airline gives him or her on-line passes that are good for free flights wherever the airline goes. Employees fly coast to coast for less than five to 15 percent of what a similar ticket could cost the general public. Close relatives pay a little bit more than the employee pays. Some carriers, resorts, and cruise ship lines extend discounts to a "friend" who shares an employee's room or flies with the employee. These passes are on a space-available basis, which means that Mark's employer won't bump a paying passenger so Mark, their accountant, can fly to Miami to see Mom. If the plane is full, he has to wait for another flight.

After retiring, an airline employee can spend his or her days using airline passes. One retired TWA mechanic from Illinois studied geology at nightschool. The classes weren't held at his local school. They weren't even held in the Midwest. This dedicated student used his free lifetime pass on TWA to commute 4,200 miles a week to Eisenhower High School in Rialto, California.

In addition, most airlines make interline agreements with other air carriers so that their employees can travel free or nearly free to just about any place that has an airport. An interline agreement says, in effect, "If you give our people a free flight or let them fly at a big discount, we'll fly your people on the same terms." Like on-line passes, interline fares are usually subject to space availability. Some carriers declare blackout periods—peak seasonal travel months, Christmas, and spring academic break—during which passes or discounts are unavailable. So if Mark wants to go to Florida beaches along with tens of thousands of college students who are taking the week off to attend the annual spring Beer and Hormone Festival, he has to pay regular fare.

Because airline personnel are normally given vacations at times other than peak travel periods and are able to go where they please without much thought to airfare, the travel industry (hotels, resorts, cruise ships) relies on them to help fill empty hotel beds, bus seats, rental cars, and train compartments during slack periods.

The bible of airline personnel freebies is the *ASU Travel Guide,* a book that contains hundreds of pages packed tightly with discount offers. Let's have a look at a few:

- Fly from Madrid to Cairns, Athens, Kuwait, or Vienna for under $150.

- Fly from the United States to Japan, Hong Kong, Taiwan, or other Asian destinations for well under $900—land package included.

- Get a 40 percent discount on cruises on a *positive space basis,* which means that your spot is reserved;

- Fly from Miami to Bonaire in the Dutch West Indies and stay at a beach hotel for three nights, all for less than $250.

- Pay $100 round trip from New York or Philadelphia to Kingston or Montego Bay, Jamaica; kids go for half price.

- For $230, fly from Los Angeles, New York, or Miami to Buenos Aires, Argentina; Guayaquil or Quito, Ecuador; or to Lima, Peru.

Airline discounts amount to 50 to 75 percent; hotels give 20 to 50 percent off; and most rental car companies take about a fifth off their rates. No airline employee should be without the *ASU Guide.* For the current price, write to ASU Guide, 1325 Columbus Ave., San Francisco, CA 94133.

- *Airfare: The Magazine for Airline Employees* is a trip-discount periodical. An ad in one edition offered 40 percent off the retail price on a *Queen Elizabeth II* world cruise. Another ad offered employees a 40 to 50 percent reduction on a cruise on the SS *Norway* in the Caribbean. For the price, write to Airfare, 25 W. Thirty-ninth St., New York, NY 10018.

"Coffee or Tea? I Travel Free!"

Members of the general public often see flight attendants as the glamorous substars of airlines who have almost as much fun and see the same fabulous locales as pilots, who are the brightest stars in the airborne constellation. Others see them as flying waiters and waitresses. The truth lies somewhere between these two perceptions.

The nearly 200,000 attendants for the commercial airlines have often grueling schedules. They might be away four to 10 days at a time, still paying rent or making mortgage payments for a condo that they see all too little of. Those just hired will need roommates or to live with Mom and Dad, because the airlines pay not a whole lot more than the minimum wage to start; senior attendants, on the other hand, make an impressive salary. On some long-haul international flights, attendants can be scheduled for 16-hour stretches at a time. They can serve as sole attendant on small local carriers, or they may be part of a platoon of up to 18 on mammoth planes who serve as many as 400 tired and occasionally demanding passengers. Some flight attendants jet back and forth, seeing nothing more than St. Louis and Houston. Others enjoy layovers in world-class spots such as Cancun, Copenhagen, Tokyo, Auckland, or Paris. According to the Association of Flight Attendants, 84 percent are female. The oldest is 74; the youngest, 19.

Two legal decisions improved the lives of flight attendants immeasurably: In 1968 the courts struck down the mandatory resignation ages of 30 to 35; and in 1990 smoking was banned on all domestic flights. Thus an attendant can serve, if he or she chooses to do so, to age 74 (and presumably beyond that) and have a good chance in a smoke-free environment to live at least that long.

According to the Association of Flight Attendants, carriers look for candidates with good communication skills, who can adjust to changes, can work well with others and without direct supervision. For international flights, bi- or trilingual applicants are preferred. While most attendants have at least some college, applicants need a minimum of a high school diploma or a GED certificate. They complete four- to six-week training courses with the airlines to learn what to do in case of an emergency and how best to serve passengers.

In addition to landing in interesting places, flight attendants, like other airline employees, are in line for great additional free and cheap travel perks.

"This Is Your Captain Speaking"

Commercial airline pilots, those steel-nerved drivers who have control of the lives of as many as 400 passengers and flight crew, make the big bucks—more than $100,000 a year for many captains. In charge of flying more than 3,000 aircraft owned by American commercial airlines, they're professionals chosen for their judgment, excellent health, skill, education, and—above all—experience. Captains are 48 years old on average with an average of 20 years of piloting experience. They've reached the top spot. Although most can afford to pay for their vacation travel, they enjoy all the perks that other airline personnel enjoy.

The path to becoming an airline captain is long: Armed with the four-year university diploma that's preferred, but not always required, and a Federal Aviation Administration certificate, which requires 1,500 hours of flying time, they start up the ladder. About 75 percent get much of their required flying time out of the way in the military. Others take commercial aviation courses in flight schools or in colleges.

The flight engineer, known as the second officer, has the entry-level position among the cockpit crew. The average new hire for the cockpit crew at a commercial airline has about 4,000 hours of flying experience. He or she doesn't actually fly the plane but makes certain that mechanical and electronic devices are operating perfectly. The first officer ranks just above the flight engineer. With an average age of forty and with an average of 10 years' experience, this officer assists and relieves the captain in operating the aircraft.

For further information on becoming a pilot, contact:

- Pilot Information Program, Education Department, Air Line Pilot Association, 535 Herndon Parkway, P.O. Box 1161, Herndon, VA 22070. Phone: (703) 689-4356.

- Aerospace Education Foundation, 1501 Lee Highway, Arlington, VA 22209. Phone: (703) 247-5800.

- Director of Education, Department of Transportation, Federal

Aviation Administration, 800 Independence Ave. SW, Washington, D.C. 20590. Phone: (202) 366-4000.

PREPARING AND APPLYING FOR AIRLINE JOBS

So many different jobs exist in the airlines that it's impossible to generalize about the preparation necessary for them. According to Lise A. R. Archambault, who operates a travel agency and teaches travel and tourism courses, an important reason some applicants are hired over others is that they have "the ability to communicate clearly in at least two languages." The applicant who's fluent in three major languages probably has a better chance than someone who is bilingual, assuming their other qualifications are more or less equal.

Hundreds of airlines streak the skies daily. Many do commuter hops, but major airlines have a number of routes and often land in the places you want to visit. Here are the top five airlines in the United States in mid-1997, ranked in order of millions of passenger miles:

- Delta Air Lines, Inc., Employment Office, Hartsfield International Airport, Box 20530, Atlanta, GA 30320. Phone: (404) 715-2600.

- American Airlines, Inc., Box 619616, DFW Airport, Dallas, TX 75261-9410. Phone: (817) 967-2640.

- United Airlines, Inc., P.O. Box 66100, Chicago, IL 60666. Phone: (708) 952-4000.

- U.S. Air, Inc., Attn.: Employment Services, Pittsburgh International Airport, Pittsburgh, PA 15231.

- Southwest Air, Attn.: People Dept., P.O. Box 36644, Dallas, TX 75235-1661. Phone: (214) 263-1717.

Send your resumé also to some of these others:

- Air South, Attn.: Employee Relations Dept., P.O. Box 1129, Columbia, SC 29211.

- Alaska Airlines, Attn.: Human Resources, P.O. Box 68900, Seattle, WA 98168.

- Aloha Airlines, Inc., Attn.: Human Resources, P.O. Box 30028, Honolulu, HI 96820.
- America West Airlines, Inc., Attn.: Employment, 4000 E. Sky Harbor Blvd., Phoenix, AZ 85034.
- Carnival Air Lines, Attn.: Personnel, P.O. Box 9013, Dania, FL 33004.
- Continental Airlines, Inc., P.O. Box 4748, Houston, TX 77210-4748.
- Continental Express, 15333 JFK Blvd., Houston, TX 77032.
- Frontier Airlines, Attn.: Director-Human Resources, 12015 E. Forty-sixth Ave., Denver, CO 80239.
- Hawaiian Airlines, Inc., Attn.: Human Resources, Box 30008, Honolulu International Airport, Honolulu, HI 96830.
- Horizon Air, Attn.: Human Resources, 19521 Pacific Highway South, Seattle, WA 98188.
- North American Airlines, Bldg. 75, Suite 250, JFK International Airport, Jamaica, NY 11430.
- Reno Air, Inc., Attn.: Human Resources, P.O. Box 30059, Reno, NV 89520-3059.
- Northwest Airlines, Inc., 5101 Northwest Dr., St. Paul, MN 55111-3034.
- Tower Air, Inc., Hangar 17, JFK International Airport, Jamaica, NY 11430.
- U.S. Air Express/Allegheny Airlines, Inc., Attn.: Human Resources, 1000 Rosedale Ave., Middletown, PA 17057-0432.
- U.S. Air Express Piedmont Airlines, Inc., 5443 Airport Terminal Rd., Salisbury, MD 21801.
- World Airways, Inc., Attn.: Human Resources, 13873 Park Center Rd., Suite 490, Herndon, VA 22071.

Getting More Information about Airline Careers and Perks

Contact one or more of these organizations and ask for information about airline careers, desirable training, and—above all—travel perks.

- Airline Pilots Association International, 1625 Massachusetts Ave. NW, Washington, D.C. 20036. Phone: (202) 328-5400 or (703) 689-2270.

- Association of Flight Attendants, 1625 Massachusetts Ave. NW, Washington, D.C. 20036. Phone: (202) 328-5400.

- The Future Airline Professionals Association, 4959 Massachusetts Blvd., Atlanta, GA 30337. Phone: (800) JET-JOBS. FAPA publishes a directory of airlines that hire.

- International Flight Attendants Association, 2314 Old New Windsor Pike, New Windsor, MD 21776.

- International Society of Women Airline Pilots, P.O. Box 66268, Chicago, IL 60666-0268.

More homework—find these books in the library:

- *Flight Attendant* by David Massey, Arco/Prentice Hall, 15 Columbus Circle, New York, NY 10023. Phone: (212) 373-8500.

- *Flight Attendant Interview Handbook,* by Ken Rebalais, State of the Art, 1625 S. Broadway, Denver, CO 80210. Phone: (303) 722-7177.

- For addresses and names of key personnel from the entire industry, find the *World Aviation Directory* at your library. It's published twice a year by Ziff-Davis Publishing Co., One Park Ave., New York, NY 10016.

TRAVEL FREE AS A TOUR MANAGER

Tour director, courier, escort, and manager are titles for essentially the same job. The man or woman who does this job is a well-traveled individual. He or she usually meets a group of tourists—any number from six to sixty or whatever the bus or van will hold—at the airport, accompanies them throughout the set itinerary, and sees them off at their departure airport. The tourists may all be from the same city or they may be from all different nations and do Tower of Babel imitations.

On the bus tour, in addition to providing road commentary, the tour director will see that the group is checked into a hotel that's been booked in advance by the head office and will make certain each night that they are housed in singles or in doubles. The tour director will take them to all meals that are included and give the restaurant staff the meal voucher or payment. The director will meet local guides and ensure that the group receives the city sight-seeing as outlined in the firm's brochure. The director will make certain the bus driver takes the group to each stop on the itinerary and will pay admissions for those attractions that are included in the tour price.

In addition, the manager will see that each passenger is enjoying the experience of traveling and offer advice on local customs, on exchanging currency, purchasing postcards and souvenirs, or phoning home. If necessary the manager will help replace a lost passport or arrange for medical care if a passenger becomes ill. The tour director does whatever is necessary to ensure that the tour is carried out as planned by the company staff and ensures the group gets everything its members have paid for.

These guides might work with groups for a day or two and more likely for a week or longer, occasionally for as long as six weeks. This can be a seasonal job or a year-round job, depending on the travel season in that part of the world. A guide can work year round if he or she can do summer tours and ski tours. Some work in both Europe and Southeast Asia on a rotating seasonal basis.

The advantage of being a guide is that you visit the same places as the travelers, you get your hotel room and whatever meals the passengers get, and you earn a salary and tips. Getting a job entails applying to some of the more than 3,000 tour operators in North America. Knowledge of foreign cultures, history, architecture, and art is often necessary. Sufficient language ability, especially for Europe, Asia, or Latin America, is essential. Unless you guide in the United States, you must be multilingual in order to deal with hotel and restaurant staff, drivers, and local guides in their own languages.

On the Road with Jacob the Tour Guide

Jacob, a recent Dartmouth graduate who had lived in Europe when his father was an officer on an American military base in Germany, was hired by a medium-sized tour company to accompany a group of 36 American and Canadian travelers through Europe during a recent summer. Following intensive training at company headquarters in New York, Jacob met his group at London's busy Heathrow Airport. After he ascertained all had their luggage, he shepherded them onto buses to go to their hotel. Working closely with the desk clerk, Jacob checked the arrivals into their rooms, recommended they rest for three hours, and then took them for their arranged dinner.

After dinner Jacob held a brief meeting with his group. During the meeting, he outlined the program for the next few days and answered questions. The next morning he met his travelers after breakfast, introduced them to a local guide to whom Jacob gave a voucher for services, met them when they had completed their city sight-seeing, recommended places where they might have lunch on their own, and outlined the basics of an optional theater evening and of an optional tour to Stratford-on-Avon the next day. That evening Jacob took most of the group to a theater to see a production of Agatha Christie's *The Mousetrap*. Because he'd had only four hours of sleep the night before, he fell asleep during the first act—in fact, as soon as he sat down. His ticket, from which he received little benefit, was free.

Two days later, Jacob and his group were driven to the English Channel on a bus, after which Jacob purchased ferry tickets at Dover and took his group to Calais, France. He then shepherded them on the train to Paris and performed most of the same duties he had performed in London, but this time in his very best high-school French. Instead of falling asleep in the theater, he took a brief nap in his seat while taking his group on a *bateau mouche,* a riverboat on the River Seine.

From Paris the group went to Brussels, where Jacob's French

was still useful. In Germany, Switzerland, and Austria Jacob continued to perform his duties, but they were easier because he spoke German pretty fluently. As the tourists rolled across green countrysides on their air-conditioned coach, Jacob outlined the history of places through which they were passing. When they reached Italy, Jacob had a misunderstanding with a restaurant manager because he had only recently completed a crash-course in Italian; but a waiter, who spoke good English, straightened the matter out and the group enjoyed an excellent meal.

When the Americans and Canadians departed at Leonardo da Vinci Airport in Rome at the end of the tour, each client thanked Jacob for his expert knowledge of Europe and for making their vacation a success. Three women hugged Jacob and by the time he counted his tips, which included Austrian schillings, Italian lire, British pounds, French francs, German marks, travelers' checks, lots of dollars, and an incongruous Mexican peso, he had $1,378 for his 12 days on the road. Moreover, he had visited Lucerne, Innsbruck, and Venice, places he had never been to before but had read about carefully as part of his preparation. He had read so carefully that when he gave detailed road commentary about history and culture, his group was convinced he had been to those places numerous times.

Jacob met his next group that same afternoon at the airport near Rome and began escorting them on the reverse route of the trip he had just completed. Jacob feels that doing five 12-day trips was a lucrative and educational way to spend the summer between his first and second year of graduate training at Yale. Jacob feels he now knows parts of Europe quite well.

Learning More about Traveling Free As a Tour Manager

Write to these organizations and ask about jobs, working conditions, and how to break into the field.

- International Association of Tour Managers, 65 Charnes Dr., East Haven, CT 06513-1225. Phone: (203) 466-0425.

- National Tour Association, 546 E. Main St., Lexington, KY 40508. Phone: (800) 755-8687.

- United States Tour Operators Association, 211 E. Fifty-first St., Suite 12B, New York, NY 10022. Phone: (212) 750-7371.

These companies and organizations employ tour managers. Write to them about job possibilities.

- AIFS (American Institute for Foreign Study) arranges tours of Europe for American students and adults. They hire tour directors to lead these educational programs. AIFS, 15-17 Young St., London W8 SEH, U.K. Phone: (011) 44-171-376-0800.

- Experiment in International Living/World Learning, Kipling Road, Box SALTA, Brattleboro, VT 05302-0676. Phone: (800) 345-2929. Experiment hires tour managers to lead groups of high-school students in one of 19 countries in the summer.

- Interlocken International, RR 2, Box 165, Hillsboro, NH 03244. Phone: (603) 478-3166. Interlocken recruits group leaders to escort high-school students on tours all over the world.

- Specialized Travel Ltd., 12-15 Hanger Green, London W5 3EL, U.K. Phone: (011) 44-181-991-2200. They need tour escorts for choirs and orchestras that travel and perform in Europe.

MANAGING AN OVERLAND EXPEDITION

Here's a job that requires the patience of Job, a cast-iron stomach, and—conceivably—a bulletproof vest. For the adventuresome, the experience is incomparable. You can manage tours for one of a dozen or more companies that take tourists across Africa or Asia in overland vehicles such as four-wheel-drive trucks that carry 12 to 25 people. Laura Resnick, writing in *Travel Bargains Worldwide,* compiled by *Transition Abroad* magazine, traveled for eight months from Morocco to the Cape of Good Hope and camped in wildlife preserves, interfaced with pygmies, met West African chiefs, whitewater rafted on the Zambezi, and drank tea in Berber homes.

Resnick advises that overland companies hire tour managers for nine to 12 months or longer. These managers have to be over 24 and have leadership qualities and travel experience. She calls it "an excellent way to spend a year or more being paid to travel." Your food, shelter, and transportation are taken care of on the road, and you get salary and tips. The manager (or campmaster as he or she is sometimes called) does road commentary, helps the group cross international borders, and makes certain the trip progresses as it was planned at company headquarters. Headquarters is often in England, to which applicants may have to travel for an interview.

Sources for brochures and further information are

- Adventure Center, 1311 Sixty-third St., Suite 200, Emeryville, CA 94608. Phone: (800) 227-8747. Adventure Center is the U.S. booking agent for Guerba Expeditions, Encounter Overland, and Dragoman, the three leading overland companies.

- Guerba Expeditions, 40 Station Rd., Westbury, Wiltshire BA13 3QX, U.K.

- Kumuka Africa, 40 Earls Court Rd., London W8 6EJ, U.K.

LIVING AND WORKING ABROAD

"Forget vacation travel!" you say. "I demand the Whole Eggroll—to work and live in a foreign country during all my working years. If I want a vacation I'll come back to the States or explore the world from my vantage point abroad." That's not a bad move. There are cultural, educational, and financial advantages to permanent work abroad. It could be a savvy career move: Many observers find it interesting that friends from college get better jobs overseas than they get in the States. Working in an expatriate community, they are closer to the decision makers and get promoted faster.

Full-time overseas jobs for North Americans are usually of three types:

1) Working for a U.S. company with full benefits. According

to the editors of the *International Employment Gazette,* the typical compensation package for an expatriate American executive may include extra pay for being away from the States, a housing allowance, a car or assistance shipping the executive's car from home, tuition and required school books for the children, one or two annual paid-for trips back home for the executive and family, relocation expenses, and tax assistance. In addition, the IRS gives expatriate workers profitable breaks. The executive may also accrue up to 40 days vacation and a contract-completion bonus. The alert executive also has the pleasure of widening his or her perspective of the world. Finally, a history of having made important decisions for an organization overseas shows well on a resumé.

2) Working for a foreign firm with nationals of that country, for a foreign salary, which is probably less than they'd get working for a U.S. firm.

3) Working free-lance, as a consultant, journalist, etc.

Preparing for an Expatriate Career

Whatever your goal, you may want to know what career you might prepare for to raise your chances of traveling outside North America. Some of these positions are in government service, dealing with international issues; the diplomatic service is a prime example. Others are working in importing and exporting; doing a job in an American business that has overseas interests; or in cultural areas such as teaching, painting, music, or writing. You might work for a foreign firm or government as a technical consultant. There's no simple formula for all of the above, but in general, experts agree that graduate degrees in international relations or international business will enhance one's potential, as will the ability to speak another language.

Where can you obtain the best graduate degree to get hired for a good job abroad? Dr. Bob Sanborn, Associate Dean for Student Affairs at Rice University, has rated the top ten schools for international studies as follows:

1. University of Pennsylvania, Wharton School: The Lauder Institute, Philadelphia;

2. Columbia University, School of International & Public Affairs, New York City;

3. INSEAD, Fountainbleu, France;

4. Princeton University, Woodrow Wilson School, Princeton, NJ;

5. Johns Hopkins University, SAIS, Washington, D.C.;

6. Georgetown University, School of Foreign Service, Washington, D.C.;

7. Tufts University, Fletcher School, Boston;

8. IMD, Lausanne, Switzerland;

9. University of California, San Diego, School of International Pacific Rim Studies;

10. Thunderbird-American School of International Management, Phoenix, AZ.

Honorable mentions include Monterey School of International Studies; London Business School; Harvard University, JFK School of Government; University of Washington, Jackson School of International Studies; and the University of South Carolina, College of Business, Program in International Business.

Finding the Right Overseas Position

Whatever your training, you have an idea of where you'd like to work and where you wouldn't want to work. Our friend Dr. Bill has always said if they didn't have palm trees, it was too cold for him. Once you've narrowed down a list of locations, use similar methods of getting a job as you would back home:

• Send resumés in advance of your coming, but these may not be any more effective than they are in America; that is to say, you may get only a handful of responses in return for a gargantuan mailing and horrendous postage bill. E-mail is less expensive and could catch an employer's attention more readily than mail.

- Tell everyone that you're going to Lima or Darjeeling, or wherever. Somebody you know probably knows someone who has a friend there to put you up for a few days or to arrange a job interview for you. Maybe the friend will hire you.

- Go to work for U.S. companies in the U.S. that have operations in the place you want to go and try to work your way into a job in the overseas branch. If your burning desire is to live in Kazakhstan, for instance, apply to a large American oil company that has operations there. If you want to supervise banana cultivation, apply to a firm with interests in Central America.

- Go to your country of choice to pound the pavement, leave resumés, and try to arrange interviews.

- When you arrive, try to meet as many people in the expatriate community as possible—in their favorite bars, restaurants, gyms, clubs, etc. Tell everyone you meet what you're looking for. It makes no difference if they are employers; they may know someone who can help you.

- Learn the language, or at least enough to get by. Bilingual employees are valuable.

- If you're self-employed as a consultant, journalist, business owner, etc., take your expertise and aspirations abroad. Check first to see what restrictions there are on your operating your business in that place.

- Subscribe to the *International Employment Gazette,* 220 N. Main St., Suite 100, Greenville, SC 29601. Phone: (800) 882-9188. This newspaper contains more than 400 job announcements in each biweekly issue. Some ads are for volunteer positions, some are for au pairs, and a few are for teachers and for ESL specialists. A substantial number are for technical personnel in Saudi Arabia and the Persian Gulf's United Arab Emirates. The highest-paying contracts get signed by engineers, project managers, administrators, medical and dental personnel, and computer experts, among others.

- Look in English-language publications such as *Athens News* and *Anglo Portuguese News* (Lisbon) for ads. Many big cities have such papers for English-speaking residents and visitors.

- Take with you the *Tax Guide for U.S. Citizens Abroad,* Publication 54, free from Forms Distribution Center, P.O. Box 25866, Richmond, VA 23260.

What to Read to Find Out More

These books should be available from your local library. If they are not there, you can request that they be brought to your library on an interlibrary loan. If they are unavailable for free, you may order them through *International Employment Gazette,* 220 N. Main St., Suite 100, Greenville, SC 29601. Phone: (800) 882-9188.

- *Jobs Worldwide,* by David Lay and Benedict A. Leeburger. Lay and Leeburger tell the key employers in each country. They focus on engineering, construction, petroleum operations, management, and on key technical positions.

- *Almanac of International Jobs and Careers: A Guide to Over 1001 Employers!* by Dr. Ron Krannich and Dr. Caryl Krannich. The Krannichs list job opportunities offered by government, business, consulting firms, nonprofits, and universities. They spotlight internships and teaching jobs.

- *Complete Guide to International Jobs & Careers,* by Dr. Ron Krannich and Dr. Caryl Krannich. The Krannichs disclose successful overseas job-getting strategies, assess the international job outlook, key in on specific opportunities, and reveal major employers' addresses and fax numbers.

- *Jobs for People Who Love to Travel,* by Dr. Ron Krannich and Dr. Caryl Krannich, tells what jobs in what industries to prepare for. It includes numerous addresses and phone numbers and gives valuable tips on getting the job you want.

ONCE YOU FIND THE RIGHT JOB—THEN WHAT?

If you commit yourself to being an expatriate American worker abroad, you'll want to protect or even improve your tax status, get Medicare benefits, and make sure that the folks in Washington, D.C., count you as an important constituent, although you'll be nowhere in the United States for the foreseeable future. Two organizations work on these projects. You'll be eligible to join one or both:

- AARO (Association of Americans Resident Abroad), 49 rue Pierre Charron, 75008 Paris, France. Phone: (33) 1 42 56 10 22. Fax: (33) 1 43 59 77 03.

- American Citizens Abroad, Box 321, 1211 Geneva 12, Switzerland. Fax: (4122) 347-6847. They also offer *The Handbook for Citizens Living Abroad,* which deals with banking, health insurance, citizenship, taxes, voting, etc.

FREE TRAVEL AS A CAREER

Whether you work in the travel industry in the United States or Canada, or whether you opt to work as an expatriate overseas, your life will be enriched by your travel experiences. And unlike workers in most other industries, you won't have to go into debt or wait for retirement to see the world.

CHAPTER 15

"Have B.A., Will Travel": Teaching Overseas

McCheap's Fifteenth Law of Travel:
With generous vacations and overseas starting points,
teachers who work abroad see a big chunk of the world.

PRODUCING CHALKDUST IN FOREIGN CLASSROOMS

U.S. residents with college degrees have a good opportunity to teach American pupils overseas. The pupils' parents may be diplomats, businesspeople, in the military, or they may live abroad for any number of reasons. They send their children to mostly, but not exclusively, elite private schools. These schools' administrators hire educators whose experience ranges from being a recent college graduate to having many years in teaching, counseling, library management, or administration.

Tens of thousands of American kindergarten through high-school students attend such schools in Germany. Thousands more are enrolled in Japan, Singapore, Mexico City, Guam, the Persian Gulf, Paris, and London—wherever numbers of Americans live.

You can choose to teach third grade back in Humdrum Corners where the most exciting community event may be the opening of a Dairy Queen, or in a city like Stockholm, Madrid, or Kyoto where museums, concerts, and universities help define cultural life. In the American schools abroad, the salary, benefits, subject matter, and students are much the same as they are at home; nevertheless, as a result of overseas cultural opportunities, you may ultimately consider your teaching time in another country as the highlight of your career.

INTERVIEW WITH JANELLE, OVERSEAS TEACHER

Overseas teachers can take advantage of virtually unlimited travel possibilities, as our interview with former overseas teacher Janelle shows. Today, back in the States, Janelle is a superb community college basic skills and English-as-a-Second-Language instructor. She's one of those well-traveled people who doesn't need to read *You Can Travel Free*.

YCTF: How long did you teach overseas?

Janelle: Nineteen years.

YCTF: Where did you teach?

Janelle: I taught in Beirut, Lebanon, for four years; that was before the troubles. I liked it there but I had to leave when the shooting started. I taught briefly in Puerto Rico, one year in Guatemala, and in Dubai on the Persian Gulf for 14 years.

YCTF: Why did you teach overseas rather than in the States?

Janelle: I *did* teach in a public school in California for eight years after college graduation. But I wanted to see the world and I wanted to support myself while I was doing it.

YCTF: That's what a lot of *You Can Travel Free's* readers want to do. How did you get your first overseas assignment in Beirut?

Janelle: I wrote letters to schools everywhere and I got four responses. I heard from American schools in Athens, Berne, Bucharest, and Beirut. I might have taken the job in Berne, but with the salary they offered it would have been hard to live in the Swiss economy. Things were too expensive, so I chose Beirut. They wanted experience, which I had, and they wanted a credential and I had one. My credential was for secondary teaching and I ended up teaching middle school. It probably doesn't make much difference what kind of credential you have for lots of overseas schools, so long as you have one.

YCTF: So it's hard to live on the pay?

Janelle: It depends. Lots of schools pay housing and even

travel back home or to London once a year. And if you live outside the U.S. for 18 months or more you don't pay income tax. My pay was fine. I was able to live well and to travel a lot.

YCTF: You stayed 14 years in Dubai. Do most American teachers stay that long in overseas schools?

Janelle: Most will stay two to six years at the same post and then go somewhere else because they want to see other parts of the world. Americans working in two-teacher schools in places such as Chad or the Amazon are out of there after a year or two. I stayed in Dubai 14 years because I married a European who worked in the Gulf and because it was an excellent place to live and teach.

YCTF: How did your pupils compare with those back in the U.S.?

Janelle: They were fine. In overseas posts you have really close-knit communities. Parents get involved in the schools and are concerned that their children do well. The kids were seldom a problem of any kind.

YCTF: What places did to you get to visit besides the cities where you were teaching?

Janelle: From Dubai my girlfriends and I would fly off to Pakistan on weekends just to go shopping in Karachi. When I was in Beirut, I took trains or taxis to Damascus, Syria, once a month to poke around in the souks. I went to Istanbul a lot and once I took a two-week bus trip through Cappadocia and Ankara in Turkey. I've been to Turkey a lot. Once I took a train to Aleppo, Syria; it was so slow that passengers could jump off, pick wild flowers along the way, and jump back on.

YCTF: That's slow.

Janelle: It was always an adventure. From Beirut I went all over the whole Mediterranean to Middle Eastern countries and to Western European countries, but the only North African county I went to was Egypt. When I taught in Dubai I went to Kenya eight times. One time another teacher and I took the entire sixth-grade class to Kenya for a two-week safari. I love Kenya. I even went overland to Ethiopia from Beirut and then to Tanzania and on to Kenya. That was in the early 1970s before the Ethiopian revolution.

YCTF: Did you go to India?

Janelle: Oh, many times! I went to India and the Far East on home leave on my way back to California. I'd start in Delhi, go to Thailand, Singapore, Hong Kong, Indonesia, the Philippines, Hawaii, and California. On the way back I'd stop in New York to see friends and then go on a train ride in Switzerland. I basically went around the world because I'd come back through Europe.

YCTF: Why did you finally return to California to teach?

Janelle: I left Dubai because of my husband's job. If it hadn't been for that, I would have stayed.

YCTF: Would you do everything the same if you had your life to live over?

Janelle: Absolutely. I just found teaching overseas so much fun.

YCTF: Do you have any advice for young people who might be considering teaching overseas?

Janelle: Go ahead and do it while you're young. When you're young you can travel more easily.

YCTF: Where haven't you been that you'd like to go?

Janelle: South America. I've never touched foot on that continent. I want to see Machu Piccu and the Amazon.

YCTF: I'm sure you'll make it. Thanks for the interview.

Janelle: Thank you.

FINDING OUT ABOUT OVERSEAS TEACHING POSITIONS

Getting a teaching job in an English-speaking school abroad isn't automatic. As teacher shortages develop in the United States, job hunting abroad may become easier. But for now, don't expect to show up in Lima or even Liberia and nail down a job just after you've arrived. It's possible to do, but most hirings are arranged before you leave home. As a result, teaching candidates need to send resumés, travel for interviews, attend hiring fairs, and do a lot of networking.

Before you apply, decide where you want to go. The candidate who is willing to go anywhere may end up in a job no other rational applicant has been willing to accept. The school may be in some terribly lonely backwater with weather that would challenge King, the Yukon wonder dog, or that could melt asbestos in full sun. Decide how long you want to stay. Contracts are generally for a year and sometimes for two. Once you've done that, go for the best school in the best location on your list of acceptable locales. Find out the school's salary range, learn about the cost of living there, and try to determine if you can support yourself in that location on the salary. The hiring officials can usually tell you about local costs. To get started in your search or exploration of possibilities, contact one or more of the following organizations.

ORGANIZATIONS THAT CAN HELP YOU GET A TEACHING JOB OVERSEAS

The agencies and publishers listed here are of several types. Some are employment agencies that will help you get a teaching job abroad; most charge a fee. Some schedule job fairs to which applicants and hiring administrators come to meet. They charge fees. Some are compilers of data, publishers who will send you periodically updated lists of job openings in educational institutions abroad. Most charge fees. Others are government agencies that hire educators directly to staff their overseas schools. The rest are governmental organizations that facilitate overseas teaching by American academics. Most don't charge fees.

Association of American Schools in Mexico

Soft winds, excellent food, exotic music, lovely people: Mexico. If you'd like to teach in the land of our immediate southern neighbors, contact the Association of American Schools in the Republic of Mexico, APDO 6-1074, Guadalajara, Jalisco, Mexico. Phone: (011) 593-2472-974. The association publishes a directory of American schools.

Association of American Schools in South America

Association of American Schools in South America, Regional Development Center, 14750 N.W. Seventy-seventh St., Suite 210, Miami Lakes, FL 33016. Phone: (305) 821-0345. Fax: (305) 821-4244. E-mail: aassa@gate.net. The AASSA holds recruiting fairs where staffers hire teachers to teach in Rio, Buenos Aires, Santiago, and elsewhere. How's your Spanish or Portuguese? That may be one of the first questions you're asked.

China: State Bureau of Foreign Experts

China! Want to teach there? These jobs aren't in expatriate American and Commonwealth schools, but they're jobs for English speakers to teach Chinese pupils. If you're interested, apply to State Bureau of Foreign Experts, Box 300, Beijing 100873, People's Republic of China. Fax: (8610) 684 68001. Not long ago the State Bureau was looking for two foreign coaches for weight lifting, wrestling, boxing, judo, tae kwon do, and swimming. These coaches now work with provincial teams on year-long contracts.

Chronicle of Higher Education

The Chronicle of Higher Education lists overseas teaching and administrative positions in each of its weekly editions. These announcements are for college, university, foundation, and research personnel. Institutions that recruit through *The Chronicle* are mostly foreign universities in which English is either the language of instruction or which require English-speaking instructors. Contact them at P.O. Box 1955, Marion, OH 43306-2055 for subscription information.

Department of Defense Dependent Schools

Department of Defense Dependent Schools are on U.S. military bases abroad. Contact the Department of Defense Dependents Schools, 4040 N. Fairfax Dr., Arlington, VA 22203-1634. Phone: (703)-696-3269. You can just as easily teach Britanny or Damon in an exotic locale where to put commas and semicolons as you can back home. Locations of defense schools are wherever one finds large numbers of U.S. armed forces personnel: Belgium, Great Britain, Iceland, Netherlands, Norway, Bermuda, Newfoundland, Cuba (Guantanamo Bay), Panama, Germany, Bahrain, Greece (Crete), Italy, Portugal (Azores), Spain, Turkey, Japan, Korea, or Okinawa.

To apply you need at least a bachelor's degree with 18 units of education courses. Teaching experience can be a real plus. Every school position you'd find in the states is available, from teaching high school computer science or geography to being an elementary resource specialist or principal. Assignments are for one or two years, and salaries are comparable to what urban school districts offer in the United States.

Living accommodations may be in dormitories, apartments, hotels, converted office buildings, or in modern facilities. Housing is often available without charge, and when it's not available, our Uncle Sam pays an allowance to cover rent and utilities. And our beneficent uncle will send your household goods and personal effects to your overseas destination.

Our friend Irene says: "When I taught for two years in Germany, I'd take trips in Germany, France, Italy, Belgium, Luxembourg, and the Netherlands during my vacations. It's amazing how far you can get and how much you can see in even a week at Easter and Christmas. My German is pretty good now, because I'd go off base and practice as much as I could. I also saved a lot of money because I used public transportation instead of having a car and I didn't have to pay rent. I did most of my shopping in the base PX, which was a lot cheaper than shopping in town. And on the whole, I found the pupils better behaved than they were back home where I'd done my student teaching. I recommend the experience to any teacher."

Department of State Overseas Schools

Department of State, Office of Overseas Schools, Room 245, SA 29, Washington, D.C. 20522-2902. Phone: (703) 875-7800. Fax: (703) 875-7979. The U.S. State Department will send you a list of independent overseas schools that children of Americans in foreign countries attend and that receive U.S. government assistance. These schools hire their own staff and some send representatives to recruiting fairs in the United States to do so.

The extensive list the Department of State will send gives the name, address, administrator, phone and fax numbers, and—when available—e-mail address of schools in virtually every country where you'd find enough Americans to field a baseball team.

It's your big chance to teach in Albania, Azerbaijan, or Belarus. In addition, the level of the school—elementary, immediate, or high school—is indicated, as is the current enrollment. Thus, if you wanted to teach in Madagascar, you could e-mail the director of the American School of Antananarivo at asamad@boardfs.mg. Similarly, you could phone the principal of the International School of Ulaanbaatar at 976-1-52959, if you had a burning desire to teach grades seven to 12 in Mongolia.

Education Information Services

Education Information Services can give you dates and places of recruiting fairs to which representatives of overseas schools come to hire. Prospective teachers and administrators normally need to register in advance of these events, so receiving this timely information is vital. Contact EIS at P.O. Box 620662, Newton, MA 02162-0662. Phone: (781) 433-0125.

Friends of World Teaching

Friends of World Teaching (P.O. Box 1049, San Diego, CA 92112-1049; phone: [800] 503-7436) publishes *Overseas Teaching Opportunities*. Friends provides lists of more than 1,000 English-speaking schools in more than 100 countries where U.S. and Canadian children are enrolled. These lists include positions for administrators, counselors, librarians, nurses, secretaries, and teachers.

Friends of World Teaching, which has sent such data to job seekers since 1969, will, for a nominal fee, send a listing of jobs that are open in three countries of your choice; you can add countries for a small amount. Send a SASE for further information.

HMS Education Personnel

HMS Education Personnel, 58-60 Berners St., London W1P 3AE, U.K. Phone: (01) 144 171 636 7030. Fax: (01) 144 171 637 0262. This is a fee agency that places elementary and secondary teachers in schools in England. It's not necessary to have had prior teaching experience to apply.

The International Educator

TIE, *The International Educator,* P.O. Box 513, Cummaquid, MA 02637. Phone: (508) 362-1414. Fax: (508) 362-1411. TIE calls its newspaper, which features "help wanted" ads placed by more than 200 schools worldwide, "the best and least expensive route to securing an overseas appointment." For the subscription price, you receive four quarterly issues, a "Jobs Only" supplement, and the brochure *Guide to Finding a Job Abroad.* Write, call, or fax for the up-to-date subscription price.

International Educators Cooperative

International Educators Cooperative, 212 Alcott Rd., East Falmouth, MA 02536. Phone/fax: (508) 540-8173. IEC holds recruitment fairs in the United States.

International Schools Services

International Schools Services, Educational Staffing Department, P.O. Box 5910, Princeton, NJ 08543. Phone: (609) 452-0990. Fax: (609) 452-2690. E-mail: ISS@ISS.edu. ISS, founded in 1955 as a nonprofit organization, states that it places more than 500 educators in American and international schools worldwide. It's one of the major agencies in the nation. Schools are located in Africa, Asia, Latin America, Europe, and the

Middle East. English is the language of instruction, but all students aren't necessarily American.

ISS charges a fee for establishing a permanent file and an additional fee if you attend one of their International Recruitment Centers to which headhunters from international schools are invited. Candidates are furnished comprehensive information on overseas educational job searching and counseling as well as a subscription to ISS's newspaper, *NewsLinks*. No other fees are charged to those placed.

The client schools are particularly looking for instructors in math, science, and computers and for elementary teachers. ISS advises that teachers must have at least two years of relevant teaching experience; they specify that the word *relevant* excludes time tutoring or working as a teaching assistant. Contracts, normally for two years, usually include round-trip transportation for the teacher and his or her family. ISS warns, however, that typical overseas teaching pay won't support a family and that "most schools cannot consider teaching candidates with two or more dependents."

Overseas Academic Opportunities

Overseas Academic Opportunities, c/o Susan Towey, 72 Franklin Ave., Ocean Grove, NJ 07756. Phone: (908) 774-1040. OAO publishes the monthly *Bulletin of Overseas Teaching Opportunities*. "Little or no teaching experience [is] required," states Towey, for positions available in all parts of the world. The *Bulletin* lists openings for K-12 subjects and grades; most openings don't require a foreign language or a state certificate.

Overseas Placement Service

Overseas Placement Service for Educators, University of Northern Iowa, Cedar Falls, IA 50615. Phone: (319) 273-2083. Fax: (319) 273-6998. E-mail: overseas.placement@uni.edu. Overseas Placement Service invites applicants to placement fairs to which overseas schools send recruiters. In order to participate, candidates need to be certificated to teach in one of the 50 states and to be willing to sign a contract for two years if they get a suitable job.

Candidates who have no dependents or have a spouse who is an educator, and candidates with at least a couple of years of teaching experience have an inside track.

A recent recruiting fair that OPS held in Iowa welcomed administrators from a hundred international schools in more than 60 countries. In addition, OPS performs other services for registrants: maintaining a credential file, referring suitable candidates to employers, publishing a fact book and mailing out *Overseas Placement Matters* (a newsletter). There are fees.

Search Associates

Search Associates, P.O. Box 636, Dallas, PA 18612. Phone: (717) 696-5400. Fax: (717) 696-9500. E-mail: 76770.3322@compuserve.com.

Search Associates offers one-year positions for bachelor's-degree holders through its International Schools Internship Program. Entry-level teachers are offered airfare, salary, and housing. This organization holds job fairs to match applicants with hiring administrators. These fairs are held not only in the United States but in Kuala Lumpur, Malaysia; Dubai, Persian Gulf; Toronto, Canada; and Oxford, England. There's a fee.

Teachers of the World

Teachers of the World, Inc., P.O. Box 83, Kent Store, VA 23084. This agency helps educators find jobs overseas in all subject areas, at all levels, including jobs teaching English to non-English speakers. It is a non-fee agency, but there's an application processing charge.

U.S. Territorial Schools

Here's an opportunity to sit under a palm tree or splash in the surf between classes. If a job in the Virgin Islands, Samoa, Guam, or Puerto Rico sounds interesting, read on. These places are all U.S. territories and possessions. Applications for positions in the American Empire can be requested from the following officials:

- Director, Department of Education, Pago Pago, American Samoa 96799;

- Director, Department of Education, Box DE, Agana, Guam 96910;

- Secretary of Education, Box 759, Hito Rey, Puerto Rico 00919; and

- Director, Department of Education, Government of the U.S. Virgin Islands, St. Thomas, U.S. Virgin Islands 00801.

University of Maryland

University of Maryland runs overseas higher education programs mainly for military personnel. This gives servicemen and -women a chance to earn degrees after work or during their lunch break while on duty away from the States. The University of Maryland hires U.S. citizens with doctorates to teach accounting, astronomy, biology, business subjects, chemistry, computer studies, criminology, economics, English, government, history, math, physics, psychology, sociology, and speech.

Lecturers serve for one academic year with an opportunity to renew their contracts one year at a time for up to four years. The university has centers in the Azores, Belgium, Germany, Greece, Iceland, Italy, the Netherlands, Spain, Turkey, the U.K., Australia, Guam, Hong Kong, Japan, the Marshall Islands, South Korea, and Thailand. Salaries are "generally comparable" to those of faculty at lower-division or undergraduate colleges in the States. University of Maryland assists with transportation to and from the overseas campus.

Our acquaintance Ed taught accounting at a U.S. base in Japan for two years and used his vacations to see as much of the rest of East Asia as he could. When we last caught up with him, he was setting out on a tour of Vietnam and Malaysia. Except for the Japanese winters, Ed loved his experience; his students were eager, and travel opportunities were plentiful. Write to

Overseas Programs, University of Maryland, University Boulevard at Adelphi Road, College Park, MD 20742.

World Learning, Inc.

Professional Development Resource Center, World Learning, Inc., P.O. Box 676, Kipling Road, Brattleboro, VT 05302. Phone: (802) 258-3248. World Learning issues a monthly newsletter with information on teaching positions worldwide. There's a fee.

EXCHANGING TEACHING POSITIONS

If you already have a job in education, it may be possible to go to another country for a semester or a year to replace a teacher there. That teacher will come to your school or college and take your job. It's an exciting chance to travel and to experience another culture at little or no cost. Another advantage: Your teaching experience abroad looks good on a resumé. These organizations can help you make the switch:

Faculty Exchange Center

Faculty Exchange Center, 952 Virginia Ave., Lancaster, PA 17603. Phone: (717) 393-1130. College or university educators such as professors, instructors, counselors, librarians, and administrators have an opportunity to chuck it all temporarily and go to another part of the country or of the world for a semester or year. If that sounds appealing and if you're a college-level educator, consider trading your job with that of a distant colleague.

The FEC facilitates exchanges by publishing a directory of names, areas of specialization or current assignments, addresses, and phone numbers of personnel who want to participate. Members, having received the directory, write to other members whose jobs are similar to theirs and suggest an exchange. For example a biology instructor in a Florida community college notes that a biology instructor from Scotland would like to trade jobs and that one of his geographical preferences is the

U.S. Southeast. If the Floridian and the Scot come to an agreement, each remains on his or own salary from the home institution during the exchange. Whether each of the universities will offer to help defray airfare is up to the regents or administration.

A major way the exchangees save money is by trading their homes as well. As a result, the Floridian can teach in Scotland and pay about what he or she would pay in the States for living costs, although he keeps up his mortgage payments, taxes, and condo dues back home.

The FEC will send a pamphlet listing institutional members. If you work for an institution that doesn't belong, perhaps you can convince the administration that it ought to join. An exchange can be as mentally refreshing as a sabbatical.

Fulbright Teacher Exchange

Opportunities Abroad for Educators is a publication full of program descriptions and application forms for teachers (kindergarten through grade 12) who want to exchange with teachers in more than 30 countries. It's free from the U.S. Information Agency, Fulbright Teacher Exchange Program, 600 Maryland Ave. SW, Room 235, Washington, D.C. 20024.

NAFSA Job Registry

Job Registry, NAFSA: National Association of International Educators, 1875 Connecticut Ave. NW, Suite 1000, Washington, D.C. 20009-5728. Phone: (202) 939-3131. This bulletin, issued 10 times a year, is aimed at educators who want temporary exchanges with other educators. If you're currently under contract, and your school board agrees, you could teach abroad for a year. The teacher whose classroom you're taking over replaces you.

TEACHING ABROAD: READ ALL ABOUT IT

What follows are books about teaching abroad and lists of schools that hire abroad.

- *Directory of Resources for International Cultural and Educational Exchanges,* U.S. Information Agency, Room 212, 301 Fourth St. SW, Washington, D.C. 20547.

- *Schools Abroad of Interest to Americans* is from Porter Sargent Publishers, 11 Beacon St., Suite 1400, Boston, MA 02108; it lists 800 K-12 schools that enroll English-speaking pupils in 130 countries.

- *Teaching Abroad: Opportunities for U.S. Educators Worldwide* is published by the Institute of International Education, 809 United Nations Plaza, New York, NY 10017.

When you teach overseas, you learn as well.

CHAPTER 16

Teaching Your Own Language

McCheap's Sixteenth Law of Travel:
When people in other countries are eager to give you money
to speak English, say something.

SATISFY A NEED AND PAY FOR YOUR TRIP

If you're reading this book, chances are you read, write, and speak English well. If English is your native language or you speak it like a native, you can probably get a job teaching abroad with non-English speakers as your pupils. Chances are that you can teach as you travel, paying for your footloose life-style as you go.

The mother tongue of the Anglo-Saxon countries has become the international language of commerce and of tourism. It's absolutely essential that businesspeople in most nations be able to communicate well in English. Even those whose alphabets are frustratingly exotic to us have to be able to converse in English before they can even apply for a job in some businesses, even in their own countries. Others need to learn the language of international commerce well and quickly in order to get promoted. Workers who can't communicate in English have lost their jobs in some places. Fortunately for American travelers, American English is widely preferred in businesses abroad.

English, as you well know, is a major literary language as well. Millions on all continents aspire to read Shakespeare, Dickens, Jack London, Hemingway, and other giants in the language in which they wrote. Moreover, people everywhere, from Afghanistan to Zululand, fall in love with American entertainment; in the last several decades they've been learning English by listening to tapes and CDs of popular musicians from Paula Abdul to Frank Zappa. Young people whose native alphabets don't progress from A to Z wear T-shirts that announce they have "No Problem," that they root for the San Francisco 49ers, and that the wearer is the "World's Greatest Lover." English, then, with its quirks and myriad rule exceptions that keep teachers and professors fully employed, is the world language of choice and of necessity.

The world needs and wants to learn what you learned as a child. Your ability to do what came naturally to you can be your passport to paying for travel as you travel. As an honored teacher, you can live abroad in an astonishingly pleasant environment.

YOUR CHOICE OF ASSIGNMENTS

The beauty of paying for travel by conversing in your own language is that opportunities are varied. You can be a formal classroom teacher or a free-lance private tutor. You can work full- or part-time. You can opt for a temporary or long-term assignment. You can teach or tutor virtually anyplace where English isn't the native tongue and lots of places where it is. You could work under a contract for a year or more, or you can be free to leave when you wish.

If your teaching is conducted in a school, following a formal lesson plan, that institution could be a language school attended by adult learners, a private academy for children, or a public grammar or high school. You could have 40 pupils whose desks are rigidly and geometrically spaced, or you could sit with and teach a small informal discussion group while splashing at the beach.

Or you may be asked to conduct your classes in a business setting and train employees. Some instructors work part- or full-time in foreign cities for companies that encourage their employees to take courses before or after work. Some teachers are asked by the companies to do lucrative translations or editing work on the side.

Depending on your qualifications, you could be a professor of English in an overseas college or university.

Listening to Teachers

Let's catch up with a handful of teachers of English and find out what sort of fun, trials, tribulations, and adventures they've been having overseas. These traveling instructors are graduates of New World Teachers, based in Boston, San Francisco, and Puerto Vallarta; it's a prominent training school for instructors. Each of these Americans has earned a certificate to teach English to speakers of other languages:

With Megan in Ecuador

Megan, a teacher of English from Seattle, writes from Cuenca, Ecuador: "It's so lovely here. Eighty-three hundred feet up in the mountains, a beautiful river, cobblestone streets, and pretty old buildings with red-tiled roofs. I found a nice apartment, five minutes from the school, so things are going great.

"I went to Colombia to see beautiful pre-Inca ruins scattered in a gorgeous landscape. I flew to Cuzco, Peru, and hiked the Inca trail to Machu Picchu—what a great experience! The nature amazes me. I hiked around an island on Lake Titicaca where the Incas thought the sun was born. There's so much I want to see, but for now I'm content to be in Cuenca thinking of fun lessons to try out on my students."

With Melissa in Madrid

Melissa, of San Diego, reports: "I am alive and well and living in Madrid. . . . It's absolutely amazing what a hot commodity speaking English is in Spain. The unemployment rate seems to make the demand even higher because everyone is forced to be more competitive globally.

"Also, I have already been able to save enough money for a

five-day trip to Greece with my friend from Zimbabwe. Next weekend is followed by two public holidays, so we will spend it in Athens and on the island of Mykonos."

In China with Penny

Penny, of Santa Barbara, writes from China: "I wanted to tell you that I indeed got the job. Not only are they going to fly me down to Guangzhou to visit the school and look over the contract, but they are also going to pay me to fly home from China to Santa Barbara to say my good-byes, then fly me back by October 1! I'm very excited because I love China so much. It is more than I had ever imagined!"

Teaching in Tokyo with Lee

Lee, of Portsmouth, Ohio, reports from Tokyo: "I didn't have to search very far. I just walked into the Kimi Information Center and the manager asked me if I wanted to teach a class that night. I said sure and have been working there ever since. I teach one children's class and the rest of my students are adults.

"I thought moving to Tokyo would be a lot more challenging, but it was easy. In addition to getting a job, I have found a nice place to live. I am renting a room in Tokyo for only $200 a month. I should be paying a little more, but I teach my landlord's friends how to use computers for two hours each week."

With Jeff in Brazil

Jeff, of Madera, California, writes from Recife, Brazil: "Greetings from the land of *Carnaval*. I am only working part-time and make quite a bit of money by Brazilian standards . . . and not a day goes by that somebody doesn't inquire about being tutored. Native American speakers are in great demand here.

"Recife is a fantastic city. It is everything I expected and more, and less. Pre-*Carnaval* celebrations have been terrific and it is not uncommon to find me dancing in the streets with my Brazilian friends until the wee hours of the morning."

WHERE IN THE WORLD?

In a number of less affluent countries of Eastern Europe, Asia, Africa, and Latin America, fluency in English is all that you may need to land a job. Your pay may be small or nonexistent, you may receive only room and board. But room and board and an opportunity to get to know the people of the place and being of assistance can often add up to free travel at its best.

In some areas of the world where poverty is more noticeable, you may be asked to pay for your airfare and your rent and food during your stay. These jobs are actually volunteer positions. Volunteer positions are discussed in some detail in chapter 11, "Volunteering to Travel."

If you need to pay for your trip by teaching English, look toward richer industrial nations. In more affluent areas of Asia, such as Japan, Taiwan, and South Korea, in most of Europe, and in parts of Latin America, the pay can be quite good. Jobs in Western Europe may be difficult, but far from impossible, for North Americans to get. That's because British and Irish citizens are members of the European Community and they don't need work permits to teach English in member nations on the Continent.

DO YOU NEED A CERTIFICATE?

It's not always necessary to have a teaching certificate to get a job teaching English abroad, but it usually helps and sometimes is essential. To qualify for a superior wage teaching English in rich industrial or petroleum-producing countries, you'll probably be required to have at least a bachelor's degree. Some schools insist the degree be in English, but often any subject will do. Some schools that pay well and offer benefits and some job security require, in addition to your degree, a certificate in teaching English to non-English-speaking people.

There are several recognized certificates. These include certification in ESL (English as a Second Language), EFL (English as a Foreign Language), and TEFL (Teaching English as a Foreign Language). Still others are TESL (Teaching English as a Second Language), TESOL (Teaching English to Speakers of Other

Languages), and in Britain, RSA (Royal Society of the Arts) issued by Cambridge University. A newer certificate is CELTA (Certificate in English Language Teaching to Adults). The CELTA certificate appears to be the preparation of choice today. Some teachers attain M.A. degrees in teaching English as a foreign language. In general, the more qualified you are in terms of degrees, certification, and experience, the better your pay will be and the easier it will be to land a job where you want to be.

Getting Certified

Certification will make you a more proficient instructor and will give you a profession with which to finance your travels as long as you want to travel. A valuable certification to earn is the CELTA. Another is TESOL. Those who earn master's degrees in teaching English to foreign language speakers often do so because they want to do research, to train teachers, or to become administrators. When you have more degrees than a thermometer and lots of experience, you'll have enough credibility to open your own training school.

As the popularity of going abroad to teach English balloons, the number of schools that offer courses and certificates in teaching English as a foreign language or as a second language grows. Many of these schools advertise small classes, and intensive courses of about four weeks. Many also schedule part-time programs that take about three months. Most make lists of overseas job listings available to their graduates and give guidance in finding jobs. Some offer counseling in negotiating work contracts. None is particularly cheap, but perhaps you should look at tuition as a good investment in qualifying for unlimited pay-as-you-go travel.

Training schools award grades that are recognized by teaching professionals everywhere. These include "Pass A," "Pass B," "Pass," or "No Pass." Graduates with A's and B's are the most sought after. How are grades arrived at? At least one school counted the final examination for 10 percent of the grade and practice teaching counted for much of the rest.

A comprehensive list of training schools can be found in the *Directory of Professional Preparation Programs in TESOL in the U.S. and Canada.* The directory lists more than 400 programs. Find it in a university library or get the current price and order it from Teachers of English to Speakers of Other Languages, Inc., 1600 Cameron St., Suite 300, Alexandria, VA 22314. Phone: (703) 836-0774.

Where to Get Certified

A selection of schools follows. Check out carefully the ones that interest you. Before you sign on, ask for phone numbers or addresses of those who have taken the course. Contact several graduates and ask questions. Your questions should be about the effectiveness of the training and about whether the training has led to good jobs for them.

American English Programs of New England

American English Programs of New England, Old School Commons, 17 South Street, Northampton, MA 01060. Phone (413) 582-1812 for a brochure. E-mail: eflworld@crocker.com. Website: www.crocker.com/eflworld. A bachelor's degree is preferred but is not required of pupils. Full-time students need four weeks to complete the certification; part-timers will put in twelve weeks.

Center for English Studies

The Center for English Studies, International House USA, 330 Seventh Ave., New York, NY 10001. Phone: (212) 629-7300. Fax: (212) 736-7950. E-mail: CESNY@TIAC.NET. The Center offers the CELTA (Certificate in English Language Teaching to Adults) course in teaching English to non-English speakers. Its administrators promise "intensive teaching practice."

Coast Language Academy

Coast Language Academy, 501 Santa Monica Blvd., Suite 403, Santa Monica, CA 90401. Phone: (310) 394-8618. Fax: (310)

394-2708. It's also located at 200 S.W. Market St., #111, Portland, OR 97201. Phone: (503) 224-1960. Fax: (503) 224-2041. After 140 hours of training, graduates receive the RSA University of Cambridge Certificate in English Language Teaching to Adults (CELTA). The school provides assistance in finding that first overseas teaching job.

English International

English International, 655 Sutter St., Suite 200, San Francisco, CA 94102. Phone: (415) 749-5633. E-mail: 103326.1743@ compuserve.com. English International offers four-week courses leading to the RSA/Cambridge CELTA certificate in TEFL to Adults. They ask that their students have a degree and some knowledge of a foreign language. Courses begin every month.

International Language Institute

International Language Institute, 5151 Terminal Rd., 8th Floor, Halifax, Nova Scotia, Canada B3J 1A1. Phone: (902) 429-3636. Fax: (902) 429-2900. E-mail: study@ili.halifax.ns.ca. This school features the CELTA (Certificate in English Language Teaching to Adults) Program. CELTA emphasizes extensive supervised teaching practice with adult pupils. ILI's 120-hour course gives you an opportunity to live and learn in historic Halifax, Nova Scotia. More information is on ILI's website: http://www.ili.halifax.ns.ca.

ITC Prague

ITC stands for International TEFL Certificate, and its courses are in Prague, Czech Republic. ITC offers four-week courses followed by a "job guarantee." To find out more about studying in Prague, call the San Francisco information office, 655 Powell St., Suite 505, San Francisco, CA 94108. Phone: (415) 544-0447. You can phone their "hotline" for a recorded newsletter: (415) 789-8336. The website is: http://www.vol.cz/ ITC. Or e-mail ITC at praginfo@mbox.vol.cz. In the Czech

Republic, contact ITC Prague, Spanielova 1292, 163 00 Prague 6, Czech Republic. Phone: (42) 2-96-14-10-14. E-mail: praginfo@ mbox.vol.cz. No matter how much you learn, you'll more than likely love Prague, arguably Europe's most beautiful city.

New World Teachers

New World Teachers, 605 Market St., Suite 800, San Francisco, CA 94105. Phone: (800) 644-5424. E-mail: TeachersSF@ aol.com. "Teaching your way around the world will be as much fun for you as it will be for your students," promises NWT literature. NWT provides monthly four-week intensive certificate courses. These courses are taught in Boston, San Francisco, or in Puerto Vallarta, Mexico. During the North American winter, Puerto Vallarta can serve as a credible substitute for paradise. No second language or teaching experience is required. Their ads promise "lifetime job placement assistance." Check out NWT's website: http://www.goteach.com.

St. Giles Language Training Center

St. Giles Language Teaching Center, One Hallidie Plaza, Suite 350, San Francisco, CA 94102. Phone: (415) 788-3552. Fax: (415) 788-1923. E-mail: sfstgile@slip.net. RSA University of Cambridge teacher training courses are for four weeks in San Francisco, London, or Brighton (England).

Typical courses are teaching vocabulary, lesson planning, error and correction techniques, language awareness, phonology, working abroad in EFL, and using songs in the classroom. St. Giles turns out enthusiastic graduates. Grad Jennifer writes from Poland: "I've been here a couple of weeks and I am surprised by how much I like it. My classes are wonderful. I'm teaching ages nine to adults. The students are a joy to teach. . . . The mountains are only a 10-minute bus ride away. Plenty of skiing in winter."

The School of Teaching ESL

The School of Teaching English as a Second Language, 2601 N.W. Fifty-sixth St., Seattle, WA 98107. Phone: (206) 781-8607.

Fax: (206) 781-8922. E-mail: tulare@seattleu.edu. Your credits will be from Seattle University. Courses bear titles such as Methods of Language Acquisition, Teaching English Pronunciation, and Teaching Grammar to ESL Students. To enroll, you must have a bachelor's degree. You can earn initial or advanced certificates in TESOL or TEFL as well as a master's degree in Teaching English to Speakers of Other Languages.

Worldwide Teachers Development Institute

Worldwide Teachers Development Institute, 266 Beacon St., Boston, MA 02116. Phone: (800) 875-5564. Fax: (617) 262-0308. E-mail: BostonTEFL@aol.com. Twelve students in a class study for the TEFL Certificate. The intensive immersion program requires at least 100 hours of classroom instruction. Located in Back Bay by Charles River, the school offers a "holistic communicative approach" as well as "global placement guidance." In addition, students who are deficient in a particular language skill receive special tutoring at no extra charge. No second language is required. Ask about the *distance learning option* and about classes in Chicago.

Here's what one happy graduate had to say: "Thailand is the land of smiles, and although I had never taught before my TEFL-certificate experience in Boston, I felt well prepared and easily found a job. I had plenty of time for my other passion of scuba diving off the southern coast of Thailand." Visit their website at http://www.to-get.com/BostonTEFL.

BECOMING A TEACHER WITHOUT CERTIFICATION

Here's what the experts—those who have actually free-lance tutored abroad—have to say about preparing without obtaining a certificate. In fact, it's good advice even if you have, or plan to earn, a certificate.

Few good teachers are born. Not all experienced teachers are good, but all good teachers have some experience. Just because you can speak English like a native and because you received A's in everything from freshman comp to morphology doesn't mean you can teach. To find out that you can't teach on the first morning you're standing before an expectant crowd of 50 students in a classroom in rural Nigeria can be a stunning blow. Get some teaching experience first. You don't have to be a schoolteacher to do that, although formal paid classroom experience may help a lot.

It's helpful to arrive in your foreign city or town of choice with references that state you have some experience teaching, especially if you don't have a formal ESL certificate. Here are some things you can do to get references and experience:

- Take an ESL methods teaching course at a local college or university.

- Take a training workshop offered by a local college, school district, adult school, or literacy council for those who want to teach ESL. It's usually a free or minimal-cost, 12- to 15-hour class.

- Volunteer to tutor pupils whose language is that of people in the places you want to travel. For example, if you want to support yourself by tutoring in Cambodia, ask to be a teacher's aide or volunteer ESL tutor in a school or reception center for recent arrivals from Cambodia.

- Volunteer as a tutor in a local literacy program and ask to be paired with students who know little English.

- Volunteer as an aid in an ESL class in a local K-12 school.

Contact these organizations for information about literacy tutoring opportunities in your neighborhood or city:

- Literacy Center, P.O. Box 81826, Lincoln, NE 81826. Phone: (800) 228-8813.

- Literacy Volunteers of America, 5795 Widewaters Parkway, Syracuse, NY 13214. Phone: (315) 445-8000.

Read *Teaching Conversation Skills in ESL,* which is available from your public library or from Center for Applied Linguistics, 3520 Prospect St. NW, Washington, D.C. 20007.

THE JOYS OF FREE-LANCING

Many instructors opt to be free-lance teachers, without a contract and without assignments from a school. My former student Dori didn't want a teaching contract and she didn't want the rigidity of a classroom. She wanted to be free to come and go as the spirit moved her. Because she had always desired to visit the "lost city" of Petra in the Jordanian desert, she taught English in Aqaba, Jordan, for three months one spring. She scoured bulletin boards and English-language newspapers in Aqaba for the phone numbers of people who wanted tutoring. She ran an ad in local papers. She pieced together a sufficient number of pupils, and working about 25 hours a week she was finally making good money. She not only supported herself in the pleasant seaside town where she could have good access to Petra for weekend exploring and scuba diving after work, but she saved enough that she was able to travel in Egypt and Israel for a month before looking for pupils to tutor in Tel Aviv.

Like Dori, as a free-lance, you don't have the security that a contract and pre-enrolled pupils provide. Let's say you arrange to visit the office of a professional to conduct private lessons during his or her lunch hour or after the business day; if your pupil has to fly to Frankfurt, you don't get paid while he or she's gone. Your lesson could be as casual as speaking English to a few teen-agers in and around a family pool or on a ski slope, but if your pupils don't show up, you don't get paid.

FINDING ENGLISH TEACHING ASSIGNMENTS

Some would-be instructors simply turn up in a foreign city and advertise for pupils in local periodicals; often, like Dori, they get enough students to support their stay. Others get jobs by word of mouth or by turning up at the right time at English-language schools. Graduate Colleen writes to St. Giles' staffers in San Francisco where she recently completed the CELTA program: "Hello! I made it to Spain and everything is great. I've been here for two weeks and not only found a job the first day I looked for one, but started teaching that same day. It's absolutely incredible. In the middle of the [job] interview the phone rang and [the school's director] sounded quite upset at whomever she was talking to. She was speaking in Spanish. It turned out that the teacher for the 4 P.M. class said he wasn't going to be able to teach the class. It was 1:30 P.M. She was in a panic. So, I looked at her and told her I would teach it. And I did! That's how I got my job."

How many hours a week do you want to work? How much money do you need to make in order to live and to continue your travels? As a free-lancer, you can adjust your hours and income.

TEACHING ENGLISH IN AN OVERSEAS LANGUAGE SCHOOL

Let's say you've completed a certificate in teaching English to people with foreign tongues. Most of the certificate-issuing schools listed above will provide assistance in finding at least your first teaching assignment overseas. In areas where native English speakers are scarce, if you have no certificate, a bachelor's degree will often help you get a teaching job. If you're on your own, without the help of a school from which you've been certificated, the information below on finding English teaching assignments should prove useful.

GETTING THE JOB

Few people are hired at a school overseas without first showing up and presenting themselves to the director. That means you must have some faith and a reserve of cash to go abroad and find your job. Make sure you'll have health (including medical evacuation) insurance before you go.

You can herald your arrival by writing the director in advance. Is writing ahead necessary? It's impossible to generalize about myriad cities in nearly 200 countries. It's quite possible that you can get a job by simply showing up at a language school abroad and asking for an interview, particularly when native English speakers are in short supply. But you can increase your advantage, particularly where competition is keen, by writing in advance.

Go to the library and find a phone directory for the place you want to teach. Look up the heading Schools in the commercial listings; look up the equivalent of the word *school* in the language of the country and write down the addresses and phone numbers. Send a resumé or *curriculum vita* to the director. Highlight any teaching, tutoring, or volunteering in a literacy program that you may have done. Be certain your college degree is easily found on the page. Highlight your degree with bold letters or by underlining it. List other languages you know or language classes you've taken; linguistic ability is prized by proprietors of these schools.

If you've taken courses in a subject with a specialized vocabulary, list those courses. Schools may hire you because you've taken medical terminology, economics, accounting, introduction to business, computer technology, engineering, and any science courses. Your knowledge of arcane vocabulary could be your key to employment, because the school's pupils need to form a vocabulary that includes terminology in their fields of employment.

In your brief cover letter (in English) tell the director or manager when you'll be in town and that you intend to stop by. Don't expect a reply and don't expect red carpets and caviar, but when you do turn up, the manager may recall having received your resumé.

Be sure to bring copies of your diplomas, transcripts, birth certificate, passport, letters of recommendation, and any lesson plans you may have developed. Lesson plans will show the director that you're well prepared and have some idea of what you want to do in the classroom.

Don't underestimate the importance of first impressions, particularly in countries where people dress more formally than they do back home. Your clean and neat appearance will be indispensable for getting you past the director's receptionist at many schools.

Sources of Information about Openings

Knowledge of job openings will give you a decided advantage in nailing down the English teaching job you want. The organizations that follow can get that essential information to you. One could hire you. Contact one or more:

Berlitz

Berlitz, 400 Alexander Park Dr., Princeton, NJ 08540. Phone: (609) 514-9650. This premier language school looks for university graduates who can be trained in the Berlitz Method for placement in Latin America, Korea, and Europe.

Educational Information Services

Education Information Services offers a list of openings in American overseas schools and an additional list in more than 100 schools in Central Europe that seek teachers of English. Send a SASE to EIST, P.O. Box 620662, Newton, MA 02162-0662.

Overseas Academic Opportunities

Overseas Academic Opportunities, 72 Franklin Ave., Ocean Grove, NJ 07756. Phone: (908) 774-1040. Each month this organization publishes *Bulletin of Overseas Teaching Opportunities*. There's a focus on TESOL teaching at the elementary and secondary levels. One issue listed openings in Abu Dhabi, United Arab Emirates; Istanbul, Turkey; Jakarta, Indonesia; Milan, Italy; San Miguel, Spain; Trabzon, Turkey; Zaragoza, Spain; and Zug, Switzerland. Write or call for subscription details.

TESOL Placement Bulletin

TESOL: Members of TESOL (Teachers of English to Speakers of Other Languages, Inc.) have access to the TESOL Placement Bulletin. For membership applications, contact TESOL, 1600 Cameron St., Suite 300, Alexandria, VA 22314. Phone: (703) 836-0774. E-mail: publ@tesol.edu. Their website can be found at www.tesol.edu. TESOL also maintains a resumé referral service; they send your resumé to employers and recruiters. Their job bulletin, issued six times a year, lists teaching positions and grant announcements. This organization also publishes a directory of schools.

Teaching English Abroad

Teaching English Abroad is published by the magazine *Transitions Abroad* and contains firsthand reports by those who have taught overseas, as well as information on how to get certified and find a job with or without certification. Call (800) 293-0373. E-mail: trabroad@aol.com. Or write to *Transitions Abroad,* P.O. Box 1300, Amherst, MA 01004-1300.

U.S. Information Agency

If you have certification and a bachelor's degree, you can apply to teach in overseas programs administered by the U.S. Information Agency. Contact the English Language Program Division, USIA, 301 Fourth St. SW, Washington, D.C. 20547. Phone: (202) 619-5869.

GENERAL BOOKS ON TEACHING ENGLISH OVERSEAS

Those who want to plan carefully for teaching English abroad should read one or more of the following:

- *Teaching Abroad* by Sara Steen, IIE. This book is the most authoritative U.S. guide to teaching opportunities for TESL, K-12, and university teaching. Contact IIE, P.O. Box 371, Annapolis Junction, MD 20701. Phone: (800) 445-0443. E-mail: iiebooks@iie.org. Website: http://www.iie.org.

- Susan Griffith, *Teaching English Abroad: Talking Your Way Around the World.* Peterson's Guides. Phone: (800) EDU-DATA.

- *Teaching English Abroad: First-Hand Reports and Resource Information.* From Transitions Abroad, P.O. Box 1300, Amherst, MA 01004-1300. Phone: (413) 256-3414. E-mail: trabroad@aol.com. In fewer than a hundred pages, veterans of overseas English teaching describe opportunities, placement organizations, training centers, and still more resource books; they also share firsthand reports.

- *Teach American English around the World* by Thomas A. Kane, Ph.D., with Cheryl De Jong; Abbott Press, 266 Beacon St., Boston, MA 02116. Dr. Kane and Ms. De Jong explain how to support your travels through teaching. They reveal how to get a certificate in a short-term course, and they give strategies for targeting the job you want.
- *Native Speaker: Teach English and See the World* by Elizabeth Reid. It's available from In One Ear Publications, 293461 Manzanita Dr., Campo, CA 91906.

OPPORTUNITIES EVERYWHERE

Teaching English in Latin America

In Latin American countries, where the height of summer coincides with Christmas and New Year's, the academic year stretches from February or March to November or December. Some schools offer programs year-round. Depending on the city you choose to work in, most teachers can find a few hours of work each day.

General

- Association of American Schools in South America, 14750 N.W. Seventy-seventh St., Suite 210, Miami Lakes, FL 33016. Phone: (305) 821-0345. This organization recruits and places certified English teachers for 32 schools in 11 countries of Latin America.

Argentina

- ESL International (5761 Buckingham Parkway, Culver City, CA 90230) is affiliated with English language schools in Buenos Aires and Rio.
- The Language Training Center for Management hires U.S. and Canadian teachers with degrees and TEFL certificates. They provide salary, vacation, sick leave, and insurance. Contact LTCM at Maipu 742, Piso 8 H, Buenos Aires 1006, Argentina.

Brazil

- In Brazil, hordes of children study English in schools. But don't count on the general population being able to speak to you in your own tongue. If you can speak Spanish, you'll be able to read many signs and even make yourself understood, although you may not understand the response to what you've just asked. You would do well to listen to language tapes to learn the basic phrases necessary to get by.

According to Volker Poelzl, writing in *Transitions Abroad* (November/December 1996), you can earn enough by teaching English to cover living expenses and have money left for some travel in return for teaching at least 20 hours a week. Most courses in language schools last only a month or two, so you don't have to sign a long contract. You can travel, return to your base city, and teach another course. ESL training and ability to speak Portuguese are not necessary but are pluses in getting hired or finding your own students. Look for teaching jobs in the want ads of papers such as *O Globo, Jornal do Brasil,* and *O Dia.*

Some English language schools to contact in Rio de Janeiro are

- Ace American Center of English, Avenida Beira Mar 406, GR. 207, Castelo, Rio, RJ, CEP 20025-900, Brazil. Phone: (011) 55-21-220-3345.

- Beeline, Avenida 13 de Maio 23, GR 429, Centro, Rio, RJ, CEP 21031-000, Brazil. Phone: (011) 55-21-222-7238 or 532-5792.

- Brasas English Cours, Avenida Graca Aranha 19, 3 andar, Centro, Rio, RJ, Brazil. Phone: (011) 55-21-532-0761.

- English Center, Rua Toneleiro 219, Copacabana, Rio, RJ CEP 22030-000. Phone: (011) 55-21-255-0014.

- Fisk English School, Avenida 13 de Maio 33, SI. 306, Centro, Rio, RJ, Brazil.

Chile

- See Argentina, ESL International.
- Alliance Abroad, 18 Buena Vista Terrace, San Francisco, CA 94117. Phone: (415) 487-0691. Volunteers are placed as English teachers in Chile, Uruguay, Ecuador, and Mexico.

Colombia

- Centro Cultural Colombo Americano, Carrera 43, 51-95 Barranquilla, Colombia. This school needs teachers of English in Baranquilla, Cali, Bogota, Medillin, and other notoriously exciting places.

Costa Rica

- World Educational Forum, Box 383-4005, San Antonio de Belen, Heredia, Costa Rica. Phone: (800) 689-1170. Live free with host families and teach English without pay in Costa Rica or Mexico.
- World Teach, Harvard Institute for International Development, One Eliot St., Cambridge, MA 02138. Phone: (800) 4-TEACH-0. World Teach makes one-year appointments of teachers in Costa Rica and Ecuador. Costa Rica, a nation surrounded by neighbors with problems, seems to do most things right. In this land of pristine rain forest and idyllic cottages, you'll feel as at home as you ever will in Central America.

Ecuador

- See Costa Rica, World Teach.

Teaching English in Western Europe

The good news is that teaching English is probably the most pleasant work for which most North Americans in Western Europe are qualified, and there are openings in Europe. The bad news: Large numbers of native English speakers, many of them certificated to teach English as a foreign language, live in Continental cities. As a result, the competition for teaching jobs is fierce. Language schools have a plethora of applicants for part- and full-time faculty positions. Note in this section how many more agencies and schools are actively recruiting in Eastern than in Western Europe. To paraphrase Horace Greeley, "Go east, young man [or woman], go east."

It is, however, possible to earn some money teaching English as a free-lance tutor in Western Europe. Susan Griffith, author of *Teaching English Abroad: Talking Your Way Around the World*, warns that it could take several months to find enough private clients to make a decent living. Griffith suggests that in order to attract pupils, you publicize yourself shortly after you arrive in your city or town of choice. Put up notices on bulletin boards anywhere you can. Send notices to public schools, to professionals such as lawyers; send notices to businesses that depend on foreign contacts. Your best advertising, however, will come through word of mouth, because if you're good at what you do, *word* (hopefully in coherent English) will get around.

It's also possible to exchange English lessons for room and board. Again, put ads in papers and on bulletin boards. Print cards with your name, phone number, and credentials and hand them out.

Austria

- English for Kids, A. Baumgartnerstr. 44, A/7042, 1230 Vienna, Austria. Phone: (011) 43-1-667 45 79. This residential summer program hires instructors. You'll need a TEFL certificate.

Spain

- O'Neill School of English, Ibarluce 20, 48960 Galdakao, Spain. Phone: (011) 34-44-456 49 17. The O'Neill School helps arrange placement of English speakers in Spanish homes. You'll live in the home and converse with children in English.

- Alexandria Abramian, who had taught English in Spain for three years, counsels that generally, you should show up in person to get a job in Europe. The school operators want to meet you first. Secondly, they want to make certain they have adequate enrollment before hiring; therefore late summer and early autumn is the best time to look for work. In Spain, Abramian suggests looking for job ads in the Sunday papers, in Barcelona's *La Vanguardia* and in *El Pais* in other parts of Spain.

Switzerland

- Institut du Hau-Lau, 1831 Les Sciernes d'Albeuve, Switzerland. Phone: (011) 41-260928 42 00. They need teachers for summer language schools.

Teaching English in Eastern Europe

The nations of Eastern Europe—Poland, Latvia, Lithuania, Estonia, the Czech Republic and Slovakia, Hungary, Romania, Bulgaria, the former Yugoslav republics, Albania, Belarus, Ukraine, Moldova, and Russia itself—are trying desperately to reap the largess of capitalist economies after 35 or more years of communism. In order to do that, they must train businesspeople to converse and write in the language of international business. That's where you could come in.

You'll find jobs are easier to get here than in Western Europe. They often pay less, but the requirements may be less stringent than in the West. Try to arrange employment before you go to Eastern Europe. In your cover letter, if you've never taught, tell about volunteer activities you may have done that are similar to teaching: counseling at summer camps, literacy tutoring, etc. Business English and English for children are particularly popular specialties for teachers of English in Eastern Europe.

Public schools will take teachers, often whether they're certified or not. In some cases, depending on how desperate schools are for teachers, you need not speak the local language to get hired. Language schools in the major cities of Poland, the Czech Republic, Slovakia, and Hungary hire at various times during the year.

General

- InterExchange, 161 Sixth Ave., New York, NY 10013. Phone: (212) 924-0446. Fax: (212) 924-0575. Interexchange helps place teachers of English for a year in the Czech Republic, Hungary, and Poland, and for a semester or a year as teaching assistants in Finland. Certification (TEFL) isn't required, but at minimum a B.A. is preferred. English is sufficient except that German could be helpful in Central Europe. InterExchange also sponsors a homestay program in Finland in which Americans teach English to a family in return for room and board and some pocket money. Males and females between 18 and 24 may apply. InterExchange charges program fees.

- Soros Professional English Language Teaching Program (SPELT) 888 Seventh Ave., 31st Floor, New York, NY 10106. Phone: (212) 757-2323. Soros looks for experienced teachers of English for most Eastern European nations.

Baltic Nations

- See Czech Republic, Fandango.
- See Russia, Project Harmony, Travel Teach USA.
- See Bulgaria, Teachers for Central and Eastern Europe.

Bulgaria

- Teachers for Central and Eastern Europe, 21 V S Rakovski Blvd., Dimitrograd 6400, Bulgaria. Phone: (011) 359-391 24787. Fax 391-26218. Native speakers teach English in Bulgaria, the Czech Republic, Hungary, Poland, and Slovakia. Call (512) 494-0392. E-mail: jbmorrow@mail.utexas.edu.

Czech Republic

- Academic Information Agency, Dum zahranichnich styku, MSMT CR, Senovazne namesti 26, 111 21, Prague 1, Czech Republic. Inquire about their placement fee.

- See Bulgaria, Teachers for Central and Eastern Europe.
- Caledonian School, Vlatavska 24, 150 00 Prague 5, Czech Republic. Phone: (011) 42-2 57 31 36 50. This school employs 80 English speakers to teach.
- English for Everybody, 655 Powell St., Suite 505, San Francisco, CA 94108. Phone: (415) 789-7641. E-mail: praginfo@mbox. vol.cz. For an "assistance" fee, the school states it can deliver "guaranteed jobs, housing, airport greeting" in Prague and other Czech cities. They also place teachers in Turkey, Russia, Austria, and other Eastern European nations. You must have a bachelor's degree and TEFL/ESL certificate; their business is to train you to achieve a certificate.
- Fandango (1613 Escalero Rd., Santa Rosa, CA 95409; phone: [707] 539-2722) is involved in recruiting EFL teachers for the Czech Republic, Russia, Poland, Hungary, and the Baltic nations.
- Foundation for a Civil Society, 1270 Avenue of the Americas, Suite 609, New York, NY 10020. Phone: (212) 332-2890. The Foundation recruits teachers for summer and year-round ESL positions in the Czech and Slovak republics. It provides a stipend and a stay with a family that wishes to improve their English skills.
- InterExchange, 161 Sixth Ave., New York, NY 10013. Phone: (212) 924-0446. Fax: (212) 974-0575. InterExchange places teachers in Prague and Budapest for a semester or a year.
- ITC Prague. If you don't have a TEFL certificate, consider obtaining one in Prague through ITC Prague, Narodni 20, 11672 Prague 1, Czech Republic. Phone: (011) 42-2-96-14-10-14. You may find it significantly cheaper than pursuing a similar month-long program in North America.

Finland

- Center for International Mobility, PB 343, 00531 Helsinki, Finland. Phone: (011) 358-0-7747-7033. Stay with a Finnish family and teach them English.

- InterExchange, 161 Sixth Ave., New York, NY 10013. Phone: (212) 924-0446. Fax: (212) 974-0575. InterExchange places teachers in Finnish elementary and high schools. It provides a stipend and housing. They charge a "program fee" for placement and orientation.

Hungary

- See Czech Republic, InterExchange, Fandango.
- Teach Hungary, 700 College St., Beloit, WI 53511. Phone: (608) 363-2619.
- See Bulgaria, Teachers for Central and Eastern Europe.

Moldova

- See Russia, Travel Teach USA.

Poland

- English School of Communication Skills, ul.sw. Agnieszki 2/lp, 31-068 Krakow, Poland. Phone: (011) 48-12-22 85 83.
- World Teach, Institute for International Development, One Eliot St., Harvard, Cambridge, MA 02138. Phone: (800) 4-TEACH or (617) 495-5527. WT offers placement in Poland and Lithuania for those with 25 or more hours experience and a university degree.
- See Bulgaria, Teachers for Central and Eastern Europe.
- See Czech Republic, Fandango.
- For information on English teaching opportunities in Poland, contact The National Ministry of Education, Department of International Education, Al Szucha 25, 00-918 Warsaw, Poland.

Romania

- See Hungary, Teach Hungary.
- See Russia, Travel Teach USA.

Russia

- When you arrive in St. Petersburg, look in *The Neva News* and the *St. Petersburg Press* for the names and numbers of people who require someone to teach them English. Look too for the names and locations of schools to which you might apply for a job. You might also arrange to swap language lessons for sleeping bag space or for food.

- American Academy of Foreign Languages, Moscow, needs English instructors with some knowledge of Russian. Send a resumé, photo, and cover letter. Send them to the American Academy of Foreign Languages, Post International Box 421, 666 Fifth Ave, Suite 572, New York, NY 10103.

- American Council of Teachers of Russian, 1776 Massachusetts Ave. NW, Suite 700, Washington, D.C. 20036. Phone: (202) 833-7522. Fax: (202) 833-7523. The Council places English teachers in schools in Moscow and St. Petersburg. It charges no fees and provides airfare, housing, a stipend, and some insurance.

- See Czech Republic, English for Everybody.

- Language Link Schools, Novoslobodskaya ul. 5 bid. 2 101030 Moscow. Telephone or fax: (011) 95-973-2154. This agency hires 40 English language teachers in a number of schools.

- Project Harmony, Six Irasville Common, Waitsfield, VT 05673. Phone: (802) 496-4545. The Project makes placements in Russia, Uzbekistan, Kirghizia, Kazakhstan, Latvia, and Lithuania.

- Travel Teach USA, P.O. Box 357, Rigby, ID 83442. Phone: (208) 745-7222. Travel Teach offers "working holidays" in Russia, Ukraine, Moldova, Romania, and Lithuania.

Slovakia

- For information about teaching English, contact the Slovak Academic Information Agency, Hviezdoslavovo nam, 14 Box 108, 810 00 Bratislava 1, The Slovak Republic.

- Slovakia: See Czech Republic, Foundation for a Civil Society; see Bulgaria, Teachers for Central and Eastern Europe.

Slovenia

- Mint D.O.O., Jeranova Ulica 1, Ljubljana, Slovenia. Phone: (011) 386-61-133-8456. Teach English, German, Italian, Spanish, French, or Russian at the Mint School in Ljubljana, a vibrant city in the former Yugoslavia. The pay in a recent year was reportedly three times comparable with pay in other East European countries. This school wants to interview you in person first.

Ukraine

- Mir V Mig, Box 1085, 310168 Kharkov, Ukraine. Phone: (011) 7-0572-653141. Places teachers in schools and universities in Kiev and Kharkov in the Ukraine.
- Ukraine: See Russia, Travel Teach USA.
- Ukrainian National Association, Inc., 30 Montgomery St., Jersey City, NJ 07302. Phone: (800) 253-9862. Fax: (201) 451-2093. Teach for four weeks in the summer if you have a bachelor's degree. Students are usually adults or high school age. Your classroom may be a school or factory cafeteria. The Association provides room and board with a host family.

Teaching English in the Middle East

Kazakhstan, Kirghizia, Uzbekistan

- Project Harmony, Six Irasville Common, Waitsfield, VT 05673. Phone: (802) 496-4545. PH places teachers of English in former-Soviet Central Asia and in Latvia, Lithuania, and Russia.

Syria

- American Language Center Damascus, c/o USIS, Box 29, Damascus, Syria. Phone: (011) 963-11-332-7236 or c/o USIS, Department of State, Washington, D.C. 20521-6110. This organization employs 40 English-speaking teachers.

Turkey

- English Fast, Burhaniye Mah-Resmi Efendi Sok No 4, Beyler-beyi, Istanbul, Turkey. Phone: (011) 90-216-318-7018 or 7019. English Fast needs teachers in Istanbul, Ankara, and Izmir, Turkey.
- Saday Educational Consultancy, Necatibey Caddesi 92/3, Karakoy, Istanbul, Turkey. Phone: (011) 90-212 243 2078. Saday provides Turkish families with live-in English tutors. It's a great opportunity for cultural immersion.

Yemen

English-language schools are looking for teachers in Yemen, one of those exotic nations virtually tucked into the cuff of a much larger country, Saudi Arabia. Yemen lies, awash in history, near the mouth of the Red Sea.

- Contact The British Council for information on part-time teaching. Interviews can be completed in the United States. British Council, Box 2157, Sana'a, Republic of Yemen. Phone: (011) 967-1-244-121. Fax: (011) 967-1-244-120.
- Contact Modern American Language Institute, which provides a stipend, free housing, and food for two hours of teaching a day. Box 11727, Sana'a, Republic of Yemen. Phone or fax: (011) 967-1-241-561.

Teaching English in East and South Asia
What to Read

- *Teaching English in Asia: Finding a Job and Doing It Well,* Pacific View Press, P.O. Box 2657, Berkeley, CA 94702. This comprehensive manual tells where and how to find job openings and how to obtain visas, and it details proven teaching methods.
- *Teaching English in Asia,* by Jerry and Nuala O'Sullivan, tells about jobs in China, India, Indonesia, Japan, South Korea, Malaysia, Philippines, Singapore, Taiwan, Thailand, and Vietnam. It's published by Passport Books, c/o NTC Publishing,

4255 W. Touhy Ave., Lincolnwood, IL 60646-1975. Phone: (800) 323-4900.

- Potential teachers of English in China will want to see *Living in China: A Guide to Teaching and Studying in China including Taiwan,* by R. Weiner, M. Murphy, and A. Li. It's from China Books, 2929 Twenty-fourth St., San Francisco, CA 94110. Phone: (415) 282-2994. E-mail: chinabks@slip.net. It includes directories of schools, colleges, and organizations that employ teachers of English.

- Teaching English in Japan is the subject of *Make a Mil-Yen: Teaching English in Japan,* by Don Best. It can be ordered from Stone Bridge Press, P.O. Box 8208, Berkeley, CA 94707. Phone: (800) 947-7271.

- *How to Get a Job and Teach in Japan,* by Bonnie Kuraoka is available from the author at 3595 S.E. First St., Gresham, OR 97030.

China

According to the Council on International Educational Exchange, 450 million Chinese are studying English and there's a growing need for native English speakers. A 12- to 16-hour teaching week will result in contact with more than 150 eager students. Pay is poor, but it's higher than the Chinese receive; and living costs are low, so you should be able to cover expenses and complete some extensive travel within the PRC. If you have a bachelor's, TEFL or TESL certification, or teaching experience, you should be able to find a job. Teachers in some schools receive airfare. Most teachers don't know much Chinese before they arrive, but you'll have the opportunity to learn.

These agencies can help you arrange a teaching job:

- American Field Service International, 313 E. Forty-third St., New York, NY 10017. Phone: (212) 949-2630.

- China Teaching Specialist Program, Western Washington University, Old Main 530A, Bellingham, WA 98224. Phone: (206) 676-3753.

- Chinese Education Association for International Exchange (CEAIE), 37 Damucang Hutong, Beijing 100816. Phone: 011-86-1-602-0731. This organization can help you land a year-long contract. The teaching week is approximately 15 hours in the classroom, but class sizes can be quite large.

- CIEE facilitates placement for teachers of beginning English in China. The academic year begins in August. Teachers work 10 to 20 hours a week and receive a salary and free housing. TESOL instruction is provided during a short training course and orientation in the United States. You need at least a bachelor's degree in any subject. Contact CIEE: (888) COUNCIL. E-mail: inro@ciee.org.

- Embassy of the PRC, Education Office, 2300 Connecticut Ave. NW, Washington, D.C. 20008. Phone: (202) 328-2563. Ask for information on teaching English in mainland China.

Indonesia

Indonesia is a cultural smorgasbord, or rather *rijsttafel.* Its hundreds of cultures, hundreds of languages, and diversity of religons distract one from the fact that Indonesia's swiftly becoming an economic power. Manufacturing, petroleum, and agriculture make Indonesia a major trading country whose leading businesspeople must know English. Here, then, is your opportunity to get to know these lovely islands.

- International Language Programs, ILP Centre, J1, Raya Pasar Minggu, No. 39A, Jakarta, Indonesia. Phone: (011) 62-21-798-5210. They are looking for qualified teachers to teach English in Indonesia.

Japan

You may work for a company that provides English instruction for its employees, in a vocational school where all students must learn English, or in a public or private school. If you work for a language school or public school, you'll probably be asked to sign a one- or two-year contract. The school that hires you can arrange for your full-time working visa. You generally need a four-year degree, but not necessarily in English. Teaching experience is not always required. You may end up teaching young children or adults. Many schools will either furnish housing, help you find housing, and/or subsidize housing. Make certain the place you'll stay is livable; standards in a few Japanese communities may not be the same as your standards.

Check too to make certain that you have a reasonable teaching schedule. A seven-hour teaching day could be split between morning and evening classes, leaving you with a double commute and midday time to kill. Remember too that the cost of living is astonishing, but so are salaries. If you're careful, you may well be able to save money.

To find a job without applying to an agency, go to your library and find the *Japan Times.* Look for ads in the Monday edition that ask for teachers of English. Also look into

- *O-Hayo Sensei: The Newsletter of Teaching Jobs in Japan,* edited by Lynn Cullivan, is published biweekly. It's by subscription. Contact O-Hayo Sensei, 1032 Irving St., Suite 508, San Francisco, CA 94122. Phone: (415) 731-1113. E-mail: editor@ohayosensei.

- When you arrive in Tokyo looking for an English-teaching job, go to the Kimi Information Center, Kimi House, K57 Building, 6th Floor, 2-54-3 Ikebukoro, Toshima-ku 171. Phone: (011) 81-3-3986-1604. Kimi lists job openings and places to stay. Kimi will fax your resumé to four dozen English conversation schools in the Tokyo area.

- If you're already in Japan looking for a job, inquire from other job seekers at a *gaijin* house—a hostel for foreigners that's found in most major urban centers. In Tokyo you might go to the Okuba House, 1-11-32 Hyakunin-cho, Shinjuku-ku; or the English House Ryokan, 2-23-8 Nishi-Ikebukuro, Toshima-ku. Check the notice boards in these houses and in tourist offices. There, you may find clients looking for teachers.

- Pick up a copy of *Teach English in Japan* by Charles Wordell and Greta Gorsuch, published by *Japan Times;* it's available from Konokuniya Book Store, 10 W. Forty-ninth St., New York, NY 10020. Phone: (212) 765-1461. With all of these leads, you can probably piece together enough private teaching sessions to pay for your stay.

The following are schools, agencies, and other organizations that can place you:

- AEON actively recruits English speakers to teach in their 225 schools within Japan. A bachelor's degree is necessary. If you enjoy writing essays, you'll be happy to know that AEON will ask you to write on the topic, "Why I want to live and work in Japan"; but you need to do this only if you want to be hired.

  The company offers salaries, benefits, return airfare on completion of the contract, and housing assistance. Contact AEON, 9301 Wilshire Blvd., Suite 202, Beverly Hills, CA 90210. Phone: (310) 550-0940. AEON, 203 N. La Salle, Suite 2100, Chicago, IL 60601. Phone: (312) 251-0900. AEON, 230 Park Ave., Suite 1000, New York, NY 10169. Phone: (212) 808-3080. Website: www.aeonet.com.

- American English Institute, 1833 Kalakaua Ave., Suite 1000, Honolulu, HI 96815. Phone: (808) 942-5881. It places teachers in mostly small towns.

- ASA Community Salon, ASA Staff Center, Toota Building 10, 3-72-7, Sendagaya Shibuya-ku, Tokyo 107. Phone: (3) 3796-4488. This organization employs English teachers.

- Berlitz Schools of Languages (Japan), Inc., Kowa Bldg., 1, 5F, 11-41, Akasaka 1-chome, Minato-ku, Tokyo 107. Phone: (3) 3589-3525. Berlitz employs several hundred teachers. Send or bring around a resumé.

- ECC Foreign Language Institute, Skikata Bldg., 1F, 4-43 Nakazaki-Nishi, 2-chome, Kita-ku, Osaka 530. Phone: (6) 359-1596. Send or carry your resumé to their hiring staff.

- The English Club, Inc., Naritaya Bldg, 2F, 1-2-2 Tsukagoshi, Warabi City, Saitama T335 Japan. Phone: (48) 432-7444.

- Geos Language Corp., Ontario Simpsons Tower, Suite 2424, 401 Bay St., Toronto, ON M5H 2Y4, Canada. Phone: (416) 777-0109. Fax: (416) 777-0110. Geos offers one-year contracts for 26 hours per week of teaching. It provides return airfare, salary, housing, and insurance.

- Interact Nova Group, 2 Oliver St., 7th Floor, Boston, MA 02109. Phone: (617) 542-5207. Fax: (617) 542-3115. Students come in all sizes from age 12 to adults. Teachers teach them 33 to 35 hours a week with no more than three or four students per class. This organization places teachers in 230 different locations.

- Interface Company, Lifepia Motoyama 3F5-21-5, Nekoga-hora-Dori, Chikusa-Ku, Nagoya 464, Japan. Phone: (011) 52-781-2001. Teachers work six hours a day with Japanese children and receive monthly compensation and a bonus after the first year. Two two-week vacation periods and all Japanese holidays are paid. But Interface doesn't pay airfare to and from Japan.

- International Education Services, Rose Hikawa Bldg., 22-14 Higashi 2-chome, Shibuya-ku, Tokyo 150. Phone: (3) 3498-7101.

- JET stands for Japan Exchange and Teaching Program. Phone: (800) INFO-JET. The "JET" program is sponsored by the Japanese government. More than a thousand American college graduates and young professionals are invited to share language and culture with Japanese youths.

  You must be between ages 18 and 35 to apply. You must indicate a strong interest in Japanese culture. Americans serve for a year in junior and senior schools and government offices in Japan. JET provides airfare, housing, a salary, and health care. Interviews are held at Japanese consulates in North America. Contact the Japanese Embassy, 2520 Massachusetts

Ave. NW, Washington, D.C. 20008. Phone: (202) 234-2266. The pay is said to be quite good. More than 4,000 teachers are employed.

For more information on JET, use your Internet: listserv@ listserv.arizona.edu. This is a discussion group in which those thinking about signing up with the JET program can ask questions of those who have returned.

- MIL the Language Center, 3F Eguchi Bldg., 1-6-2 Katsutadai, Yachi Yo-Shi, Chiba T276, Japan. Fax: (474) 85-7875. MIL has 2,000 students at five schools. Their ages range from four to 70. MIL offers good compensation, a 10 percent raise for the second year, low-cost furnished housing, and a contract-completion bonus (in lieu of airfare).

- The Overseas Service Corps of the YMCA recruits English teachers for language schools in Taiwan and Japan. Contracts are usually for a year. They provide a stipend, housing, insurance, and return airfare on completion of the contract. Contact International Office for Asia, YMCA of the USA, 909 Fourth Ave., Seattle, WA 98104.

- Nova Intercultural Institute is a large English-language school in Japan. Potential teachers may apply at their U.S. office, 2 Oliver St., Suite 7, Boston, MA 02110. Phone: (617) 542-5027. Or contact the Canadian office, 1881 Yonge St., Suite 700, Toronto, Ont. M4S 3C4. Phone: (416) 966-6682. Nova signs teachers to one-year contracts.

- YMCA International Office for Asia, 909 Fourth Ave., Seattle, WA 98104. Volunteers teach in a Japanese YMCA for two years.

Korea

Koreans want to become competent English speakers. It's a good place to find a good job teaching English. South Korea's Foreign Capital Inducement Act frees American workers from paying income tax to South Korea for a specific period. Those with TESOL or RSA certificates and some experience receive quite good pay. They work 16 to 20 hours a week and many earn accrued vacation time. In some cases it's possible to negotiate for airfare. You may find ads requesting English teachers in the English-language *Korean Times* and *Korean Herald*. Try applying at some of the *hogwons* (language schools) in Seoul and Pusan.

- Academy of Foreign Languages, 7B-4L Daebang-Dongchang-won City 641-100, Kyungnam Province, South Korea. Fax: (011) 8255-1810-600. They offer one-year contracts with possibility of renewal.

- Best Foreign Language Institute, 98-3 Jungang-Dong, Chang-won City, Kyungsangnam Province, 641-030, South Korea. Their pupils are at levels from preschool to high school. In return for teaching six hours a day, teachers get a week's vacation, half of their health insurance premium paid, free rent on living quarters, and the opportunity to eat subsidized meals at the institute. In addition, the academy provides round-trip airfare.

- Culture Connect International, 211 N. Union St., Suite 100, Alexandria, VA 22314. Phone: (703) 684-4886. Fax: (703) 684-4887. E-mail: culture@erols.com. Culture Connect requires a bachelor's degree and it bases salary on degrees and experience. "Our language centers are luxurious with state-of-the-art equipment," states a Culture Connect representative. They encourage teaching couples to apply.

- ELS, 5761 Buckingham Parkway, Culver City, CA 90230. Phone: (310) 642-0988. Fax: (310) 649-5231. ELS places teachers in Seoul, Taegu, and Pusan for one year. It provides salary, housing, insurance, and round-trip airfare.

- English Friends Academy, c/o Stefan Carpenter, 733 Shin-donga-4, Banghak-3 Dong, Dobong-gu, Seoul 132-023, South Korea. Fax: (011) 822-956-8847. This private academy has 350 students. It also runs a summer camp program. They provide teachers an apartment, flight to Korea and return, and a salary plus a month's bonus on completion of the contract.

- English Language Recruitment Center, Inc., 4344 S. Archer Ave., Suite 131, Chicago, IL 60632-2827. Phone: (312) 843-9792 or (312) 843-9723.

- Good Teacher's Center, 271-19, Dongin 3-GA, Jung-Ku, Taegu 700-423, South Korea. Fax: (8253) 427-8295. Phone: (82) 53-427-8291. Homepage: http://bora.dacom.co.kr/-gta. E-mail: gta@chollian.dacom.co.kr. Good recruits teachers to teach conversational English throughout the year. They ask for at least a bachelor's degree and offer "good" pay, housing, and airfare.

- Korea Academy Consultants, Ju-kong Apt. #105-711 Kum-kok Dong, Puk-ku, Pusan 616-130, Korea. This agency advertises for teachers of English and places them in private language schools. "Experience and/or TESOL certificate [are] preferred but not required." There's a placement fee.

- Korean Services Group, 147-7 Bun Jeon Dong, Jin-ku Pusan 614-060, South Korea. Fax: (011) 82-51-817-3612. This organization places teachers in 120 schools.

- SISA America, P.O. Box 4679, Cerritos, CA 90703-4679. Fax: (310) 404-9513. Website: www.ybmsisa.com. You should have a bachelor's degree and excellent English. In return for teaching English to Koreans, you receive a salary, bonus, airfare, housing, relocation allowance, health insurance, vacation, and sick leave. Positions are available year-round. Fax your resumé.

Siberia

- Work in Siberia? A year in Asiatic Russia would give you plenty to tell the folks back home. If hired, you get the title of *professor* at Tomsk Polytechnical Institute or at Tomsk State University. The pay, although small by American standards, allows North American teachers to live better than average Russian college teachers do. Free housing is provided. You work from 8:30 A.M. to noon, with an hour of preparation time, teaching five English classes from September to early

June. Contact the English Department, Tomsk Polytechnic University, International Studies, 30, Lenina Ave., Tomsk, 634004, Russian Federation. Phone: 001-738-222-69669. E-mail: tpu@tpu.tomsk.su.

Taiwan

Taiwan is a major trading partner with the United States and an economic powerhouse. In addition, there's a labor shortage and Taiwan needs lots of teachers of English. "The Taiwanese," writes former ESL teacher Deborah Lockwood, "cling to the ancient Confucian model of passive learning," where the teacher holds forth and the pupils remain silent. "As a result," continues Lockwood, "everyone in Taiwan studies English but very few can speak it." If you speak English as a native, you should be able to land a job teaching English for about 20 hours a week. Because you'll encourage your students to speak in class, they'll learn to speak English well and you'll be in great demand. Right? In addition, some companies need people with perfect English skills to proofread business communications, so you can make a good income on the side. Some schools and organizations that can place you are

- ELS International, 12 Kuling St., Taipei, Taiwan. Phone: (011) 886-2-321-9005. ELS hires 200 English teachers for its 12 schools in Taiwan.

- Hess Language Schools, 83 Po Ai Road 2F, Taipei, Taiwan. Hess hires 200 teachers for 40 of its schools in Taiwan. Details may be obtained from 4 Horicon Ave., Glen Falls, NY 12801. Phone: (518) 793-6183. Hess provides a salary, assistance in finding a place to live, and insurance. Hess has 662 locations where teachers work with children about 20 hours a week.

- Overseas Service Corps YMCA, OSCY Manager, International Division, YMCA of the USA, 101 N. Wacker Dr., Chicago, IL 60606. Phone: (800) 872-9622. Teach English in Taiwan for the minimum of a year. It recruits 25 English teachers for a year for nine schools. A bachelor's degree is required, preferably in English. Teachers receive salary, return airfare, bonuses, paid vacation, health insurance, and "more."

Thailand

According to working-abroad writer Susan Griffith, "Anyone who is determined to teach in Thailand and prepared to go there to look for work is virtually guaranteed to find opportunities." Jobs are principally in Bangkok, Chiang Mai, and Songkhla. The latter two cities are delightful; Bangkok is smog- and traffic-bound most of the time, yet vibrant and pulsating. Place an ad in English-language papers such as the *Bangkok Post* and *Nation* and check hostel bulletin boards for offers. Visit language schools; their addresses are in the phone directory.

- CIEE, 205 E. Forty-second St., New York, NY 10017. Phone: (212) 661-1414 ext. 1439. CIEE can help place English teachers in elementary and secondary schools for the academic year.
- English and Computer College, 430/17-24 Chul Soi 64, Siam Square, Bangkok 10330, Thailand. Phone: (011) 66-2-255-1856. Half of ECC's 60 schools are in the capital. They hire native English speakers.

YOUR LANGUAGE—AND THEIRS

Those who travel abroad to teach their own language to others inevitably receive for their time and expertise far more than pay. Whether the teachers enjoy their assignment or not, they're never the same afterward, for they gain as much as they give. Teaching English helps them learn about the culture of their host country, and perhaps even a bit of its language. Most of all, these teachers—like all good travelers—return home having learned something valuable about themselves and their own society.

CHAPTER 17

A Wealth of Free Information

McCheap's Seventeenth Law of Travel:
Learning as much as you can about your destinations costs nothing,
and can make your free travels a success.

TRAVEL FACTS FOR FREE

Getting good information is a major necessity for any traveler, and particularly for the free traveler. Free public libraries and university libraries, if you have access to them, can supply most of the books mentioned in *You Can Travel Free*. The Internet is a marvelous source of travel information. National, state or provincial, regional, and metropolitan governments fund tourist bureaus; many of those bureaus will gladly send you, at no charge, information about visiting their areas. Some countries have no tourist bureaus in North America, but their embassies will often supply the needed information. This chapter contains recommendations on books and periodicals, Internet sources, and addresses of tourist bureaus and foreign embassies.

THE BEST GUIDEBOOKS FOR BUDGET TRAVELERS

A good guidebook will be up-to-date and will include not only the top sights in major cities, but it should explain in some detail what to see and do in out-of-the-way places. It should include, at least, a comprehensive rundown of the history and culture of the place or area, good directions, admissions costs, and opening times of places you might want to visit. Budget guides will differ from standard guides in that they'll exclude excruciatingly expensive hotels and restaurants. Budget guides include information about taxis, but they'll tell you how to use cheap public transportation as well.

The good news about travel guides is that they've been getting increasingly better and better. In fact, the current crop of guides is excellent. Competition for the traveler's guidebook dollar is so intense that the travel sections of major bookstores and even libraries are crammed with a variety of titles sufficient to cause buyers to be perplexed by the decision of which to buy or to check out. Most of the best guides are updated annually.

What are some of the best budget guides today?

- Berkeley guides include titles for Europe and individual countries; e.g., France, Great Britain, etc. They're written by well-traveled University of California students and published and sold by Fodor's Guides, 201 E. Fiftieth St., New York, NY 10022. Phone: (800) 733-3000.

- The *Let's Go* series, c/o St. Martin's Press, 175 Fifth Ave., New York, NY 10010. *Let's Go* guides are written by Harvard and Radcliffe students who roam the world to update the series annually. These books cover Europe, Central and North America, the Middle East, and Asia. *Let's Go: Europe, Let's Go: Eastern Europe,* and specific country and city guides are increasingly popular, accurate, and easy to use. All are written by fun- and culture-loving but penny-pinching pupils for the financially challenged.

- Lonely Planet Publications, Embarcadero West, 155 Filbert St., Suite 251, Oakland, CA 94607. LP's *On-a-Shoestring* series covers the world with more than 150 titles. They include regional (e.g., *Mediterranean Europe on a Shoestring*), country (Peru and lots of others), and city (Cape Town, etc.) guides. The series includes language phrasebooks (*Japanese Phrasebook* and other languages), audiotapes (*Thai Audio Pack*), travel atlases, and travel literature. These are highly accurate and detailed sources that have been carefully researched.

- Maverick Guide Series, Pelican Publishing Co., P.O. Box 3110, Gretna, LA 70054. Phone: (800) 843-1724 or (888) 5-PELICAN. *Maverick Guide* authors are experts on the areas they write on and their descriptions are not only detailed but honest. These guides cover transportation, sight-seeing, where to stay and what to eat, culture, geography, history, and entertainment. The Maverick Series includes guides to Hong Kong, Macau, and South China; Bali and Java; Malaysia and Singapore; Hawaii; Vietnam, Laos, and Cambodia; the Great Barrier Reef; New Zealand; Australia; Thailand; Prague; Berlin; and Barcelona. A recent addition is a guide to an area all-too-few Westerners visit: The sheikdom of Oman. *The Maverick Guide to Scotland* is another recent addition.

- Moon Travel Handbooks, 722 Wall St., Chico, CA 95928. Phone: (916) 345-5473. Moon has brought out more than 50 titles covering Asia, the Pacific, the Caribbean, and the Americas. When you're finished reading a Moon guide you'll think you've been there. The authors definitely have. Probably the most meticulously accurate travel guidebook we've ever used is David Stanley's *South Pacific Handbook;* Stanley's footprints must have dented the sand on virtually every atoll in the region. The scope is unbelievably detailed.

- Rough Guides, c/o Penguin Books USA, Inc., 375 Hudson St., New York, NY 10014. Rough publishes more than 60 titles for traveling worldwide. Rough covers countries (Australia, etc.), cities (Amsterdam and others), regions (e.g., Barcelona and Catalunya). and specialties (Mediterranean Wildlife, women's travel interests). The accuracy is excellent.

The free traveler owes it to him or herself to go to the free public library, check out guidebooks for the areas to be visited, and make copious notes before returning the books. If you plan to stay in hostels and eat food you buy in grocery stores or public markets, you don't need to haul a heavy volume that includes posh hotels and three-star restaurants. In fact, you'll probably be interested mostly in the major sights you expect to visit. In that case, go to the Salvation Army Thrift Shop—or any thriftshop or store that sells used paperbacks dirt cheap. Buy a guide to Europe if you're going to Europe, or a two-bit guide to wherever you want to go. Even if you have a three-month Eurail Pass, you probably won't get to half the places covered in the book. Let's say you're going to England, Netherlands, Germany, and Denmark. Tear those pages out that cover the sights in the four countries you plan to see. Leave the posh hotel and budget-busting restaurant sections in the book; when you're rich and famous you may want them. Leave the rest of book home. Some other year you'll need the sight-seeing sections for other countries. The major advantage is that you'll have a light-weight, made-to-order guide book. To make it lighter, leave the pages about England in a dustbin when you leave England, and discard the Dutch pages as you cross the border to leave.

In addition, contact tourist agencies for free pamphlets and maps that cover your destinations. This chapter contains the most important addresses and phone numbers.

INFORMATION FROM THE INTERNET

- A valuable Internet archive is rec-travel at ftp.cc.umanitoba.ca. There you'll find advisory information from the U.S. State Department and other useful travel updates.

- Addresses, phone numbers, e-mail addresses, and websites are available for government tourism offices and/or U.S. embassies. Punch in http://www.towd.com.

- Books on travel, or on any subject: Find the names and authors of more than a million titles listed by subject. You can purchase these books as well—http://www.amazon.com.

- CIA: On the Internet look for the CIA World Factbook— http://www.odci.gov.94fact/fb94oc/fb94toc.html.

- Cities: For information on more than 2,000 cities, punch in http://www.city./net.

- Currency: How much will drachmas or lire cost you when you want to visit Greece or Italy? For these and most other currencies, see this site, which offers current exchange rates—http://www.dna.1th.se/sgi-hin/kurt/rates.

- Distance finder: You want to fly from Oporto, Portugal, to Sofia, Bulgaria. You want to know how many miles that is. Enter the longitude and latitude and this Internet location will give you the answer—http://www.indo.com/distance/.
- Foreign language: Want to find out how to ask "Where's the potty?" in Dutch? This site offers lots of phrases in languages one most often uses when traveling—http://www.travelang.com/language/. You can also access www.travelang.com.
- Geography: Let's say you have an assignment to make big bucks photographing penguins in the Kerguelen Islands. The problem? You don't know where these islands are. Look up the Kerguelens, or any place on the globe, in Geography Nameserver—http://www.mit.edu8øø1/geo.
- Hostels all around the world—all affiliations—can be found on the Web at http://www.hostels,com.
- Recreation travel: Find the rec.travel library—http://www.solutions.net/rec-travel/.
- Students should look for *The Student and Budget Travel Resource Guide,* which is available at http://asa.ugl.lib.umich.edu/chdocs/travel/travel-guide.htm.
- For all sorts of travel information, try Travelocity—http://www.travelocity.com.
- Weather—http://cirrus.sprl.umich.edu/uxnet/. This site gives you current weather conditions throughout the country and the world. Should you take an umbrella to Marbella? Find out.
- Yahoo Travel Directory—http://www.yahoo.com/Recreation/Travel.

MISCELLANEOUS:
BARGAIN GUIDES, FREE SAMPLES, ETC.

- The Barge Lady, 101 W. Grand Ave., Suite 200, Chicago, IL 60610. Phone: (800) 880-0071. Fax: (312) 245-0952. An expert on barge travel in Europe will send you a free newsletter that highlights barge vacations.

- *Big World.* Write to Big World, P.O. Box 21, Coraopolis, PA 15108. Website: bigworld@x.netcom.com. Ask for a sample copy of this low-budget travel magazine.
- *Consumer Reports Travel Letter,* P.O. Box 53629, Boulder, CO 80322-3629. Phone: (800) 234-1970. It's published by Consumer's Union. A sample issue is free.
- Customs: Get a free pamphlet explaining your Uncle Sam's customs regulations. U.S. Customs Service, P.O. Box 7407, Washington, D.C. 20044. Phone: (202) 927-6724.
- Hosteling: Don't use fuel—walk, backpack, or bicycle. For information on more than two dozen trips in United States, Canada, Europe, Israel, and Costa Rica, contact HI-AYH Programs Dept., 733 Fifteenth St. NW, Suite 840, Washington, D.C. 20005. Phone: (202) 783-6161 or e-mail them at dkalter@attmaill.com.
- *La Belle France,* P.O. Box 3485, Charlottesville, VA 22903. Phone: (800) 225-7825. Fax: (804) 296-0948. It's a monthly newsletter on travel in France. A sample issue is free.
- Moon Publications, P.O. Box 3040, Chico, CA 95927. Phone: 800-345-5473. E-mail: travel@moon.com. Website: www.moon.com. Moon publishes a free travel newsletter, *Travel Matters.* It highlights their travel handbooks for various regions of the world.
- *Passport.* 350 Hubbard St., Suite 440, Chicago, IL 60610. Phone: (312) 464-0300. Fax: (312) 464-0166. It's a monthly newsletter on foreign and domestic hotels, restaurants, and shopping. A sample issue is free.
- Rick Steves' *Europe Through the Back Door Newsletter,* 120 Fourth Ave. North, P.O. Box 2009, Edmonds, WA 98020-2009. Phone: (206) 771-2009. Fax: (206) 771-0833. E-mail: ricksteves@aol.com. Website: www.ricksteves.com. Rick will send you a free 64-page quarterly magazine that includes budget travel tips.
- *Scenic Walking,* 703 Palomar Airport Rd., Suite 200, Carlsbad, CA 92009. Phone: (800) 473-1210. E-mail: lajolla@bctwalk.

com. Website: www.bctwalk.com/lajolla. A tour company publishes this free newsletter about walking trips in places such as Europe and New Zealand.

- *Transitions Abroad,* 18 Hulst Rd., P.O. Box 1300, Amherst, MA 01004-1300. Ask for subscription information. The articles are addressed to university study-abroad advisors and to students who want to study, work, volunteer, or simply travel. It's full of valuable tips, addresses, and phone numbers.

- The Travel Channel has a homepage that provides up-to-date travel news and information from selected newsletters. E-mail: info@travelchannel.com.

- *The Thrifty Traveler,* P.O. Box 8168, Clearwater, FL 34618. E-mail: thrifty@aol.com. Ask for a sample copy.

- *Travel Smart,* 40 Beechdale Rd., Dobbs Ferry, NY 10522. Phone: (800) 327-3633. It's full of bargains and tips. A sample is free.

- *Travel Tips for Senior Citizens* is free from Bureau of Consular Affairs, U.S. Department of State, 2202 C St. NW, Washington, D.C. 20520.

- U.S. Government travel advisories and warnings, as well as passport and visa information, can be obtained from the State Department at (202) 647-5225.

- University dorm rooms: British Universities Accommodation Consortium Ltd., Box 1355, University Park, Nottingham NG7 2RD, U.K. Phone: (011) 44-115-950-4571. You can save money by renting a dorm room when students are on break.

- *U.S. and Worldwide Travel Accommodations Guide,* from Campus Travel Service, P.O. Box 5486, Fullerton, CA 92635. Phone: (800) 525-6633. The guide lists 700 places worldwide that offer inexpensive bed and breakfasts.

- Women's Travel: *Maiden Voyages, The Indispensable Guide to Women's Travel,* has gone online at http://maiden-voyages.com. It's an opportunity for women to read about and communicate about travel issues that concern them. It also provides a bulletin board through which women can search for suitable travel companions. For information about the quarterly magazine, call (800) 528-8425.

ATTENTION SENIORS

- Senior discounts are reported in *The Mature Traveler,* P.O. Box 50400, Reno, NV 89513.

- AARP (American Association of Retired Persons) has arranged discounts on car rentals, airfare, hotels, etc., for members. Applicants must be at least 50. Phone: (202) 434-2277.

- National Council of Senior Citizens, 1331 F St. NW, Washington, D.C. 20004. Phone: (202) 347-8800. If you join you get travel discount coupons.

- *101 Tips for the Mature Traveler.* Request this free pamphlet from Grand Circle Travel, 347 Congress St., Boston, MA 02210. Phone: (800) 248-3737.

- *Unbelievably Good Deals and Great Adventures That You Absolutely Can't Get Unless You're Over 50,* by Joan R. Heilman, Contemporary Books, 180 N. Michigan Ave., Chicago, IL 60601. Phone: (312) 782-9181. Bet it's in your public library.

MEDICAL CARE ABROAD

- U.S. Federal Center on Disease Control can give you prevention checklists and suggest inoculations and other precautions for overseas travel. Phone: (404) 332-4559.

- Health advisories for most countries in the world are on the Internet. Check the website at www.hs.unt.edu/clinics/itmc/travel.htm.

- You can have a free membership in IAMAT (International Association for Medical Assistance to Travelers). IAMAT provides access to 3,000 English-speaking physicians in countries everywhere. These practitioners have agreed to a standard list of fees. You get a membership card, a world immunization chart, a series of risk charts, and a directory of doctors in 125 countries and territories. Member physicians' services are not free. Contact IAMAT, 40 Regal Rd., Guelph, Ontario

N1H 1BS, Canada. Phone: (519) 836-0102. Or write IAMAT at 417 Center St., Lewiston, NY 14092.

- See Shoreland's Travel Health Online (http://www.triprep. com) for free, detailed information on health concerns, preventative medications and vaccines, and travel illnesses in more than 200 countries.

FREE TOURIST INFORMATION

Write, call, fax, or drop by these tourist bureaus or embassies. Most will send you relevant information on how to get there, where to stay, what to do, and where to eat. Don't expect them to feature the Rock-Bottom Hotel or the Cheap Eats Cafe, however. They want you to show up and spend, spend, spend. But that's no reason not to get wonderful, free maps and brochures.

Africa

- African Travel Association, 347 Fifth Ave., Suite 610, New York, NY 10016. Phone: (212) 447-1926.
- Africa—particularly Kenya, Tanzania, Uganda, Zambia, Zimbabwe, Malawi, Botswana, Namibia, and South Africa—can be found on the Web at www.onsafari.com.
- Angola—U.S. Office, 1050 Connecticut Ave. NW, Suite 760, Washington, D.C. 20036. Phone: (202) 785-1156. Fax: (202) 785-1258.
- Botswana Department of Tourism, Private Bag 0047, Gaborone, Botswana. Phone: (267) 353024.
- Chad Embassy, 2002 R St. NW, Washington, D.C. 20009. Phone: (202) 462-4009. Fax: (202) 265-1937.
- Comoros Islands Permanent Mission—USA, 336 E. Forty-fifth St., 2nd Floor, New York, NY 10017.
- Djibouti Republic Embassy—USA, 1156 Fifteenth St. NW, Suite 515, Washington, D.C. 20005. Phone: (202) 331-0270. Fax: (202) 328-7950.
- Egyptian Tourist Authority, 630 Fifth Ave., New York, NY 10111. Phone: (212) 246-6960.

- Ethiopia Embassy—USA, 2134 Kalorama Rd. NW, Washington, D.C. 20008. Phone: (202) 234-2281. Fax: (202) 328-7950.
- Gabon Tourism, 347 Fifth Ave., Suite 1100, New York, NY 10016. Phone: (212) 447-6701.
- Ghana Tourism, 407 S. Dearborn St., Chicago, IL 60605. Ghana Embassy—USA, 3512 International Dr. NW, Washington, D.C. 20008. Phone: (202) 686-4500. Fax: (202) 686-4527.
- Guinea Embassy—USA, 2112 Leroy Pl. NW, Washington, D.C. 20008. Phone: (202) 483-9420. Fax: (202) 483-8688.
- Guinea-Bissau Embassy—USA, 918 Sixteenth St. NW, Mezzanine Suite, Washington, D.C. 20006. Phone: (202) 872-4222. Fax: (202) 872-4220.
- Ivory Coast Tourism, 2424 Massachusetts Ave. NW, Washington, D.C. 20008. Phone: (800) GO-ABIDJAN. Fax: (202) 387-6381.
- Kenya Tourist Office, 424 Madison Ave., New York, NY 10017. Phone: (212) 486-1300.
- Malawi Tourism, 600 Third Ave., New York, NY 10016. Phone: (212) 949-0180.
- Mali Tourism, 111 E. Sixty-ninth St., New York, NY 10021.
- Mauritius Government Tourist Information Service, 15 Penn Plaza, 415 Seventh Ave., New York, NY 10001. Phone: (212) 239-8367.
- Morocco National Tourist Office, 20 E. Forty-sixth Ave., New York, NY 10017. Phone: (212) 557-2520.
- Nigeria Tourism, 575 Lexington Ave., New York, NY 10022. Phone: (212) 715-7200.
- Senegal Tourism, 888 Seventh Ave., New York, NY 10106. Phone: (212) 757-7115.
- Seychelles Tourist Board, 820 Second Ave., Suite 900F, New York, NY 10017. Phone: (212) 687-9766.
- South African Tourism Board, 747 Third Ave., 20th Floor, New York, NY 10017. Phone: (212) 838-8841.
- Tanzania Tourism, 205 E. Forty-second St., Suite 1300, New York, NY 10017. Phone: (212) 972-9160.

- Togo Tourist Information, 1706 R St. NW, Washington, D.C. 10009. Phone: (202) 667-8181.
- Tunisia Embassy, Tourist Section, 1515 Massachusetts Ave. NW, Washington, D.C. 20005. Phone: (202) 862-1850.
- Uganda Tourism, 336 E. Forty-fifth St., New York, NY 10017. Phone: (212) 949-0110.
- Zaire Embassy, 1800 New Hampshire Ave. NW, Washington, D.C. 10009. Phone: (202) 234-7690.
- Zambia Tourist Office, 237 E. Fifty-second St., New York, NY 10022. Phone: (212) 308-2155.
- Zimbabwe Tourist Office, 1270 Avenue of the Americas, Rockefeller Center, Suite 1905, New York, NY 10020. Phone: (212) 307-6565.

Asia

- Afghanistan Islamic State Embassy—USA, 2341 Wyoming Ave. NW, Washington, D.C. 20008. Phone: (202) 234-3770.
- Armenian Tourism, Embassy of the Republic of Armenia, 122 C St., Washington, D.C. 20001. Phone: (202) 393-5983.
- Bahrain State Embassy—USSA, 3502 International Dr. NW, Washington, D.C. 20008. Phone: (202) 342-0741.
- Bhutan Travel Agency, 120 E. Fifty-sixth St., #1130, New York, NY 10011. Phone: (212) 838-6382.
- China National Tourist Office (People's Republic), 350 Fifth Ave., Room 6413, New York, NY 10118. Phone: (212) 760-9700. Fax: (212) 760-8809.
- Dubai Tourism, 8 Penn Center, Philadelphia, PA 19103.
- Hong Kong Tourist Association, 590 Fifth Ave., New York, NY 10036. Phone: (212) 869-5008.
- India: Government of India Tourist Association, 30 Rockefeller Plaza North, Mezzanine Room 15, New York, NY 10112. Phone: (212) 586-4901.
- Indonesia Tourist Promotion Office, 3457 Wilshire Blvd., Suite 102, Los Angeles, CA 90010. Phone: (213) 387-2078.

- Israel Ministry of Tourism has an information hotline: (800) 596-1199.
- Japan National Tourist Organization, One Rockefeller Plaza, Suite 1250, New York, NY 10020. Phone: (212) 757-5640.
- Jordan Information Bureau, 2319 Wyoming Ave. NW, Washington, D.C. 20008. Phone: (202) 265-1606.
- Kazakhstan Embassy—USA, 3421 Massachusetts Ave. NW, Washington, D.C. 20007. Phone: (202) 333-4507. Fax: (202) 333-4509.
- Korean National Tourist Corp., Two Executive Dr., 7th Floor, Fort Lee, NJ 07024. Phone: (201) 585-0909.
- Kuwait Embassy—USA, 2940 Tilden St. NW, Washington, D.C. 20008. Phone: (202) 966-0702. Fax: (202) 966-0517.
- Laos People's Democratic Republic Embassy—USA, 2222 S St. NW, Washington, D.C. 20008. Phone: (202) 332-6416. Fax: (202) 332-4923.
- Macau Government Tourist Office, P.O. Box 350, Kenilworth, IL 60043-0350. Phone: (800) 331-7150 or (847) 251-6421. Fax: (847) 256-5601. E-mail: asiatour@aol.com.
- Malaysian Tourist Information Center, 818 W. Seventh St., Los Angeles, CA 90017. Phone: (213) 689-9702.
- Myanmar Tourism, 2514 University Dr., Durham, NC 27707. Phone: (919) 493-7500.
- Nepalese Embassy, 2131 Leroy Place NW, Washington, D.C. 20008. Phone: (202) 667-4550.
- Pacific Asia Travel Association, 71 Stevenson St., Suite 1425, San Francisco, CA 94105. Phone: (415) 398-4295.
- Pakistan Tourism, 12 E. Sixty-fifth St., New York, NY 10021.
- Singapore Tourist Promotion Board, 590 Fifth Ave., New York, NY 10036. Phone: (212) 302-4861. Also, 8484 Wilshire Blvd., Suite 150, Beverly Hills, CA 90211. Phone: (213) 852-1901.
- Saudi Arabia Tourism, 601 New Hampshire Ave. NW, Washington, D.C. 20037.
- Taiwan Republic of China Tourism Bureau, One World

Trade Center, Suite 7953, New York, NY 10048. Phone: (212) 466-0691.

- Tajikstan Permanent Mission—USA, 136 E. Sixty-seventh St., New York, NY 10021. Phone: (212) 472-7645.
- Turkmenistan Permanent Mission—USA, 136 E. Sixty-seventh St., New York, NY 10021. Phone: (212) 472-5921.
- Uzbekistan Tourism, 60 E. Forty-second St., New York, NY 10165. Phone: (212) 983-0382.

Canada

- Canadian Tourism Commission, 235 Queen St., 4th Floor, Ottawa, Ontario K1A OH6. Fax: (613) 954-3964. E-mail: otc.cct@ic.gc.ca.
- Alberta Travel, Box 2400, Edmonton, Alberta T5J 2Z4. Phone: (800) 661-8888. Fax: (403) 427-0867.
- British Columbia Tourism, Parliament Bldg., Victoria, British Columbia V8V 1X4. Phone: (800) 663-6000.
- Manitoba Travel, 155 Carlton St., 7th Floor, Winnipeg, Manitoba R3C 3H8. Phone: (800) 655-0040.
- New Brunswick Tourism, Box 12345, Fredericton, New Brunswick E3B 5C3. Phone: (800) 561-0123.
- Newfoundland and Labrador Tourism Marketing, Box 8730, St. John's, Newfoundland A1B 4K2. Phone: (800) 563-NFLD.
- Northwest Territories Tourism, Box 1320, Yellowknife, Northwest Territories X1A 2L9. Phone: (800) 551-0788.
- Nova Scotia Department of Tourism, Box 130, Halifax, NS, Canada B3J 2M7. Phone: (800) 565-0000 from Canada, or (800) 341-6096 from USA.
- Ontario Travel, Queen's Park, Toronto, Ontario M7A 2E5. Phone: (800) ONTARIO. Fax: (613) 952-7906.
- Prince Edward Island Tourism, Box 940, Charlottetown, Prince Edward Island C1A 7N8. Phone: (800) 463-4PEI. Fax: (902) 368-4438.
- Quebec Tourisme, CP 979, Montreal Quebec H3C 2W3. Phone: (800) 363-7777. Fax: (514) 864-3838.

- Saskatchewan Tourism, 500-1900 Albert St., Regina, Saskatchewan S4P 4L9. Phone: (800) 667-7191. Fax: (306) 787-5744.
- Yukon Tourism, Box 2703, Whitehorse, Yukon Territory Y1A 2C6. Phone: (403) 667-5340. Fax: (403) 667-3546.

Caribbean

- Anguilla Tourist Information:
  —c/o Medhurst & Associates, 271 Main St., Northport, NY 11768. Phone: (800) 553-4939.
  —Anguilla Tourist Board, Box 1388, The Valley, Anguilla, B.W.I. Phone: (809) 497-2759. Fax: (809) 497-2710.
- Antigua and Barbuda Department of Tourism and Trade, 610 Fifth Ave., Suite 311, New York, NY 10020. Phone: (212) 541-4117. Fax: (212) 757-1607.
- Aruba Tourism Authority, 1000 Harbor Blvd., Weehawken, NJ 07087. Phone: (800) TO-ARUBA. Fax: (201) 330-8757.
- Bahamas Tourism Authority: Website—http://www.inter-knowledge.com/bahamas.
  —8600 W. Bryn Mawr Ave., Suite 820, Chicago, IL 60631. Phone: (312) 693-1500. Fax: (312) 693-1114.
  —3450 Wilshire Blvd., Suite 208, Los Angeles, CA 90010. Phone: (213) 385-0033. Fax: (212) 383-3966.
  —19495 Biscayne Blvd., Suite 809, Aventura, FL 33180. Phone: (305) 932-0051. Fax: (305-937-0585.
  —150 E. Fifty-second St., New York, NY 10022. Phone: (212) 758-2777. Fax: (212) 758-6531.
  —121 Bloor St. East, Suite 1101, Toronto, ONT M4W 3MS, Canada. Phone—Canada only: (800) 968-3777. Fax: (416) 968-6711.
- Barbados Tourist Authority:
  —800 Second Ave., New York, NY 10017. Phone: (800) 221-9831 or (212) 986-6516. Fax: (212) 573-9850.
  —3440 Wilshire Blvd., Suite 1215, Los Angeles, CA 90010. Phone: (800) 221-9831. Fax: (213) 384-2763.

—5160 Yonge St., Suite 1800, North York, ONT M2N 6L9, Canada. Phone: (800) 268-9122. Fax: (416) 512-6581.

- Belize Tourist Board, 421 Seventh Ave., Suite 201, New York, NY 1001. Phone: (800) 624-0686. Fax: (212) 563-6033.

- Bonaire Tourism Corp., 10 Rockefeller Plaza, Suite 900, New York, NY 10020. Phone: (800) U-BONAIR. Fax: (212) 956-5913.

- British Virgin Islands Tourist Board:
  —370 Lexington Ave., Suite 313, New York, NY 10017. Phone: (800) 835-8530 or (212) 696-0400. Fax: (212) 949-8254.
  —1804 Union St., San Francisco, CA 94123. Phone: (800) 835-8530. Fax: (415) 775-2554.

- Caribbean Tourism Association, 20 E. Forty-sixth St., New York, NY 10017. This association represents 30 islands. Phone: (800) 356-9999. Fax: (212) 697-4258.

- Cayman Islands Department of Tourism:
  —9525 W. Bryn Mawr, Suite 160, Rosemont, IL 60018. Phone: (847) 678-6446. Fax: (847) 678-6675.
  —Two Memorial City Plaza, 820 Gessner, Suite 170, Houston, TX 77024. Phone: (713) 461-1317. Fax: (713) 461-7409.
  —420 Lexington Ave., Suite 2733, New York, NY 10170. Phone: (212) 682-5582. Fax: (212) 986-5123.
  —3440 Wilshire Blvd., Suite 1202, Los Angeles, CA 90010. Phone: (213) 738-1968. Fax: (213) 738-1829.
  —6100 Blue Lagoon Dr., Suite 150, Miami, FL 33126-2085. Phone: (305) 266-2300. Fax: (305) 367-2932.

- Costa Rica Tourist Board. Phone: (800) 343-6332.

- Curacao Tourist Board:
  —475 Park Ave., Suite 2000, New York, NY 10016. Phone: (800) CURACAO. Fax: (212) 683-9337.
  —330 Biscayne Blvd., Suite 808, Miami, FL 33132. Phone: (305) 374-5811. Fax: (305) 374-6741.

- Dominica: Contact Caribbean Tourism Association.

- Dominican Republic Tourist Information Center:
  —1501 Broadway, Suite 410, New York, NY 10036. Information Hot Line: (800) 752-1151. Fax: 212-575-5448.

—2355 Salzedo St., Coral Gable, FL 33134. Phone: (305) 444-4592. Fax: (305) 444-4845.

—2080 Crescent St., Montreal, Quebec, H3G 2B8. Phone: (800) 563-1611 (Canada only). Fax: (514) 499-1393.

- French Government Tourist Office, 444 Madison Ave., New York, NY 10022. Phone: (900) 990-0040. Fax: (212) 838-7855.

   $$$—Cousin Thrifty McCheap says, "Beware of 900 numbers—They're not for tightwads."

- Grenada Board of Tourism:
  —820 Second Ave., Suite 900D, New York, NY 10017. Phone: (212) 687-9554 or (800) 927-9554. Fax: (212) 573-9731.
  —469 University Ave., Suite 820, Toronto, ONT M5G 1Y8, Canada. Phone: (416) 595-5164. Fax: (416) 595-8278.

- Guadeloupe. Write to French Government Tourist Office.

- Haiti Department of Tourism, 18, rue Legitime, Port-au-Prince, Haiti. Phone: (011) 509-23-2143/5631/0723.

- Jamaica Tourist Board:
  —3440 Wilshire Blvd., Suite 1207, Los Angeles, CA 90010. Phone: (213) 384-1123.
  —801 Second Ave., 20th Floor, New York, NY 10017. Phone: (212) 856-9727 or (800) 233-4582.
  —500 N. Michigan Ave., Suite 1030, Chicago, IL 60611. Phone: (312) 527-1296.
  —One Eglinton Ave. East, Suite 616, Toronto, ONT M4P 3A1, Canada. Phone: (416) 482-7850.

- Martinique Promotion Board, 444 Madison Ave., 16th Floor, New York, NY 10022. Phone: (800) 391-4909. Fax: (212) 838-7855.

- Montserrat Tourist Board, c/o Medhurst & Associates, Inc., 775 Park Ave., Huntington, NY 11743. Phone: (516) 425-0900. Fax (516) 425-0903.

- Puerto Rico Tourist Company, 575 Fifth Ave., 23rd Floor,

New York, NY 10017. Phone: (212) 599-6262 or (800) 223-6530. Fax: (212) 818-1866.

- St. Barts. Contact French Government Tourist Office.
- St. Eustatius, c/o Caribbean Connections, P.O. Box 261, Trumbull, CT 06611. Phone: (800) 692-4106.
- St. Kitts and Nevis Tourism Office, 414 E. Seventy-fifth St., New York, NY 10021. Phone: (800) 582-6208. Fax: (212) 734-6511.
- St. Lucia Tourist Board, 820 Second Ave., New York, NY 10017. Phone: (800) 457-3984 or (212) 867-2950. Fax: (212) 867-2795.
- St. Maarten Tourist Office:
  —675 Third Ave., New York, NY 10017. Phone: (800) 786-2278 or (212) 953-2084. Fax: (212) 953-2145.
  —243 Ellerslie Ave., Willowdale, Toronto, ONT M2N 1Y5, Canada. Phone: (416) 223-3501. Fax: (416) 223-6887.
- St. Martin. Contact French Government Tourist Office.
- St. Vincent and Grenadines Tourist Office, 801 Second Ave., 21st Floor, New York, NY 10017. Phone: (800) 729-1726 or (212) 687-4981. Fax: (212) 949-5946.
- Trinidad and Tobago. Phone: (800) 595-ITNT. E-mail: tourism-info@tidco.co.tt. Website: http://www.tidco.co.tt.
- Turks and Caicos Tourist Board, Box 128, Pond St., Grand Turk. Phone: (800) 241-0824. Fax: (809) 946-2733.
- U.S. Virgin Islands Division of Tourism, 1270 Avenue of the Americas, Room 2108, New York, NY 10020. Phone: (212) 332-2222. Fax: (212) 332-2223.

Europe

- Andorra Tourism, 6800 N. Knox Ave., Lincolnwood, IL 60648. Phone: (708) 674-3091.
- Austrian National Tourist Office, 500 Fifth Ave., Box 1142 Times Square, New York, NY 10110. Phone: (212) 944-6880. E-mail: antonyc@1x.netcom.com. Or P.O. Box 491938, Los Angeles, CA 90049. Phone: (310) 477-3332. Website: http://www.anto.com.

- Belarus Embassy, 1619 Hampshire Ave. NW, Washington, D.C. 20009. Phone: (202) 986-1604. Fax: (202) 986-5491.
- Belgian Tourist Office, 780 Third Ave., Suite 1501, New York, NY 10017-0799. Phone: (212) 758-8130. Fax: (212) 355-7675. Website: http://www.visitbelgium.com.
- British Tourist Authority, 551 Fifth Ave., Suite 701, New York, NY 10176-0799. Phone: (800) 462-2748 or (212) 986-2200. Fax: (212) 986-1188. Website: http://www.bta.org.uk.
- Britain on a Budget. Website: www.budgetbritain.com.
- Britain—*Time Out* magazine tells what's on in London. Website: www.timeout.co.uk.
- Bulgarian National Tourist Agency, 20 E. Forty-sixth St., New York, NY 10017. Phone: (212) 822-5900.
- Croatian National Tourist Office, 300 Lanidex Plaza, Parsippany, NJ 07054. Phone: (888) 462-7628. Fax: (973) 428-0707. Website: www.htz.hr.
- Cyprus Tourist Organization (Greek Cyprus), 13 E. Fortieth St., New York, NY 10016. Phone: (212) 683-5280. Fax: (212) 683-5282.
- Czech Tourist Authority, Czech Center, 1109 Madison Ave., New York, NY 10028. Phone: (212) 288-0830. Fax: (212) 288-0971.
- Denmark—see Scandinavian Tourist Board. Website: http://www.deninfo.com.
- Estonian Consulate, 630 Fifth Ave., Suite 2415, New York, NY 10111. Phone: (212) 247-0499.
- Europe Travel Commission has a website featuring information on traveling in 26 member nations. Type http://www.visiteurope.com.
- Finland—see Scandinavian Tourist Board.
- French Government Tourist Office, 444 Madison Ave., 16th Floor, New York, NY 10022. Phone: (900) 990-0040. Website: http://www.fgtousa.org.

- German Tourist Information Office, 122 E. Forty-second St., 52nd Floor, New York, NY 10168-0072. Phone: (212) 661-7200. Fax: (212) 661-7174.

- German Information Center, 950 Third Ave., New York, NY 10022. Phone: (212) 888-9840. Website: http://www.germany-tourism.de. The center publishes weekly newsletter *The Week in Germany;* it's about government and business affairs and it's free.

- Gibraltar Information Bureau, 1155 Fifteenth St. NW, #710, Washington, D.C. 20005. Phone: (202) 452-1108.

- Greek National Tourist Office, 645 Fifth Ave., Olympic Tower, New York, NY 10022. Phone: (212) 421-5777. Fax: (212) 826-6940.

- Greenland Tourism, Box 1552, DK 3900 Nuuk, Greenland. Phone: (299) 2 28 88. Fax: (299) 228 77.

- Hungarian National Tourist Office, 150 E. Fifty-eighth St., New York, NY 10155. Phone: (212) 355-0240. Fax: 207-4103. Website: http://www.hungary.com/-tourinform.

- Iceland—see Scandinavian Tourist Board.

- Irish Tourist Board, 345 Park Ave., New York, NY 10154. Phone: (800) 223-6470 or (212) 418-0800. Fax: (212) 371-9052. Website: http://www.ireland.travel.ie.

- Isle of Man Tourist Information Center, Sea Terminal Building, Douglas, Isle of Man IM1 2RG U.K. Phone: (011) 44 1624 686766. Or in the U.S.: c/o Travel Connoisseur, 1011 Camino De Rio South, San Diego, CA 92108. Phone: (619) 294-2444. Fax: (619) 294-2445.

- Italian Government Travel Office, 630 Fifth Ave., Suite1565, New York, NY 10111. Phone: (212) 245-4822. Fax: (212) 586-9249.

- Latvian Embassy, 4325 Seventeenth St., Washington, D.C. 20011. Phone: (202) 726-8213. Fax: (202) 726-8213.

- Liechtenstein—see Swiss National Tourist Office.

- Lithuanian Embassy, 2622 Sixteenth St., Washington, D.C. 20009. Phone: (202) 234-5860.

- Luxembourg National Tourist Office, 17 Beekman Place, New York, NY 10022. Phone: (212) 935-8888. Fax: (212) 935-5896.
- Malta National Tourist Office, 350 Fifth Ave., Suite 4412, New York, NY 10118. Phone: (212) 695-9520.
- Monaco. Website: http://www.monaco.mc/usa.
- Monaco Government Tourist Bureau, 565 Fifth Ave., New York, NY 10017. Phone: (800) 753-9696.
- Netherlands Board of Tourism, 355 Lexington Ave., 21st Floor, New York, NY 10017. Phone: (212) 819-0300.
- Northern Ireland. Website: www.interknowlecge.com/northern-ireland.
- Norway—see Scandinavian Tourist Board. Website: http://www.norway.org.
- Polish National Tourist Office:
  —275 Madison Ave., #1711, New York, NY 10016. Phone: (212) 338-9412. Fax: (212) 338-9283. Website: http:www.polandtour.org.
  —Poland Orbis, Polish Travel Bureau, 342 Madison Ave., Suite 1512, New York, NY 10173. Phone: (800) 788-7247.
- Portuguese National Tourist Office, 590 Fifth Ave, 4th Floor, New York, NY 10036. Phone: (212) 354-4403. Fax: (212) 764-6137.
- Romania National Tourist Office, 573 Third Ave., New York, NY 10016. Phone: (212) 697-6971.
- Russian National Tourist Office, 800 Third Ave., Suite 3101, New York, NY 10022. Phone: (212) 758-1162. Fax: (212) 458-0933.
- Scandinavian Tourist Board (Denmark, Finland, Iceland, Norway, Sweden), P.O. Box 4649, Grand Central Station, New York, NY 10163. Phone: (212) 885-9700. Fax: (212) 983-5260.
- Scotland. Website: http://www.scotourist.org.uk/stb.
- Slovakia Travel Service, 10 E. Fortieth St., Suite 3601, New York, NY 10016. Phone: (800) 753-0582.

- Slovenian Tourist Office, 345 E. Twelfth St., New York, NY 10003. Phone: (212) 358-9686. Or 2826 E. Commercial Blvd., Ft. Lauderdale, FL 33308. Phone: (305) 772-9200. Or 10662 El Adlante Ave., Fountain Valley, CA 92708. Phone: (714) 378-0510.

- Spanish National Tourist Office, 666 Fifth Ave., New York, NY 10103. Phone: (212) 265-8822. Fax: (212) 265-8864.

- Sweden—see Scandinavian Tourist Board.

- Swiss National Tourist Office, 608 Fifth Ave., New York, NY 10020. Phone: (212) 757-5944. Fax: (212) 262-6116. Website: http://www.switzerland-tourism.com.

- Turkish Ministry of Tourism, 821 United Nations Plaza, New York, NY 10017. Phone: (212) 687-2194. Website: http://www.turkey.org/turkey.

- Ukrainian Embassy, 3350 M St. NW, Washington, D.C. 20007. Phone: (202) 333-0606. Fax: (202) 333-7510.

- Wales Tourist Authority. Website: www.tourism.wales.gov.uk.

Latin America

- Argentina National Tourist Office, 12 W. Fifty-sixth St., New York, NY 10019. Phone: (212) 687-6300.

- Belize Tourist Board, 415 Seventh Ave., New York, NY 10011. Phone: (212) 268-8798.

- Bolivian Embassy, 3014 Massachusetts Ave. NW, Washington, D.C. 20008. Phone: (202) 232-4828. Fax: (202) 328-3712.

- Brazilian Tourist Information Office, 551 Fifth Ave., Suite 519, New York, NY 10176. Phone: (212) 286-9600.

- Chilean National Tourist Board, 510 W. Sixth St., Suite 1210, Los Angeles, CA 90014. Phone: (213) 627-4293.

- Colombia Government Tourist Office, 140 E. Fifty-seventh St., New York, NY 10022. Phone: (212) 688-0151.

- Costa Rica Tourist Board, 1101 Brickell Ave., BIV Tower, Suite 801, Miami, FL 33131. Phone: (800) 327-7033 or (305) 358-2150.

- Ecuador—FEPROTUR, 7270 N.W. Twelfth St., Suite 400, Miami, FL 33126. Phone: (305) 593-9955.
- El Salvador Consulate, 46 Park Ave., New York, NY 10016. Phone: (212) 889-3608.
- Guatemala Tourist Commission, P.O. Box 144351, Miami, FL 33144. Phone: (305) 854-1544.
- Guyana Tourism Association, 228 South Rd., Lacytown, Georgetown, Guyana. Phone: (011) 592-50807. Fax: (011) 592-50817.
- Honduras Tourism Institute, 2100 Ponce de Leon Blvd., Suite 1175, Coral Gables, FL 33134. Phone: (800) 410-9608.
- Mexico Tourism. Phone: (800) 44-MEXICO.
  - —1911 Pennsylvania Ave., Washington, D.C. 20006. Phone: (202) 728-1750.
  - —70 E. Lake St., Suite 1413, Chicago, IL 60601. Fax: (312) 606-9012.
  - —5075 Westheimer, Suite 975W, Houston, TX 77056. Fax: (713) 629-1837.
  - —1801 Century Park East, Suite 1080, Los Angeles, CA 90067. Fax: (310) 203-8319.
  - —2333 Ponce de Leon Blvd., Suite 710, Coral Gable, FL 33134. Fax: (305) 443-1186.
- Nicaragua Consulate, 1627 New Hampshire Ave. NW, Washington, D.C. 20009. Phone: (202) 939-6531. Fax: (202) 939-6574.
- Paraguay Tourism, 2400 Massachusetts Ave. NW, Washington, D.C. 20008. Phone: (202) 483-6960.
- Peru: c/o FOPTUR, 50 Biscayne Blvd., Suite 123, Miami, FL 33132. Phone: (305) 374-0023.
- Suriname Consulate, 7235 N.W. Nineteenth St., Suite A, Miami, FL 33126. Phone: (305) 593-2163. Fax: (305) 599-1034.
- Venezuela National Tourist Office, 7 E. Fifty-first St., New York, NY 10022. Phone: (212) 826-1660.

South Pacific

- American Samoa. Phone: (684) 633-1093.
- Australian Tourist Commission:

—489 Fifth Ave., 31st Floor, New York, NY 10017. Phone: (800) DOWNUNDER. Call (847) 296-4900 to speak with a travel counselor. Fax: (847) 635-3718.

—1212 Avenue of the Stars, Los Angeles, CA 90067. Phone: (310) 552-1988.

- Cook Islands Tourist Authority, 1000 San Clemente Way, Camarillo, CA 93010. Phone: (805) 388-4673.
- Fiji Visitors Bureau, 5777 W. Century Blvd., Suite 220, Los Angeles, CA. Phone: (213) 568-1616.
- Guam. Phone (800) US3-GUAM.
- New Zealand Tourism Board. Phone: (800) 388-5494.

—501 Santa Monica Blvd., Suite 300, Santa Monica, CA 90401. Phone: (310) 395-7480. Fax: (310) 395-7480.

—1111 N. Dearborn St., Suite 2705, Chicago, IL 60610. Phone: (312) 440-1345. Fax: (312) 440-3808.

—780 Third Ave., Suite 1904, New York, NY 10017-2024. Phone: (212) 832-8482. Fax: (212) 832-7602.

- Northern Mariana Islands, Box 861CK, Saipan, MP 96950. E-mail: mvb@saipan.com. Website: www.visit-marianas.com.
- Palau Visitors Authority, Box 256, Koror, Palau 96940. Phone: (011) 680-488-2793.
- Papua New Guinea Tourist Office, c/o Air Niugini, 5000 Birch St., Suite 3000, Newport Beach, CA 92660. Phone: (714) 752-5440.
- Tahiti Tourist Promotion Board, 9841 Airport Blvd., Suite 1108, Los Angeles, CA 90045. Phone: (213) 649-2884.
- Tonga Consulate General, 360 Post St., Suite 604, San Francisco, CA 94108. Phone: (415) 781-0365.
- Vanuatu Tourism Office, 520 Monterey Dr., Rio Del Mar, CA 95003. Phone: (408) 685-8901.

United States: State Tourist Bureaus

- Alabama: 532 S. Perry St., Montgomery 36104. Phone: (800) ALABAMA.
- Alaska: P.O. Box E, Juneau 99811. Phone: (907) 465-2010.

- Arizona: 1100 W. Washington, Phoenix 85007. Phone: (602) 230-7733.
- Arkansas: Department of Parks and Tourism, One Capitol Mall, Little Rock 72201. Phone: (800) NATURAL. Website: www.ono.com/arkansas.
- California: P.O. Box 9278, Van Nuys 91409. Phone: (800) TOCALIF.
- Colorado: P.O. Box 38700, Denver 80238. Phone: (800) COLORADO.
- Connecticut: 865 Brook St., Rocky Hill 06067. Phone: (800) CTBOUND.
- Delaware: P.O. Box 1401, Dover 19903. Phone: (800) 441-8846. Website: www.state.de.us.
- Florida: P.O. Box 1100, Tallahassee 32302-1100. Phone: (904) 487-1462. Website: www.goflorida.com.
- Georgia: P.O. Box 1776, Atlanta 30306. Phone: (800) VISITGA.
- Hawaii: Waikiki Business Plaza, 2270 Kalakaua Ave., Honolulu 96815. Phone: (800) 464-2924.
- Idaho: 700 W. State St., Boise 83720. Phone: (800) 635-7820.
- Illinois: 310 S. Michigan Ave., Suite 108, Chicago 60604. Phone: (800) 2CONNECT.
- Indiana: One North Capitol, Suite 700, Indianapolis 46204-2288. Phone: (800) 289-6646.
- Iowa: 200 E. Grand Ave., Des Moines 50309. Phone: (800) 345-IOWA.
- Kansas: 700 S.W. Harrison, Suite 1300, Topeka 66603. Phone: (800) 2KANSAS, ext. 131.
- Kentucky: Phone, Capital Plaza Tower, 22nd Floor, Frankfort 40601. Phone: (800) 225-TRIP.
- Louisiana: P.O. Box 868, Covington 70434-0868. Phone: (800) 964-7321. Website: www.louisianatravel.com.
- Maine: P.O. Box 23000, Hallowell 04347. Phone: (800) 533-9595.
- Maryland: 217 E. Redwood St., Baltimore 21227. Phone: (800) MDISFUN.

- Massachusetts: 100 Cambridge St., Boston 02202. Phone: (800) 447-MASS.
- Michigan: P.O. Box 30226, Lansing 48909. Phone: (800) 5432YES.
- Minnesota: 375 Jackson St., Room 250, St. Paul 55101. Phone: (800) 657-3700.
- Mississippi: P.O. Box 1705, Ocean Springs 39566-1705. Phone: (800) WARMEST. Website: www.mississippi.org.
- Missouri: Truman Office Building, Box 1055, Jefferson City 65102. Phone: (800) 877-1234.
- Montana: Room 010, Deerlodge 59722. Phone: (800) VIS-ITMT.
- Nebraska: P.O. Box 94666, Lincoln 68509. Phone: (800) 228-4307.
- Nevada: Capitol Complex, Carson City 89710. Phone: (800) NEVADA8.
- New Hampshire: P.O. Box 856, Concord 03301. Phone: (800) FUNINNH, ext. 159.
- New Jersey: 20 W. State St., CN 826, Trenton 08625-0826. Phone: (800) JERSEY7, ext. 7963. Website: www.state.nj.us/travel.
- New Mexico: Joseph Montoya Bldg., 1100 St. Francis Dr., Santa Fe 87503. Phone: (800) 545-2040.
- New York: One Commerce Plaza, Albany 12245. Phone: (800) CALLNYS.
- North Carolina: 430 N. Salisbury St., Raleigh 27611. Phone: (800) HELLOND.
- Ohio: P.O. Box 1001, Columbus 43215. Phone: (800) BUCK-EYE.
- Oklahoma: Dept TN57R, P.O. Box 60789, Oklahoma City 73146. Phone: (800) 652-6552. Website: www.otrd.state.ok.us.
- Oregon: 775 Summer St. NE, Salem 97310. Phone: (800) 547-7842.
- Pennsylvania: Room 456 Forum Bldg., Harrisburg 17120. Phone: (800) VISITPA, ext. 109. Website: www.state.pa.us.

- Rhode Island: One West Exchange St., Providence, 02806. Phone: (800) 556-2484. Website: www.visitrhodeisland.com.
- South Carolina: P.O. Box 71, Columbia 29202. Phone: (803) 734-0122.
- South Dakota, 711 E. Wells Ave., Pierre 57501. Phone: (800) SDAKOTA. Website: www.state.sd.us.
- Tennessee: P.O. Box 23170, Nashville 37202. Phone: (800) 836-6200.
- Texas: P.O. Box 12728, Austin 78711. Phone: (800) 888-8TEX, ext. 728. Website: www.TravelTex.com.
- Utah: Capitol Hill, Salt Lake City 84114. Phone: (800) 200-1160.
- Vermont: 134 State St., Montpelier 05602. Phone: (800) VERMONT.
- Virginia: 1021 E. Carey St., 14th Floor, Richmond 23219. Phone: (800) VISITVA. Website: www.virginia.org.
- Washington: 101 General Administration Bldg., Olympia 98504. Phone: (800) 544-1800.
- Washington, D.C., 1212 New York Ave. NW, Suite 600, Washington, D.C. 20005. Phone: (202) 789-7000. Website: www.washington.org.
- West Virginia: 2101 Washington St., East Charleston 25305. Phone: (800) 225-5982.
- Wisconsin: P.O. Box 7606, Madison 53707. Phone: (800) 432-TRIP.
- Wyoming: I-15 at College Dr., Cheyenne 82002. Phone: (800) 225-5996. Fax: (307) 777-6904.

THE LAST ADDRESS

Got a free travel adventure you'd like to share? Got a good idea that belongs in the next edition of *You Can Travel Free?* Something need correcting? Send it to Dr. Bob Kirk, c/o Pelican Publishing Co., P.O. Box 3110, Gretna, LA 70054-3110. You'll have my thanks.

Index